INDIAN TRADER:

THE LIFE AND TIMES OF J. L. HUBBELL

D1446271

INDIAN TRADER:

THE LIFE AND TIMES OF J. L. HUBBELL

Martha Blue

KIVA
PUBLISHING, INC.
Walnut, California

First Edition
ISBN 1-885772-17-3

Library of Congress Cataloging-in-Publication Data

Blue, Martha, 1942–
    Indian trader : the life and times of J.L. Hubbell / Martha Blue
    p. cm.
    Includes biographical references and index.
    ISBN 1-885772-17-3 (cloth) – ISBN 1-885772-21-1 (pbk.)
    1. Hubbell, John Lorenzo. 2. Indian traders–Arizona–Ganado–Biography. 3. Navajo
Indians–Commerce. 4. Navajo Indians–Social life and customs. 5. Hubbell Trading Post
National Historic Site (Ganado, Ariz.)–History. I. Title

E99.N3 H923 2000
979.1'37–dc21
[B]
                                                            00-024704

A portion of the author's proceeds from this work go to support Indian-related programs at
the Museum of Northern Arizona, which serves the Colorado Plateau.

All photographs, unless otherwise indicated, are from the photographic collection archived at
Hubbell Trading Post National Historic Site in Ganado, Navajo Indian Reservation, Arizona.

Grateful acknowledgement is made to the following for permissions and use of photographs and materials:
Hubbell Trading Post National Historic Site for use of the photographs in the collection of the site and access
to portions of the microfiche reproducing the originals which form the Hubbell Papers, Special Collections,
University of Arizona, Tucson, Arizona; to Special Collections, University of Arizona, Tucson, Arizona, for
permissions for photographs and use of collections relative to Hubbell trading; photographs from the Kansas
State Historical Society, Topeka, Kansas; photographs from the Museum of New Mexico, Santa Fe, New Mexico;
photographs and materials from the Hubbell Family Papers and the McNitt Papers from the New Mexico State
Records Center and Archives, Santa Fe, New Mexico; and photograph courtesy of the Southwest Museum,
Los Angeles, California. Specific photographs are identified in the photograph list in the appendix.

Cover design: Bob Jivanjee

Printed in USA by Ali Graphic Services, Inc.
9 8 7 6 5 4 3 2 1

To my blood and spirit sister Marlene and to the memory of my sister Michele and my brother Quentin, Jr.

Indian history inspired the development of ethnohistory, which places actions and events in a carefully explored context of culture and world view. Ethnohistory reaches its peak when its techniques are applied across the board, when white people as well as Indians are cast as actors in complex cultural worlds, and when no point of view is taken for granted.

—Patricia Nelson Limerick, *The Legacy of Conquest: The Unbroken Past of the American West*

CONTENTS

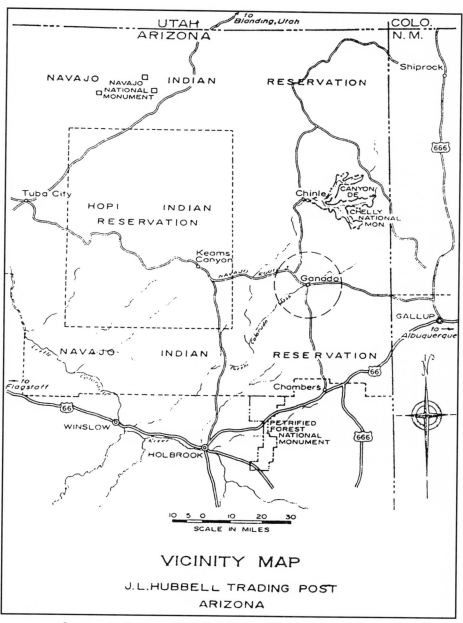

VICINITY MAP

J. L. HUBBELL TRADING POST

ARIZONA

Interpretative Prospectus for Hubbell Trading Post National Historic Site by
Superintendent John E. Cook and Regional Historian William E. Brown, April, 1967.

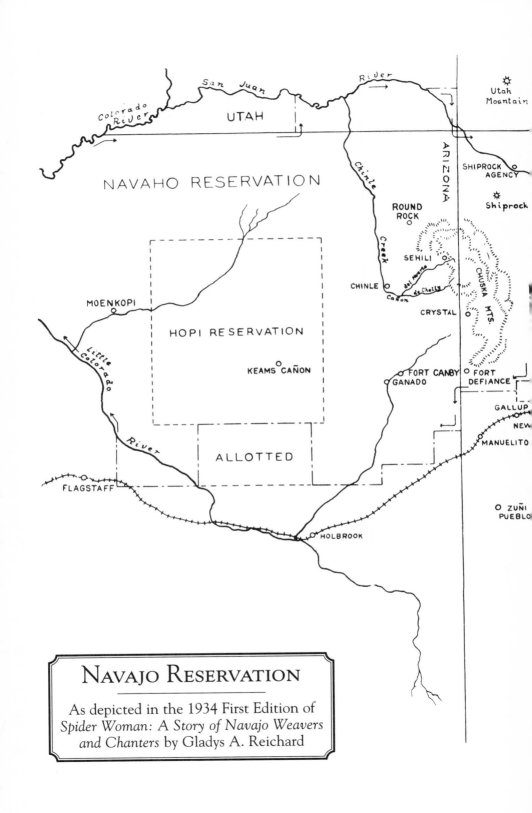

Navajo Reservation

As depicted in the 1934 First Edition of
*Spider Woman: A Story of Navajo Weavers
and Chanters* by Gladys A. Reichard

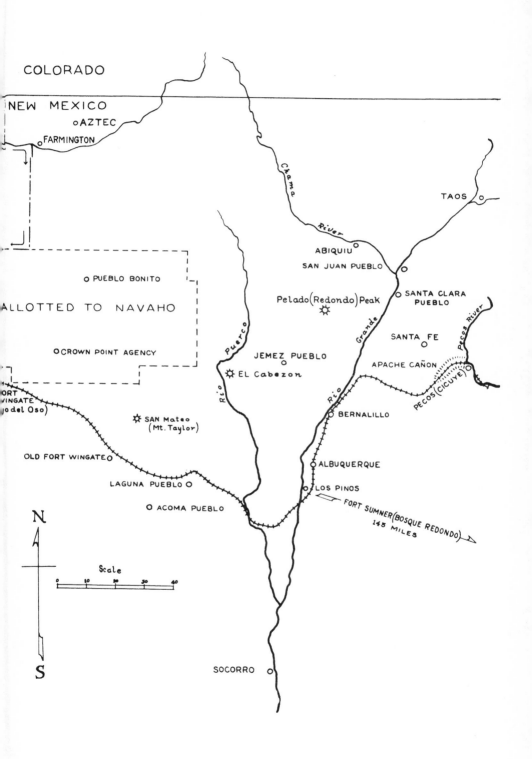

COLORADO

NEW MEXICO
o AZTEC
o FARMINGTON

Chama

River

TAOS o

ABIQUIU
SAN JUAN PUEBLO

O PUEBLO BONITO

ALLOTTED TO NAVAHO

Pelado (Redondo) Peak
☼

SANTA CLARA
PUEBLO

O CROWN POINT AGENCY

Rio Puerco

JEMEZ PUEBLO

Rio Grande

SANTA FE

Pecos River

☼ EL Cabezon

APACHE CAÑON

ORT
WINGATE
(Ojo del Oso)

☼ SAN Mateo
(Mt. Taylor)

PECOS (CICUYE)

Rio

OLD FORT WINGATE O

BERNALILLO O

LAGUNA PUEBLO O

ALBUQUERQUE O

O ACOMA PUEBLO

LOS PINOS O

FORT SUMNER (BOSQUE REDONDO)
145 MILES

N

Scale

0   10   20   30   40

SOCORRO O

S

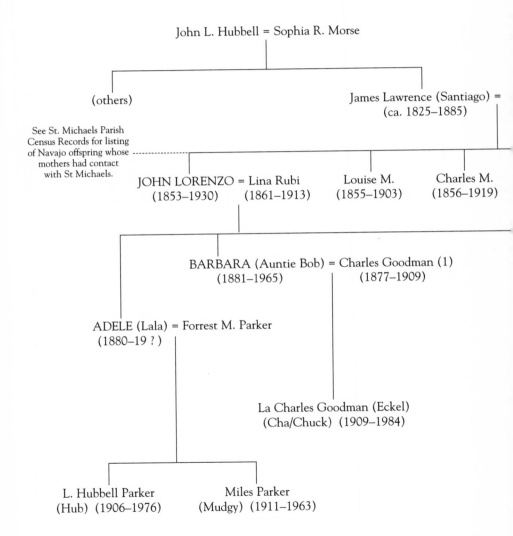

Immediate Family Tree of J. L. Hubbell including some of his Navajo offspring

John L. Hubbell = Sophia R. Morse

(others)

James Lawrence (Santiago) =
(ca. 1825–1885)

See St. Michaels Parish
Census Records for listing
of Navajo offspring whose
mothers had contact
with St Michaels.

JOHN LORENZO = Lina Rubi
(1853–1930)   (1861–1913)

Louise M.
(1855–1903)

Charles M.
(1856–1919)

BARBARA (Auntie Bob) = Charles Goodman (1)
(1881–1965)   (1877–1909)

ADELE (Lala) = Forrest M. Parker
(1880–19 ?)

La Charles Goodman (Eckel)
(Cha/Chuck) (1909–1984)

L. Hubbell Parker
(Hub) (1906–1976)

Miles Parker
(Mudgy) (1911–1963)

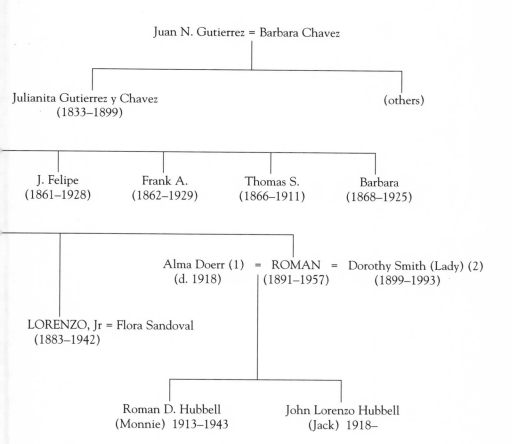

Juan N. Gutierrez = Barbara Chavez

Julianita Gutierrez y Chavez
(1833–1899)

(others)

J. Felipe
(1861–1928)

Frank A.
(1862–1929)

Thomas S.
(1866–1911)

Barbara
(1868–1925)

Alma Doerr (1) = ROMAN = Dorothy Smith (Lady) (2)
(d. 1918)   (1891–1957)   (1899–1993)

LORENZO, Jr = Flora Sandoval
(1883–1942)

Roman D. Hubbell
(Monnie) 1913–1943

John Lorenzo Hubbell
(Jack) 1918–

Adapted with corrections and additions from Appendix I: *A Genealogy of the Immediate
J. L. Hubbell Family*, Outline of Hubbell Papers, Special Collections, University of Arizona

J.L. Hubbell (Card No.1) (naꞏkai sání No.1)   Xox White Man
        John Lorenzo   Mexican

Fa: Ca:
Mo:
Ho: Ganado, Ariz.
Bs: Died November 12, 1930
Bp: Buried on Hubbell's Hill Noveember 14, 1930
FC: by Fr. Jerome
Cr:
Sr:

Wi: Ca: tábąhá

Ch: naꞏkai sání bici' No.1

Wi: ꞏyiłxabaꞏ No.14-hastiꞏn žin   Cl: bįꞏh bitoꞏni

Ch: 38878   Maud Hubbell, Mar.23,1906, Bp.
Ch: 38749   Tom McCabe, 1908

Wi: bidáɣa łání bici' No.2   Cl:tódíč 'íni

Ch: 24377   John Shirley, 1900, Bp.

Wi: ꞏyiłhanazbaꞏ No.4   Cl:tódíč 'íni
Ch: 54074   Peter Lee, 1893

J.L. Hubbell   (Card No.2)   White Man

Wi:?59320   asžéꞏ néꞏz No.18-holḱiḣi   Cl: bįꞏh bitoꞏni

Ch: Mildred Hubbard, 1902

Wi: Cl: tódíč 'iꞏni

Ch: 58797   Roman Hubbell, Mar.10,1904

Prepared by J. Andrews, St. Michaels Archivist, May 1, 1986

PREFACE AND ACKNOWLEDGMENTS

THIS WORK REALLY BEGAN with my childhood fascination with Indians and pioneers. My family's 1950s Sunday drives from Prescott, Arizona, up to Navajo and Hopi country fueled this fascination. As an adult, my work as a legal services lawyer in the late 1960s in Tuba City, Navajo Indian Reservation, Arizona, a government agency town serving Navajos and Hopis, solidified my interest. At the legal services office, I worked with both Navajo and Hopi clients and handled a variety of matters, including complaints about traders. I also received assistance from traders on cases as varied as land disputes and valuation of Indian livestock for welfare eligibility purposes. In my personal life, a neighbor in the Navajo farming community of Moenave taught me to card and spin wool, and I took weaving classes.

My most profound Navajo country historical experience occurred the first time I attended the Honorable Chester Yellowhair's court in Tuba City. Opposite Judge Yellowhair's bench was a wall-sized photograph of ration day for the Navajos in the mid-1860s at Bosque Redondo, also called Fort Sumner. This was, in effect, the concentration camp to which the American military exiled thousands of Navajos. The view—numerous gaunt Navajo people standing and on horseback by the fort's buildings—haunted me.

During my twenty-seven years' practice of Indian law in northern Arizona, I used historical documents and oral histories, read ethnographies and histories of the area, interviewed Indians and traders about the past, and researched archival material relative to Navajo-Hopi-Havasupai life. Early on in my legal career, I decided that if I could have stepped back into the nineteenth century, I would have been an Indian trader.

What developed for me, then, was a curiosity about the Southwest's trading-post era and about Navajo-Hopi history. I was bothered by the Eurocentric orientation of trader literature (and its "Wild West" style) as well as its treatment of Indians as objects, not as subjects/actors. In the interviews I conducted and in oral histories I located, I found a much different tenor. I was provoked and stimulated by the Indian narrators' viewpoints of their lives, causes and effects, and the minor importance of Euro-Americans to Indian life before and after the century turned.

Indian oral histories about the Ganado area and the Hubbell Papers at the University of Arizona provided starting places for my efforts to synthesize diverse viewpoints about traders, or, at least, place them side-by-side for readers to evaluate. Additional information spanned a long period, from the Hubbell family's colonization of the Southwest in the early eighteenth century to the creation of the Hubbell Trading Post National Historic Site (HTPNHS) at Ganado, Arizona, in the twentieth. From this mass of information, I selected words from many sources: the Hubbell Papers, hundreds of boxes of documents in Special Collections at the University of Arizona; the Working Papers at HTPNHS; and government documents, diaries, visitor correspondence, social reports, court records, and oral histories. The oral histories number more than fifty (I consider these to be the single most important contribution to this ethnobiography), and were taken primarily in the late 1960s and early 1970s from Navajos and Euro-Americans connected to Ganado and Hubbell's trading ranch. In the mid-1980s, as part of the Hubbell Rug Study, another thirty or so interviews were conducted with Navajo weavers, both female and male. The Navajo interviews memorialized Navajo perceptions of Hubbell and the trading era and gave us a fresh look at both topics.

In weaving together J. L.'s ethnobiography, I have also used the words of Navajo headmen; a Hopi traditional leader; the daughters of a well-known Navajo weaver; J. L.'s Navajo employees; a crazy artist who drew Conté crayon Indian portraits; a flamboyant American president's travel memoirs of Navajo and Hopi country; a telegraph operator-turned-trader then banker, wholesaler, and wool merchant; an ex-Franciscan brother and photographer-turned-trading post manager; and others.

Particular note must be made of the Hubbell Papers at the University of Arizona. In 1959, when National Park Service historian Robert M. Utley visited the Hubbell trading ranch at Ganado, he found one hundred crates, boxes, and trunks—loaded with sand and suffering from rodent attacks—in the barn and on the home's back porch. A dozen years later, this material was deposited with Special Collections at the University of Arizona, and by 1978, Special Collections personnel, under the leadership of Clint Colby, had sorted the material into five hundred and seventy-three boxes. (The finding aid alone runs one hundred forty-one pages.) Additionally, Clint Colby prepared a lengthy

HUBBELL
T P VISTOR CENTER
GANADO   AZ 86505

DATE: 03/21/04   TIME: 10:52
MER#: 347500115279   TER#: 0001
        S-A-L-E-S D-R-A-F-T

REF: 0007   BCH: 025
CD TYPE: VI
TR TYPE: PR
INV#: 3089
AMOUNT: $46.45

ACCT: ************3089   EXP: ****
AP: 044552
NAME: LINDA E   ORWOLL

CARDMEMBER ACKNOWLEDGES RECEIPT OF
GOODS AND/OR SERVICES IN THE AMOUNT OF
THE TOTAL SHOWN HEREON AND AGREES TO
PERFORM THE OBLIGATIONS SET FORTH BY THE
CARDMEMBER'S AGREEMENT WITH THE ISSUER
THANK YOU FOR USING VISA

X _Linda Orwoll_____
TOP COPY-MERCHANT BOTTOM COPY-CUSTOMER

03-21-04

1 TX *3.95 1
1 TX *18.00 1
1 TX *24.50 1
   *46.45 ST
   *0.00 TX 1

        3 Q
   *46.45 CH

   10-52
150-2166

list of the personnel at the various trading posts and businesses owned by the Hubbell family. My very warm thank-you to Mr. Colby, his staff, and the University of Arizona's Special Collections for their Herculean work.

As Navajo historian Jennifer Denetdale once pointed out to me, non-Indians listing their credentials for writing about Indian people mention associations with Indian individuals and workplaces in Indian country. I have touched on the latter already. In regard to the former, I extend my everlasting appreciation to the many Navajos, Hopis, and others who shared their cultures with me, including, to name just a few: the late Cleopatra Anthony; Bill and Dollie Beaver; Gevern Begay; Margaret Begody; Roberta Blackgoat; the late Mike Brodie; the late Gilbert Brown; the reservation-wide staff of DNA, then known as *Dinébeina Nahiilna be Agaditahe* (attorneys who contribute to the economic revitalization of the Navajo people) and now called DNA People's Legal Services. I thank as well the visionary first director of DNA, Inc., Theodore R. Mitchell, who always emphasized justice for Navajos (thank you, Ted, for your mentoring) and who made possible my entry into Indian country; the always generous and patient Dorothy and Richard George; Nancy Howard; the late Charles Loloma; Marie Mitchell; the late Clyde Peshlakai; Jim and Mae Peshlakai and their extended family; Merrill Sandoval; and Sally Yazzie.

In the dozen years since I started working on this particular book (while I also practiced law, made art, published other books and articles, and cut this manuscript several times from its Tolstoyan size to the current version), I have been helped by countless institutions, agencies, and people. It is a pleasure to acknowledge the late Dorothy S. Hubbell, J. L. Hubbell's daughter-in-law, who was generous with her time, letters, enthusiasm, energy, and information for this project. Likewise, I thank David M. Brugge, former curator at Hubbell Trading Post National Historic Site, who unstintingly shared his knowledge in his own considerate and thorough way and commented on early drafts, as did my good friends Barbara Lacy and Carolyn Niethammer on later drafts. David deserves special thanks, too, for the consummate work he has done for years on Navajo matters, including both his published and unpublished work on slave trafficking, Navajo biographies, eastern Navajo history, and various aspects of trading.

For earlier drafts, Irene Silentman, Dr. Ellavina Perkins, and Peggy Scott reviewed the Navajo vocabulary and Navajo chapters and deserve special mention. As the work expanded and contracted, I could not always follow Navajo orthography according to current Navajo dictionary publications, and opted instead to follow the spelling of names as they appeared in interviews and certain words as they appeared historically. Any Navajo orthographic inconsistencies are solely mine. And, while fluency in Navajo phonetics has always eluded my grasp, I thank a multitude of Navajo language teachers for giving me some familiarity with the language.

The Navajo Studies Conference, The Heard Museum in Phoenix, Arizona, and the Museum of Northern Arizona in Flagstaff influenced this work by giving me the opportunity to present papers on certain aspects of my research, as did the now-defunct Colorado Plateau Studies at Northern Arizona University.

I would also like to thank Anna L. Walters and the Diné College Press for publication of my monograph on the Navajo witchpurge of 1878, and the Museum of Northern Arizona and James Babbitt, who spearheaded *Plateau*'s "Historic Trading Posts" issue, which contained my first conceptualization of the Indian view of traders.

Without the work of those ahead of me, this work could not have been done. The late historian and trader expert Frank McNitt (with whose romantic views of Indian traders I do not always agree) had gathered numerous research files for a J. L. Hubbell biography; these papers are now part of the New Mexico State Library and Archives (others are in the archives at Hubbell Trading Post National Historic site). Likewise, the same archive provided an excellent resource in its Hubbell Papers collection. I am indebted as well to the works of other scholars, including Dr. Charlotte Frisbie, Dr. Kathleen M'Closkey (and our voluminous correspondence), the late Dr. Gladys Reichard, and Dr. Gary Witherspoon.

For interviews, insights, correspondence, encouragement, and other assistance, I must thank Dr. Val Avery; Judy and Mike Andrews; the late John Adair; Susan Lamb Bean, who was always there as both a friend and writing colleague; Loretta Begay; Thrude Breckenridge; Joanie Brundige-Baker; Dr. Robert W. Robin and his late wife Dr. Barbara Chester (both mentors); Marion Davidson; Sam Day III; Jennifer

Denetdale; Lynn Galvin; Dr. Laura Graves; Fran Joseph; Martin Link; my stepfather, David Manning; Marlene McGoffin; Dr. Robert S. McPherson; Dr. Edgar W. Moore; Gary Morrison; Judith Nies; Michelle Osborn, who as my last typist was also enthusiastic about the project; the late P. T. Reilly; Steve Udall, who shared information about gambling in St. Johns among the non-Mormons; Jeri Tisdale; Ken Van Houten, who located and gave me an original J. L. Hubbell business card and catalogue; Adelle Verkamp; Roy Ward; Jeanne Williams; and Teresa Wilkins.

This project unfolded as a gift of relationships and place tied to Ganado. Just as J. L. Hubbell symbolized Southwestern hospitality, so have the National Park Service (NPS) and Southwest Parks and Monuments Association (SPMA) at Hubbell Trading Post National Historic Site (HTPNHS) in Ganado shown their interest, assistance, and enthusiasm for this project on every level. I thank all the superintendents and staff, present and past, at this unique place, with special emphasis on Liz Bauers, Gino Bahe, Clarinda Begay, curator Edward M. Chamberlin (for whom no request was considered minor), trader Bill Malone, Marietta Oskey, Kathy Tabaha, Superintendent Nancy Stone, Maralyn Yazzie (whose boundless enthusiasm for this project often buoyed me), and those many Ganado-area Navajos who assisted the NPS in its first years of HTPNHS operation by participating in an oral history project. T. J. Priehs, SPMA's Executive Director, shared with me Dr. Charles S. Peterson's excellent unpublished manuscript on the Hubbell farm. I thank Dr. Peterson (whom I have never met) as well.

While the names of many of the Navajos who encouraged me to include Hubbell's Navajo family in this book have not been listed, they also have my warm thanks.

For their informed assistance, whether or not I excerpted material from their collections, I thank the curators, librarians, archivists, and staff at the Arizona Historical Society in Tucson; Special Collections Department of the University of Arizona, Tucson (most recently, the assistance given to me by Roger Meyers); the Special Collections Department and the Arizona Historical Foundation in the Hayden Library, Arizona State University, Tempe; Connie Menninger, the Kansas State Historical Society; the Special Collections Department,

Zimmerman Library, University of New Mexico, and the Albuquerque Public Library, Albuquerque; the New Mexico State Records Center and Archives, Santa Fe; Special Collections Department, Cline Library, Northern Arizona University, Flagstaff (particularly director Karen Underhill); the library at the Museum of Northern Arizona, Flagstaff; the Sharlot Hall Museum, Prescott, Arizona; the Arizona State Department of Archives and Libraries, Phoenix; the Bancroft Library, University of California, Berkeley; and the county recorders, probate courts, clerks of the court, and treasurer's offices in the counties of Coconino, Apache, and Navajo in Arizona and Bernallilo in New Mexico. All the background information helped me understand the era (though most was cut from the original lengthy draft and only a select portion of the data collected is in this work).

A warm thank-you goes to Stephen Hill of Kiva Publishing for publishing this manuscript, and to Erin Murphy and Susan Tasaki, who helped along the way.

And finally, my appreciation goes to my daughter Zoe Moreno, who encouraged me, and to my husband Oliver W. Johnson, who assisted me in every way in this project, from photographing historic photos to cooking chili for five hundred people for a Hubbell Friends event. Without Ollie, there would have been no finished manuscript.

Any errors in this book are solely mine.

INTRODUCTION

AS THE ROVING TRADER faded from the trans-Mississippi West in the 1850s, the era of the reservation trader began. The government-licensed reservation trader established a fixed trading post site on an Indian reservation and supplied Indians with Euro-American goods. These reservation traders shaped an economy adapted to Indian culture and reservation life. At the same time, they transmitted Euro-American material culture; aided—in the opinion of the government—in controlling and "civilizing" the Indians; and represented the Indians' most common and consistent Euro-American contact.

From about 1876 (or 1878) to 1930, Juan Lorenzo Hubbell traded at Ganado, Arizona, in Navajo country. Sentiment about him varied. Euro-Americans viewed him as the premier, indeed the dean, of Indian traders in the Southwest. Some Navajo customers said it was good to have trader Hubbell as a friend, while others said Navajos did everything around his Ganado trading ranch for low wages.

While J. L. Hubbell's life story tells the larger tale of the settlement of the West, the reservation trader, and the Indian economy, certain factors distinguish his life from those of other traders: his heritage, land acquisition, longevity, entrepreneurial spirit, politics, and influence on Navajo textiles.

His mother's family came from Spain to the Southwest after the Pueblo Revolt of 1680. His Spanish ancestors established a Big House tradition and rooted themselves in the area nearly a century and a half earlier than those of other Southwestern traders. His Yankee father came to the region during the Mexican-American War (1846-1848).

The two cultures, Spanish and Yankee, melded in J. L. Hubbell. Much of his life was dominated by practices common in Hispanic society: social position and responsibilities inherent to landowner status and the maintenance of a dependent and supportive family and community. These mixed with Yankee business ethics, aggression, and his effort to live up to the particularly American myth of the self-made man.

If these dual traditions were the underpinnings, or the warp, of his life, land was the weft.

J. L. turned a mere one hundred sixty acres of land—the American symbol of national identity and social status—into an entrepreneurial base with tentacles over, through, and past Navajo and Hopi country. An inventory of Hubbell family operations through 1967 catalogued some thirty-two trading posts and stores; only six were acquired after J. L.'s death. To that number must be added his scores of other business activities, which ranged from a saloon/billiard hall to stage/freight lines. He personally influenced the evolution of a native economy on the Navajo and Hopi reservations for over fifty years, and his descendants continued the family tradition for nearly forty years more until the National Park Service acquired J. L.'s Ganado trading ranch in 1967.

He left his mark in politics as well, heading the Republican party in a Democratic territory (and later, state) and losing a bid to be the state of Arizona's first elected United States Senator. On the commercial side, during the first decade of the 1900s, when Sears Roebuck and Co. sold reversible silk ties for twenty-nine cents, J. L. Hubbell often had Navajo rug sales in excess of forty thousand dollars yearly. (Today, the Navajo textile style identified with his trading ranch, the Ganado Red, has achieved international distinction.)

Though he defined himself as an Indian trader, he imaginatively composed his own life at every opportunity. He reveled as a raconteur and the most interesting actor in his own Wild West stories. He collected fine art, ethnographic objects, photographs, old Navajo blankets, Indian baskets, the friendships of Indian leaders and presidents, famous and common house guests, and liaisons. He had a designer's eye; old blanket designs and architecture fascinated him equally and he expressed that fascination in the textiles he commissioned and in the expansion of his trading ranch. Likable, he could wring at least some advantage out of any situation (he once enlisted a visitor, the wife of the Assistant Commissioner of Indian Affairs, as one of his rug ambassadors, and she sold the textiles he sent her from Ganado to her friends in Washington, D. C.). He was trustworthy, old-fashioned, and a believer in American myths and in Euro-American superiority over Indians.

The conflicts and complexities of the Southwest were woven into J. L. Hubbell's life: the Navajos' repatriation and economic recovery, the era of the reservation trader in frontier history, the tourist explosion wrought by the Santa Fe Railway and the Fred Harvey Company,

Arizona's quest for statehood, water development in its desert plateau country, the transition of the Navajo blanket to rug, and the image-makers' (artists, writers, and photographers) portrayals of the Southwest.

This book also addresses the conflict (identified by Larry McMurtry in "How the West Was Won or Lost," *The New Republic*, October 22, 1990), between the Triumphalists' "recognition that the winning of the West was in large measure an imaginative act," and the Revisionists' view (thoroughly expressed by Patricia Limerick in *The Legacy of Conquest: The Unbroken Past of the American West*, W. W. Norton and Co., 1987), that the West was a

> mosaic of failure, financial and personal, but also... moral... an irresponsible white male's adventure, hugely destructive of the land itself, of the native peoples, and even the white males' own women and children.

If one looks at J. L.'s life through revisionist glasses, he was a lady's man, a gambler, too family-oriented in business, a power monger, a resource extractor and exploiter, a federal bounty recipient, and a sometime toady. He grabbed land and water use by carefully fusing his aims with those of the Indians and publicly minimizing his direct benefit. A study of his life, set in the history and personalities of the Spanish/Mexican/American periods and the Navajo and Hopi pre- and post-reservation periods, is a story with multiple layers of reality. Add to it the public's view of the trader, the Indians' view of the trader, and trader's view of himself, and we have an ethnobiography—a complex portrait of an era as exemplified in the life of one man.

The "I came, I saw, I traded, I saved the Indians" theme in trader-related literature needs squaring up. It is my purpose here to include in J. L. Hubbell's life story not just the standard version of a trader's life, but also the Indian (primarily the Navajo) story. Indian adaptation, borrowing, innovation, and tradition (activities that are not mutually exclusive) explode Euro-Americans' view of Indians as a dying race. Indian leaders, such as the Navajo headmen and medicinemen, charted their way through a difficult terrain in the late 1880s and the early 1900s, and their paths mirrored and often crossed that of J. L. Hubbell. These complex cultural worlds and multiple cultural viewpoints, unsettling as they may be, are woven throughout Hubbell's life and give us a fresh angle on an old story.

At the 1997 Navajo Studies Conference in Albuquerque, one Navajo attendee commented that writing down a story freezes it in that version, when, in fact, different versions exist. As an independent scholar with a pro-Indian predisposition, my goal is to tease out the different versions of Hubbell's story, even though the versions are disharmonious—in essence, to "unfreeze" it.

I have opted to use the word "Indian" to refer to America's indigenous people, since it was the vernacular of Hubbell's time. For the same reason, I have left within quotation marks such derogatory referencing terms as "bucks" and "squaws." When the tribal affiliation is named or known in reference material, it is identified in the text. The term "Euro-American" sweeps in both Anglo-Americans and Hispanic-Americans, though at times I refer specifically to Anglos and Hispanics. Hubbell and his brother Charlie generally referred to themselves as "white men," although as Hubbell aged (or if circumstances warranted), he referred to himself as being of Spanish descent. The term "trading ranch" includes his farmland, residences, barn, warehouse, post, corrals, and the old Leonard building, while "trading post" generally refers to just the land and buildings involved in the trading aspect of his enterprises.

When quotes attributed to J. L. Hubbell are from an "as told to" biographical interview that appeared in the magazine *Touring Topics* shortly after Hubbell's death in 1930, they are marked as such in the text.

This book's six-part organization reflects the pattern that names played in the trader's life. He was christened Juan Lorenzo Hubbell. Throughout his life he acquired other names: the Navajos called him *Nakeznilih* ("Double Glasses" or "Wearing Spectacles") at first and then *Naakaii Sání* ("Old Mexican") as the century turned. His business acquaintances, correspondents, and fellow politicians called him J. L. Hubbell. Hispanic relatives and the coterie of visitors to whom he extended his renowned hospitality called him Don Lorenzo. And Teddy Roosevelt apparently gave him the title of Lorenzo the Magnificent. In this text, Juan Lorenzo Hubbell is most often referred to as J. L., sometimes as Hubbell, the trader, or even J. L. Hubbell. (Hubbell Parker, his grandson, is mentioned by his full name.) "J. L. Hubbell" was the name he chose for his fancy and plain business letterheads, the name he signed to all his correspondence, a name minimizing his Hispanic background, and a name that does not create confusion between him and his trader son Lorenzo.

Since I started work on J. L.'s life story, I have become aware of the fact that several periodicals, books, and even films have confused the correspondence, events, and likenesses of J. L. and his son Lorenzo. Usually, this has been done by erroneously identifying J. L. as the person in the material, when it was actually his son Lorenzo. Since son Lorenzo's business stationery did not indicate his "Jr." status, some of this confusion is understandable. However, only J. L. Hubbell's very closest friends called him "Lorenzo"; Hispanic friends and relatives (and his many guests) called him "Don Lorenzo." During his lifetime, and in this work, the name "Lorenzo" refers to J. L. Hubbell's oldest son, not to Juan Lorenzo Hubbell.

Each of Hubbell's names had its own social context, geography, and role. Each required a different response from the trader. Like an old eye-dazzler blanket, the names collected and reflected viewpoints and perceptions that place him in the larger context of a Western entrepreneur in multiple cross-cultural settings and Southwestern history.

No name appears on J. L. Hubbell's grave marker.

PART ONE
JUAN LORENZO

Hubbell, John Lorenzo, Arizona State Senator and Indian Trader, Ganado, Apache County, Arizona, was born in Pajarito, New Mexico, November 27, 1853. He is of Danish and Spanish descent, the son of Sentiajo [sic] L. Hubbell and Julianita [Gutierrez] Hubbell.... The Senator's forbears were men of great fighting qualities; on the paternal side he is a lineal descendant of Danes, who, centuries ago, won part of England from King Alfred the Great; his maternal ancestors came out of Toledo, Spain, three generations back, and settled in New Mexico.

—*Notables of the West*

The Westward course of population is neither to be denied nor delayed for the sake of all the Indians who ever called this country their home. They must yield or perish.

—U. S. Commissioner of Indian Affairs, 1870,
quoted by J. E. Chamberlin in *The Harrowing of Eden*,
requoted in Hugh Brody's *Maps and Dreams*

CHAPTER ONE
Eighty-four Pairs of Ears

BLOOD SPRAYED over the doorway of Juan Lorenzo Hubbell's trading post on May 31, 1878, the day a group of Navajos killed Hastiin Jieh Kaal/Dejolie for practicing witchcraft, or *antiih*. The trading post was on the lake near Ganado (then called Pueblo Colorado) in Navajo country, Arizona Territory.

That same day, or perhaps the next, J. L. Hubbell's friend Ganado Mucho (also known as Many Cattle), a Navajo headman or *naat'áanii*, led a horde of fifty or more armed Ganado-area Navajos to nearby Cornfields. Ganado Mucho was considered to be the Navajos' western chief by the U. S. government. In a 1970 oral history, Amos Johnson, a Cornfields man whose grandfather participated in the drama, described the event.

Medicineman Hastiin Biwosi (Mr. Shoulder, also known as Hombro or Hombre), a Navajo treaty signer like Ganado Mucho, just happened to be at Cornfields conducting a ceremony in a forked-stick, teepee-shaped hogan. The mob planned to kill Hastiin Biwosi because, over a period of time, he had buried certain Navajos' belongings, a sorcerer's practice that was believed to have led to the deaths of leaders, children and sheep.

When the frenzied crowd arrived at the Cornfields hogan, those inside—except for Hastiin Biwosi—hurried out with the medicine pouch. Shouting riders circled the hogan, lassoed the poles that stuck out of its smoke hole, and toppled it. The mob found Hastiin Biwosi hiding among the log poles and shot and wounded him. As Amos Johnson's grandfather dragged Hastiin Biwosi out, the crowd ignored the man's pleas for clemency. They stoned him with such violence that his corpse was unrecognizable.

When Ganado Mucho and his people received word that a Chinle Navajo war party was organizing to avenge Hastiin Biwosi's death, the Ganado Navajos apparently turned to J. L. Hubbell for assistance. It is said that Hubbell volunteered to ride alone toward Chinle to parlay with the war party, which apparently he did. After talking to the Chinle group, Hubbell managed to gather the regional leaders together for further discussion and thus averted bloodshed. In essence, Hubbell restored harmony by following a long-standing Navajo approach to managing conflict: instructive and creative speech in a public setting. Despite his no doubt primary desire to protect his fledging store and inventory, the incident stamped him as a daring friend of the Navajos. And as witchpurge turbulence continued, Hubbell stayed involved on several levels, which both exposed him to danger and garnered him praise. Hubbell's behavior was consistent with his Hispanic heritage and its Big House tradition, which mandated that those in positions of power exercise their authority in service to the community.

There is compelling evidence to indicate that the Navajo people were the threads that whipstitched together the lives of Juan Lorenzo Hubbell's family, on both the maternal Gutierrez and paternal Hubbell sides in Pajarito, a few miles from Albuquerque's "Old Town" area. His great-grandfather Don Lorenzo Gutierrez participated in an 1805 raiding/slaving clash; in the 1850s, father James Hubbell retaliated for Navajo stock raiding; uncle Charles Hubbell was involved in the Navajo Roundup and Long Walk of the 1860s; and Juan Lorenzo himself exerted his influence in tribal affairs and trading beginning in the 1870s.

For decades, in response to the advancing Spanish frontier, Navajos had been moving west and southwest from Dinétah (their ancestral homeland), the area originally considered "Navajo country" in modern-day northern New Mexico. Following a treaty with the Navajos, a Spanish governor of the New Mexico province urged that the tribe be driven across the Colorado River into California. The Spanish failed in that effort, and, ultimately, the Navajos checked Spain's westward expansion. They also resisted "missionizing," one of Spain's methods of taming and colonizing new lands.

However, the first Spanish colonizers in 1598 had provided an economic godsend for themselves and for the tribes that already lived in the area. These colonizers had brought with them several hundred head of livestock, including churros, a disease-resistant, common breed of Spanish sheep that could exist in the semi-arid climate and produced a nearly greaseless, long, straight wool that could be woven without washing.

During the tumultuous Pueblo Revolt of 1680, Puebloans and Navajos pushed the Spaniards out, seized their abandoned sheep and horses, learned shepherding, and managed increasing flocks and herds. By the time the Spanish re-entered the area, sheep were an integral part of the ever-adaptable Navajo way of life. Sheep—most especially their wool and

4

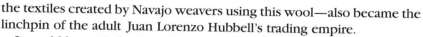

the textiles created by Navajo weavers using this wool—also became the linchpin of the adult Juan Lorenzo Hubbell's trading empire.

It could be said that Hubbell's success was the sum of his ethnically diverse heritage combined with his own ability to seize the moment and work it to his advantage.

Pajarito, New Mexico Territory, November 27, 1853

Lively with the Spanish language's trilled r's and v's, Pajarito, or "Little Bird," and its village households were typical of many Hispanic settlements along the Rio Grande Valley, in what was to become the American Southwest. Within the adobe walls, dried anise and coriander hung from the *vigas* (roof beams) and scented the air; burros and roosters vied with each other at dawn and bullfrogs held forth at dusk; and alfalfa, chile peppers, corn, geraniums, and grapes colored the irrigated river lands.

As a settlement, Pajarito was maintained by Indian labor, captive or convert, complemented by the eighteen or so poor families who serviced the households and ranching interests of the Gutierrez-Hubbell families as well as those of Pajarito's other landed citizens. The landed families owned hundreds of cattle and horses, plus thousands of sheep. Some managed their sheep by "sharecropping" wool and mutton with shepherds, and others used slaves, *peons* (unskilled laborers), and *mestizos* (people of mixed Indian and Mexican ethnicity).

Following the annulment of peonage (which took place in 1867 under the New Mexico Territorial Legislature), the poorer villagers switched to laboring for the Pajarito-area landowners on a share system. Phillip Hubbell, Juan Lorenzo's nephew, described some of this work. For example, the members of the community whitewashed the mile-and-a-half of high adobe walls surrounding the Pajarito homestead, as they depended on the "family for their living. So, to do something—if they weren't working the livestock or the farm or the things that went along with the property, they were working on the property itself, to keep it in repair." Some of the village women served as babysitters/governesses or chichiguas (wet nurses), for all the Gutierrez-Hubbell children and grandchildren.

This was the world into which Juan Lorenzo Hubbell was born on November 27, 1853, the third child of Yankee entrepreneur James Lawrence Hubbell, "a native of Vermont, whose parents were English," and Juliana Gutierrez, "the daughter of a proud old Spanish pioneer family," according to Juan Lorenzo's *Touring Topics* interview. They had married on March 31, 1849, when Juliana—who according to family history was a striking blue-eyed blond—was sixteen. Their union gave their son a Yankee squatter's mentality—vitality and an entrepreneurial hunger—plus Hispanic grace, spirit, and the landed class's tradition of a dependent community. Altogether, James and Juliana had twelve children, four of whom died in infancy, according to the Hubbell family Bible.

The Spanish Legacy

Juliana's ancestors had emigrated from Spain's Toledo-Aragon region, an area that in many ways mirrored New Mexico Territory's topography of basin and range, plateaus with open space and light, and green-ribboned waterways. Unlike Spain, however, here communal Pueblo Indian villages hugged the banks of the broad, brown Rio Grande, and family groups of Navajos and Apaches lived in its valley.

The Gutierrez Pajarito Grant Claim No. 157 petition, filed in 1887 with the U. S. government, provides insight into Juan Lorenzo's Hispanic ancestry. These proceedings confirmed the validity of the Pajarito land grant, although not as a Spanish crown grant (as family lore boasted), but rather, through purchase, occupancy, and continued use. The proceedings also recorded a maze of partial interests inherited, purchased, and sold. By the time it reached Juliana and her relatives, the Pajarito grant measured four miles from north to south (near Isleta Pueblo on the southern extent) and fourteen miles east to west. It was bounded by the Rio Grande and the Rio Puerco.

As stated by the land-grant claimants, the first mention of the Pajarito land grant came in Dona Josepha Baca's 1746 will. Josepha's granddaughter Apolonina, who inherited a portion of Pajarito, married Clemente Gutierrez. Their son, Don Lorenzo Gutierrez, later sired Don Juan Gutierrez, Juliana's father. (When their third child was born, Juliana and James named him for both his grandfather and his great-grandfather.)

Don Lorenzo Gutierrez had figured prominently in a successful Spanish clash with the Navajos in 1805, a clash that gave the Spanish captives for the slave trade. Slave trafficking not only dovetailed with the Spanish government's Indian policy of playing the tribes against each other, it also punished Indians (often Navajo), for resistance and occasional livestock raids. Between 1700 and 1870, some sixteen hundred Navajos (mostly women, who were prized for their weaving skills, and children) entered Hispanic households as slaves. The Gutierrez family was among those who benefited.

The 1805 conflict in which Don Lorenzo distinguished himself began in mid-January, during *Yas Nilt'ees*, the Navajos' "Time of Crusted Snow." Lieutenant Colonel Antonio Narbona, an Indian fighter from Sonora, Mexico, along with influential provincial leaders including Captain Don Lorenzo Gutierrez, led an expedition of three hundred troops about two hundred miles west of Albuquerque, piercing the Navajo heartland in Canyon de Chelly. (Within less than a century, Canyon de Chelly would be one of Juan Lorenzo's trading sites.)

According to Navajo oral tradition, most of the Navajo men were away hunting at the time. Those who remained in the canyon split up when the Spanish expedition arrived. Some climbed into a cave high up the canyon walls and were killed (the cave was later named "Massacre Cave"). Narbona reported killing one hundred fifteen Navajos. He gave eleven children and wounded prisoners to the Sonorans, and the Navajos' horses to the auxiliary forces. The expedition cooked and ate the recaptured sheep. Narbona brought back twenty-four captives and lamented that there were only

> eighty-four pairs of ears of as many [Navajo] warriors and that six are lacking...because the subject that I encharged with them lost them.

It was customary for government officials to reward campaigners who presented them with warriors' ears and captives.

Don Lorenzo Gutierrez may have kept one or more of the Navajo captives for himself, as slave baptismals appeared in Spanish parish records, including Pajarito's nearby Isleta, in spring of that year. As though describing Don Lorenzo's great-grandson seventy-five years

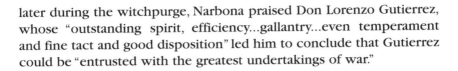

later during the witchpurge, Narbona praised Don Lorenzo Gutierrez, whose "outstanding spirit, efficiency...gallantry...even temperament and fine tact and good disposition" led him to conclude that Gutierrez could be "entrusted with the greatest undertakings of war."

Don Lorenzo, Mexican Rule, and Yankee Trade

When the Mexican government took the Southwest from Spain in 1821, Don Lorenzo Gutierrez figured heavily in the new political order, as did Juliana's paternal grandfather, who served as the provincial governor. Both men were *patróns*, persons of substance who belonged to socially prominent families and provided social and economic security and leadership to others. However, Don Lorenzo died before the end of Mexican rule in 1846.

On the authority of a property statement dated January 7, 1829, by Juliana's father, Don Juan Gutierrez, he inherited from Don Lorenzo Gutierrez one-half of the dwelling house and land (rancho), mules, pack saddles and oxen, the garden, a saddle, a silver-hilted saber, pistols, and debts—money and sheep—owed to his father. Don Juan affirmed his obligation to carry out his father's many demands: paying for numerous masses for his father and "the Blessed souls in purgatory," financing bi-weekly masses using tithes from the "fruits of the garden" unless a disaster prevented production, and funding a hundred masses for those "who had served him [Don Lorenzo] and with whom he had business" from debts owed the deceased don.

Whereas in his bequests Don Lorenzo cobbled together family, social, business, and religious matters, a heritage tied to the land, he wisely allowed for change. For over two centuries, the Spanish had bound their future to the land and its people, creating a legacy of exploitation of the natural environment and of the indigenous people. This legacy was zealously carried forward by Yankee merchants, who caravanned goods from Missouri to Santa Fe. As though blown by a "So'wester" that had abruptly stopped and dropped them to the ground, many Yankee traders stayed in Santa Fe, married Hispanic or Indian women, and immersed themselves in the area's cultures. These resettled Yankee merchants welcomed the American military's takeover during the Mexican-American War, the war that drew James Lawrence Hubbell, Juan Lorenzo's father, to the Southwest.

Yankee Ancestry and the Mexican War

Claiming William the Conqueror as an ancestor, the Protestant Hubbells had emigrated from Denmark to New England, where they pursued mercantile and fur trading ventures. James Lawrence Hubbell mustered into the army on July 20, 1846, at Fort Leavenworth, Kansas. He joined the Second Regiment of the Missouri Mounted Volunteers, who looked like a combination of American trappers and Mexican vaqueros (cowboys). Led by Colonel Sterling Price, the twelve hundred mounted Missouri Volunteers and five hundred Mormon Battalion infantrymen traveled across eight hundred dusty, hot miles of plains and deserts in fifty-three days. Private James Lawrence Hubbell arrived in Santa Fe in late September 1846, after the initial American conquest of the territory, and by September 1847, had been honorably discharged.

James stayed in the Southwest, and over the course of years, supplied the army with cattle, learned Spanish, re-enlisted and fought in the Civil War, acted as sheriff in Valencia County, served as a council member/porter in the American military government's first legislature and as a judge in the probate court, and attended seven Republican National Conventions. Along with these public activities, he married, tended to personal business, fathered children, and took care of his family.

Whether James's three brothers and parents followed him west before or after his marriage is unclear. Of his brothers, Charles M. served with Kit Carson; Sydney officiated as an assistant Supreme Court Justice of New Mexico Territory, married into a prominent Hispanic family, and argued in favor of slaveholding; and John R. drowned in 1865 in a river crossing two years after he resigned from the army following a court-martial. By 1880, according to the census, James's parents, John L. Hubbell and Sylvia R. Morse Hubbell, were living with James and Juliana at Pajarito.

Assimilation and Expansion

While Pajarito remained the heartland of the Gutierrez-Hubbell families, James pursued activities outside the village and participated in the tumultuous life of the territory: the "Navajo problem" (as New

9

Mexicans considered it), the Civil War, and the roundup and incarceration of the Navajos.

Hispanic demands for protection from Navajo livestock raids provided the impetus for construction of the American outpost at Fort Defiance in 1851, sited at the Navajos' *Tse hootsooi* ("Green Place in the Rocks," or more literally,"Meadow in a Canyon").That year, Navajo raiders filched livestock belonging to James and his father-in-law. Persistent and bold, James gathered ten men, and the group took out in pursuit of the raiders. As their pursuers closed the gap to a mile, the Navajos lanced the stolen livestock. When their horses played out, the pursuers gave up and went back to camp. An American military commander, late in joining the chase, wrote in his report that from a distance, the returning horsemen all seemed to be Hispanic—their sombreros, buckskins, serapes, and horse trappings marked their ethnicity, he thought. To the army man's surprise, as the horsemen came closer, their leader (James Hubbell) hailed the commander in unaccented English.

James, who could move gracefully between "good morning" to "*buenos días*" and from "mister" to "*señor*" and back again, was heavily relied upon by his in-laws for his bilingual skills. These, coupled with his vigor in pursuing his various private endeavors—freighting and sheep-raising—rapidly carried him up the Southwest's ladder of success.

In the 1850s, using twelve six-mule-team wagons, he freighted heavy mining equipment from Texas to southern Arizona's Heintzelman Mines. On his way back, he carried rawhide bags stuffed with ore. Sheep, another source of wealth, provided two staples of the Southwestern economy: mutton and wool. Land grant families, who owned most of the sheep, regularly increased their flocks. At least once, in 1858, James drove the Gutierrez-Hubbell flock to California to sell. On those occasions when James and Juliana or their relatives, like many New Mexicans, did not sell all their wool clip, Juan Lorenzo may have watched Hispanic weavers produce fine Rio Grande textiles. It can also be supposed that Navajo women in the Pajarito households wove slave blankets. Thus, Juan Lorenzo could have become familiar with textiles and Navajo weaving at an early age. (In support of this supposition is his description of the "stockings with feet" made by the Isleta Indians and traded to the Navajos—something he apparently had observed as a child.)

In 1859, James again complained to the army about Indians (locals said they were Navajos) killing herders and driving off livestock. Based on James's charge, the army pursued and killed Navajos, took Navajo war leader Manuelito's sheep, and burned his camp at Pueblo Colorado Wash. (In less than twenty years, Juan Lorenzo would befriend Manuelito and trade with him at Pueblo Colorado, later called Ganado.)

Throughout, Juan Lorenzo's extended family held to the Big House standard of their maternal Hispanic ancestry. This went beyond economics and included social responsibility. For example, within Pajarito, Juliana (often called "Julianita"), who had a share in a number of land grants, was a matriarch. The community called Juan Lorenzo's mother *mi mama* or *mi Tia Julianita*, "my mother" or "my Aunt Julianita," and came to her for guidance and help. Phillip Hubbell, Juan Lorenzo's nephew, recalled her culturing his smallpox vaccination and making enough serum to vaccinate the whole community. She was known for her generosity, Phillip said, as "she figured it was the best way to invest it [money]—in people."

James and the Civil War

By late 1861, as patriotism was running high and people were aligning themselves with the Union or the Confederacy, James assembled a troop of New Mexico Territory men and re-enlisted, this time in the Union army. He went in as a captain. The army valued his horse at fifty-five dollars and his equipment at twelve dollars. His brother Charles, age twenty-one, enrolled as a first lieutenant, and Cruz Rubi, age thirty (later to be Juan Lorenzo's father-in-law) enrolled as private.

James was quick to note (and chafe at) the military's discrimination against Hispanic-Americans, which surfaced more openly during the Civil War, as well as its failure to treat him as an officer and gentleman. In January 1862, James griped in writing to the territorial governor. His lengthy charges included the military's poor treatment of him even though he was an officer of the Volunteers, the Confederate Texans' being allowed to capture some territorial forts, and the regular army commanders' inability to speak Spanish to the volunteer troops. While views at the time differed, some American army commanders did indeed rate the territorial Hispanic volunteers as deficient in self-reliance, military spirit, English, and intelligence.

James had other difficulties that year. In April, Colonel B. S. Roberts of the Fifth Regiment of New Mexico Volunteers arrested James for having a laundress in his wagon. James insisted that he had permission. Roberts denied this, saying the orders of "no laundresses" were long-standing. James pressed his argument, saying that she was the wife of his saddler rather than a prostitute as had been intimated. The saddler, explained James, had enlisted as a married man under the condition that his wife was taken care of and received rations as a laundress.

James requested a release from arrest to tender his resignation, but the laundress problem must have resolved itself. In June, the army arrested James again, this time for the illegal disposition of public property, and confined him to the area within the Albuquerque city limits. In late July, he requested leave for shoulder injuries so he could seek relief from his pain at Luna Hot Springs.

By fall 1862, the territorial general had turned his attention back to Indian hostilities, and James campaigned against the Mescaleros with Kit Carson, who headed five companies of New Mexico Volunteers. Finally, at the end of November, James tendered his unconditional resignation, giving as his reason private affairs that required his attention. During this time, Juliana gave birth to their eighth child, Frank, and the couple's two oldest sons, Santiago and Juan Lorenzo, attended school in Santa Fe.

Juan Lorenzo's Education

Juan Lorenzo's recollections of his education vary considerably from information found in available records. In writing to a political correspondent, Juan Lorenzo described himself as one-half Mexican and said he could not speak a word of English until he was thirteen years old. In the 1930 *Touring Topics* interview, he recollected that he learned Spanish before English and that his early education,

> private tutoring, was in Spanish. My father, however, clung to the traditions of his English ancestry, and when I was twelve years old sent me to Farley's Presbyterian School in Santa Fe. I spent four years in that school and the instruction there was in English.

Earlier, in *Notables of the West*, he had recollected a total of nineteen months' attendance at St. Michaels and McFarland's schools in Santa Fe. The records of Santa Fe's St. Michaels School and College listed nine-year-old Juan Lorenzo, along with his older brother Santiago, in attendance for thirty-eight months, commencing December 1862. (This was only three years after Archbishop Lamy, who would later be eulogized in Willa Cather's *Death Comes to the Archbishop*, established the school.) St. Michaels' 1865 prospectus listed the courses of study as

> reading, writing, grammar, geography, the use of the globe, history, arithmetic, bookkeeping, algebra, geometry, measuring, surveying, drawing, logic, French, Latin, Greek and music.

The prospectus further noted:

> Each pupil should be provided with sufficient clothes, mattress, bed clothes, napkins and towels, a knife, fork, spoon and glass: brushes, basin, soap and combs. On the first Thursday of the month, the pupils may go to the city if their parents come for them. The scholastic year begins on the first of November and ends on the last Thursday of August.

The *Rio Abajo Weekly Press* confirmed this schedule, reporting on September 1, 1863, that "the children of Santiago [James] Hubbell arrived in town last week from the Brothers and Sisters School at Santa Fe." The school year was arranged to accommodate the boarders' need to be home in time for the fall harvest.

The Long Walk

That same year, as the people of Pajarito prepared for winter, federal military authorities in New Mexico Territory planned a campaign to finally deal with their "Indian problem." Kit Carson and his troops would round up the Navajos and the government would imprison them on a flat, desolate expanse of land, forty miles square, by the alkaloid Pecos River. Here, in the territory's east-central region, federal authorities would fashion a model farming community as well as isolate the Navajos from incoming American settlers.

The Americans called this place Fort Sumner, and the Hispanics,

Bosque Redondo or "Round Grove," after a circle of green cotton-wood trees. The Navajos dubbed it *Hwelte* or *Hwééldi*, a Navajo form of the Spanish word *fuerte*, or "fort." Whatever it was called, Fort Sumner (and the roundup) soon became synonymous with suffering.

Many Navajos fled westward to escape Carson and his troops; among the army troops was Charles Hubbell, James's younger brother. Fleeing headmen Manuelito and Ganado Mucho were joined by a Navajo mother and her young son, Henry Chee Dodge (who would later be Juan Lorenzo's friend, business contemporary, and the first Navajo tribal chairman). It is said that Chee's mother climbed up to a Hopi village to get food and never returned; Chee then ended up at Fort Sumner in the care of various Navajo relatives. (Henry Chee Dodge's father may have been a captive of Hispanic descent, Juan Cocinas, who was killed in the Navajo wars. Or, he may have been Navajo Indian agent Henry L. Dodge, murdered by the Apaches in 1856.) It is possible that Chee journeyed to Fort Sumner as part of one of Charles Hubbell's convoys.

According to letters written years later, Charles Hubbell visited the Gutierrez-Hubbell family while serving under Kit Carson during the roundup. He is sure to have regaled the Pajarito household with his stories about getting lost and then wounded at Pueblo Colorado Valley; about the army's winter attack on Canyon de Chelly, when Kit Carson and his men—including Charles—broke the starving Navajos' resistance; and about the forced marches of Navajos to Fort Sumner, some of which he led. (The Navajos call this collection of marches "The Long Walk," and the number of Navajos who suffered or perished on the way is appalling.) Charles might also have told about his rescue of Navajo children stolen from a convoy by New Mexicans, or that he ignored army orders to proceed with haste on the final march because he wanted to be sure that the last thousand Navajos he ushered to Fort Sumner arrived in fair condition.

James may have cashed in, as did his brother, Judge Sydney Hubbell, on the bonanza New Mexicans experienced in supplying Fort Sumner. While the Fort Sumner Navajos were acquiring a taste for American food goods, however, limited rations and crowding were causing illness and death among the people. Of the approximately nine thousand people who were marched to Fort Sumner, nearly two thousand died, generally of dysentery and pneumonia. The Navajos wanted to return home, and by 1868, the government wanted out of the Fort Sumner experiment as well.

Before the Navajos met with the U. S. government's representative, General William Tecumseh Sherman, for treaty-making in May 1868, tribal leader Barboncito conducted the Navajo "Put In the Bead" ceremony, which involved placing a white shell in a female coyote's mouth. When she ran westward to Navajo country, it was taken as a sign to the Navajos that they would return to their high-desert homeland.

The treaty signed between the United States of America and the Navajo Tribe on June 1, 1868, which had a multitude of provisions, established the boundaries of the original Navajo reservation. It was to be eighty by sixty-five miles in size, running along the Arizona-New Mexico border and sweeping in Canyon de Chelly. Those boundaries omitted much of the pre-Fort Sumner Navajo homeland, including the farmlands around Chinle Valley, Pueblo Colorado Valley, and important grazing lands. The treaty also provided for distribution of annuity goods and livestock as well as the establishment of a Navajo agency (which was ultimately sited at Fort Defiance). The distributions pointed the Navajos again to a pastoral life and to a continuation of their Fort Sumner reliance on Euro-American food goods. Both of these circumstances opened entrepreneurial doors for Juan Lorenzo when he started trading.

Amazingly, a count of returning Navajos was found in a bill (totaling $968.80) presented by James to the U. S. government. The 7,136 returning Navajos, their 564 horses, and 4,190 sheep crossed a toll bridge/dam that was 75 feet long and 18 feet high and built by James and Juliana's brother, Roman, on the Rio Puerco. Whether or not fifteen-year-old Juan Lorenzo saw the blanket-wrapped Navajo men clasping their bows and arrows and the women in worn *bils* (blanket dresses), he must have heard the details when his father raged over the unpaid government claim.

The same year the Navajos were allowed to return from Fort Sumner, James not only incorporated a mining venture but also finished remodeling the second of Juliana's family homes. (In 1841, Rio Grande floodwaters had washed away what remained of Juliana's ancestors' first Pajarito house, which was built in 1825.) The March 28, 1868, edition of the *Rio Abajo Weekly Press* described the additions. After reporting on the series of improvements that Juliana's brother, Juan N., made at Pajarito, the article went on to note that James Hubbell

> has finished there one of the largest, most convenient, and comfortable buildings for a residence that we know of in New Mexico.

In addition to the living area, the residential complex included a large storeroom for mercantile purposes, a walled-in corral, plus extensive sheds and areas for stables and wheat. The article noted that "farming seems to be the order of the day," and that the family planned to supplement Pajarito's new vineyards by "several thousand more grape vines to be set out this spring." Nor did the Gutierrez-Hubbell families neglect their civic duty. They donated land to widen the village of Pajarito's main street, and James set out fifteen hundred cottonwoods to green the area.

In his youth, Juan Lorenzo said, he worked for his father, presumably on many of these endeavors. By age seventeen or so, however, he left Pajarito and his father's authority. His own life story began.

Santiago Hubbell in Civil War uniform; from the New Mexico State Records Center and Archives, McNitt Collection and Hubbell Family Papers Santa Fe, New Mexico. John L. Hubbell, Juan Lorenzo's paternal grandfather. This photo is from the photograph collection archived at HTPNHS. All photos hereafter unidentified are from that collection.

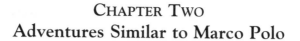
CHAPTER TWO
Adventures Similar to Marco Polo

ABOUT 1870, JUAN LORENZO SAID, he set out to seek his "fortune in the world." He was muscular—a wrestler and swimmer—not tall, not yet hefty. His light complexion offered no clues to his Hispanic ancestry, nor did his brown hair. He probably wore the thick, rimless eyeglasses he had on in an 1873 photograph.

Like a loose warp, the picture of Juan Lorenzo's life up to his twenty-fourth year is distorted by his varied and multiple retellings of its details. In the frontier tradition, he remade himself in each story. Writers later embroidered these stories even further. As a result, his early life comes to us like a series of legends.

Leaving Home

The January 1931 issue of *Santa Fe Magazine* reported that Juan Lorenzo began work at "the age of twelve, clerking in the post office in Old Albuquerque" and "was an all-around athlete." The 1870 New Mexico census listed him at home at age sixteen, and he often spoke of working for his father before starting out on his own. In *Notables of the West*, he said he received an appointment at age eighteen as assistant postmaster in Albuquerque, then moved a year later to clerk in the Santa Fe post office. In the *Touring Topics* interview, he related clerking at the Albuquerque post office at age seventeen and saving money from his forty-dollar-a-month salary. Regardless of when and where, clerking in a post office gave J. L. experience in recordkeeping, service-oriented business, and contract mail.

In the early 1870s, Juan Lorenzo finally left his "indoor life as a postal clerk" in Albuquerque to satisfy his "craving for romance and adventure" by setting out for the "virgin land" of Utah Territory with a saddle horse and outfit he bought with his savings. This journey by horseback of "500 miles through little-known country and along uncertain trails," far from the "outposts of white civilization," also took him through unfriendly Indian territory. At that time, the New Mexico and Arizona territories were deemed lawless places where residents lived in fear of what they considered Indian "menaces": Comanches and Apaches.

Between Albuquerque and his destination in Utah Territory, red-and-buff sand and rock defined a parched land of few springs. Seasonal winds whirled sand into travelers' eyes, clothes, and gear. Spring often brought late snows. If it rained, the earth deepened its color and trails became soupy clay messes that sucked at each step of horse or man. Washes turned into roaring streams. In summer, the sun broiled those crossing this "Painted Desert."

He probably traveled up the valley bordering Tanner and Hamblin washes below northern Arizona's Echo Cliffs, a rusty sandstone escarpment (now Highway 89), then dropped down to the copper-ribboned Colorado River as it crossed into Utah. John D. Lee's oasis hideout marked this crossing. Juan Lorenzo remembered staying there several weeks. At the time, federal authorities were dogging Lee for his role in the infamous September 1857 Mountain Meadow Massacre. Lee had been the captain of the Mormon Militia that attacked an Arkansas-Missouri wagon train (as ordered, he said, by the Mormon authorities) and killed one hundred persons. To avoid federal officers, Lee took up the church's charge to develop the isolated southern route from Utah to Arizona.

In an 1875 photograph, the unsmiling Lee, sixty-three years old, is dressed in ill-fitting clothes, and his unruly white hair is bunched up in cowlicks. In the *Touring Topics* article, Hubbell said that this man, portrayed by others as the devil of his time, was

> a thoroughly likable sort of fellow, hospitable, kind-hearted, intelligent, and with utterly none of the traits of character later attributed to him.

Lee had built a ferry to take wagons over the rough crossing at Lonely Dell (now called Lee's Ferry), for the sum of three dollars each; the toll for horses was seventy-five cents. Sometimes he took the fee as barter: chickens, dried fruit, soda, soap, sugar, matches, and once, a scythe. He ferried the Indians and traded with them as well, turning Lonely Dell into Navajo-Hopi-Paiute country's first stationary trading post/ranch.

During his weeks with Lee, Juan Lorenzo probably observed in Lee characteristics that early Navajo agent John H. Bowman noted about the Mormons in general: they acquired Indian languages; treated

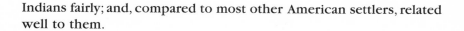

Indians fairly; and, compared to most other American settlers, related well to them.

Paiutes and Hopis

In *Touring Topics*, Hubbell said that after he left Lee's Lonely Dell, he worked in Kanab, Utah, until difficulties in early 1872 forced him to flee. These "difficulties" left him with bullet wounds in his leg. (In his old age, he limped and showed a scar from the wounds to his doctor.) The Paiutes found him wandering in delirium and nursed him back to health, a debt he repaid, he said, again and again to all Indians. He quit Utah by swimming the Colorado River at the bottom of the Grand Canyon, something, he boasted, that "not many white men have done and lived to tell about."

Pushing on to Hopi country, Juan Lorenzo stayed there from early spring until late summer 1873. While at Hopi, *Touring Times* reported, he "acquired a smattering of the very difficult Hopi language" and established himself "on friendly terms" with the Hopi people.

The Hopis live in villages atop three finger-like mesas in the middle of Navajo country. At that time, they were called *Moquis*, a term spelled and pronounced "Moki" by Euro-Americans. The term is similar to a Hopi word for "dies" or "is dead." Anthropologists urged the use of Hopi (meaning "good in every respect"), which is the Hopis' name for themselves.

Until the late 1800s, the Hopis lived in isolation on their mesa tops in multistory, pueblo-style dwellings, in sharp contrast to Juan Lorenzo's earlier hosts, the scattered Paiutes, who were considered by whites to be impoverished. The Hopis' complex religion, social organization, and political structure dictate the mainstream of tribal life. Juan Lorenzo observed the dolls carved from cottonwood roots into the likenesses of *katsinas*, figures personifying the spirits of the Hopi way; Hopi men weaving; and Hopi women preparing the plant materials for coiled and wicker basketry and processing clay for pottery.

Then as now, using the technique of dry-farming, Hopis raised abundant crops in spite of scant rainfall, and Juan Lorenzo stayed long enough to observe their full agricultural cycle: preparing seed, terracing, planting, weeding, hoeing, and harvesting. Some agricultural figures for 1893, twenty years later, are graphic indications of Hopi industriousness. According to census figures, they planted 3,600 dry acres in corn; of the 2,500,000 pound crop, the Hopis consumed 1,150,000 pounds and sold 100,000 pounds to traders. They bartered 500,000 pounds to the Navajos for sheep, traded another 150,000 pounds, and stored 600,000 pounds as surplus.

They planted 2,000 acres with other staples—beans, melons, squash, pumpkin, chiles, onions, and gourds (which were made into ceremonial rattles)—as well as sunflowers and cotton, and tended 1,000 acres of peach and apricot orchards. The fecundity the Hopis wrought from the parched land must have impressed Juan Lorenzo's agrarian sensibilities.

An older Hubbell stands in a cornfield at Keams Canyon.

The government had appointed the first Hopi agent in 1864, and the Church of Friends established a Moravian mission at the village of Oraibi in 1870, so it is likely that the young Hubbell associated with other Euro-Americans during his stay. In his *Touring Topics* narrative, however, he focused on the Hopis' allowing him to watch the snake dance ceremony from "beginning to end—the washing of the snakes, the dance, and the final liberation of the snakes as messengers in their [Hopi] prayers for rain." He commented that he was "probably one of the first white men to witness such a spectacle." (In actuality, the snake ceremony, an hour or so public rite, is only the culmination of a complex, solemn, and symbolic nine-day event.)

Juan Lorenzo would have seen the washing of the snakes in the kiva, a rectangular subterranean room accessed by a ladder through a trap door in the roof and usually open only to male members of the kiva's clan. Ceremonial activity was indicated by attaching a bow standard with red horsehair or animal skins and feathers to the ladder. The Snake Society ceremony began with a four-day gathering of snakes from the four directions. In the plaza, a green bower of cottonwood boughs and reeds in the shape of a shuck of corn held the snakes during the dance. Dancers wearing white hand-woven wool kilts and antelope-horn headdresses, their mouths lined with white paint, stood by the bower beating time with their rattles. Each snake dancer received a live snake at the bower, placed it in his mouth, stepped on a wood plank symbolizing the sipapu, the earth's navel, and then danced around the plaza alongside a companion who stroked the snake with a feather. At the conclusion of the dance, the snakes were released to each of the four directions.

Eventually, like the snakes slithering away from the plaza, young Hubbell moved on.

After Hopi

Hubbell, by now as adventurous as his father, conversant with many cultures, and wiser, ended his *Touring Topics* coming-of-age memoir:

> After nearly five years of wandering and the collection of experiences somewhat similar to those of Marco Polo, I drifted back into New Mexico again, and then into the Navajo country.

Other memoir versions differ in the details: the trip's length, his age, his trip's purpose (sometimes said to be a horse-buying expedition), his killing of the pursuers in Utah, and his rescue from his Paiute nurses by military intervention. Even though Hubbell embellished his personal history and confused his dates, every version was faithful to the patterns he wove and rewove into his life: his romantic view of the Southwest, his love of characters and cultures, his constant motion and restlessness, his penchant for being the first in anything, his ease in making friends, his willingness to expose himself to danger, his resourcefulness, and his courage. By the time he arrived at Fort Defiance, Bureau of Indian Affairs (BIA) Indian agent headquarters for "the people," or *Diné*, as the Navajo call themselves, young Hubbell possessed a strong sense of self. He considered himself to be physically powerful, an all-around athlete, and a fighter.

The biographical sketch in *Notables of the West* matches some of the documentary evidence of Hubbell's activities until his mid-twenties: clerking at Henry Reed's posts in Fort Wingate and Fort Defiance, traveling to Utah on a horse-buying expedition, and serving for about three years as an interpreter and labor superintendent with the BIA, both mundane and exciting, certainly involved Hubbell with all the players in Navajo country.

For example, from late 1873 to early 1874, Hubbell verified the distribution of treaty-issue annuity goods from the Fort Defiance Indian trader's inventory to Navajo leaders. In the same documents, Hubbell swore that he interpreted Navajo agent W. F. M. Arny's explanation to the Navajo leaders from English to Spanish and that another person (probably a Navajo, who signed with an x) translated the Spanish into Navajo. J. L. wrote out vouchers for labor and witnessed the marks of Indian laborers on the vouchers: Jim Navajo for night-watchman work, Peter Naigely for wood chopping, Charley Navajo for herding, and others.

Juan Lorenzo as a young man

Southwest historian Frank McNitt, in *The Indian Trader*, dubbed Arny a "hypocritical rascal, a Bible-pounding moralist who plotted larceny." Agent Arny spent the first few months of his tenure as agent (late 1873 to early 1874) purging the agency of employees he considered immoral for cohabiting with Indian women; this included Juan Lorenzo's friend, one-time acting agent Thomas Keam. Arny also harangued leaders Ganado Mucho and Manuelito and their followers to move onto the reservation, and otherwise managed to alienate the non-Navajo and Navajo community alike. (Paradoxically, he also sent the half-Navajo boy, Henry Chee Dodge, to school because he believed the boy to be the son of early Indian agent Henry L. Dodge.)

Navajo unrest swelled in the spring of 1874 over the off-reservation killing of three Navajos and the wounding of a fourth, supposedly by Mormons. The Navajos, members of a trading party caught in a snowstorm, were reported to have killed some livestock. Back on the reservation, Navajos wanted the Mormons to pay for deaths, while the Mormons insisted that non-Mormons had killed the three members of the trading party. Arny sent Hubbell and Ganado Mucho as couriers to meet with Utah-based Mormon leader and mediator Jacob Hamblin in an effort to quell the unrest.

By late May 1875, the Navajos began to petition the Commissioner of Indian Affairs for Arny's removal. On July 15, 1875, at Fort Wingate, Hubbell acted as interpreter and probably drafted the removal petition sent to President Ulysses S. Grant by a group of about thirty Navajos. This aligned Hubbell with tribal leadership. The petition's eloquent conclusion asked for an agent "who will take less and do more, give us less show and more justice. We believe Thomas Keam to possess all we ask for." Arny railed against Thomas Keam, who owned the Fairview Trading Post, south of Fort Defiance and east of the Hopi First Mesa. Though Keam had married a Navajo woman in a Navajo ceremony, Arny considered him a "squaw man," and Arny made no secret of his opinion.

According to some accounts, Hubbell's government employment was followed by work in Albuquerque, both before and after he opened his own trading posts. What we do know is that Hubbell clerked for traders to the Navajos, worked the BIA, and befriended key people in Navajo country during a tumultuous time (it was Keam who, in October 1876, guaranteed Hubbell's contract to supply the Navajo Agency with one hundred thousand pounds of corn.)

Hubbell was aware of the Navajos' insufficient reservation land base, which forced many individuals to live outside its boundaries. He observed Navajo leaders smoothing over the problems that inevitably arose with government agents when individual Navajos failed to keep the peace according to treaty provisions. He knew that Navajos had survived defeat and exile to return to Navajo country hungry and poor. Yet they refused to vanish, and indeed appeared to be flourishing. As Juan Lorenzo cast about for a suitable enterprise, Navajo country in the mid-1870s must have looked good.

He knew the smells of a Navajo sheep camp: pungent wool, oiled saddles, and mutton stew. He heard the sound of wind kicking sand, the staccato thump of a weaver's fork beating the weft into a blanket, the bleats of corralled sheep, and the rhythms of the Navajo language—

nasal, tonal, and glottal. He tasted ashy coffee, roasted corn, and sweet Navajo tea. He watched the landscape's wash of colors: alkali patches, crimson mesas, apricot sand dunes, evergreen forests, green-gray junipers, and khaki sage.

By the time he finished with government work and trading-post clerking, he had experienced the crowded New Mexican pueblos, the Paiutes' bare homeland, the Hopis' agricultural industriousness, and the Navajos' adaptability. He burned to begin a trading post in Navajo country, with its handful of government employees and buildings at Fort Defiance, its scattered Navajo camps, flocks of sheep, and eight thousand or so Navajos led by Manuelito and Ganado Mucho

Manuelito and Ganado Mucho

In the Navajo historical and cultural perspective, *naat'áanii* (headmen) obtained and held power through charisma, leadership, and persuasive abilities. This echoed the situation of the Hispanic *patrón*, who brought to his position a sense of obligation and service. Two men, both naat'áanii and both friends of young Hubbell, dominated Navajo-Euro-American relationships from the post-*Hwééldi* period until their deaths in 1893.

Manuelito, who stood more than six feet tall, was known as *Hastiin Ch'il hajain* ("Man of Blackweed") or *Dahaana baa daané* ("Son-in-Law of Late Texan"), and as a Navajo war chief. Bristling with aggression, he headed the short-lived tribal police force, the Navajo Cavalry. The cavalry was created at the urging of acting Indian agent Thomas Keam in 1872 to patrol Navajo country and

Manuelito as a young man.

Manuelito and wife Juanita

return stolen property, which was most often livestock.

Ganado Mucho, in Navajo, *Tótsohnii Hastiin* ("Big Water"), was known also as "Lisper" or "Talks With His Tongue" and to Euro-Americans as the peace chief. He may have been part Hopi, though he joined Manuelito in the assault on Oraibi in 1837. Escaping Kit Carson's roundup, he later brought part of his family to Fort Sumner when New Mexican citizens took his daughters and held them captive. Ganado Mucho consistently pressed Navajo interests with the various government agents; for example, he demanded that the death of two Navajos at the hands of Mexicans be satisfied by the return of captive Navajos and stock. Always, he petitioned for more land.

Ganado Mucho

25

The Navajos' pleas (plus their Euro-American friends' lobbying efforts) clearly had an effect, for to the treaty reservation's original 3.4 million acres, another million was added in 1878 and 1880; 2.3 million in 1882 and 1884; 1.5 million in 1900; and less than a half million in 1901. In the 1870s, like Manuelito, Ganado Mucho ignored agent Arny's instructions to return to the reservation with his band. He also refused the agent's demands to stop trading with the Mormons.

A fierce-looking Ganado Mucho (center) of this group portrait of Navajo headmen.

Like almost all members of their tribe, neither man spoke English.

The Language and the People

Navajo was an unwritten language until Washington Matthews (an army doctor and ethnologist at Fort Wingate in the late 1880s who used Henry Chee Dodge, commonly called Chee Dodge, as one of his interpreters) began keeping linguistic notebooks and making word cards. As late as 1880, government records listed a Hubbell, this time J. L.'s brother Charlie, interpreting English into Spanish for government business. It was 1910 before a standard linguistic reference for non-Navajos became available.

Navajo spellings varied (as they still do today). For instance, the Navajo words *bilagáana*, *bilacaana*, or *belagana* all mean "Anglo-American."

The workhorse of the language, the Navajo verb, is likened by some to "a tiny Imagist poem" because it contains the verbal idea, the subject and the object, and prefixes. Essentially, it represents a complete sentence. Compact, precise, and finicky, verbs tell a large story: *dadiikah* is "we will go one after another, in succession." Navajo vowels are short, long, doubled, and nasal (indicated by a hook mark) in quality, and low, high, rising, and falling in tone (variations indicated by accent marks). The Navajo language's glottal stop represents a small clutch of breath that changes a word's meaning—*tsin* ("log" or "tree") and *ts'in*, ("bone"). With typical Navajo flexibility, new ideas are incorporated with a twist: *bíchíih yei ádilohii* is "its nose-with it-it lassoes-the one" or "one that lassoes with its nose." Or, in more traditional English, "elephant."

Just as the language incorporated new ideas, so did the Navajos incorporate annuity goods, which were issued to them as part of the terms of the 1868 treaty, into their lives. According to textile expert Charles A. Amsden in *Navaho* [sic] *Weaving*, the annuity distribution of clothing and goods during the first ten years of the Treaty of 1868 (approximately 1868 to 1878) created a demand for American goods that idled Navajo looms.

Previously used to weave clothing items, the loom ultimately figured in what Amsden called the "economic vassalage" of the tribe; weavers began creating textiles to trade for American-made goods, which replaced material previously manufactured by the weavers for their own use. For instance, the May 1874 annuity issue included thirty thousand yards of calico and some factory-manufactured clothing. By 1879, an Indian agent described the incorporation of these treaty goods into Navajo attire:

> Most of the males wear pants and shirts made of woolen cloth and cotton goods, and the women are for the most part dressed in skirts and waists [blouses] of calico and woolen cloth, the latter of their own manufacture; also, both men and women knit stockings which they wear with moccasins on their feet.... On dress-up occasions the men wear leggings or pants elaborately trimmed with buckskin fringe and silver buttons, and the women wrap their ankles in thick and even folds of nicely tanned goat and buckskin reaching from below their ankles to the knee.... They all wear blankets and mantles used as shawls.

When they dressed up, men wore red silk turbans decorated with feathers and silver ornaments, silver earrings, and belts of oval plates, *heishi* (round, flat pieces of shell) and turquoise necklaces, bright calico shirts, and loose cotton pants. For festive occasions, the women wore *bils*—woven, knee-length, dark-blue dresses with scarlet designs along the borders—and cinched their waists with woven belts over which they wore silver concho belts. In the late 1800s, Navajo men and women wore their hair tied back in an hourglass-shape called a *chonga*. (In contrast to the Navajos, Hubbell always dressed in dark, nondescript clothes.)

In the late nineteenth century, Navajos were generally taller than other American Indians. Some, such as headman Ganado Mucho, were of stocky build, while others were raw-boned, leaner types. Some men wore mustaches. Women were small-boned, with facial features ranging from thick lips to delicate features and doe eyes. Navajo skin color depended on ethnic mixture and sun exposure; some Navajos were light complected, others dark and ruddy. However, regardless of attire and physical attributes, Navajo individuals—then and now—inevitably coalesce into kinship groups.

A flock of Navajo sheep near Ganado

Kin, Home, and Sheep

Navajo society revolves around the relationship between an individual, his or her biological and extended family, and clan relatives, all of whom must be treated peacefully, with kindness, cooperation, and thoughtfulness. Navajos tried to establish this same sort of reciprocity of merit, mutual advantage, and obligation with government agents and traders. An Indian agent might be able to ignore this, but for a trader to be successful, he had to be aware of kinship obligations as well as certain primary Navajo social premises. These included positive behavior and values, goodness, productivity, the ability to get along, dependability, helpfulness, and generosity in giving and spending. Some ran counter to Euro-American conventions, especially the general Navajo concept that what is good for the individual is good for everyone, and vice-versa.

Juan Lorenzo's Spanish Big House tradition gave him an edge when it came to Navajo values, as did his Pajarito family's sheep operation. In fact, the Navajo word for mother, *shimá*, includes flocks of sheep, the earth, and the cornfield. For the Navajos, *dibé* (sheep) proved to be a more reliable food source than hunting or agriculture provided. Sheep provided fleece for bedding and weaving, and wool and skins for trading.

The Navajos integrated into their lives the shepherd's daily routine of herding the sheep to fresh pastures at dawn (desert areas in winter and high mountain valleys in summer), watering them, bedding them down in corrals at night, and protecting them from predators. Shepherding became another indicator of what anthropologists labeled "Navajo adaptability," or the ability of Navajos to recast a foreign element into their own pattern.

The sheep transfer provided for in the 1868 treaty took place in November 1869, in a high adobe-walled corral adjacent to the Fort Defiance agency building. There, Navajo Indian agent Captain Frank Bennett, *Chaa'tsoh'ii* or "Big Stomach," disbursed fourteen thousand sheep and one thousand goats to the Navajos. When Bennett wrote to the BIA, he noted the Navajos' anxiety, then gratitude, during the sheep issue. In *If You Take My Sheep* by L. R. Bailey, the Navajo perspective on this distribution is recounted.

Barboncito, a Navajo headman and treaty signer, after tying a battered ram to the fort corral, reminded his clansman that we lost everything...do not fight. See how it [the ram] breaks its horns and bruises its head. This is what will happen to you if you fight the white man's government....Take care of the sheep...as you care for your own children. Never kill them for food. If you are hungry, go out after the wild animals and the wild plants. Or go without food, for you have done that before. These few sheep must grow into flocks so that we, the People, can be as we once were.

The Navajos learned well. They took their excess wool—in the early years, only a pound or two sheared from each sheep with tin cans—to the traders. The traders sent it to market, first shipping it east to carpet manufacturers. By 1886, the Navajos were trading a million pounds of wool; four years later, they had doubled that amount. One of the Ganado-area oral history participants, Tully Lincoln, commented on these changes. He viewed the Navajo return from Fort Sumner as an introduction "to a civilized life. The government issued farm tools and sheep." Navajos were "to devote" themselves to these things and "never take up their previous ways of life."

Sheep, coupled with Navajo and Hispanic social behavior, greased the ultimate operation of all of Hubbell's trading posts, including his sales of Navajo textiles. Similarly, sheep pens, whether at family hogans or near trading posts, were the focal points around which reservation economic life rotated.

A fork-stick hogan, an old-style dwelling without a ceiling; later,
walls and a cribbed log ceiling became common.

The traditional Navajo dwelling, a round earthen structure called a *hooghan* (hogan), dominated the cultural and geographic landscape of Navajo country. The hogan doubled as a ceremonial house, and as such, neatly stitched the secular to the spiritual.

Hogans (first round and later, polygonal) consist of one room with a central hearth. Easily heated and dimly lit by natural light coming through the smoke hole, they are a place of easy congregation. In the heat of the day, their dirt floors are cooled by sprinkling them with water, and their eastern-facing doors catch the blessing of the sun's first rays.

Family belongings crowd shelves and cupboards nailed to walls; wooden pegs or nails driven into ceiling-crib logs provide suspended storage. The social division of hogan space, with its rear area opposite the doorway reserved for the family's patriarch or matriarch, was repeated in the trading post. In the post, individuals congregated in front of the trading counter in an area called the "bullpen." At the back of the trading room, behind the counter, the trader and his clerks occupied the position of authority.

The government discounted the comfort of hogans, overlooking the dilapidated and vermin-infested condition of most government-employee quarters, such as those Hubbell had lived in at Fort Defiance. In the Fort Defiance Indian agent's 1874 annual report, he reported that only six houses were occupied by the Navajos and insisted that "the most important step...is to induce them [the Navajos] to build permanent houses."

Hogans, houses, and government quarters were connected to each other by rough foot trails that zigzagged over Navajo country.

Navajo Country, The Physical and Cultural Landscape

The term "Navajo country" or "Navajoland" means lands used by the Navajo—an area that at any given time was always larger than the acreage within legal reservation boundaries.

The whole of Navajoland (after their return from Fort Sumner) was called *Diné Bikeyah'* and fell within the center of the Colorado Plateau, a region of rocks cut by canyons and surrounded by mesas and buttes. Extreme elevations mark its harsh physical geography—from 2,800 feet near the Little Colorado River to the 10,416-foot peak of Navajo Mountain. Mountain ranges stretch from northwest to southeast, physically slicing its high desert-to-mountainous terrain. The original Navajo Reservation, established in 1868, extended from the Shiprock, New Mexico, area west to Canyon de Chelly, Arizona (near Chinle), with a southern border above Window Rock. It did not include the Pueblo Colorado Wash slightly to the west of the original reservation boundaries where Hubbell established an early post.

Two rivers in Navajo country provided the people with their only steady supplies of water: the very large San Juan near Farmington, New Mexico, to the northeast, and the Little Colorado, often just a trickle, in the southwest near Cameron, Arizona. Most Navajos depended on uncertain seasonal creeks, streams, springs, seeps, and rock reservoirs for their water supply. A scant eight inches of annual rainfall wets half of Navajo country; the rest receives slightly more—twelve inches on the slopes and twenty-two inches in the mountains. (Once Hubbell settled in Navajo country, he thought about water development, and in his reports to correspondents, often wrote about the weather, precipitation, and their effect on the Navajos and his own farmland.)

In Navajo country, rain comes in late summer; Navajos designate a rain accompanied by lightning and thunder as a male rain, and a gentle downpour as a female rain. Droughtlike conditions occur every three to eight years. Even in normal years, months of drought are spread between seasons punctuated by too much snow, barrages of hail, or sudden flattening downpours.

The Navajos live in a land of sunshine for three hundred days a year, a blue bowl of sky covering the palest peach sand dunes and carmine mesas and buttes. Temperatures plummet to below zero and soar to over one hundred when southwestern spring winds storm across the land.

Scrub oak grows in patches in the ponderosa pine forests that blanket the elevations at about seven thousand feet; piñon pine and juniper trees dot the lower slopes. Cottonwood, box elder, alder, walnut, and peach trees thrive in the mountain canyons. The valleys of Navajoland, like Hubbell's Pueblo Colorado Valley, are broad, rolling, and spotted with sagebrush, cactus, grasses, yucca, greasewood, and, if there is underground water, cottonwoods. To Euro-Americans of the nineteenth century, the absence of green deciduous trees and grass-covered rolling hills made the area a bleak moonscape. To the Navajos it was—and is—beautiful.

To Navajos, the physical landscape includes and is bounded by the sacred mountains that surround Navajo country. In *Between Sacred Mountains*, George Blueeyes, Navajo *haťaalii* (a medicine-man sometimes called a singer) said that the Navajos' sacred mountains, which represent Navajo law, were Blanca Peak, Mount Taylor, the San Francisco Peaks, Hesperus Peak, Huerfano Mountain, and Gobernador Knob. These mountains are adorned respectively by white shell, turquoise, abalone, jet, precious fabrics, and sacred jewels. The Navajos connect their minds, hearts, and imaginations to land and to their landscape—to the space between their sacred mountains. Through song and prayer, they recount their origins and re-enact the world's creation. The physical context of Navajo life in Hubbell's time, as now, mirrored the mythological landscape; as an example, the sacred *Dook'o'oosłííd* (known to non-Navajos as the San Francisco Peaks near Flagstaff, Arizona), is the western sacred mountain and is always represented by the color yellow and abalone shell.

Raised a Catholic in rural New Mexico near various pueblos, each with its own ceremonials, young Hubbell would have been familiar with the phenomena of rituals and ceremonies that tied Indians to seasons, events, and the earth. For Hubbell, Navajo ceremonial life undoubtedly fit a familiar pattern. He most likely witnessed the Navajo Blessingway rite, which identified the patient with, and through, the earth:

> Earth's feet have become my feet
> by means of these I shall live on.
> Earth's legs have become my legs
> by means of these I shall live on.

The refrain's repetitive verse adds Earth's body, mind, voice and so on until in its concluding verse, *hózhó* has been restored. According to anthropologist Gary Witherspoon, *hózhó* represents the Navajos' ideal state of beauty, harmony, and happiness (a state to which Hubbell also aspired). This cultural view emphasizes the power of thought encompassing good and not allowing bad thoughts to enter the mind. It stresses never having a bad dream or planning for a rainy day, because the dreaded event might happen.

Too, the Blessingway rite's refrains about feet and legs emphasize the significance of movement in Navajo life. Walter Van Dyke's book, *Son of Old Man Hat.* Van Dyke's transcription of Lefthanded's, an elderly Navajo man's, oral autobiography underscores motion as a cultural theme in post-Fort Sumner Navajo life. Here for water. There for good grazing. A visit to a relative. To a ceremony. Or to trade. Early government agents recorded the tribal leaders' continual movement: at Fort Defiance and then a day or two later at Fort Wingate or Pueblo Colorado and back. Although some classified Navajos as nomadic, they were actually pasturalists, moving their herds to fresh grass and water.

The principal Navajo verb is *naaghá,* "to go," which can be contrasted with the principal verb in the English language, "to be." This sense of motion runs through the Navajos' ancestral wanderings, ceremonies such as the Mountain Chant hero's travels, seasonal migrations, and later occupational migrations (such as the railroad work Hubbell arranged).

Movement characterized Navajo country's government employees and Juan Lorenzo's ventures into trading as well.

PART TWO
WEARING SPECTACLES

The stories that go with these places [in Navajo country], and with the mortals and immortals who have come together there, are a large part of Navajo chronicles of the origin and evolution of the Navajo world, people, and customs. These chronicles are Navajo "history" as Navajos themselves have told it from older to younger, first by word of mouth, now also in writing.

—Klara Bonsack Kelley and Harris Francis,
Navajo Sacred Places

I know a lot of people have the idea that an Indian trader is a first class scoundrel—a man who attains financial prosperity by fleecing the Indians. There may have been some that have, but they didn't last long. I've been an Indian trader for fifty years, but I've dealt honestly with them. I've never taken a dollar from an Indian without giving the Indian value received, and I've often given the Indians what should have been my own legitimate margin of business profit just to help them when they needed it.

—J. L. Hubbell, *Touring Topics*

CHAPTER THREE
Lók 'aahnteel: Place of Wide Reeds

A NAVAJO LOOM consists of two uprights and two crosspieces of heavy wood, a simple configuration that also framed J. L. Hubbell's trading life. The uprights represented the trader and his trade location, and the crossbeams, his trade goods and customers.

Hubbell's First Trading Post

Clouds of time and mythmaking obscure the literal truth of J. L. Hubbell's first venture as an Indian trader. Sometimes he gave 1876 as the date he started trading at his ultimate location in the Ganado area; on other occasions, he said it was 1878. Some of the existing records concur with the later date for the establishment of Hubbell Trading Post. In *Notables of the West*, J. L. recounted establishing his first trading store among the Navajos at Manuelito Springs, outside of military protection, some forty miles east of Fort Defiance and twenty-five miles north of Gallup.

Before 1880, when he applied for a trader's license at Manuelito Springs, his correspondence was marked "Manuelito," apparently referring to Manuelito Springs. A few years later, government records noted Manuelito's large number of Indian farms and its good trade location. They also recorded the lawless disposition of the local Indians. "No one had been brave enough to keep a store there." In any event, by 1880, J. L. had focused his trading attention to the Ganado area, then called Pueblo Colorado.

J. L. said that when he came to the Ganado area, it was known to the Indians as *Lók 'aahnteel*, which means "Place of Wide Reeds." For many years, the United States Post Office listed it as Pueblo Colorado until the confusion between it and the settlement of Pueblo in the state of Colorado necessitated a name change. At that point, it was designated, J. L. said, as Ganado, Spanish for "cattle." Hubbell's granddaughter, La Charles Eckel, wrote that her grandfather chose the name Ganado as a tribute to Ganado Mucho, since the Navajo leader headed up several hundred Navajos in the area.

The trail running through Pueblo Colorado Valley and eastward over the Defiance Plateau led to Fort Defiance and Fort Wingate, respectively thirty and seventy miles away. Historically, the Pueblo Colorado Valley marked both the western boundary of Zuni land and the eastern Hopi boundary; it also became the mid-region of Navajo land.

Two washes—the Chinle and the Pueblo Colorado—create a massive watershed forty miles wide and one hundred miles long that extends from Round Rock, north of Ganado, to Sanders, Arizona, south of the Navajo Reservation boundary. The nature of this watershed dictated Navajo settlement patterns.

Thirteen, perhaps more, archeological sites can be found within the boundaries of today's Hubbell Trading Post National Historic Site. An Anasazi site, Wide Reed Ruin, dates to the thirteenth century. Abandoned the following century, it contains seventy rooms with plazas, and kivas with human burials. Eckel wrote that, according to local Navajos, the ruins, located three hundred yards from the store, once were the domain of a gigantic Navajo chieftain, Jiilwol, whose harem wives had separate rooms facing onto a courtyard. Navajo interviewees described Jiilwol as a big-footed giant, a great thinker, and an untiring runner over an area called the Race Track, whose route can still be traced in the Pueblo Colorado Valley.

Sometime before the Spanish came to the Southwest, and long before the Americans' arrival, raiding Apaches destroyed Navajo corn supplies near Ganado. This forced local Navajos to visit the Hopis at one of their mesa villages to obtain planting seeds. After feeding the Navajos, the Hopis bound them and threw them off a village cliff. The Hopis then traveled to the Pueblo Colorado Valley and killed more Navajos. Navajo stories of the Pueblo Colorado Valley area are numerous, and mention a sequence of events tied to a place, like the story at Apaches Coming Down the Slope (*Azil gha'ii adajaii*).

Navajo place names describe locales pictorially: Dead Tree Stands Up, Red House, Tree Holding Up a Load, and Lake With Weeds in the Surface. Place, which was a crucial element to both the Navajos and Hubbell, rendered the niceties of dating events, a critical factor in most Anglo histories, unimportant. Sometimes within a place's name is a picture of the event. In Klara Bonsack Kelley and Harris Francis's *Navajo Sacred Places* stories, the authors discovered place names that interrelated the speaker, his/her home, the Navajo social structure, the land, the present world's origin, Navajo deities, and the moral imperatives of these relations. Thus the Navajo stories about Lók 'aahnteel have great importance.

Escalante and Dominquez traversed the area in 1776, and Hispanics raided there for slaves. In 1858, an American commander avenged the death of a black slave at Fort Defiance by destroying cornfields and burning hogans along Pueblo Colorado Wash. As late as the fall of 1860, Indian fighter and scout Manuel Chavez and his troops hunted for Navajos, capturing thousands of head of livestock and one hundred women and children. In retaliation, the Navajos stampeded Mexican herds, then Chavez's troops looted a thousand sacks of corn from Pueblo Colorado Valley.

Joseph C. Ives's peaceful exploratory expedition stopped in the valley to trade with the hospitable Navajos there and swapped the last of the expedition's goods for goat's-milk cheese and other items. In his 1860 report, Ives described the wash as "a pretty creek running between steep earth banks ten or twelve feet high" and the valley bottom as a "brilliant sheet of Verde [green]," welcome after the arid country he had just traversed.

Elderly Navajos from the Ganado area, interviewed in the late 1960s and early 1970s, portrayed the Pueblo Colorado Wash area as less eroded and more forested prior to J. L.'s late nineteenth-century trading ranch expansion. Mrs. Yazzie Holmes, born in 1890, claimed there was no wash; Hubbell's neighbor, Dolth Curley, born in 1884, said "water just ran over the land when it rained." Friday Kinlicheeny, born in 1895 and a Hubbell Trading Post employee for fifty-five years, recalled that the post's fenced area was once "full of juniper trees growing close together, and I was present when they felled them. The fence was built when Hubbell was young." Navajos and Hispanics hired by Hubbell took out the trees to make way for alfalfa patches, which the trader irrigated with water from Ganado Lake.

Posts at Pueblo Colorado

First Hubbell located a post or trading stand along Pueblo Colorado Wash (Spanish for "Red Town"), by what is now called Ganado Lake,

about three miles upstream from the present post. Before that, in 1871
or 1872, Charles Crary probably also started a post along the wash, but
downstream from the lake. In 1875, William Leonard, the agency
trader at Fort Defiance, bought out Crary and turned the management
of that post over to George M. "Barney" Williams. (This accounts for
references to a post along the Pueblo Colorado Wash called "Barney's"
or "Leonard's.")

When Hubbell purchased Leonard's store, the present site of
Hubbell Trading Post, everyone called the building—a rather slapdash,
low-roofed juniper log-and-sod structure doubling as post and living
quarters—the Leonard Building.

The Leonard Building, located across the wash from Hubbell Hill.
Many Horses stands with Hubbell in front of the gate.

LaCheenie Blacksheep (also known as Hastiin Díbetlizhini), one
of the many oral history project interviewees, described the building's
interior as awkwardly arranged, with merchandise at one end and a
small space used as a post office at the other. Some Navajos say that in
later years, the Leonard Building was torn down; others say it burned.
J. L. said that "two years later [he] went there [Ganado, at the Leonard
site] to manage it" and sold out his interest at Manuelito Springs.

While Euro-American entrepreneurs say they just chose whatever trading spot they wanted, Navajos viewed the placement of a trading site as a matter requiring their permission. In fact, Navajo leaders Manuelito and Many Horses (Ganado Mucho's son) said "no" twice, the second time in 1893, to the location of a Presbyterian mission along the Pueblo Colorado Wash. One Ganado-area interviewee, T'Ahashaa' Slivers, commented that long ago, Navajo leaders (including Ganado Mucho, Many Horses, Small Whiskers, and others) agreed that J. L. could move down to the Pueblo Colorado Wash area to trade, and gave him land for a trading post.

The Person Who Sits for Things of Value

By the time Juan Lorenzo Hubbell opened his own store in Navajo country, his eyeglasses had caught the Navajos' fancy. They called him *Nák'ee sinilí, Nakeznilih, Nikhaeznili,* or *Nakhaaz nili,* which can be commonly rendered as "Double Glasses," "Wearing Spectacles," and the "Man Wearing Glasses" (literally translated, "that particular thing placed on the eyes").

Navajos' use of descriptive language mixes with their sense of humor in the names they give themselves and others: *Achídahilawho,* "One Who Hurries to War," was Barboncito's Navajo name; *Éé' neishoodii* (priest), meant "one who drags the dress"; and *Béésh biwoo'ii* ("Iron Teeth," the Navajo's name for C. N. Cotton, Hubbell's business partner) meant "one who has gold-filled teeth" or "one with metal teeth."

Choice of nomenclature also illuminates nineteenth-century Navajo thinking about traders, trading posts, and trade goods. Navajo words for trading—*naalyéhé, naalyéhé bá hooghan, naalyéhé yá sidáhí*—literally translated mean "things of value," "a house with things of value," and "a person who sits for things of value." Popularized and shortened equivalents became "merchandise," "trading post," and "trader." The literal translations are also indicative of the relevance these things had to Navajos in those early years and of the importance of traders, not just to individual Navajo consumers, but to Navajo leaders as well.

While the Navajo definition of a trader emphasized the concept of material goods, the traders themselves put a high value on their role in the community. Hubbell commented in the *Touring Topics* article that Easterners visualized a trader as a Sir Thomas Lipton fellow in India, making money from products of the Orient. He felt that what he called the dictionary definition—one who isolates himself from his race to establish trade relations with American Indians—fell *muy corto* (very short) of the traders' real role. Hubbell defined this true role as everything from merchant to father confessor, justice of the peace, judge, jury, court of appeals, chief medicineman, and *de facto* czar of the domain over which he presided.

J. L.'s friends and occasional guests, Dane and Mary Roberts Coolidge, in their work *The Navajo Indians*, named traders as one of the three most important types of individuals on the reservation; Indian agents and Navajo leaders completed the list. They said that the Navajos would travel long distances to trade with a personable trader in whom they had confidence. Among the traders' functions were acting as a local newspaper; as a mortician; as a doctor by bandaging wounds and providing pharmaceutical products; and as an advisor. On the other side, traders served all non-Indians—government or private—on the reservation by interpreting, advising, and making Indian contacts in matters such as sheep buying and dam construction.

In her book *The Navajo*, Ruth Underhill called reservation traders "Navajo Shoguns," similar in many ways to the Japanese shoguns who guided their local populations. And Joseph Schmedding, who traded at Chaco and bought the Hubbells' Keams Canyon post, took to task the more common view of traders in his book *Cowboy and Indian Trader* when he wrote that "a trader's life is not just standing behind a store counter and selling merchandise at exorbitant prices to untutored savages."

A House with Things of Value

Prior to stationary trading posts, the Navajos manufactured most of what they needed, or made infrequent trading trips for food, medicine, or clothing. However, many of the goods provided by traders had obvious practical, if not aesthetic, advantages over those made by hand. For example, the fifteen-cent tin cups available at the trading post became more popular than the wooden cups manufactured by the Navajo. To make a wood cup meant finding a wood burl, removing a plug from it, seasoning it, smoldering hot coals in the burl cavity, and finally scraping away the charcoal. The last two steps were repeated until the cavity was the size desired. Weavers also came to prefer the traders' wire-toothed tow cards over wild thistles to smooth out their tangled, clipped wool.

Before the late nineteenth century, traders sometimes roamed the countryside with wagons of goods. Then came seasonal trading tents (Hubbell's brother Charlie clerked at one in Washington Pass, north of Fort Defiance, in 1884), and the more common two-room structures. These stationary posts and trade goods revolutionized Navajo material culture at a faster pace than the government could manage with its proselytizing, educating, and making farmers out of the subjugated tribe.

While trading posts emphasized the rectangle and hogans, the circle, both used the same building materials—posts, logs, rocks, and earth—and both emphasized a central activity area. Most trading posts boasted a trading room separate from a warehouse.

The post's womblike central area, called the bullpen, was warm, snug, and close like a hogan. Both bullpen and hogan smelled of burning juniper and faintly musty wool. Shelves full of commercial food products lined the trading room's walls. Flour sacks and bags of sugar shared space with bolts of fabric and canned peaches. Unsold saddles, bridles,

In this painting by E. A. Burbank, which records the bullpen of Hubbell's Ganado trading post, Hubbell is standing in the corner behind the counter, and the man resting his feet on the stove is thought to be his brother Charlie.

and enamel coffee pots dangled from the ceilings or overflowed into the trader's office and living quarters or outbuildings—thus following a century-old trading post maxim:"customers won't buy what they can't see."

A wooden plank counter, worn smooth and concave like the stone steps to an old church, separated the trader, clerks, and shelves of goods from the bullpen, the area where the Navajos congregated and socialized around a wood-burning stove. Navajos pushed native goods—wool, hides, silverwork, and rugs—across the yard-wide, chest-high counter, and the clerks (who were generally Euro-American) slid back calico, coffee, and other products of an industrial society in return.

Bullpen of Hubbell Trading Post

Though traders like Hubbell clearly met a need, how traders viewed this was often condescending to the Indians and biased in favor of the trader. Anglo Sam Day II (son of a St. Michaels, Arizona, settler and trader, and Hubbell's neighbor) once said, "My God, these Indians would've starved to death if it hadn't been for the traders."

Day also commented that some thought that traders robbed the Indians, but "the government never helped the doggone poor devils in any way."

While Day confused U. S. policies and the traders' economicgoals, the literal translation of the Navajos' term for the contents of the trading post does indeed partially support his view: Among these "things of value" were flour, coffee, potatoes, bacon, canned tomatoes and peaches, salt, baking powder, and beef. Some traders raised and sold pigs and turkeys. Household equipment included calico, velveteen, needles, thread, enamel and wrought-iron dinner and cooking ware, knives, shears, saddles and bridles, and shoes and hats. Indeed, trading post inventories were similar to those of any rural storekeeper a half-century earlier.

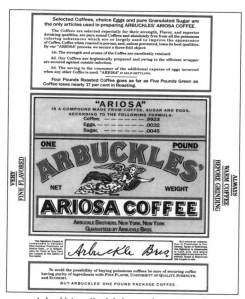

Arbuckle's coffee label, a trading post staple

The Necessities

Frank Mitchell, born in 1881 and a Navajo Blessingway singer, politician, and judge from the Chinle area, related in his autobiography, Blessingway Singer, that in his early years, the reservation lacked roads and wagons and no trader sold food in Chinle. Mitchell said the "only post we heard of was over at Ganado and that was too far away. The trader at Hubbell's in Ganado used to get his merchandise from Gallup." Mexicans ran the supply line to the post, Mitchell said, using saddlebagged mule trains or wagons.

"Store food" drew many Navajos to the Ganado area, however. Long-time Ganado resident, Ya Na Bah Winker, later a weaver for Hubbell, explained that hunger and hardship caused her family to move to

Ganado to be near Hubbell's store. Navajos who had to depend upon uncertain autumn crops and piñon harvests to get them through the winter were often starving by spring.

About the time Hubbell started trading at Ganado, agent John E. Pyle wrote in his diary (January 1 to November 27, 1878) that

> in good years, the tribe could be self-supporting, for within ten years the Navajos have grown from a band of paupers to a nation of prosperous, industrious, shrewd—for barbarians—intelligent people. It should be remembered, however, that they were paupers by disastrous warfare with the whites.

He reckoned that the Navajos' sheep numbered "not less than 550,000 head. Pretty good for savages, eh?" Pyle's journal entries for May indicated wool flowing into all the trading places, ten of which bordered the reserve. Hubbell also valued sheep and goats as Navajo assets and sources of wealth. As he noted in *Touring Topics*,

> Both animals [sheep and goats] furnish them with meat, while the wool and hides are staple articles of trade, goods to be exchanged for coffee, soda water, beans, flour and all manner of white man's products that the Indians find use for.

The seasonality of stock-raising required the trader to carry accounts, however: Navajos needed provisions to carry them from November to May's shearing time.

When Hubbell began trading, his orders reflected the goods desired by the Indians. An 1886 order placed with Hubbell's wholesale supplier reflected a wide assortment of Euro-American products: one box of ball cotton (20 cents each); five president red blankets ($5.50 each); a skein of ten pounds of red yarn (20 cents each); two dozen knives (25 cents each); a dozen red bandannas ($2 each); ten pounds of indigo ($1.50 a pound); bayeta, a red woolen cloth dyed with cochineal ($2 a yard); a half-dozen small pans of graduated sizes (from 20 to 40 cents each); thirty pounds of candy; one case of pears, which Navajos called "apples with a tail on the end" (50 cents per can); ninety-three pounds of leather ($38.61); two hundred fifty needles; shovels ($3 each); fifty boxes of sea salt (25 cents each); twenty pounds of lard ($2.60); one hundred sixteen pounds of potatoes ($4.06); one hundred pounds of flour ($4.50); sixty-one pounds of bacon ($6.10); a dozen tin cups (50 cents each); three fancy blankets ($5 each); baking soda; packs of cards (75 cents each); four large kettles ($1 each); four boxes of matches (10 cents each); and coffee sacks (35 cents each).

Some of the high-priced, small-quantity items on the order sheets were obviously meant for the trader and his family—brass kettles, a half yard of chain, a bolt lock, platform scales, two pounds of tea, a sack of cornmeal, and a string of chiles. In 1885, Hubbell's post ordered a thousand pounds of flour at a time, at four dollars per hundred pounds.

The trader's relationship with his wholesaler mirrored the trader-Indian dynamic. The supplier used credit, consignment, delivery, and marketing to bind the trader to a particular wholesaler. The trader watched the wholesaler's honesty, performance, and prices, and threatened to terminate the relationship if the wholesaler violated principles associated with these values.

The Trading Ritual

Here is Hubbell's perspective on the trading ritual, as recorded in *Touring Topics*:

> An Indian buck drives up with his wagon in front of the post. He may have several hundred pounds of wool, a bale of goat skins, several rugs that his squaws have made, and a number of articles of Indian silver jewelry. All such goods have very definite market value, and the trader who is honest will allow the Indian equal value in other staple commodities or quotations of the day.

Navajo oral history interviewees said that Hubbell would open canned goods and invite them to eat when they entered the trading post. After they ate, he would bring out his tin money and tell them what their wool was worth.

Both Navajo men and women chewed plug tobacco, which posts displayed behind the counter. A propped-up wooden box held Climax (mixed with molasses), Star, and Brown's Mule brands. While in

Customers coming and going and resting with their blanket packs at Hubbell's post.

a hospitable gesture, traders provided free tobacco to their customers, they sometimes used wooden boxes with nails mixed into the tobacco to discourage greediness. Instead of a box, Hubbell placed a Bull Durham or Duke tobacco mixture in a six-inch-wide concrete bowl and dropped into its four-inch well some matches and cigarette paper.

Hubbell, in his *Touring Topics* discourse on trading, used an example of a customer trading a hundred dollars' worth of Indian goods.

> The Indian wants to see $100 in actual money laid out on the counter...if he buys a tin of sardines costing ten cents, he demands that the purchase be paid for then and there out of his money pile...if he hands over a dollar he must receive ninety cents in change before he goes on making additional purchases.

Usually, after each transaction, Navajos would inquire "How much left?"

Occasionally, J. L. said, the trader gave his Navajo customer a written statement, or "due bill," of the credit available to them for goods traded. This due bill would be traded out over a period of time. Hubbell felt that the more astute Indians had "learned they could rely on the trader's honesty."

More than one observer of trading-post patterns commented that Navajos played traders against each other, bragged about besting a trader in a transaction, and traveled long distances to trade at a favorite post. One of the St. Michaels Franciscan fathers recounted the ending of one of those stories. A Navajo sold Hubbell a big sack of wool stuffed with a large rock. Hubbell instructed his clerk to put the rock in a sack of flour and sell that sack back to the same Navajo customer. When the Navajo bought the rock-laden flour sack, he never complained, much to Hubbell's delight. Another of Hubbell's practices was to use a bull snake to catch mice in the store and the warehouse. The snake rested behind display cases in the post and sometimes in the cash drawer. The Navajos avoided it and must have been relieved when a teamster killed it in the blacksmith shop one day. Hubbell was not happy, however.

Lefthanded, in his autobiography, *Son of Old Man Hat*, described Hubbell's trading protocol early in his trading days at Ganado. When Lefthanded arrived at Ganado with blankets full of wool,

> The trader, Wearing Spectacles, came out and started shaking hands with us, saying "Welcome, my sons-in-law." He was saying that and running around among us; he was so glad and thankful we'd come to his place. The old man, my father, said, "Yes, we've come a long way...we're all pretty hungry." "Oh, well, then," he [Hubbell] said, "Hurry and unload your horses and turn them loose. Just take them up there, and they'll have plenty to eat."

Hubbell gave them a bucket, a dutch oven, and a pan of flour with baking soda in it so they could make themselves a meal. Following the meal, Lefthanded commented that Hubbell "was a jolly fellow...talking and laughing" and telling them to bring their wool in when they were ready. The trader said "I'll give you a good price for it. I'll treat you well. I know you've come a long way." Hubbell encouraged them to spend the night "or even four because I like to have company all the time." After they finished trading, Lefthanded's father said they would leave the next morning so they would not eat up all of Hubbell's grub, though "we're thankful to you for treating us nicely." The trader said,

> "Well, I don't care about feeding you. I only care for friends, that's
> all. Even though I run out of grub I can get more because it's not
> far from here where I get it." The next morning he gave us some
> more food.

While Lefthanded's portrait of trader Hubbell revealed generosity, amiability, and courtesy (all primary Navajo values), it also bordered on ridicule. In the Navajo way, the trader made many faux-pas. He came out immediately as Lefthanded and his group arrived rather than waiting until they approached his door. The trader repeated himself, which in the Navajo way is culturally inappropriate. Hubbell used effusive words of friendship when there had been no time to develop mutual confidence and respect. The trader's use of "my sons-in-law" was a particularly inappropriate phrase for a white man to use in public with Navajos he barely knew. And finally, the trader's continual directives bordered on being overbearing.

Navajo trading behavior relied on the safety formulas for Navajo life—be wary of non-relatives and go slowly—which meant that many minutes could pass between the time a Navajo entered a trading post and trade beginning. Traditionally, only those actively trading stood at the counter; others lounged near the wall or stove. With the entire stock on display, this inspection period allowed the customer to prepare a mental shopping list.

Joseph Schmedding, who spent several years clerking for long-time trader Richard Wetherill before running the post at Keams Canyon, defined the proper standards of trading practice as

> a battle of wits, but none was allowed to have recourse to unfair
> means, to cheat, to falsify weight, or in any manner take advantage
> of the illiteracy of Indians. Fair play was the rule of the game, and
> each deal had to leave a pleasant taste in the mouth of everybody
> concerned.

Writer Hamlin Garland, who stayed with J. L. for a few weeks in 1899, commented in his essay collection *Observations* that it was pathetic to see Navajo customers' interest in the white man—they eagerly ran to the post

> because it seemed somehow to have a little touch of the great white man's world in it. There were pictures on the cans and wrappers of the groceries...pictures posted on the wall.

He also observed that the Indians "were ready to do anything they knew how, to earn a little money and also they kept their word!"

The Coolidges (Hubbell's writer friends) explained that the customers had no money, which meant the trader extended heavy credit to his customers, who paid later in sheep, wool, pelts, blankets, and piñon nuts. He loaned thousands of dollars on pawned jewelry, turquoise, silver, and saddlery without interest, and held these items for a long time. Hubbell allowed that he did "a considerable pawn-brokerage business," since the Indians were "notoriously improvident" and would pawn their jewelry and other property in order to buy goods. (His statement reflected a distinctly Euro-American point of view. Navajo culture frowns on the accumulation of wealth for its sake alone and respects sharing.)

The turquoise and silver jewelry, particularly silver concho belts, that adorned the post's pawn racks never left the trading post except for ceremonies. If the goods remained on the pawn rack past their redemption date, then the pawn was considered dead. However, if a trader sold dead pawn he would lose the customer's good will. Compassion, too, precluded some sales of dead pawn, as Maynard Dixon (an early 1900s artist-visitor) related. A visitor wanted to buy some dead pawn, so J. L. examined the pawn tickets. He then commented, "H'm—that was due last December. I know that family. They had bad luck—lot of their sheep froze to death last winter. They'll redeem it some time."

Hubbell held on to a necklace a Navajo customer valued as sacred, then decided to sell a piece of dead pawn a "no good" customer pawned when he "gambled everything away." These value judgments could be considered paternalistic, yet they also indicate that Hubbell recognized his customers who pawned items as individuals. In her work *Woman Who Owns the Shadows*, Indian novelist Paula Allen Gunn reminds readers to remember that

Indians are people too. Strong, capricious, willful, gentle, mali-
cious, kind, vicious. People. Human beings. Not noble denizens of
a long-lost wilderness.... But real live human beings, full of piss and
vinegar, as the saying goes.

Tokens, a Medium of Exchange

J. L. paid out tokens, as did other traders. Also called tin money,
trade checks, aluminum money, chips, tin trade chips, J. L. H. money,
script, and trader checks, these were minted with the name of his trading enterprise and had designated values. Navajos called the tokens
seco (dry money) or *pesh-tai* (thin metal or dry chips). He gave these
out for Indian products and in lieu of cash for Indian labor.

Minting their own money saved traders from making cash outlays
in a cash-poor business and tied the token holder to the trader's store.
Early in the trading-post era, Navajos distrusted paper money and
though this attitude changed, traders held on to the token tradition,
often ignoring government regulations prohibiting its use (Hubbell
argued for an exception for Ganado due to its location on private
land). The managers of Hubbell's outlying posts requested tokens and
fretted over their use.

Hubbell hired Indians, mostly Navajo, to work at his trading ranch
and in related post functions, such as carrying the mail. In this regard,
Hubbell's operations were thoroughly dyed with feudal and colonial
overtones. His biases toward free enterprise and his rhetoric of the
self-made man notwithstanding, he spared no effort in developing a
dependent community around him at Ganado and at his other posts
as well. According to historian Charles S. Peterson, who wrote a trea-
tise on the Hubbell farm enterprise, J. L. played the role of *hidalgo*
well, exploiting all the elements in his activities to create a form of
vassalage.

Though Hubbell said that he saved the lives of Indians who traded
with him in order to repay the debt he himself owed the Paiutes for
saving his life, he also knew that certain trading practices, such as the
use of tokens, could sometimes be equated with dishonesty. There
were, he said in *Touring Topics*, just a few "black sheep" or "dishonest
Indian traders." However, he credited most with being "too honest for
their own good."

Group of tokens, mostly Hubbell

Hubbell's metal coinage use was generally limited to his stores, though occasionally another store would take Hubbell tokens. For instance, Sam Day accepted Hubbell tin at Day's St. Michaels store when Navajos attending a ceremonial nearby had nothing else to exchange for food. Hubbell's Keams Canyon store got credit for J. L. H. tin taken at Keams. Navajo medicinemen accepted it in payment for traditional ceremonies, and churches sometimes found it in their collection plates.

Navvy

Hubbell took pride in his ability to speak the Navajo language. He often said that all trade business with the Navajos was handled in Navajo and, in *Touring Topics*, that

> the unwritten Navajo tongue is scarcely easier to the average white man to learn than Chinese. It is a rare Navajo who speaks English.

The trader who would be successful with the Indians must speak
their language well. I've been studying and speaking their language
now for fifty years, and I think I speak it as well, or possibly better,
than most men who speak it at all. Yet, I am constantly learning
new Navajo words that I've never heard before.

There were those who felt that the early traders' isolation enhanced their ability to speak Navajo. The traders, according to
anthropologist William Adams (who had been a trader's clerk),
spoke a jargon called "trader Navajo" or "Navvy," language reserved
solely for trading situations. Thus, it is likely that traders did not
understand all the conversations around them. Navajos say trader
Navvy resembled "baby talk," as it lacked the language's complex
grammar and syntax.

For example, a few Navajos opined that Hubbell's use of kinship
terms was improper, and sometimes bordered on rudeness.
Hubbell's artist friend, E. A. Burbank, painted many Navajo portraits
at Ganado and used the word *bi'ááá* to identify a Navajo man's wife;
the artist probably got the word from his host. This term actually
meant "his whoring mistress." One Navajo woman, Mrs. Ben Wilson,
whose parents were close friends of the Hubbells, said Hubbell had
a "dirty way of talking," referred to men as *do-dah-jo-baii* (He-Who-
Lacks-Generosity), and got words wrong. Apparently, J. L. also overworked Navajo exclamatory phrases such as "*doo sohodoobéezh
da*," which means "it's terrible," or "it's very different and complicated." Traders' children, who usually grew up on the reservation, were
commonly acknowledged as better speakers of Navajo.

Regardless of his facility with Navajo and his trading experience,
he still had to be baptized as a trader and had to identify an economic
venue that would benefit him and his clients. Hubbell's initiation as
a trader and his involvement with Navajo textiles and their economics completed his rather unique entry into trading post life.

CHAPTER FOUR
Witches Shot Stones into Their Bodies

LIKE A SIOUX Wintercount—a record of memorable events drawn on buffalo hide—a Navajo pictorial blanket commemorating Hubbell's first decade of trade would include his trader-coming-of-age tales, the witchpurge of 1878, the 1880 arrival of the Santa Fe railhead at Albuquerque, and his involvement with Navajo textiles commencing in 1884.

Coming-of-Age

All traders experienced one or more "baptisms" before their customers accepted them. Authors have penned dramatic retellings of Hubbell's own baptisms, and he himself observed in *Touring Topics*:

> I learned a great many things about Indian psychology very early during my first years as an Indian trader. And, one of the first things I learned was that a white man must never let an Indian know that he has the slightest fear of a single Indian, or any hundred Indians. The slightest show of fear would put the white man on the defensive, and the Indians would literally have him "on the run" from that very moment.

At the beginning of his life as a trader, so the story goes, he was loading wool into wagons by himself when a band of Navajos appeared. For no apparent reason, the angry men tied him to an oxcart and sketched in the sand their plan to hang him from a nearby mesquite tree (though none grows in Navajo country). In one version, Manuelito rode up brandishing a club and insisted that the angry Navajos release the young trader. Manuelito then berated the assembled mob, reminding them J. L. was their best friend, a fair and just white man who never lied. In some retellings, it was Many Horses, Ganado Mucho's son, who rebuked the crowd and claimed J. L. as a Navajo friend.

In 1931, Dorothy C. Mott dramatized the mesquite tree legend further: hostile Navajos attacked Hubbell at the exact spot where the hacienda, Hubbell's home, later stood; stole his goods; then tied him to a mesquite to burn him. From another Navajo band, "a stalwart buck" "slashed" the trader's "rawhide thongs" and said "You no kill him. He my brother," puzzling even J. L. until the Navajo explained: J. L. had saved him from drowning in the Colorado when the Navajo tried to swim the river. Mott wrote that Indians were

> notoriously poor swimmers in mid-river...the buck's horse had slipped and fallen, then floundered about on the rocks until he had broken his master's arm.... Don Lorenzo, on the bank, plunged in, swimming...to the Indian's side, and dragged him ashore.

Mott's retelling bristled with clichés and pidgin English—"grunts" and "sons told their sons"—a writer's license run amuck. One truth can be discerned among all the tales, however: to most Navajos of that time, J. L. was just another non-Navajo.

The Navajos were not reluctant to relieve themselves of undesirable non-Indians: in the summer of 1875, Navajo leaders took over the Fort Defiance agency buildings by force, ridding themselves of agent Arny. In May 1882, they threatened to drive agent Galen Eastman out of Navajo country.

Navajos had a reputation for testing the mettle of traders. In the *Touring Topics* article, Hubbell described an incident that occurred early in his trading career when an Indian customer demanded a free sack of flour. Hubbell refused, and the man

> picked up the sack of flour and marched out of the post.... I bounced over the counter and overtook the Indian with the sack as he went outside the door.

Though some seventy-five other Indians stood there backing up the Indian's demands, Hubbell grasped his hair and twisted him to the ground. The trader marched the Indian by his ear "like a whipped dog" back into the post. To the other Indians' amazement, the man obeyed Hubbell's order to redeposit the flour. Then, J. L. said, the other Indians threatened him and a bigger, braver Indian advanced on him. The trader

> pounced upon him, bore him to the ground and twisted his ear as

I'd done with the first man. When I let him up he whined and ran away like a rabbit. Then I challenged the whole lot of them.

He threatened, in Navajo, to twist the ears of any and all who thought they could steal from him. He recalled this as a

tremendous bluff. But, it worked successfully. Not an Indian moved. I stood there eyeing the angry throng for several minutes ready to begin twisting ears—and there were no ears to be twisted. One by one the Indians began slinking away. That lesson seemed to last. At least, I've gone along for fifty-eight years now without a repetition of any similar incident.

While it is rather odd that flour sacks were within reach rather than behind the four-foot-high bullpen counter (unless a shipment had just arrived), the feat of young and athletic J. L. jumping over the counter seems likely.

These incidents may have happened (in some form) at Manuelito Springs, and precipitated his move to Ganado. In any event, Navajos are known for their sense of humor—dry, witty, often self-effacing—and most traders' "baptismal" tales end with acceptance of the trader by the Indians, who often laughed in appreciation of the trader's besting them.

J. L. (in *Touring Topics*) insisted that to be a successful Indian trader, one needed to understand Indian reasoning. "He must cater to their whims, superstitions, and their child-like psychology." This he did, he said, in the 1886 smallpox epidemic during which the Indians credited him with "supernatural power." (This incident is not mentioned in any of the Navajo oral histories.) When the Navajos' "chants and rituals" failed, he "waded right in to help the Indians with their sick, their dead, and their dying." Hubbell himself was protected against the disease by his childhood immunization.

These stories reveal two conflicting views of Hubbell during his early trading years. One shows him as the passive recipient of Navajo aggression, saved by his inherent goodness and brotherhood. The other underscores his concept of himself, a concept he characterized as early as his "Marco Polo" journey: fearless, tough, and decisive. The latter view, however, is borne out by his involvement with the Navajo witchpurge of 1878.

The Witchpurge and Trading

Letters, journals, military reports, and Navajo oral histories concerning the witchpurge of 1878 confirm Hubbell's view of his role in Navajo society. In the witchpurge, both J. L. and his brother are prominent players in a time of tribal turmoil that threatened both the lives of non-Navajos and their property. Its ultimately successful resolution, which again involved J. L., meant that traders and their investments were relatively safe.

The great witchpurge resulted in deaths all over Navajo country— forty or so tribal members suspected of witchcraft were killed by other Navajos. The initial mention in archival records of problems with the purge and the Hubbells' involvement comes in letters hastily penned by Charlie Hubbell on May 31, 1878. Charlie, J. L.'s younger brother, clerked at what was probably the first Ganado-area Hubbell trading post situated along the lake there. Charlie appealed for ammunition, his rifle, and ultimately, military intervention. Ganado-area Navajos were killing those suspected of engaging in witchcraft, and Charlie felt vulnerable to attack.

Several Navajo accounts detail the killing of a Navajo suspected of witchcraft in front of the first Hubbell store (as described at the beginning of chapter one) at Ganado Lake, and another at Cornfields. Following the killings, Ganado Mucho convinced Charlie that Ganado Mucho's own life and "our [Euro-Americans'] lives are in danger and also the store and contents." They—apparently Ganado-area Navajos and non-Navajos—had no means of holding out against a force coming from Chinle to avenge Hombro's death. This danger perhaps dissipated with J. L.'s intervention. However, the military had already left Fort Wingate in New Mexico Territory for Ganado, with orders "to protect the whites and their property but on no account to take an active part in the difficulties between the Indians themselves." Indian agent Pyle also went to Ganado. There, both the army and the agent (each with a different view of how to respond to the Navajos' fears of witchcraft) met with local Navajos.

Then, in early June 1878, J. L. (who was apparently at his Manuelito store) wrote a letter for headman Manuelito. In it, the Navajo leader pleaded with the army to tell the medicinemen accused of witchcraft not to kill any more Navajos (he had been threatened himself). He also said that Navajos held medicinemen in the mountains north of Fort Defiance.

As a result of the letter, on June 10, J. L. accompanied a military expedition to the Tunisha Mountain valley, where they found several bound Navajo medicinemen. According to the commander of the expedition, Lieutenant Mitchell, the men were being charged with witchcraft. The Indians, he said, "called it shooting stones into bodies." The expedition spent about two days at the site; Ganado Mucho's arrival on the second day, accompanied by a hundred followers, enhanced the situation's volatility. The lieutenant lectured, and Hubbell interpreted, on the dire consequences of continued killing by either group. Mitchell quelled the disturbance and lauded Ganado Mucho's appearance—he was the only Navajo leader who came to the hostage scene. Mitchell also officially complimented J. L. on his bravery and assistance during the touchy assignment.

When the medicineman was killed at his store near the lake, J. L. relocated. (Historically, Navajos avoided the dead, as they believed that contact could cause illnesses and premature death.) He bought Leonard's one-story log post and adobe structures along the Pueblo Colorado Wash and eventually dropped the Manuelito Spring operation. Perhaps the difference in the two *naat'áaniis'* response to the Navajos' witch scare influenced this decision. In any event, the trading Hubbells managed to solidify their relations with tribal leaders and the army by helping settle the intratribal unrest. Additionally, they stabilized the reservation for trade in general, since neither the traders nor their stores became targets of Navajo violence during the witchpurge.

It is reasonable to postulate that if the Navajos had targeted traders and their posts, then traders would not have made the investments of labor, time, and money in facilities and inventory to build up a trading community. Further, by positioning themselves off the reservation, but near Navajo population centers, some of the trading posts were able to avoid the regulatory reach of the BIA.

Following the 1878 scare, the next significant event for early trading entrepreneurs like Hubbell was the railhead's arrival in

Albuquerque in the early 1880s. This drastically altered the trading game by easing the transportation of goods on and off the reservation. It also enabled J. L. to continue his role as intermediary between Navajos and non-Navajos. This time, however, the conflict was economic, among traders, weavers, and the non-Indian markets. Even as J. L. entered this fray, the Navajo blanket (a woven, soft, rectangular fabric draped around the body or used as bedding) was already well known.

Navajo Weaving History

Historians often sort Navajo weaving history into three periods, each of which touch J. L.'s life tapestry. The classic period (1650s to 1868) coincided with his mother's family's Southwest residency. Most researchers establish the Pueblo Revolt of 1680, when the Puebloans took refuge among the Navajos, as the time Navajos learned to weave. The transitional period (1868 to 1890) overlapped the railroad's southwestern expansion and J. L.'s entanglement in Navajo government and economic affairs. The rug period matched the beginnings of Hubbell's trading heyday (1890 to the 1910s) and the trading post era (1880 to 1930). During these years, the terms "blanket" and "rug" were used interchangeably as the Navajo textile metamorphosed from a wearing blanket to a rug of heavy durable yarns.

In 1795, during the classic period, Spanish Governor Fernando de Chacon recognized the superiority of Navajo textiles over Rio Grande weaving, saying that the Navajos worked their wool "with more delicacy and taste than the Spaniards."

The Navajos themselves point to their weaving origin story: Spider Man, a Navajo holy person, taught the Diné to forge sunshine, lightning, and rain into a loom, and Spider Woman taught them to weave.

Blankets and Hubbell

Just as conflicts abound in Navajo weaving origins, they also exist in the estimation of traders' influence on Navajo textile design and value. In a 1909 interview, J. L. recollected that for about ten years after he started to trade, he had no idea of the possibilities of "what might be accomplished in the way of industrial development" of the Navajos.

From 1884 on, however, he insisted that the weavers improve the design and color of their textiles. By rejecting, he said, aniline-dyed wool, cotton warps, and pound blankets, he created a market for textiles woven in the old patterns that he deemed the most artistic; pound blankets were usually ordinary textiles woven of coarse handspun, aniline-dyed yarns and paid for by weight.

Pound blankets featured in Hubbell's Navajo Blanket & Indian Curios catalogue of 1902.

His efforts at directing style and materials, he felt, translated into profits for both weaver and trader.

In 1884, the trading post at Ganado purchased only three to four hundred pounds of Navajo textiles. On September 23, 1884, C. N. Cotton, J. L.'s friend, bought a half-interest in Hubbell's Ganado post. Cotton broadened the Navajo textile market past the Southwest and Indian country by sending mimeographed circulars about Navajo blankets nationwide. At age twenty-two, the tall, lanky Cotton had arrived in

Gallup in 1881 (Hubbell erroneously recollected that their friendship turned to a partnership in 1880) to work as a telegraph operator on the rail line. The Ohioan was not only seven years younger than Hubbell; he came from a different background. For example, Cotton left school at age eleven to support his family when his father died.

While Cotton gets credit for introducing massive mail order marketing of Navajo textiles, it was Hubbell who asked artists such as E. A. Burbank (who first visited in 1897) to paint miniature rug designs for Hubbell's customers' and weavers' use. These five-by-seven to twelve-inch-square framed rug studies—variously called blanket studies, wall pictures, painted rug designs, or sketches—were executed in oil or watercolor on gray or manila paper and depicted vintage colors, designs, and patterns.

Desk in Hubbell's office with painted rug designs behind desk.

Judging from the seventy-seven signed design paintings and photographs that decorate the walls of the Hubbell Trading Post rug room today, Burbank painted most of the signed rug studies. Bertha Little, a teacher at Ganado's Presbyterian Mission School in the 1900s, signed twenty-three. H. G. Marrata, a Chicago artist/photographer/printer who printed J. L.'s only catalogue, signed three. One is signed by H. B. Judy, a Brooklyn artist. Burbank later said that he watched Hubbell's weavers, "studying the patterns and colors [of the rug sketches and photographs] and then with their hands, measuring off the size." Afterwards, presumably using the sketches as guides, they would produce a textile "exactly like the picture."

In their own oral histories, some of the weavers contradicted this, saying that they never wove from the painted rug designs. One, Ya Na Bah Winker, said weavers used the rug designs displayed on the trading post walls and "maybe for that reason he [J. L.] had them there." Asdzaa Bekashi said she wove blankets for J. L. any way he wanted because he gave the weavers mohair yarn and store credit.

Some interviewees said the trader gave them bread and canned goods before transacting business, and then gave them ten to fifteen dollars—mostly in tin money—after weighing the rug on his scale.

J. L. paid T. Slivers sixty dollars in tin money for Navajo dresses (*bils*) and bayeta rugs; the latter took two months to complete. Though Asdzaa Dloo Holoni wove white, black, red, blue, green, and gray wool rugs, most of her work had gray predominating, with a black border, white and black stripes, and a black cross in the middle. (The swastika shape disappeared during World War II, as the weavers "were told about the enemy having that design.") She purchased her dyes at the trading post and received fifty dollars in tin money for a rug.

Weavers around the turn of the century.

Sometimes Navajo women wove double-faced textiles; these complicated textiles had a different pattern on each side.

Mrs. Winker recollected that many Navajo women wove "for [Hubbell] because there was hunger—many hardships...." Since he supplied the wool, she could finish a small rug in one day and take it to the store for food. She described J. L. and his son (probably Roman) as kind and considerate; when a weaver brought in a rug, J. L. "would give you some canned goods and bread, but now they won't even do that or part with a red cent."

The Hubbell revival style of weaving associated with his trading/weaving merchandise heyday characteristically used classic to late classic-period motifs (terraced patterns from basketry designs) woven with mohair and commercial yarns and wool colored with red aniline dye. His special orders of oversized Navajo textiles (he financed the weavers during the weaving process) is typified by the famous two-faced textile known as the "1885 Staples Rug," which was twelve feet by eighteen feet, two inches.

By 1890, the Indian agent's annual report estimated the cash value of Navajo weaving at thirty thousand dollars. About this time, Cotton, who had favored commercial dyes and cotton warp, moved from Ganado into Gallup, New Mexico, and his influence among the weavers dissipated. Thereafter, J. L.'s preference for native vegetable dyes and old patterns dominated the Hubbell Trading Post market.

In 1899, in conjunction with the Hyde Exploring Expedition, Chaco Canyon trader Richard Wetherill opened an Indian curio store in New York. By the following year, an Indian decorating craze had swept the city. In 1903, the Navajo rug trade amounted to three hundred fifty thousand dollars and by 1914, seven hundred thousand dollars. It faded, however, when World War I broke out; as the price of wool rose, Navajos found it more financially beneficial to trade raw wool than to keep it back for weaving.

Just as Navajo women wove two-faced or double-sided textiles, J. L.'s attention in the 1880s was divided between marketing Navajo blankets and running businesses and politicking in St. Johns, Arizona, the new county seat of Apache County. (St. Johns was about a hundred miles south of Ganado on the Little Colorado River.) This diversion ultimately proved to be of mixed value to the trader.

PART THREE
J. L. HUBBELL

In 1882 I became sheriff of Apache County, and had I known at the time what a kettle of fish I was getting into, my political career would probably have ended at the time.... The cattle men were Texans, and they opened bloody warfare upon all the poor, ignorant Mexicans, Indians, and Spanish-Americans who were owners of sheep.... During the period of strife I'd been shot at from ambush no less than a dozen times, and my home had been converted to a veritable fort.

—J. L. Hubbell, *Touring Topics*

Senator Hubbell, who has been a factor in the politics of Arizona for about forty years, is one of the most picturesque men of the Southwest and a living link between the old and new order of things.

—*Notables of the West*

CHAPTER FIVE
A Fine Kettle of Fish: St. Johns

IN THE DECADE following the 1878 witchpurge, J. L.'s life vibrated like the serrated diamond pattern of a Navajo eyedazzler blanket. To that diamond pattern, he added storekeeper, sheep owner, wool merchant, sheriff, family man, Hispanic spokesman, saloon proprietor, and stage line operator.

St. Johns, Arizona Territory

When J. L. recollected his career, he noted opening a store in 1878 in St. Johns (originally called El Vadito, or The Crossing). In his journal entry for an early December 1879 trip to St. Johns, Mormon diarist Joseph Fish gives us a glimpse of J. L.'s Ganado store.

> [W]e stopped at Mr. Hubbell's store where we got our breakfast which was rather a poor one. There was no woman about the place and no regular cook.... We stayed all night at Mr. Hubbell's store and at a late hour he gave us the keys and went off, and it was surmised by us that he had an engagement with one of the gentler sex of the Mexican race. He returned about daylight.

J. L.'s future father-in-law, Civil War veteran Cruz Rubi, had settled his sheep at St. Johns five years earlier, built the first diversion dam, and filed claims on it. By the summer of 1877, almost all of St. Johns' one hundred families were Hispanic. Among the handful who were not was another of J. L.'s close friends, Jewish entrepreneur Solomon Barth, who had survived the Mormon pushcart caravan west, life as a rider for the Pony Express, and capture by the Apaches. Barth had also come to St. Johns and staked out land and water claims in advance of J. L.'s arrival. Not long after J. L. arrived in St. Johns, the short, handlebar-mustached Barth swapped his squatter rights to the Mormons for cattle, then stayed instead of leaving as the Mormon settlers had expected.

The territorial legislature created Apache County (which in square miles is larger than New Hampshire and Vermont combined) in 1879, and before long, its citizens were embroiled in ethnic, religious, and professional conflicts. Between the Navajos to the north and the Apaches to the south were Catholic Hispanic sheepmen and farmers, Texas cattlemen, Jewish merchants, Indian agents, traders, some outlaws and rustlers, and increasing numbers of Mormon farmers (sometimes polygamists).

St. Johns was a lawless place when J. L. first arrived he said. In the spring of 1880, when the number of Mormon settlers swelled to one hundred eighty, J. L. joined in a petition to Mormon leader David K. Udall. This petition, which J. L. may have authored, protested the Mormons' advance into St. Johns. The petitioners—thirty-one out of the thirty-three bore Hispanic surnames—said such a move endangered the town and would oppress the Mexican population. If the Mormons left, said the petitioners, difficulties and disagreeable consequences could be avoided. The Mormons stayed. As the Mormons dug in at St. Johns, they opposed a merchant group to which both Barth and Hubbell belonged, called the St. Johns Ring.

The Mormons accused Ring members of stuffing the ballot box to swing the county seat from Mormon-dominated Springerville to Catholic-controlled St. Johns, and of influencing the judiciary, law enforcement, and juries in the county. As Fish wrote, the Ring, who opposed "Mormons at every corner," drew down "the public crib...to the very bottom"; he also characterized J. L. as a "rabid anti-Mormon" who said that he would fight them "until hell froze over and then give them a round on the ice."

In Hubbell's later years in St. Johns, according to a *Notables of the West* biographical sketch, he led sheep interests in the regional war between local cattlemen and sheepmen—a natural position for one who was a "heavy owner of sheep" and "large operator in wool."

Lina

Even though Hubbell embroiled himself in land, politics, and business ventures, he found time to start a family during this period. It was during J. L.'s St. Johns years that he became involved with Lina Rubi. Though he recalled the year of their marriage to be 1879, the record shows that in 1879, Lina was married to Encamcion Lucero. Six years would pass between the time of Lina's divorce from Lucero and the time J. L. married her on July 27, 1891. For seven years after the date of her marriage to Lucero, she bore no children. Then she had three in a period of eight years during the time she was abandoned by Lucero. The last child, Roman, was born in October 1891, eight years after Lorenzo, Lina's third child. Both J. L. and Lina spoiled Roman, a beautiful baby (and ultimately, a handsome man). As the children matured, J. L. favored Roman over Lorenzo. There is a possibility that Roman was the couple's only biological child.

Lina's life resembles the Navajo wearing-blanket fragment found in Massacre Cave (the site of the 1805 death of Navajos at the hands of Spanish soldiers)—its four narrow stripes represent her children and its alternate bands of natural wool, the places she lived. The blanket fragment's frayed selvages and missing corner echo her life's obscure and missing details.

In his recollections, J. L. claimed that Lina's family lineage ran back to the Southwest's sixteenth-century Spanish settlers, and mentioned her grandfather, who fought on the Confederate side in the Civil War and lived to be one hundred three years old. Lina's father had served with James Hubbell in the New Mexico Volunteers. Issac Barth, Solomon's brother, said all the daughters of Cruz Rubi and his wife Tafayo Reyes were beautiful, and Lina was the Southwest's most beautiful girl.

Lina married Encamcion Lucero on January 1, 1873, when she was eleven. A year later, Lucero got drunk at a party and abandoned her. It is likely that she then joined her parents in St. Johns and was reclaimed by Lucero when he showed up there in 1877. Lina resumed living with him until May 1877, when, following a drinking and gambling bout in St. Johns, he abandoned her again.

The baptismal records at St. John the Baptist, in St. Johns, Arizona Territory, registered her daughter Adela's baptism on August 10, 1880; the father was given as "unknown." The Great Register of the Domiciled Inhabitants of the County of Apache for 1882 does not list J. L. but does include Lina, who is indicated as "head of household," aged twenty, residing in St. Johns with her two children, two-year-old Adela and eight-month-old Barbara (born September 1881). The same register listed Cruz Rubi, her father, as head of a separate household, as well as his wife and other family members. By April 1883, Lina had given birth to her third child and first son, Lorenzo.

Just as Lina was busy with family matters in the 1880s, J. L. did not let any sand stick to his feet during this tumultuous time in Arizona Territory. Confusion, controversy, feuds, and claim jumping over land and water abounded both in the territory and on the Navajo Reservation. On January 6, 1880, an executive order extended the reservation border six miles south; this expansion included the one hundred sixty acres Hubbell said he had taken up in 1876 along the Pueblo Colorado Wash.

Between St. Johns and the Reservation

The arrival of the Santa Fe, Southern Pacific, and Denver & Rio Grande railroads to New Mexico in 1880 and 1881 heralded growth for J. L.'s varied endeavors. In the spring of 1880, letters from Navajo City and a license to trade at Manuelito Camp (the place names were apparently used interchangeably) located on the east-west railhead axis confirm his economic interests outside of St. Johns.

In September 1880, Fish reported meeting J. L. in New Mexico, where Hubbell was working on the railroad east of the Continental Divide. The next year, J. L. hauled freight from St. Johns to Fort Defiance, and the agent ordered another shipment of beef cattle—this time sixty thousand pounds—from J. L. The trader's 1882 invoices to the Hopi Agency for transporting Indian supplies are further evidence of his wide-ranging commercial interests. (The same year, J. L.'s friend Henry Chee Dodge had J. L.'s old job of interpreter for the Navajo agency and was earning three hundred dollars a year.)

Chee Dodge as a young man dressed as an Indian scout.

70

Trading post ledgers for Ganado show that Charlie Hubbell was trading at the Leonard location in Ganado, with J. L. joining him there part of the year.

By March 1883, J. L. had been appointed to the Board of Jail Commissioners for Apache County. During this time, he began building up what he called the "trading ranch" at Ganado. To the original Leonard building, he (and later, he and Cotton) added several stone/log structures—initially the rug room and office—topped with flat roofs and protected with iron-barred windows.

In 1883, another Anglo arrived in Navajo country, Sam E. Day, Sr., who settled with his family at the spring-fed meadow called *La Cienaga* or *Cienaga Amarilla* (Yellow Marsh in English or *Tsó hotso* in Navajo) halfway between Gallup and Ganado. After the Franciscans decided to establish a Catholic mission there in 1898, this area was designated as St. Michaels. For nearly two decades, the Days were Hubbell's nearest non-Indian neighbors, and their post was a frequently used way-station for Hubbell's various transport operations.

In 1884, Apache County's Great Register placed Juan Lorenzo Hubbell, age thirty-one, and his brother Felipe Hubbell, age twenty-three, in St. Johns. Charles Hubbell was listed as residing at Pueblo Colorado.

During the early 1880s, the *Apache Chief* (a local newspaper billing itself as "the miners', stockraisers', farmers', politicians', merchants' and people's" paper) was the territory's only anti-Mormon journal. Self-described as combining "fun, sense, and careful information," this newspaper docu-

J. L. in 1885, age about 32

mented some of J. L.'s activities. For example, in April 1884, the paper carried an ad for the "Springerville, St. Johns, and Navajo Mail, Passengers & Express, L. Hubbell, Prop." and in a column, raved about the company's transportation service. By early May, the paper had reversed its opinion, reporting that the mail service was not satisfactory. At the end of that month, the ads named a new manager, and by August, a new proprietor, A. Gonzales. In early May, J. L. was reported to have solved his Ganado management situation by sending his brother Phillip (also known as Felipe) to look after his Navajo country store.

On July 13, 1884, the paper announced J. L.'s candidacy "for sheriff of Apache County, subject to the action of the anti-Mormon Nominating Convention"—no obstacle, since Barths and Hispanics dominated its membership. Before the election, J. L. acquired the Monarch Billiard Parlor and Saloon, and made Thomas Bradley manager; Bradley was one of the few non-relatives to whom J. L. entrusted a business. (Hubbell's ownership of the saloon seems to have been quite brief; by September 1885, ads indicate someone else as proprietor.) At Ganado, he had added another non-related partner, C. N. Cotton.

The Apache Chief predicted J. L.'s election win, and after the election, reported that inspectors kept Mormon polygamists from entering the polls in St. Johns and Springerville. In the *Touring Topics* article, J. L. confused both his election year—1882 (Thomas Perez, a wealthy Hispanic sheepman, was sheriff that year)—and his term of office—he served one term, not two.

On December 26, 1884, following J. L.'s successful bid for the sheriff's position, Lina filed for divorce from Lucero. She x'ed her signature (which seems to indicate that she was illiterate) on legal documents acknowledging that she had heard her complaint and that it was true. J. L. witnessed the complaint. None of the three children are mentioned in these documents.

In February 1885, when Hubbell was barely into his term as sheriff, his father died. Thereafter, J. L. added trips to New Mexico to his itinerary. A new St. Johns newspaper, the *St. Johns Herald*, which was established in January 1885 as the official county newspaper, ran a multi-column profile of Santiago Hubbell.

It was also around this time that things heated up in Apache County, according to Hubbell in *Touring Topics*, who recalled that he had

> scarcely more than taken the oath of office as sheriff before the Texans...ran off some 200 head of horses belonging to the Indian sheep men.... And, by todos santos I went [after them]—and I never let them quit running until I had chased them 125 miles and had the last Texan in jail and the stolen horses returned to the Indians.

This official assistance was an anomaly, since territorial sheriffs tended to harass Indians rather than aid them. Ganado Navajo oral histories verify Sheriff Hubbell's assistance, however, though not the numbers proffered by Hubbell

Another "Sheriff Hubbell" anecdote involved Many Horses, a Navajo headman and son of Ganado Mucho, and told of Hubbell chasing after outlaws who fled into the reservation. Many Horses, who accompanied Hubbell, recalled that as the rustlers camped and let down their guard, the pursuers closed in. Many Horses, it is said, asked Hubbell which one he should kill. To this, Hubbell responded "none," which, in turn, disgusted Many Horses, who would not have joined the pursuit, he said, if he had known that Hubbell would be so squeamish.

Following his election, J. L. said in *Touring Topics*, Texas cattlemen "opened bloody warfare upon all the poor, ignorant, sheep-owning Mexicans, Indians, and Spanish-Americans." He likened running sheep and cattle on public range to keeping "monkeys and parrots in the same cage," and sided with sheepmen since, in his opinion, sheep were better suited to the land. In his grandiose account, Hubbell claimed that while he was sheriff, he settled the range war after three years, a dozen ambushes (he barricaded his home with mattresses and sandbags), and the loss of nearly three hundred lives, including those of five deputies.

Years later, Solomon Barth's son accused J. L. of claiming success in a range war that actually happened during his successor's (Commodore Perry Owens') term. Supporting Barth's contention is the fact that none of the local newspapers reported any of these dramatic events during J. L.'s tenure as sheriff. And, as only nine county sheriffs and just a few more deputies are recorded as being killed between 1865 and 1986 in Arizona, Barth's point is well taken.

Nonetheless, Hubbell's recollections of his involvement in violent or potentially violent conflicts during his St. Johns' years were typical of his tendency to rewrite his own life story. Ridding the St. Johns area of cattle thieves and convincing the military he was right in doing so; opposing the Mormons; leading the sheepmen in a regional war; recovering Indian horses stolen by Texans; and fighting (and settling) a dispute between Texas cattlemen and local Indian and

Mexican sheepherders: J. L. was the man of the hour, the hero in his own personal drama.

As did all of Arizona's early sheriffs, J. L. charged the county for official travel—thirty cents a mile—and billed the Board of Supervisors for other duties performed. As an example, it cost the county two dollars each time J. L. served a warrant. In March, J. L. escorted two Hispanic-surnamed horse thieves to the Yuma Territorial prison, where, he quipped, they would be "entertained at the resort for a period of two years at the taxpayers' expense." He billed the county six hundred eighty dollars for this trip.

During this period, J. L. benefited from an amiable Board of Supervisors. One of them, Henry Huning of the Huning & Cooley cattle operation, had endorsed Hubbell for sheriff at the 1884 nominating convention. Ernest Tee, a wealthy and educated Englishman, and Morris Barth were also favorably disposed toward him. After Barth's death in the spring of 1885, W. B. Leonard (the man from whom J. L. purchased the Ganado post) filled the vacancy. In April, J. L. traveled with Leonard to his home at Navajo, also called Tanner Springs. The same month, the county paid J. L. approximately thirty-five hundred dollars for fees, salary, and transportation of prisoners; his annual salary was increased to five thousand dollars after 1885.

J. L. was assisted by his brothers Frank, Tom, and Felipe, who served as his deputies. Again, this was common practice; in Arizona Territory, nepotism was the rule, not the exception. Deputies did the clerical work and performed many of the sheriff's functions while the sheriff himself was away running his own business.

Sometime after April 1885, when the wool season at Ganado was in full swing, the relationship between Sheriff Hubbell and the Board of Supervisors unraveled. About that time, attorney H. V. Howard returned to St. Johns, and in May, deputy sheriff Tom Hubbell arrested six men for cattle theft. While surviving records do not clearly identify the reasons, it appears that these arrests, coupled with Howard's return and his complaints about J. L.'s job performance, precipitated a shift in Hubbell's previously close relationship with the board. The June 11, 1885, issue of the St. Johns Herald placed the two out-of-town supervisors in town, and reported that Sheriff Hubbell was expected home in a few days. On June 13, the board called for a special meeting to be held in St. Johns on June 22, 1885, to inquire and investigate "the management of certain county offices and the county jail" and to take such action "as the Board may deem requisite."

The Ouster

Though he was then at Ganado, J. L. received notice of both the meeting and the board's intent to oust him as sheriff. He learned that the board would claim that his presence at his Ganado trading post, then within the boundaries of the Navajo Reservation, placed him outside the county and the territory. Hubbell responded swiftly, selling—on paper, it seems—his remaining half-interest in the Ganado store to Cotton on June 22, 1885. The supervisors postponed the meeting scheduled for June 22 to the next day; originally scheduled to begin at ten in the morning, it was delayed until two in the afternoon, probably waiting for J. L.'s arrival.

In *Notables of the West*, Hubbell said that

> Shortly after taking office, he went to visit his store, 100 miles away from the County Seat, and during his absence his political opponents declared his office vacant and, with the aid of the courts, named another to his office. He was notified of the plan and, after riding 100 miles between suns, managed to arrive at his office a few hours between the time for transferring it.

In this version, Hubbell recollected heavily armed gunmen supporting his opponents. He gathered his own supporters and stationed them outside the court. After arguing with the judge, Hubbell took possession of the prisoners in the courtroom, put them in jail, and booted his opponents' armed men from town. This ouster attempt later inspired at least two pieces of fiction by writers who were J. L.'s guests, Hamlin Garland's "Delmar of Pima," which appeared in *McClure's Magazine* (February 1902) and Dane Coolidge's *Lorenzo the Magnificent: The Riders from Texas* (published in 1925 by Grossett & Dunlap). The latter also included other aspects of Hubbell's life: the Mexican land grant, the family residential complex, Castilian blood, Navajos, and his patrón mentality.

Since the summary minutes from the Board of Supervisors' records are missing pages three to one hundred two, (thanks, it is said, to

Solomon Barth, who cut them out to delete information about criminal matters affecting the Barths), we rely on the *St. Johns Herald.* It reported that J. L. refused to recognize the supervisors' authority, held possession of the jail and public property, and started legal proceedings to annul their actions. At this point, the supervisors unanimously declared the office vacant and appointed James E. Porter, the former county surveyor, as sheriff. As one of his sureties (a guarantor required by law), Porter used Supervisor Tee's business partner Henry Smith. On June 25, 1885, the *Herald*'s "Local News" column, said "the county court recognizes Mr. Porter," and "It looks as if Apache County will have two sheriffs instead of one."

The paper recounted the board's proceedings and Howard's litany of charges. First, he said, J. L. failed to give the proper bond, using two Mexican instead of three white sureties. Typically Arizona boards of supervisors monitored sureties closely, since they guaranteed the proper financial performance of the officeholder. For instance, in 188l, Pima County's board made the Tucson sheriff-elect muster up an additional seventy-five thousand dollars in sureties.

Howard also accused J. L. of leaving for Albuquerque in April without the supervisors' permission. He pointed out J. L.'s continued absence prior to the Board of Supervisors' meeting. The attorney further complained that J. L. had appointed as deputy his brother Frank, an incompetent, and Frank had neglected his duties by failing to serve bench warrants on two Hispanic-named men charged with rustling. J. L., Howard alleged, "refused to work in harmony with the District Attorney's office," and "had been insulting to the District Attorney's office and the judge of the County Court." J. L. purportedly told the judge, who asked him to serve some papers "to stick said subpoenas -- --- ---." Additionally, Sheriff Hubbell often let a certain prisoner run at large and become intoxicated.

In an editorial, the *Herald* called Howard's affidavit into question. It was, the paper said, conceived in malice by a malcontent short-term county resident, "who in an arrogant manner proclaims, 'the Mexicans must go'," and who belittled one of the area's most popular gentlemen, J. L. Hubbell.

The paper continued to support Hubbell. In a July 2 "Local News" column, two more tidbits appeared: "No legal business transacted by the County Judge's court this past week. Let the congregation all rise and say the Doxology!" Too, it was reported that Sheriff Hubbell had left for Prescott the previous Sunday "on business connected with that office." J. L. returned from Prescott on Sunday, July 5th, with an order temporarily enjoining Porter from acting as sheriff. He also served Porter with a complaint and summons. In its July 9 issue, the paper reported that J. L. had provided a bond and was "now in undisputed possession of his office."

The lawsuit eventually fizzled out. When J. L. summarized this incident in Farish's *History of Arizona*, he said that three men elected by his efforts—Huning, Tee, and Smith (though Smith was not a supervisor)—turned on him and wanted him out of office.

When the full Board of Supervisors met on July 7, 1885, they authorized payment to Sheriff Hubbell of $7,943.53. When the board met again two days later without the presence of Supervisor Leonard, it ordered the district attorney to bring suit against J. L. for malfeasance while in office.

The Divorce

As J. L. navigated the treacherous waters of territorial politics, Lina was also involved in her own legal problems. The record of her divorce proceedings, though couched in legal language and translated by others, provides a rare personal glimpse of her life at the time. The court papers included signatures of her relative Alfred Ruiz, court clerk, and one of J. L.'s deputy sheriff—brothers, who verified serving the papers on Lucero in Apache County after the newspaper had published the summons seventeen times between February 19, 1885, and June 11, 1885. Lucero's gross irresponsibility garnered sympathy for Lina in the Hispanic community, judging by the number of Hispanics involved in her proceedings.

On September 19, 1885, the court took Lina's testimony in a series of written questions and answers, which J. L. witnessed and probably interpreted for her.

Q: During the time you lived with him how did you conduct yourself towards the defendant?

A: I conducted myself towards the defendant like a dutiful wife would do. I did everything for him that I could and was obedient to him at all times....

Q: Was the defendant an able-bodied man capable of earning a support for himself and family?

A: He was, but he was too lazy, idle, profligate and dissipated to do so. [Nearly identical words were used by the other two witnesses].

Lina's daughters: Barbara (standing) and Adela (seated), circa 1885

Lina explained that she and her children lived off the charity of friends and relatives, as Lucero failed to provide them with life's necessaries. A couple of days later, Judge Howard granted Lina's divorce. In his decree, in addition to the usual recitals, he cited her age at marriage and dutifulness as well as the able-bodied Lucero's abandonment and neglect.

As J. L.'s fortunes with the Board of Supervisors were declining, they were rising with the Navajos. According to Hubbell in *Touring Topics*, his provision of sheriff services and assistance in the 1886 smallpox epidemic counted heavily in his favor on the reservation. But as the election approached, and probably in deference to Hubbell's conflicts with the Apache County supervisors, the letterhead for the Ganado trading ranch read "C. N. Cotton, Indian Trader, Ganado, Apache County, Arizona." This discretion seems to have had little effect, however, on Cotton and Hubbell's business relationship or on the upcoming election.

As the 1886 election neared, the supervisors continued to harass Hubbell. They ordered Hubbell in his role of jail commissioner and all the other jail commissioners to file a full report by October 1886 of bonds issued and delivered (in March 1883). Yet, the board did not wait till October and instead ordered the district attorney to file litigation to secure the report. Ultimately, the board rejected the filed report as incomplete, and then paid all county employees' salaries except Hubbell's. They put a hold on payments due him for sheriffing until he filed duplicate receipts for all monies collected by him as sheriff and due Apache County.

Aside from the problem presented by the jail bonds, J. L. faced several other re-election difficulties. Sojme say that the general lawlessness that prevailed in Arizona Territory and the suspicion that small cattle spreads harbored rustlers meant that law-and-order campaigns often succeeded as election strategies. At this time, the railroad and cattle companies challenged the Little Colorado Valley's clique of Indian traders and Hispanic sheepmen, as did the Mormons, who were still upset at Apache County's corrupt 1884 elections. Hubbell's open contempt for certain politicians, whom he called "damn rascals," probably did not help his cause.

In October 1886, law-and-order citizens and commercial interests from Apache County gathered in Winslow. This group selected Commodore Perry Owens as their candidate for sheriff. Owens, a short man with long blonde hair and a reputation as a gunman, was later eulogized as a legendary gunman and Navajo fighter by author Dane Coolidge in his 1932 book, *Fighting Men of the West.*

Though Hubbell rallied his supporters behind an Equal Rights ticket and accused the Winslow convention of "plotting to form a vigilante organization to murder 'Mexicans'," he lost the election. The Mormons felt that Owens could control the county's lawless elements, and that, without him, they would have to leave Arizona.

Hubbell's defeat did not assuage the Board of Supervisors, who continued to refuse to pay his salary "until such time as he turns over to the proper authorities all monies due the county." On July 1, 1887, they determined that they owed J. L. thirty-one hundred dollars, which included his salary for two quarters plus a charge for transporting an "insane person." However, the board found his accounts to be deficient by thirteen hundred dollars. Either needing money or resigning himself to the situation, Hubbell requested that the warrant be drawn less the disputed amount; the board so ordered and the transaction was finally closed.

Though J. L.'s law enforcement skills (and integrity) may appear problematic, in those days, sheriffs served many masters: they answered to boards of supervisors and the territorial district courts, acted as county jailers, and performed duties as ex-officio tax assessors and collectors. While Owens was given credit for taming local rowdy elements, information included in records and the amount of fees collected seem to indicate that J. L. attended to the office's routine duties. Other than among his political enemies, J. L. had a reputation for meeting his obligations.

Not long after Owens took over the sheriff's office, he consulted with the Navajo agent about matters concerning the Navajo Reservation. The agent advised Owens to talk with his predecessor for answers to any questions on Indian matters, which implies that the turmoil in St. Johns did not affect the esteem in which J. L. was held on the reservation. Owens then proceeded to use his office to harass Frank Hubbell, levying on Frank's sheep and other property even after Frank (along with Tom and Felipe) had returned to New Mexico Territory, where Santiago's death may have opened up economic opportunities for the three brothers around Pajarito and Albuquerque.

Losing the election was not the end of Hubbell's St. Johns problems. He was named as defendant in several lawsuits; one concerned his failure to deliver twenty-two thousand pounds of wool, and another, a bond he signed for the delivery of some horses. These lawsuits, in typical territorial fashion, dragged on for years in the county court and were either never resolved, or if a judgment was entered, it was not satisfied.

Apache County Mormon historians consider the late 1880s as a watershed in Mormon/non-Mormon conflicts. The issues and personalities faded away when some of the St. Johns' Ring left, a few wrongdoers got in hot water, and the power and property of St. Johns' Hispanic citizens diminished. Within four years of Hubbell's re-election defeat, the entire county boasted less than a thousand non-Indian residents. By then, only county government business livened up St. Johns, and the turmoil, growth, and economic possibilities, which had seemed so strong early in the decade, fizzled out.

No longer encumbered by his official duties, J. L. occupied himself with the Arizona Mercantile Company. The incorporators meet on January 20, 1887, in St. Johns and elected directors; J. L. was chosen to be superintendent. The incorporators gave Hubbell the responsibility of purchasing and selling general merchandise and employing clerks. The company purchased three hundred dollars' worth of goods from "Roman Lopez and Brother." Directors A. Gonzales and R. Lopez examined the building J. L. had under construction in St. Johns and recommended that the new company purchase it for twenty-five hundred dollars, with the provision that J. L. finish it by June 1, 1887, and agree to its repurchase upon dissolution of the corporation. Though still involved with Arizona Mercantile, J. L. returned his attention to trading in Indian country.

CHAPTER SIX

Long a Tremendous Gambler

AS J. L. REFOCUSED on the trading ranch at Ganado, he became the central diamond of an old-style blanket design; his partner Cotton was the border. Both gambled, one that his return to the trading ranch would pay off, the other that he could transform himself into a banker and wholesaler. Both won.

Problems and Possibilities

Contemporaries described Cotton as tall and large-boned, a bluff and hearty man who spoke loudly and chomped on a big cigar. While J. L. handled Indian problems himself, Cotton laid problems originating in Ganado at the feet of the local Indian agent, demanding that the agent recover a stolen mare or a pawned silver belt filched by the owner. On another occasion, Cotton requested the agent's help after being threatened by a Navajo. After the summer 1885 sale of J. L.'s half-interest in the Ganado post to Cotton, we find Cotton sometimes accounting to Hubbell, and referring to property—wool, for example—as jointly owned. However, many contradictory details cloud the nature of their business relationship and ownership of the Ganado trading ranch until the early 1900s.

On the other hand, there is no lack of clarity about Cotton's dissatisfaction as a trader. He complained, traded, and moaned: His bull teams, "slower than the second coming of our savior," took fifteen to twenty days' round-trip to go to Manuelito, the nearest railhead. He lacked money. Albuquerque's Jewish merchants worked unfair wool deals. The bank mixed up his and Hubbell's accounts.

The two assumed that their Ganado post's location, originally outside the reservation boundaries dictated by the treaty, exempted them from having to secure a license to trade from the Bureau of Indian Affairs. However, in 1885, both applied for a license to trade in Chinle, with Charles (Charlie) Hubbell as clerk. It appears that Cotton bought one or two more stores in Chinle, one of which was purchased during that summer of 1885. (Scanty and incomplete references to trade in Chinle make reconstruction of Cotton/Hubbell or

Cotton businesses there problematic.)

Interestingly, by the spring of 1886, Charlie was trading at Blue Canyon, west of the Hopi mesas and Ganado, under the umbrella of the Ganado store. (The Navajos called Charlie *Ja' abaani*, the Bat, either because his ears stuck out or because he traded near Bat Springs in Bat Canyon, which was part of Blue Canyon.) And while there is no record that Charlie ever returned to Chinle to clerk or to trade, even as late as 1889, both Cotton and J. L. made inquiries about a Chinle trading license. By 1887, either Cotton and Hubbell felt official trade approval was needed for their Ganado operations or the bureau changed its mind and required them to apply for a license. In any event, Cotton duly sought and was granted a license, which he retained until 1900.

In the late 1880s, Hubbell (perhaps aided by Cotton) was making improvements at Ganado: raising the office roof and adding the store, warehouse, and two-story barn. The two men continued to intermingle their business affairs. In January 1889, Cotton ordered the *New York Herald Weekly*, the *St. Louis Globe Dispatch*, the *San Francisco Chronicle*, the *New York Times*, and the *Toledo Blade* for himself in Gallup and J. L. in Ganado. In May, he offered to substitute J. L.'s note with an Albuquerque supplier with his own—it seems that J. L. had "overdrawn his account considerable."

It was Cotton who, in 1890, initiated the Ganado land claim for the trading site to be excepted from the Navajo Indian Reservation as a homestead, which would allow him to file a homestead claim on the improved land. This exception was important: though a license to trade on the reservation granted the holder the right to use the land and the buildings constructed on it for a limited period of time, without an exception, everything reverted to the Navajo Tribe once trading activities ceased. To acquire such an homestead exception, the individual had to be living on the land prior to the date the Navajo Reservation was enlarged (January 6, 1880). Though Hubbell more-or-less fulfilled that requirement, the licensing of the Ganado post had started off in Cotton's name and it must have seemed best to continue it in that manner.

The local government agent endorsed Cotton's request for the exception of land from the reservation, and erroneously stated that in spring of 1878, Cotton had erected a "large number of buildings" at that location. The agent went on to say that in his opinion, Cotton operated the "best store on the reservation."

The same year Cotton started the Ganado land claim, he and Hubbell were using separate letterheads (though Cotton's referenced a Ganado trading post). By 1894, surviving documents in the Hubbell Papers indicate that the Ganado-based Hubbell was selling wool, sheepskins, and pelts to Cotton and purchasing merchandise from Cotton's Gallup warehouse.

The C. N. Cotton warehouse in Gallup, New Mexico

An 1896 wholesale catalogue for Navajo blankets from Cotton (using a Gallup address) indicated in the text that he owned the largest trading post on the Navajo reservation, which was obviously a reference to Ganado. However, his next catalogue, *Indian Traders' Supplies & Navajo Blankets*, included in the foreword a remark that he had sold his business on the reservation in 1894 and moved into Gallup.

On Hubbell's side, the partnership data is just as confusing. He sometimes dated his permanent return to Ganado and the end of his partnership with Cotton to the late 1880s; at other times, he said it continued after Cotton's move. J. L.'s granddaughter said that Cotton moved to Gallup to take over the two men's wholesale business, and the partnership continued for a while afterward.

Whatever their exact business link at any given time, Cotton addressed his letters to Hubbell to "Friend Lorenzo" and passed on business prospects, such as a platinum sample Cotton remembered seeing near Ganado, school hauling contracts, garnet buyers, and the like. Cotton often added his opinion about prospective deals, one time warning J. L. that his health would benefit if he passed up "this particular sheep-buying deal."

After the century turned, notes totaling thousands of dollars passed between Cotton and J. L.; Cotton seems to have been functioning as Hubbell's wholesale supplier at this point. In that role, Cotton would at times ask Hubbell to "not for God's sake draw me heavier, as money is a very scarce commodity with us." One year, Cotton attributed his money scarcity to his buying commodities at "exaggerated prices from the bloody Indians at a loss" the year before.

We do know that by the time Cotton was living in Gallup and J. L. had refocused on Ganado, the trader finally married Lina.

The Family Scene

The Hubbell family's formal portrait after J. L. moved back to Ganado

85

In the summer of 1891, when J. L. and Lina married, Lina was pregnant with Roman, who was born in October of that year.

The contrast between J. L. and Lina's first husband, Lucero, was marked. Hubbell wore the laurels of an Indian trader and ex-sheriff, held the title of "Don," and employed many of Lina's relatives. He acknowledged and parented the four children born to her. While Lucero only lived with Lina for a year during their twelve-year marriage, and never supported her, J. L. provided well for Lina.

J. L. did share one vice with Lina's former husband: gambling. While the amounts of money J. L. said he gambled seem exorbitant, the leaders of St. Johns' Hispanic community often participated in high-stakes games, according to lawyer Steve Udall, history buff and descendant of the St. Johns' Udall family. The Apache County Historical Society classified "card games" in late-1800s St. Johns as a "most popular means of sociability"; refusal to join a game was "taken as an insult."

Though gambling drew Hubbell, trading, with its complex economics, left most traders cash poor. How Hubbell, who usually spread himself thin among a multitude of ventures, could wager cash of any significant sum, rather than wool or an adjunct business, is not known.

In *Touring Topics*, J. L. recollected his gambling and Lina's response to it:

> I suppose a man has to have some vices and although I never drank or smoked, I was long a tremendous gambler. As a youth, I gambled at about everything that offered a gambler's chance; and, with the usual gambler's luck sometimes I won big stakes. Many a time I cut the cards for $30,000 at a single toss, and won or lost.
>
> In 1896, however, I quit gambling and I've never gambled since! I lost $60,000 in a poker game and had to tell Señora Lina about it next morning. She was disgusted, and speaking in Spanish said: "Well, Don Lorenzo! I think it is about time for you to choose between your penchant for gambling and the questions of whether or not our children are to be educated ladies and gentlemen. I'll be pleased to hear your decision after you've had sufficient time to think it over."
>
> Coming from her, this was a rebuff that stung, and my decision was made muy pronto. I replied: "I need no time for a decision.

My decision is already made, and I give you my word of honor. I'll never gamble again!" Mrs. Hubbell lived to see that pledge carried out up to the time of her death in 1914.

That anecdote credited Lina with power on matters that directly affected their children, underscored her upper-class expectations, and showed that she had some say in J. L.'s recreational activities. (It also demonstrates J. L.'s poor memory for dates: Lina died in 1913.)

In *Touring Topics*, J. L. acknowledged his Spanish ancestry, "a race noted for fine wines and brandies," and commented that alcohol had played an important part in its history. He himself, however, "never drank a drop of liquor, nor...used tobacco"—he classified liquor "*buena por nada*." Hubbell reasoned that a "man couldn't think if he drank. He just couldn't think!" J. L. forbade drinking at the post, and fired employees (non-relatives or in-laws) who disobeyed this prohibition. It seems that his approach to his brother Charlie, who himself had a drinking problem, was to relegate him to the post furthest from alcohol (liquor was, and still is, illegal on the Navajo and Hopi reservations).

In 1897, Francis E. Leupp, then a Washington correspondent for the *New York Evening Post* and later, Commissioner of Indian Affairs, partook of the Hubbell family hospitality on his way to the snake ceremony. Certainly, Leupp represented the type of guest Hubbell often sought out, a guest who could assist him in achieving his interests. Afterward, Leupp wrote to J. L., and asked him to "Please present my kind regards to Mrs. Hubbell, whose rare Spanish courtesy I remember so well when she played the hostess to our party."

When she was in residence at Ganado, Lina actively played her role as female head of the household. Though few other guests mentioned her in their correspondence, two women artists did send her their regards. One, Cornelia Cassidy Davis, sent Lina a painting of Hopi girls, a work still in the Hubbell art collection. In a 1930s letter to Roman, another 1897 visitor, artist E. A. Burbank, recalled the family scene he found on his first visit to Ganado.

You were there then, five years old, and you and I used to take long walks. You were a lively kid in those days, and kept the old man guessing. Sometimes, Old Edward, the Mexican, a good judge of whiskey, drove the teams to Gallup and back and Owetche (Wet Baby) showed up now and then. And the man with the whiskey name, Old Burkumper [sic], came along and raised hell there until your father and Charlie, your uncle, calmed him down.

The artist also noted that J. L. "was like his two sons. He had a weak spot for the girlies, same as I was then." It is interesting to observe that in his voluminous correspondence with Hubbell, Burbank never mentioned Lina.

Lorenzo, called "Lorencito" by family members, recalled that his father moved the family from Ganado to St. Johns in the winter for schooling. The students at his St. Johns school spoke only Spanish, and Lorenzo described himself as being acutely lonely until his father took him on trading trips into Indian country and gradually introduced him to the trading game.

Lorenzo began hanging around the business area of the Ganado post when he was just six years old, and this prox-imity helped him acquire a fluency in the Navajo language. He also enjoyed

Lorenzo as a teenager, photographed by family friend Ben Wittick.

spending free time with the Indians he met at the post; when his father lost track of him, Lorenzo recalled, he just "followed his nose to where horse meat was being roasted by the Navajo and there I was feasting." When he graduated to trading behind the post's count-er, he used copper bracelets, an early trade item, to barter with the Indians. He learned his father's creed that an educated white man must never take advantage of unlettered people.

In 1892, nine-year-old Lorenzo joined his father on a two-month trad-ing expedition to Canyon de Chelly. There, Lorenzo explored the ruins while his father traded with the Indians in a high-windowed room in Chinle. That same year, his father took him to see his first snake cere-mony on the Hopi mesas. When Lorenzo was older, his parents ignored his protests and sent him study Latin and literature at Notre Dame—to be educated as a "gentleman's son should be." (For himself, Lorenzo wanted to be trader, not a scholar.)

Eventually, extended marital separations seem to have become the norm, a consequence of their children's schooling requirements and J. L.'s far-flung business interests and frequent traveling.

From Trader to Lobbyist

Boarding the train in Gallup, New Mexico, Hubbell made a quick stop in Albuquerque to check on his mother and siblings, then turned his attention to his broader Washington, D. C. agenda.

As the train clackety-clacked its way across the country, J. L. changed from a grizzle-haired trader wearing ill-fitting clothes to a well-groomed gentleman—fresh as a newly warped Navajo loom—from trader to lobbyist, from the dry Colorado Plateau to humid Washington D. C.

This photograph of Juliana and her adult children might have been taken when J. L. stopped in Albuquerque on his way east. Left, back row: Charles, Phillip, Barbara, Thomas, Frank. Front Row: Louisa, Julianita, J. L. Late 1890's.

J. L., who often said the government slipped up when it extended the reservation in 1880, made several trips to Washington, D. C., to secure the special legislation that would allow him the land exception he desired. Over the years, J. L. would also push for approval of an appropriation for the Ganado Dam project and Arizona statehood. He would visit the Postmaster General's office to discuss mail runs; post-master assignments; and, in later years, the cancelgraph, an invention in which he had invested. He went to the Bureau of Indian Affairs about his trading license and Indian needs, and then to other govern-ment and congressional offices. Sometimes he would also squeeze in a trip to the National Gallery of Art or take a train to New York City to visit an artist in his studio.

Into the Wool Bag

Hubbell's Washington, D. C., trips kept the land exception issue alive. In December 1899, Navajo agent G. W. Hayzlett urged passage of an act giving title of the land to Hubbell, saying "he [J. L.] will...give the Indians...a daily object lesson in farming and stock rais-ing." This comment was congruent with the BIA's nationwide policy of assimilation of Indians. Cotton concurred with Hayzlett's remark that the "interest of Messrs. Cotton and Hubbell are identical." In fact, Cotton said, "if Hubbell's claim is allowed it will be satisfactory to me." The agent valued the Ganado trading ranch's improvements at ten thousand dollars.

The first bill affecting his Ganado trading ranch (the one excepting from the 1880 executive order "all lands claimed by actual settlers or persons to whom valid rights attach," which passed the House of Representatives on March 5, 1900) was killed by presidential veto. It was doomed by a rider that subjected the Navajo Reservation to Unit-ed States mining laws. Marcus Smith, who would be Hubbell's oppo-nent in Arizona's 1914 Senate race, later introduced another bill "which hung fire in Washington." At the time of McKinley's assassi-nation, this bill was lying unsigned on the president's desk. It was, however, signed by Theodore Roosevelt, it is said, in his first presi-dential act.

When he signed the bill on July 1, 1902, President Theodore Roo-sevelt finally placed the Ganado property partially in J. L.'s wool bag. (It would not be completely inside until his neighbor Sam Day, Sr. completed his survey and received his patent. Unfortunately, Day's

1906 survey was flawed and had to be redone; it was 1917 before Hubbell had a legitimate patent.)

View of Hubbell's trading ranch as he expanded his complex of buildings.

Anticipating the successful issuance of his exception, J. L. started building the Big House, as the family home was called, at Ganado in 1901; he began by roofing the large middle room and five flanking rooms. From the Fort Defiance Plateau, he had his Indian laborers cut and haul by oxcart ninety-five primary roof wood beams, or vigas,

Front of Hubbell home and back of trading post building with entrance to Hubbell's office. Line drawing of aerial view of Hubbell's trading ranch and farm.

91

giving the site a total of five hundred beams, four lintels, two upright support posts, and a main auxiliary beam. The family moved into this home in 1902.

Unlike a typical turn-of-the-century trader's residence, with a connected small post/residence/warehouse complex, the Hubbell trading ranch was designed to accommodate separate functions in clearly defined spaces. The massive Southwestern-style buildings, rock set with adobe mud, protected his property from fire and vandalism and enhanced Hubbell's image as well. Measuring roughly fifty-one by eighty-seven feet, the house was dominated by what the plans called the living room and everyone else referred to as the Hall; this was approximately forty-four by eighteen feet in size.

Outside, a row of cottonwoods "all up the lane to the south" was cut out by a farm manager, and roots from a row of poplars inside the wall spread so badly that the Hubbells had them cut out as well. A stand of cottonwoods planted in the wash was removed. It is still possible to see the Russian olive trees planted near the barbecue area, and an apricot tree in the courtyard, which grew from a discarded seed. J. L. planted the walnut and mulberry trees along the ditches.

Satellite Posts and Water

The year 1902 not only saw J. L. Hubbell move his family into their new residence at Ganado, but was also the year during which Hubbell expanded his trading operations to Cornfields and into Hopi country, and began his irrigation project.

Called *K'ii'tsoitah* ("Among the Rabbit Bushes") by the Navajos, Cornfields is in the wide valley of the Pueblo Colorado Wash, about five miles below Ganado. Here, where the broad, sandy floor of the wash snakes its way to the Rio Puerco, the Navajos cultivated the bottom land that bordered the river. They raised such large corn crops that they were able to sell Hubbell their excess, which one year amounted to one hundred fifty thousand pounds of corn. On one occasion, the store was struck by lightning and lost its trade. It was reported that Hubbell loaded stock in a freight wagon, left Cornfields, rearranged the load during the night, and returned the next day with "new stock." Trade then resumed.

Cornfields was also the home of J. L.'s friend Many Horses; the people of the area were considered very industrious, perhaps due to Many Horses's reputation for encouraging hard work. He was reported to ride up and down the wash at dawn admonishing the Navajos that the white man would take sleepyheads' land and possessions and make them servants.

Another significant 1902 property transaction was Hubbell's purchase of Thomas Keam's trading post at Keams Canyon. This post, fifty miles west of Ganado, stretched the Hubbell operation into Hopi territory and added the western part of Navajo country to its trading domain. Cornish seaman, immigrant, and Civil War veteran Thomas V. Keam was not only J. L.'s friend and mentor, but also the man who had established the model for doing business on the reservation. Keam, seven years older than J. L., had served at Fort Sumner, traded with the Utes, and held the Navajo Special Agent position in 1872. In 1875, he settled on a primary trade route some fifty miles west of Ganado in Hopi country's Rounded Canyon or Pongsikiana, which was a natural boundary between the Hopis and the Navajos.

View of Hubbell's Keams Canyon trading post in the early 1900s.

As early as 1881, army ethnographer Lieutenant John G. Bourke found "civilized" life at Keams Canyon, where Keam was supporting a

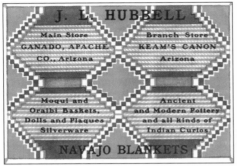

This business card was in use after Hubbell acquired Keams Canyon.

resident ethnologist/scientist, Alexander Stephans. Keam's residence showcased fine ethnographic material, the literature of Shakespeare and Dickens, and a Lilliputian flower garden brightened by candy-tuft and asters. In 1887, when the government purchased all thirteen of Keam's buildings plus his post and twenty-seven acres of land for ten thousand dollars to use for its expanded operations, Keam moved down-canyon and recreated his operation there. Finally, suffering ill-health, he sold his business to his Hubbell friends and returned to England, where he died in 1904.

More than just physical property, the purchase of the Keams Canyon post also gave nineteen-year-old Lorenzo the opportunity to start his trading career in an established location. On May 24, 1902, Lorenzo wrote his father that "I am missing you [J. L.] again." Six weeks later, he asked his father to come out to see him and to see how the business was doing. J. L.'s visits were both rare and short, and Lorenzo would repeat this refrain over the next twenty-eight years.

A Quest for Water

When Hubbell was a young man, his frequent travel was undertaken for adventure, but as he matured, he had more pragmatic motivations: land and water. The West was the country's water frontier, and use rights for this scarce commodity were being aggressively developed. For his part, Hubbell wanted water for the Ganado trading ranch.

Extreme weather conditions plagued all reservation water systems. Then as now, rain and hail hammered the arid landscape—once, four inches of rain and hail fell in an hour. On another occasion, heavy rain deluged this high desert landscape for forty-two hours. Flash flooding could be counted on to occur, heavy streams of turbulent brown water rushing down every wash. The storms also damaged ditches, often covering them with six inches of sand.

Ganado Lake

When a survey team of government engineers, led by Lieutenant C. M. Supplee, came to Pueblo Colorado Wash in 1892, they camped along Ganado Lake, a "natural lake" upstream from the Hubbell trading operation, and inspected the "Arroyo Colorado." After taking angles and measurements, they finally recommended a brush and wood dam and irrigation ditch for the farmers downstream.

In the winter of 1893, during his first term in the Arizona Territorial Legislature, Hubbell introduced bills relating to the "Appropriation of Water and the Construction and Maintenance of Reservoirs, Dams and Canals" and "Impounding and Storage of Water in Arizona Territory." Both gave the first appropriating user of the water the better rights. These were followed by a bill titled "To Encourage the Impounding and Storage of Water in Arizona." His self-interest in this legislation is clear—his trading ranch edged the Rio Pueblo Colorado, which drained in excess of two hundred twenty square miles.

In 1902, Hubbell began to develop an irrigation system for his trading ranch at his own expense. Completed in 1908, it included a diversion dam, ditch, headgates and canals, terraces, and a storage reservoir or holding pond. He also pursued a water claim separate from his homestead claim.

Weather and interest allowing, J. L. gave every visitor a tour of the complex system. One such visitor, Rufus Eley, the editor of Irrigation Age, was so impressed that he ran a feature story on Hubbell's irrigation system. Like a weaver skillfully plying yarn, J. L. turned these visitor contacts into support for his project.

Hubbell's efforts paralleled the larger course of western homesteading in the peak years between 1902 and 1910. While the federal government promoted dry-land farming, it also subsidized reclamation. True, Hubbell put in his own canal system (valued at $8,990.90 in 1918), which he financed by token-paid labor. But he also repeatedly turned to the federal government, seeking massive investments of public money in a dam that would enhance his personal project and provide increased flood control for his land.

Hubbell, in his late forties, at the time of Eley's trip to Ganado.

A Changing Economy

As Hubbell worked on water-related issues, Navajo demographics were changing, as indicated in the government agents' annual reports. These reports emphasized material changes, which according to anthropologists, precede changes in beliefs. The reports measured tribal life by white values: a rectangular house, monogamy, Christianity, education, earned wages, and manufactured clothing were given high value by the government agents.

By the early 1890s, the Navajo population had swelled to 18,000, and their herds peaked at 1,745,000. The cash value of Navajo weaving in 1890 was estimated at $30,000. The Panic of 1893 and bad weather brought that number down, however, and removal of the wool tariff further reduced the price of wool from 16.3 cents to 11.1 cents per pound. By the mid-1890s, harsh winter weather and drought worsened the Navajos' condition.

The number of Navajos who could read jumped from thirty to seven hundred. The count of missionaries and Navajo church converts started at zero and increased to six missionaries and forty-one converts. Navajo-freighter earnings rose from thirty-two dollars annually to over five thousand, and product values, from three hundred thousand to five hundred thousand dollars.

This type of report, which did not tabulate individual successes, overlooked the progress made by men such as Chee Dodge. With few exceptions, Navajos did not successfully own or manage trading posts—they believed in sharing, not bartering, with relatives. In the late 1800s, however, Chee Dodge was an exception. Employed by the Bureau of Indian Affairs for a number of years, his name regularly appears in the Apache County Board of Supervisors' minutes for approval of charges for interpreting. By 1890, Dodge managed and was in partnership with trader Stephen E. Aldrich at Round Rock Trading Post. Charlie Hubbell even clerked there for awhile.

In 1895, about the time Hubbell was beginning to build up his Ganado operation, Dodge hired a German architect from Flagstaff to design his home at Sonsola (*So'sila*, or "Stars Lying Down"). It was located between two truncated volcanic buttes nearly nine thousand feet in elevation west of the main Chuska Range and northwest of Crystal. Following long-standing Navajo custom, Dodge wed several women, most of whom were sisters or otherwise clan-related to one another, and thus expanded his livestock holdings. Though Dodge never worked for the Hubbells, a number of his tribal relatives and followers did.

Working for the Trader

When Navajo agent Hayzlett urged passage of the Ganado trading ranch act, he was reflecting the government's policies nationwide, which had Indian assimilation as one of its goals. Hubbell, however, twisted this model, creating conditions of dependency, sometimes even near-peonage, as he hired increasing numbers of laborers and paid them in tokens good only at his store.

Chee Dodge once forced J. L. to take his nephew, Joe Tippecanoe, out of the field and try him out in the store. According to Tippecanoe, J. L. grabbed his shovel, kicked it aside, and told him, "Let's go to the trading post." Tippecanoe said that Hubbell "dragged me in there and told me to stand behind the counter. There were a lot of people in the store at that time." Then, the trader said:

> this man is going to be working here and don't you ever say anything to him. You say things to the Mexicans that are working here, but not this one. I want you to treat him properly, especially women, because if you don't, his uncle Chee Dodge is not going to like it.

Tippecanoe said he was only paid in food (more probably, tokens that he spent on food), though he worked till dusk, or as late as eight in the evening if there were a lot of customers.

Other Navajo men recollected starting to work for Hubbell at a young age. Jim James said, "All my young life, I was working on the [Hubbell] farm." Net Slivers remembered that when he was thirteen he herded cattle for the trader, earning three dollars and twenty-five cents a day in tin money. J. L. paid Charlie Ganado one dollar a day in tin money for carrying the mail between St. Michaels and Ganado; to earn this, he traveled over the snow-covered summit, sometimes at night. Ganado said he could use Hubbell tokens at Cotton's store in Gallup, although others claim that Cotton allowed only fifty cents in trade for a dollar Hubbell token. Friday Kinlicheeny, another long-time Hubbell employee, carried mail and rotated his routes between Chin-le and St. Michaels. He commented,

> Sometimes the grain, hay, and the food I consumed, he didn't charge me for them.... In the winter time he said that I had a rough time and that he'd let all the charges in feed and food go and pay me $28 per month.... Tin money was all he had.

At other times, Kinlicheeny would work alongside thirty Navajos and several Mexicans in J. L.'s fields, or herd the sheep traded to Hubbell down to the railroad, an eight-day round-trip.

Sam Taliman cut and hauled timber to build bridges, the first one of which "wash[ed] away when a tornado came across the canyon." Taliman said that when he worked with other Navajos in the trader's fields "land-clearing, earth-moving, and leveling the cornfields," the foreman was a Mexican (perhaps one of Lina's many relatives).

Lina taught Loco, the Hubbells' tall, slender Navajo servant, to cook. He could prepare roast corn (J. L.'s favorite), pigeons and squab, holiday dinners with turkey and pies, and the big noon spread of roast beef, roast lamb, beans, and corn on the cob. Two Navajo interviewees—Marie Curley and Mrs. Yazzie Holms—remembered Lina.

Marie Curley's parents were Miguelito, or Red Point, and his wife, weaver Maria Antonia. They moved with Ajibaa, Maria's daughter from her first marriage, near Hubbell's trading ranch in 1898. Both Miguelito and Maria Antonia would have crossed Santiago Hubbell's toll bridge

Loco, Hubbell's cook

over the Rio Puerco when the Navajos returned from Fort Sumner in the late 1860s. Miguelito was born there in 1865 and when he was older, acquired prestigious warrior status by serving as a Navajo policeman (or scout). From a youth spent gambling and attending sings (Navajo religious ceremonies), he evolved into *hat aalii* status. Navajos called him "Red Point" after a promontory near his home. Maria Antonia was orphaned on the Navajos' return from Fort Sumner; as an infant, she was passed around among relatives and fed with a milk-filled container made from the lining of a sheep's throat. Her first husband, Sickman, abandoned her for another woman. After Miguelito and Maria Antonio moved to Ganado, they had three daughters: Alnabaa', born 1899; Marie, born 1901; and their last daughter (called Mrs. Ben Wilson in the interviews), born in 1906.

In addition to Maria Antonia's weaving, both Miguelito and she cleared land, planted, and worked for the Hubbells—Maria Antonia did washing and ironing for Lina. The two women understood each other, even though Mrs. Hubbell knew only a "little bit" of Navajo; Maria Antonia had probably also learned some Spanish. According to Marie Curley, her mother and Mrs. Hubbell and her father and Mr. Hubbell were "good friends." The women visited back and forth between their homes, though according to Marie, Lina was "so fat" that "she couldn't walk very far anyway."

Mrs. Yazzie Holmes remembered Mrs. Hubbell, called by the Navajos *Asdsa Tsoh* (as spelled in the interview and meaning "Large Woman" or "Fat Lady") making clothes and shoes for Mrs. Holmes when Mrs. Holmes' mother worked at the Hubbell home.

By the end of the century, J. L.'s Navajo name had changed, as documented by Burbank, who commented that no Navajo scene "is complete without [the presence] of J. L. Hubbell, the generous hearty Indian trader...the Navajos called 'Old Mexican'," or in Navajo,

Naakaii Sání. As he had spent a quarter-century on and around the reservation—"old" was probably an honorific, and the "Mexican" tag is obvious. For years, Hubbell had employed many Spanish-speaking male relatives and in-laws—Armijos, Rubis, and Bacas, to name a few—in his enterprises; this extended family spoke Spanish at the Ganado Big House, which the Navajos overheard.

Family sitting by the door of traders' office about the turn of the century.

In these, the middle years of his life (his forties and fifties), Hubbell's connection to his siblings in Albuquerque was augmented by his wife and children's residence there. In much the same way, his entanglements with Navajo women linked him to the Navajo people and Navajo country.

CHAPTER SEVEN
A Man Has to Have Some Vices

A TANGLED skein of yarn echoes the intricacy of J. L.'s middle years: his brothers in Albuquerque and his home there, the last years of Lina's life, his Navajo liaisons, Roman's coming-of-age and bolting from the family fold, Charlie's problems, and the Ganado dam project.

Albuquerque Connections

For years, following a pattern common to traders' wives who wanted their children to attend school, Lina spent her winters in town. For secondary education, the Hubbell children usually attended Catholic boarding schools—Notre Dame in Indiana for the boys and St. Joseph's Academy in Prescott, Arizona, for the girls.

J. L. retained strong family ties to the Albuquerque area; though his mother died at Pajarito in 1899, three of his brothers continued to live and work there. This made it a logical place for the trader to maintain a second home. By the early 1900s, when Roman was still young, the family owned a home on Albuquerque's Copper Street, and Lina lived there. Though her health was the most common reason given, the fact that J. L.'s brothers, their spouses, and children lived in the Albuquerque area may have meant more female companionship for her. Too, many of J. L.'s activities involved Albuquerque businesses or rail travel departure to the east, so the home was a convenience for him as well.

It also appears that Lina did not cotton to living on the reservation. Certainly, her personal tastes differed from J. L.'s. In J. L.'s time, workmen sat on benches and ate off an oilcloth-covered table in the Big House dining room, which also housed the churn and milk rack. The contrast between Lina's Havailand china and ornate dining room set (now displayed in the Hubbell home, though not put into service there until 1943) and J. L.'s Indian bric-a-brac and masculine furniture is marked.

Both daughters were apparently married in Albuquerque; the only similarity between the sisters' marriages was that each prospective husband requested their father's permission. Adela (or "Lala," as the family called her) married Forrest Parker in 1903 and wrote to her father immediately after the marriage that Forrest "treated her fine." Barbara wed Charles Goodman in 1906, and after an El Paso, Texas, honeymoon, settled in Albuquerque; most evenings, the Goodmans dined with Lina. Charles was one of the few in-laws who never worked for J. L.

Barbara became a young widow in 1909 when a hunting companion accidentally shot Charles. J. L. fumed about the hunting accident, calling the companion an "idiot" for handling a gun

Adela and Barbara, prior to their marriages

carelessly. (Barbara, who was also called "Auntie Bob," gave birth to a daughter, La Charles, shortly after her husband's death. Before long, mother and daughter moved from Albuquerque to Ganado.)

By the early 1900s, J. L. and Lina's adult children had become intermediaries for their parents; they also took responsibility for their mother's physical care. Some of the Hubbell family oral histories paint a picture of Lina after her daughters' marriages. While family members and even Navajo interviewees commented on her physical limitations, no one except J. L. described her as an invalid. In his oral history, Hubbell (Hub) Parker remembered his grandmother, Lina, as "a rather large heavyset woman, in fact...not real fat, but she was big, nearly as tall as [my] grandfather, Don Lorenzo." She was careful about her appearance, dressing fashionably even during the day. He recollected his grandmother's kindness in giving him money "to spend on frozen dainties...nobody...questioned her on giving us money."

Phillip Hubbell, Felipe's son and J. L.'s nephew, said that though she understood English, Lina spoke Spanish. He also recollected her as being "so kind...sitting [in] this big chair [while] they all waited on her." He said that her move to the house on Copper Street in Albuquerque was undertaken so she could be closer to medical attention—she suffered "a great deal, because she was a very big woman."

After Barbara was married and living in Albuquerque, she handled her mother's affairs. A letter she wrote to her father in February 1908 showed a sensitivity both to her father's cash situation and his need for control. Reporting that Lina had received the money J. L. sent, Barbara told him that the bills were paid and a monthly statement would be forthcoming. Then she added, "Mama needs shoes and if you want me to order them, just send the address and the number of the shoes. She needs them right badly so don't forget." In what reads like a guilty response, J. L. ordered a half-dozen small size, extra-wide shoes for Lina, a woman who could barely walk. Aside from Lina, J. L. had other family concerns in Albuquerque.

Lina in the early 1900s

Sibling Ties

Of the three brothers who returned to Albuquerque from St. Johns—Frank, Tom, and Felipe—it was Frank who stayed in closest touch with J. L. In Frank's rather terse and matter-of-fact letters, he reported the prices of wool and lambs, mentioned family members checking in on Lina, recounted his loneliness and exhaustion when his wife was absent, told of his daughters at a convent, and reminded J. L. not to forget Charlie.

By the early 1900s, Frank had became the most financially successful brother, reputedly running the largest flock of sheep in the United States. He also kept his hand in local politics, gerrymandering himself into position as Albuquerque's political boss. In 1900, he headed New Mexico's Republican party, served as county treasurer, owned a Spanish-language newspaper, and operated a political machine, disparagingly called "Hubbellism" by its detractors.

Tom served as sheriff of Bernallilo County from 1895 to 1905, and a Hubbell brother-in-law held the county school superintendent position. These careers were ended in 1905 when New Mexico governor Manuel Otero instituted an investigation of all three men for alleged mismanagement; when the investigation was completed, they were ousted. In an unsuccessful repeat of J. L.'s efforts to oppose his removal as Apache County sheriff twenty years earlier, Tom refused to relinquish his sheriff's quarters for days. In the end, however, the Hubbells never regained their political power in Albuquerque.

Thomas A. Hubbell. Alguacil del Condado de Bernalillo.

Frank Hubbell in 1901; newspaper photograph of Tom Hubbell.

When J. L.'s brother Felipe married May, an Eastern schoolteacher, Juliana built them a house next to hers at Pajarito. The few letters Felipe wrote to J. L., on stationery captioned "General Merchandise, Hay and Alfalfa, Fruits in Season," were scratchily penned and replete with spelling and grammatical errors. On occasion, Felipe arranged for men from Pajarito, who he said owed accounts at his store, to help at Ganado. Felipe, who may have had some sort of chronic health problem, was the only one of his brothers whom J. L. helped financially.

For example, J. L. mailed May Hubbell two hundred dollars in the spring of 1909, with the comment that he was "rather short of funds"; at other times, he signed notes for her. While the Hubbell family chart lists Felipe's death as occurring in 1910, there is correspondence dated 1913 in which J. L. urges May to let him know when Felipe is out of danger. After Felipe's death, May offered J. L. the first opportunity to buy the pearls his mother had given her.

The Homing Instinct

By 1905, Adela and Forrest were at back at Ganado under J. L.'s wing. This may have been due to Adela's homing instinct or perhaps to Forrest's difficulties in finding suitable employment, or both. By then, the Big House had been built and there was more room at Ganado. The couple's two sons, L. Hubbell (Hub) and Miles (Mudgy) were born in 1906 and 1911.

Forrest, a graduate of New Mexico Agricultural College, an intellectual, and an accountant, had been a shotgun messenger for Wells Fargo on the Santa Fe Railway between Albuquerque and Los Angeles. He was also a prominent male figure in J. L.'s relative/employee circle. J. L. described Forrest as "adept with a gun, not that I want anybody killed, but I do like to have a man who somebody might fear [at Ganado]." On Forrest's first day in the trading post bullpen, J. L. yanked off the younger man's necktie, saying it was inappropriate for the setting. An elderly trader recalled that, although J. L. scolded Forrest, J. L. liked him. Forrest handled inventory, bookkeeping, and some managerial duties for his father-in-law's trading enterprises; correspondents from outlying trading posts sometimes complained about the recordkeeping at Ganado.

In his unpublished story, *Chi'ndih* ("Evil Spirit"), Maynard Dixon effectively captured the dynamics of the Hubbell household in Ganado. In this account, Forrest balked at J. L.'s directive to bury a Navajo family's recently deceased young daughter. Forrest complained that there was enough to do "without playing undertaker for 'em." J. L. replied it was the custom of the country; though Forrest eventually complied, he ignored the family's request to bury their child facing a specific direction. Usually, Forrest, even if reluctantly, followed J. L.'s bidding, which could involve making a one hundred thirty mile round trip to Gallup by buggy to pick up a visitor.

On Sundays (the one day of the week that trading posts were closed), Forrest, who seemed well-liked, was often invited to socialize at other posts. He apparently reciprocated in the festivities—teetotaler Cotton responded to Forrest's October 1908 request for liquor, writing that there was "No Mt. Vernon Whiskey in town, so I send you a quart of the best I could get, as per bill herewith." J. L. was in San Francisco at the time.

Roman and the Trading Game

Before the century turned and her health declined, Lina took an active and vigorous role in matters related to her children's welfare, and it was her model and instruction that later allowed Barbara to effectively manage the Ganado home. It also enabled Lorenzo to strike out as a successful trader at the young age of nineteen. Unlike the other children, however, Roman (then in his teens) grew up during the time that his mother was ill and his father was dedicated to building up his Ganado facility, extending his trading empire, and surrounding himself with family retainers and a dependent local community. His parents may have spoiled Roman; even in 1912, a correspondent addressed him as "Dear Little Roman," begging Roman's pardon for use of the phrase but justifying it as that was what "you [are] called and it's the way your father speaks of you." J. L. was generally "Papa" to Roman and "Father" to Lorenzo.

In 1908, Roman, following in Lorenzo's footsteps, went to Notre Dame. In a letter to his father, Roman described his courses in commercial arithmetic, penmanship, bookkeeping, English, Spanish, Christian Science, and typewriting. His progress in school was apparently short-lived, however, as in a March 1909 letter to his son, J. L. wrote that he was sorry the school had dismissed Roman. J. L. also lectured his son about the fallacy of thinking that he could do as he pleased. Though he did not specify the nature of Roman's problem, J. L. said "If for such a trivial matter they sent you off, then I am not a judge of human nature." J. L. complained to Notre Dame about the triviality of reasons for his son's dismissal, demanded a refund, and threatened the school with litigation, a course of action he rarely used. He did not mention the possible litigation to Roman.

After leaving Notre Dame, Roman lived in Albuquerque with his mother and attended business school there. As they could not communicate with Lina, school administrators wrote to J. L. at Ganado about Roman's school problems: smoking and hanging around pool halls.

A month after Roman's dismissal from Notre Dame, J. L. described his own state of affairs in an April 10, 1909, letter to his artist friends Elmer and Marion Wachtel in Los Angeles:

> how many times have I longed to be able to sit in that cozy studio of yours and lay on the lounge and enjoy a good rest for the whole day. I have never been so nearly tired and worn out as I have been this spring, but we are like fools, we do not know when to stop.

Part of his activity started the year before when the federal land office demanded that Hubbell promptly process the paperwork for his formal homestead entry. In response, he filed depositions in support of his occupancy of the Ganado land. After obtaining his patent, he liked to boast that he had clear title to the only private land within the Navajo Reservation. (He was, in fact, mistaken, as St. Michaels Mission and the Presbyterian Mission at Ganado had private land titles within the eastern part of the Reservation too.)

Regardless of his poor academic performance, by the summer of 1911, Roman was responsible for day-to-day operations at the Ganado post while J. L. tended to political affairs away from Ganado. He wrote Roman many management directives and admonished Lorenzo at Keams to go down to Ganado and see Roman. J. L.'s explanation to Lorenzo regarding his decision to make Roman manager at the Ganado post provides insight into his preference for relatives as employees:

> It is best to give the boy an opportunity to show what he is made of, although a 19-year old boy is rather of an optimistic turn of mind and may make some mistakes, but it is best for him to make mistakes than to put a man in charge who would not conduct the business with as much interest as he will.

J. L. not only directed Lorenzo to watch over Roman's management, but also asked either his nephew, Elias Armijo, or his artist-friend Burbank (then at Ganado) to write to him twice a week about how the business was doing. Roman himself often wrote to his father about business matters; for example, in November 1911, he reported shipping ten thousand pounds of piñon nuts to Cotton for the eastern market.

However, complaints (not all related to Roman's management) from other employees and managers against the mother store at Ganado soared in J. L.'s absence: no money, no trade goods, and erroneous statements. One Hubbell employee/relative, Andy Romero, disagreed with a statement about his employment dates at Ganado. Others asked Roman "what has become of your father?" as J. L.'s Washington, D.C. trips were extended longer than expected.

J. L.'s letters on management to Roman also showed some of the trader's thoughts on life and principles. On one occasion, when he was stuck with the bill from a lawyer to whom he had directed a family member, J. L. commented to Roman "it is simply another experience of which I have had many in my life and we won't know anything about it 100 years from now."

Roman fretted that his father needed to let him know when the Indians should shear, for "they say I lie if you are not here." J. L. responded from Phoenix that Roman should neither encourage or discourage the Indians from starting to shear, as "they have got to get out of the idea that I am the only person who can buy wool and they [can]...sell it to you." In fact, Chee Dodge that summer sold two lots of wool to the trading post: one shipment of seventy-eight bags for $2,2886.75 and another wool lot for $2,553.00.

In 1912, Roman eloped with Alma Doer, a dancer. As reservation resident (and later, a trader at Shonto) Elizabeth C. Hegemann wrote in *Navajo Trading Days* that Roman married a "very pretty girl who had come west first as secretary" to J. L. when he "held an important appointive position in Washington D. C." Hegemann said she was told that they had

Alma with her baby son

108

a Hopi marriage ceremony performed at Oraibi before the civil service. Cornelia Cassidy Davis, an artist/correspondent/visitor, wrote to J. L. from Cincinnati on September 24, 1912, included a clipping from a Cincinnati paper and commented that, "If he is as good looking now as when he was a little boy, no wonder the girl ran away with him." She wished them every joy.

Alma and Roman.

On their honeymoon, Roman and Alma picked out jewelry at Bingham Jewelry in Los Angeles; Bingham wrote to J. L. asking him if he wanted the items charged to his account. Eventually, the couple had two children: Roman D.(Monnie) on December 30, 1913, and John Lorenzo (Jack) on March 19, 1918.

During Roman's management of the Ganado post, he often questioned his father's trading practices. For instance, he inquired whether or not they had to keep sending their wool to Cotton, as sometimes Cotton did not fix his wholesale buying price until late in the wool season. J. L. insisted that the Hubbells stood by old friends; after all, though J. L. never wrote this, Cotton had forfeited his interest in the Ganado homestead. His father also nixed Roman's idea of printing blanket patterns and colors on cards to give to the weavers; J. L. was concerned that the weavers would show the cards to other traders. Roman argued against his father's reducing the prices at the

Ganado store. Rather, in a February 19, 1913, letter, Roman insisted that the Hubbells' Cedar Spring store manager "sell sugar for ten dollars a sack, let them [Navajos] kick all they want on the price of things, skin them every chance that you get."

By spring 1913, Lorenzo was expressing concern to his father about his continued absence, for "Cotton has been pressing Roman every little chance he gets and Roman is getting so that he is mighty timid." Cotton felt pushed enough himself to write J. L. directly about matters of disagreement between himself and Roman. The correspondence between family members (Charlie, Lorenzo, and Roman) and Cotton was barely civil. In one letter, Charlie griped to Cotton that the salt bacon the wholesaler sent was okay for Indian trade, but Charlie wanted "breakfast bacon" for white people like himself. Cotton testily replied that he himself ate salt bacon.

Alma apparently suffered poor health, for letters such as those written in September 1912 by family members often mentioned her sickly condition. Roman consulted with doctors about Alma's health and in early 1913, a San Francisco laboratory was analyzing Ganado well water for typhoid or other disease-producing organisms. The laboratory did not find typhoid, and suggested that the sewage could be contaminated.

Whether or not motivated by the overbearing demands of trading with a shortage of money under his father's written directions, sometime between the end of April and the first of June 1913, Roman took his pregnant wife and bolted from the Ganado post. They gypsied across the Southwest, first to El Paso and onto Clifton, Arizona, where Roman got a job with the Shannon Copper Company. By September, they were in Douglas. J. L. tried to help Roman by suggesting names of legislative cronies who could assist him.

The Trader and the "Beauties"

The year that Roman and Alma left the reservation, a Navajo child named Roman Hubbell had his ninth birthday. As a young man, J. L. had seen mentor Thomas Keam and his brother called "squaw men," and watched authorities hound them, even though both of the Keam men married according to Navajo custom. Just as J. L. generally reject-

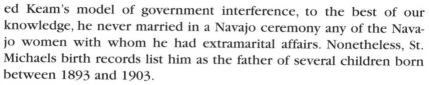

ed Keam's model of government interference, to the best of our knowledge, he never married in a Navajo ceremony any of the Navajo women with whom he had extramarital affairs. Nonetheless, St. Michaels birth records list him as the father of several children born between 1893 and 1903.

It was not uncommon for J. L.'s correspondents, diarists, and authors to note that the trader liked the ladies. More than one visitor commented on how cheaply J. L. sold blankets to favored women guests. Eleanor, the wife of J. L.'s nephew Tom Hubbell, remembered J. L.'s stories of hiding in Utah and the "wonderful girls he had their [sic] and about foot racing...." J. L.'s daughters told her not to "pay attention to Papa, he [is] just spinning yarns...."

Many of Hubbell's male visitors confided in him about their own troubles with women. Ed Sawyer, a sculptor specializing in medals including Indian subjects, wrote to "My dear Hubbell" in July 1904 from Paris. Sawyer was clearly familiar with Ganado, as he speculated that

> Ganado is awfully hot now and soon your visitors will be coming for the Snake Dance.... I wish you could know a chance to have a vacation and come over here and see fine pictures and sculpture to say nothing of the fine little girls and all you want....

In another letter, Sawyer reported that his wife thought nicely of the beautiful turquoise stones he sent and said, "I try to tell her Mr. Hubbell's a man who is very good to all the ladies."

Artist Maynard Dixon wrote that he hoped his friend was still handling the Navajo beauties deftly. Another artist, Phillip Mills Jones, who came out in the early 1900s, wrote to the trader that as it was spring, he would like to head for the desert for a good play.

> I don't think I know of anything more delightful than to see the feeling manner in which you converse with the Navajo beauties— and how they seemed to like it! I rather surmise from some of your letters that you are trying to reform and lead a different life.

Hubbell's practice of commandeering all types of resources in Indian country seems to bear out historian Kirkpatrick Sales' comments about non-native men's attitude toward native women. According to Sales, this attitude represented

> the masculine attitude toward the feminine, the acquisitive toward the desired, the dominant toward the weak, the civilized toward the natural: the women of America were as much a part of the bounty due the conquering Europeans as the other resources.

Though this could certainly be applied to Hubbell, some writers have presented a different twist on the subject. In *The Navajos*, Ruth Underhill made the following point, a perspective confirmed by Ganado oral histories. Underhill said,

> Squaw men...were sometimes a godsend to the Navajos. The Indian woman acted, to her people, as a privileged interpreter, not only of the white man's words but of his feelings and the reasons for them. More than that she turned a remote official into a relative. To...the Navajos, there can be no real friendships with anyone but a relative, real or symbolic...they react successfully only in intimate face-to-face relationships.

It is interesting to note the position that J. L. took in a 1915 dispute regarding an Anglo trader's Navajo heirs. After trader Curt Cronemeyer was murdered, his Navajo wives and children interceded in the Apache County estate proceedings, "In the matter of the Petition of Hoskay Yee Chee Nea for Partial Distribution of the Estate of Curt Cronemeyer, Deceased." Though Dan DuBois, an old-timer and friend of Hubbell's who lived near Zuni, testified in support of Cronemeyer's Navajo children and their mothers, J. L. claimed in an affidavit that the deceased never acknowledged to him that he had fathered these Navajo children. In spite of this, the Navajo heirs prevailed, and the court appointed the Navajo agency superintendent, J. L.'s friend Peter Paquette, as the children's guardian.

The "Stealing Wives"

Navajo oral histories repeatedly reference J. L.'s relationships with Navajo women; the implication is that he thus became a symbolic relative. Weaver Ya Na Bah Winker noted J. L.'s generosity and observed, "Maybe for that reason, some women had children for him, but now they are older people, too." Another, Asdzaa Bekashi, reported that Navajo women around the Ganado area said, "This is Naakaii Sání's [Old Mexican's] child." She too linked his kindness to the Navajos with his siring "a lot of children." Several elderly women remembered that the trader "went for young Navajo girls" and "sired sons." Indeed, his predilection led to many local stories. In one, all the blue-eyed Navajo children in Ganado are Hubbell descendants; in another, his burial site on Hubbell Hill was chosen to keep all his "Navajo beauties" in sight.

A few female interviewees found his attention troublesome. Asdzaa Dloo Holoni recollected that J. L. stared at her, and she avoided his trading post. Other Navajo women interviewed also commented that his staring made them uncomfortable. One of the Day granddaughters, whose mother was Navajo and father, Anglo, said when she and her sister visited the post in their teens, "Old Man Hubbell" chased them about, teasing that he was "going to pinch their titties."

In Navajo culture, a woman who has a child by a man married to someone else is called a "stealing wife." J. L. must have done a lot of stealing, as the careful records kept by Hubbell's friends, the Franciscans at St. Michaels Mission, record six Navajo women as J. L.'s Navajo wives. These are *Yiłxaba* (*Yilhaba* or *Yilxaba*) No. 14, meaning "Coming Out to War"; *Bidáya łání Bici'* No. 2, "Daughter of the Man with Lots of Beard"; *Yiłhanazba'* No. 4, "Going Off to War Again"; *Aszá' né z* No. 18, "Tall Woman"; and two unnamed women. The first unnamed wife's child has a Navajo name *Na kai Sání Bici* No. 1, or "Old Mexican's First Daughter." The record lists the mother's clan as *Tábahé*, the Near or Edge of Water clan.

Only the second stealing wife, Yilyaba No. 14, of the *Bi h bito ni* (Deerwater) clan, bore him more than one child. Their daughter, Maud Hubbell, was born in 1906, and their son, Tom McCabe, in 1908. The fifth wife, Tall Woman, had a daughter, Mildred Hubbard, born in 1902; Tall Woman belonged to the Deerwater clan, and the *Tódíc 'íní* (Bitterwater) clans, claimed the rest of the offspring. Yihanazba's son, named Peter Lee, was born in 1893. Daughter of the Man with Lots of Beard gave birth to John Shirley in 1900. The last, "an unnamed woman," gave birth in 1904 to a boy she named Roman Hubbell. Family records for these six women all listed the father as John Lorenzo, sometimes parenthetically as Nakai Sání No. 1, whose clan was "white man" or "Mexican"; the abbreviation J. L. H. was also used. (This list should not be considered exhaustive.) A review of the descendants of Hubbell's children on the Franciscans' census records reveals names of some twentieth-century Navajo leaders and professional people.

Word of a biography-in-progress on J. L. often generated comments by one or more Navajos, who would mention that their grandmother or great-grandmother had had a child "for" J. L. (Most of these Navajo Hubbell children were not part of the St. Michaels records.) There is also some bitterness about non-Navajos' lack of formal recognition of these Navajo Hubbell children and grandchildren. At the Hubbell family reunion in Arizona in the late 1980s, conference organizers discouraged Hubbell's Navajo descendants from publicizing their claims to be added to the formal family tree until Dorothy Smith Hubbell died.

J. L.'s generosity with all women, the kind of generosity that implied an expectation of reciprocity, may have been part of his relationships with Navajo women. Navajo interviewees specifically tied J. L.'s generosity to liaisons. General references are still made to "flour" or "baking-powder" blankets, small pieces woven to take to traders, leading to sexual liaisons and yielding groceries. Since the spelling of early Navajo names varies so, trading post account books, which could indicate preferential financial treatment for specific individuals, are inconclusive. The interviewees usually designated their mothers' names at the beginning of an interview, but the names rarely sounded similar to those on the Franciscans' list.

On the other hand, it is said that J. L. put at least one of the children listed by the Franciscans, Maud, through nursing school. Supposedly, when the government bought the trading post from the Hubbell family heirs (Dorothy, et al.), Maud's family made a claim that resulted in an out-of-court settlement with some of J. L.'s Navajo heirs.

The weight of the Franciscans' records; the frequency of this theme in the interviews regarding both J. L. and Roman; J. L.'s contemporaries' comments; and his marriage to Lina, strained perhaps by distance, satisfies us that liaisons did occur. The details—exactly who is a Navajo Hubbell descendant and what responsibilities, if any, Hubbell assumed for his Navajo children—are subjects worthy of further exploration, particularly by a native Navajo speaker. Then the J. L. Hubbell family tree can be updated.

Rise and Decline

As J. L.'s world broadened from provincial to national politics, as he traveled more, as he hobnobbed with people of note, Lina's world was narrowing, partly due to her inability to communicate in English and partly due to her health, although her specific maladies are never explained in detail. Nevertheless her daughters and Lorenzo were devoted to her. In what was perhaps her last non-family trip, Lina had a three-week stay at Faywood (presumably a health resort). From Albuquerque, Barbara wrote her to father on June 16, 1910, that the stay had not improved her mother's condition.

By the fall of 1911, Lina may have needed more care, as by this time, she was staying at Keams Canyon with Lorenzo. Lorenzo included word about his mother's condition in his intra-post correspondence (primarily with Ganado). In November 1911, he wrote, "Mother is feeling very well," and in early December 1911, the same message plus, "[she] is happier every day and so am I." On December 27, Lorenzo said that he was glad his father was back; J. L.'s letters during that month appear to have been sent from Phoenix and concerned political matters. Lorenzo hoped his father would visit Keams Canyon soon, as his mother appeared better than she had been for years, was in good humor, and "she sends you her love." But by February 1912, Lorenzo wrote Roman, "father was detained in Washington...Mother is well—as well as can be expected in her condition; but she is very anxious to leave." Family visitors paraded through Lorenzo's post during Lina's stays. Lorenzo sometimes reported that Lina was out of bed and feeling well, though the general tone of his correspondence seems to indicate that his mother's health was deteriorating.

J. L.'s brother Tom, who suffered from a painful terminal illness, committed suicide in 1911. Surviving him were his son Tom, Jr. from his first marriage and Sophia, his second wife. After his brother's suicide, J. L. became the executor of Tom's estate and guardian of his son. In 1912, J. L. was embroiled in a thousand-dollar claim Frank Hubbell made against Tom's estate. J. L. wrote to the estate's attorney that he would avoid this problem if it only affected himself. However, J. L. would go to court if necessary to protect Sophia and Tom, Jr.'s rights. While we do not know the matter's resolution, it did not seem to estrange the brothers.

Tom, Jr. moved to Ganado and in 1913, J. L. sent him to the University of Arizona in Tucson. The Hubbell Papers include "lecture" letters from J. L. to similar to those expressions of parental concern that the trader had sent to Roman a few years earlier. Finally, J. L. gave up on Tom and his continual financial woes and Lorenzo took over for several years.

While J. L. fretted over his Albuquerque relatives' problems, he worried about Lina as well. He instructed Lorenzo in March 1912 to give his "kind regards to your mother," and added his hope that her health was improved. He also asked Lorenzo to send him weekly updates on Lina's condition. In what seems to have been a defensive mode, J. L. explained to Lorenzo that the doctors told him not to take Lina to a low altitude because of her asthma; therefore he believed the Phoenix climate would not agree with her. On May 7, 1912, J. L. wrote Lorenzo to give his "love to Lorenzo's mother if she [is] still with [you] at Keams Canyon," and "hope that she doesn't think I've entirely deserted Ganado, but tell her I will come back as usual, even at the eleventh hour." This message would seem to indicate that J. L. did not know his wife's whereabouts, as well as a pattern of neglect in their relationship.

By J. L.'s own estimation, he spent three months in 1911 and two months in early 1912 in Washington, D. C., lobbying for a Ganado reservoir project. Following a decade of political maneuvering, J. L. wrote an unusual letter to Lorenzo on April 6, 1912. In a glow of accomplishment, with overtones of fatherly advice and a statement of his philosophy of life, he said:

> The appropriation for the Ganado Reservoir passed the House...passed the Senate, so at last after many years, my dream has come true and under adverse circumstances and with opposition that no one thought could be overcome. This will show you through life that what you always want, if it is right, persist in it, and you will accomplish anything you start to do but first be right, then go ahead.

Left: *Chee Dodge in formal portrait.*

Below: *Just as J. L. was busy politicking, so were Chee Dodge and other Navajo headmen. In early February 1912, a gathering of tribal leaders and probably government officials shows Chee in the forefront in the dark suit and white hat (sixth Navajo from right).*

This letter may have caused Lorenzo to recall the words of a female acquaintance from Keams Canyon, who reminded him that when she had last seen him in 1910, he had longed to study law at Ann Arbor and said that he had given up the dream because of family duty and love for his father.

The plan J. L. promoted was to build a dam at Ganado Lake, make canals and ditches that would connect to his own water system, develop Indian farms, and keep a continual stream of water flowing downstream, which included his property. When Hubbell first proposed the dam's construction in 1907, he must have been anticipating long work days for Indian laborers; in 1910 he proposed to increase the project's price by fifteen per cent if the government limited him to working the Indians only eight hours a day. When the dam project started, Charlie Ganado, a local Navajo, recollected that Many Horses and his brothers had acted as foremen.

Hubbell capitalized on this captive market by opening a small store that sold feed for Navajo teams as well as food and clothing for the workers. The dam store absorbed much of the Navajos' pay; historian Peterson's opinion was that those who had worked for Hubbell earlier on his own irrigation project were "caught even more closely in the web of credit and tin money that prevailed on the reservation

117

generally." He described this as a form of vassalage, and further notes that Hubbell's Hispanic background and paternalistic relationship with "his Indians,"—though leavened by his altruism and goodwill—exploited the Indian community.

The year after the project was approved, J. L. worked out an agreement with the Department of the Interior (the Bureau of Indian Affairs was within the jurisdiction of this department) for his own water usage. H. F. Robinson, an engineer for the BIA's Indian Irrigation System who had met J. L. years before, oversaw the Ganado irrigation project. This project was the star of the bureau's Navajo water projects, just as J. L.'s trading operation represented the best and most extensive of the Southwestern trading posts.

Family Concerns

In May 1912, J. L., who was worried about his daughter Barbara's isolation at Ganado, asked her to join him in Phoenix, if only for a week. He dismissed her excuse that she had no stylish clothes, saying "the people here don't use many clothes in the summer, all they use is just enough to keep them out of the gaol." In his next letter, he said he was sorry that she did not come, as she had been penned up at the trading ranch for over a year. He insisted that "when I come back from Chicago, you have to take a short trip somewhere"; six months later, she did join her father on another of his Chicago trips.

By January 1913, Adela had joined Lorenzo (and apparently Lina) at Keams, and together, they traveled to Winslow to bring Lina's parents back to Keams Canyon. At the end of February, Lorenzo wrote that "mother and the old folks are well." In mid-May, J. L. wrote a correspondent about his three-year absence from Ganado and joked that since his return, he had had to "work like a good old plow horse."

During this time, J. L.'s brother Charlie was plaguing him for assistance. Charlie was usually assigned the management of the post furthest from Ganado, which may have been to keep him from the temptation to drink. Charlie's correspondence often started off "Dear Bro." and included a general comment on trade: "good," "picking up," "dull," "awfully slow," "brisk." Then he would list his order for goods and perhaps mention family news. Usually there was some ribbing, and always some fretting: he had no stove and he was freezing; he had not received a single magazine in nine months from Lorenzo or J. L.; reminders that he and Lorenzo "would like to see" J. L., and requests for him to "come up someday." On one occasion, the trader, apparently alarmed at his brother's emotional state and isolation, had arranged a trip for him—among Hubbell's papers is a telegram sent from a California resort hotel to Ganado saying that Charlie had arrived safely.

Charlie's specific complaints in a May 28, 1913 letter to J. L. give a sense of the understaffing and cash shortages J. L. faced when he once again took up his trading reins:

> I am doing better trade this month than ever before, but I tell you it is telling on me as I have to do all the work and I am liable to break down before this wool season is over. I have a crowd of Indians with blankets and pelts here over night and not a cent in the house...strange how you people want me to do business...drop me a line.

Charlie was J. L.'s perfect counterpoint; a drinker, unmarried, no known children, no known affaires, mostly a store employee or a manager in an outlying post, and no political or financial reputation or aspirations. And Charlie, unlike his brother, picked up official complaints as wool picks up burrs. One involved his denying water to area Navajos and another, drinking.

J. L. was so vehemently opposed to alcohol that, according to the *Touring Times* interview, he dumped visiting soldiers' liquor-filler canteens into the Pueblo Colorado Wash when they stopped at Ganado to eat. Another time, it was said that he destroyed a still at a post he bought. However, long work hours and solitary days could exacerbate a man's problems with alcohol, and Charlie's drinking problem was probably more serious than J. L. realized. In June 1913, Charlie pressured his nephew Lorenzo to "take a move on yourself and come to see us. I have got the blues and I am awful dry." Another time, Charlie suggested that he and Lorenzo make a quick weekend trip into Gallup, with the stipulation that they bypass Ganado.

The letters that burned in and out of Ganado about money problems that summer (1913) also indicate that J. L. was not faring well on the family front. Except for his brothers, who had left J. L. and returned to Albuquerque from St. Johns twenty-five years earlier, no other relative had abandoned J. L. as Roman did. Charlie was upset. All his relatives were fed up with his friend Cotton. Lina was still with Lorenzo at the Keams Canyon post; the correspondence indicates that Adela was there as well, but it is not known how long she had been there or if she stayed to help care for her mother. It is also not known whether or not the trader had, or made, time to visit with Lina or Charlie. A mid-summer letter in the intra-post correspondence from Ed Thacker, Lorenzo's employee and friend, referred to Lina. Thacker wrote that he had sent "a few things for your mother, and Mrs. Parker, and a box of cigars" from Gallup.

Not long after this was written, however, Lina died at age fifty-one. What remains of the outgoing correspondence from J. L. following Lina's death concerns post business, Theodore Roosevelt's visit, and long letters to the absent Roman. Although condolence letters came in following a newspaper article reporting Lina's death, there is no surviving correspondence in which J. L. comments on it. The governor of Arizona wrote to "my dear Senator Hubbell...I take occasion to express my deep sympathy for you in your bereavement." (Years later, an aunt wrote that Lorenzo, Jr. was the family star "because he was so good to his mother.")

The family buried Lina on cone-shaped Hubbell Hill, across the Pueblo Colorado Wash from the trading ranch. The hilltop affords a panoramic view of the changing seasons, from winter white to spring's potpourri of colors at the trading ranch. At the hilltop burial site, where lichen-covered boulders topple over one another, Lina's tall sandstone grave marker sweeps up to a parallelogram topped by a cross so crude it looks like a spade. Professionally carved on her marker is "Lina R. Hubbell September 20, 1861 July 13, 1913." Viewed at a certain angle, the headstone resembles a Hopi maiden with a butterfly-whorl hairdo. It remains the hill's most prominent grave site.

As mentioned, J. L. did not reveal any of his innermost thoughts about his wife's death in surviving letters to other family members. Instead, he wrote to Roman that he was hammering at collecting accounts receivable and managed a good financial return from handling the tourist traffic at the Hopi's snake ceremony in August. In fact, J. L. specifically reported to his son that during that month, he made a thousand dollars from his autos, seven hundred fourteen dollars from fares, four hundred-fifty dollars from mail, a couple of thousand dollars from the repair of others' rigs, and four hundred dollars net from out-fitting two groups. (While Hubbell did not charge his guests, tourists were charged thirty dollars a day for either a team and driver or auto and driver between Gallup and Keams Canyon, fifty dollars for a special car, and twenty dollars to hop on the mail line.)

Roman seems to have been more interested in his own disastrous management experience at Ganado, for he included some bitter comments about his father's business practices in a September 9, 1913, letter to J. L.

> By the way who is now taking care of the books? I hope that you now have someone that can keep them straight...a first class bookkeeper can be had for $75 a month room and board to keep the books straight.... By the way, I have this craw in my gut or my throat. Did you get someone as dumb as me to take over, someone drunk enough to do that thankless job?

J. L.'s management style crippled Roman's first trading venture and may have turned him against trading altogether. Lorenzo had started at Keams Canyon at about the same age (nineteen) as Roman, but under more advantageous conditions—he was single and had a degree from Notre Dame. Also, at that point, his father had only three posts and Lorenzo was fifty miles from the Ganado mother store. There was little reservation competition, and cash shortages were not so severe and frequent. Lorenzo, however, would have never written his father such an acerbic letter, even if his father had deserved it. One theory of birth order and personality fits Roman like a hide cover on a pottery drum: the last-born tends to have certain attributes, among them, being fun-loving, personable, spontaneous, caring, tolerant, and affectionate. In adult life, the last-born expects everyone to continue looking after him as they had during his childhood. This profile is a close match with Roman's behavior.

In spite of, or perhaps because of, this turmoil, for the next decade and a half, J. L. drew his extended family to the Big House at Ganado.

CHAPTER EIGHT
The Big House

J. L. USED HIS TRADING RANCH at Ganado and Big House like spindles (long sticks with disk-shaped whorls used to twirl wool into strands of yarn): twirling multiple trading posts employing family members into a trading conglomerate, and twirling his adult children, their spouses and offspring, and other relatives into a family whose size expanded and contracted around him at the Ganado trading ranch.

Conglomerate

"Big" described both J. L.'s trading operations and his family home. In the 1915 edition of *Notables of the West*, the trader's biographical sketch (probably written the year before) listed four posts—Cedar Springs, Cornfields, Keams Canyon, and Oraibi—complementing his Ganado headquarters. Over the years, the Hubbell family added trading posts to this list and dropped others—always keeping the post operations at Ganado and Oraibi.

No later than 1914 (fifteen or so years after Cotton's Gallup beginnings), J. L. also opened a business in Gallup; this was primarily a freighting center, as Hubbell was still buying goods from Cotton. Every bit as adaptable as the Navajos, J. L. grasped the opportunities presented by the reservation's population and government-service growth to transport goods and people, both for business purposes and sight-seeing in Indian country.

His letterhead offered motorized transportation, including stage line services to "St. Michaels and Fort Defiance Daily. Stage to Ganado, Chin Lee, Keams Canyon, Hopi Villages and Oraibi Tuesday, Thursday, and Fridays." It also promoted "Hubbell's Garage. First Class Repairing and Storage, Gallup, New Mexico." Special trips could be arranged to Canyon de Chelly, Zuni, Hopi, the Painted Desert, and the Grand Canyon.

As a familial group, the Hubbells and their in-laws felt they had special attributes. J. L. once said that to be a trader on the reservation, a man had to be a lawyer, a miner, and "all kinds of things." In a 1914 letter requesting a job with Lorenzo, George Hubbell (J. L.'s cousin and

Sydney's son) linked his experience with livestock and general merchandise to a quality that the Hubbell men apparently considered uniquely theirs: "Being a Hubbell I can adjust myself to any circumstance or condition."

Once Roman returned to the family fold, he and his father often traded responsibilities between Ganado and Gallup (December 24, 1914 correspondence refers to Roman's being at the Gallup branch of the Hubbell operation). In addition to Roman, Charlie, and Forrest, many other Hubbell relatives and in-laws worked for the Hubbells in several capacities at various stores. In the early twentieth century these included, among others, Claudio Romero, P. Rubi, Policarpio Garcia, Thomas Armijo, Empimenio Armijo (he lived in the Ganado manager's house and his youngest son attended the Hubbell school), Indelicio (Andy) Romero, Charles E. Rubi, Walter Hubbell, George Hubbell, G. B. Pete, Elias Armijo (a fiddler), and John Golino.

Some of the Hubbell family members resided at the Ganado trading ranch for long or short stints; those who did not, stayed there when they traveled between Gallup and their outlying posts. The family was accustomed to the route and to the Big House, so, for a description of what it was like to make that trip and how the trading ranch struck people, we look to visitor descriptions.

Arriving at the Big House

Two early visitors created colorful word pictures of the St. Michaels-Ganado journey and their arrival at Hubbell's Big House.

View of the Hubbell trading ranch

Rufus Eley, editor of Irrigation Age, described his circa 1901 trip from Gallup, a "little town of two thousand," to Ganado as an interesting, sometimes grand, route. Passing fantastically shaped rocks, the journey included an evening camp at St. Michaels. Early the next morning, their group climbed the divide between Gallup and Ganado. At the Fort Defiance summit, the long descent came into view.

> The winding way of the stream of living water that flows by Ganado is seen.... Toward evening Ganado comes into view. The large low, one-story buildings, the public well with its old fashioned bucket and pulley, the rivers and the ford make an impressive scene.

Agnes Laut, in her 1915 book *Through Our Unknown Southwest*, said that she left St. Michaels by mail wagon driven by a "one-eyed Navajo"; the mailbags were stacked behind the passengers. By sunset, the route was descending steadily in loops and twists. Finally, they were going "up a dry arroyo bed to a cluster of adobe ranch houses and store and mission." She recalled that her first sight of the Hubbell trading ranch included thousands of bleating goats and sheep standing by the watering pool in the wash and

> Navajo men...as graceful and galee [sic] caparisoned as Arabs rode the arroyo or lounged in front of the store smoking. Huge wool wagons loaded three layers deep with the season's fleece stood in front of the rancho. Women with children squatted on the ground.

The early-1900s traveler coming up Hubbell's lane saw first the trading post warehouse and barn. At a distance, the stone/log/adobe buildings of Hubbell's trading ranch were fort-like: flat-roofed with small iron-barred windows. At the north end of the trading post was the office/rug room, then the store, double-doored and high overhead, and the warehouse. All told, the structure measured about forty-five by one hundred five feet. J. L. used the rug room as a bedroom at times; later it served as the storekeeper's apartment. A few personal effects were kept there—a wash basin, pitcher, soap, towels—and a Navajo blanket and Pendelton robe covered the single bed.

A narrow alley ran between the barn (roughly seventy-five by sixty-five feet) and the store/warehouse, separating the functions of trade and transportation. Past the barn, an L-shaped jumble of corrals and stock sheds infused the air with agitated dust and the smell of alfalfa and draft animals. Corn husks and stalks filled the area between the barn ceiling's latillos (wooden strips), the stalks dangling down like Spanish moss.

Until the Presbyterian Mission enlarged its operation, which occurred after J. L.'s death, the complex at Hubbell's trading ranch overshadowed all others. Within an area west of St. Michaels, south of Chinle, north of Chambers, and east of Keams Canyon, roughly sixty by eighty-five miles or five thousand square miles, J. L. had created the most substantial conglomeration of buildings.

To put Hubbell's 1902 trading ranch in perspective, we can look at a 1930s government survey of fifty Navajo Reservation trading posts. During this era, nearly thirty years after Hubbell's pioneering period, thirty-seven of the traders quartered their families in the trading post building itself. The residence portion of the building was usually small, and most commonly constructed with chiseled stone, adobe bricks, and Ponderosa pine logs. Only four traders operated tourist enterprises; most served meals and provided places to sleep at nominal cost as a convenience to government employees.

The Big House

Hilda Faunce Wetherill's husband managed one of J. L.'s outlying posts, one where only a couple of rooms served all functions; during 1914, Hilda made a two-week visit to the Big House and must have been struck by the contrast. In her autobiography, she described the Hubbells' living quarters as

> a house with five-foot-thick adobe walls, with a beamed ceiling of two foot logs and a living room thirty by eighty feet. Between the ceiling logs Indian baskets of value were nailed to the ceiling; the walls were entirely covered with etchings of Indian heads, family portraits, and every possible southwestern scene done in oils.
>
> Of all the treasures in the room, I...remember the saddle pockets or panniers of bull's hide with brass locks and hinges. My host told me these had been used by his grandfather to pack "pieces of eight," the gold doubloons of the good old pirate days. Now they

125

held only the dust cloths used by the Navajo maids.

Four bedrooms opened off the west side of the Hall and three off the east side. By the late 1910s, some of Hubbell's adult children, a spouse or two, their children, and a resident teacher made Ganado much more than a family's summer residence. From the archival material, a typical day at Ganado can be reconstructed.

A Day at the Trading Ranch

A summer day at the Hubbell trading ranch begins before dawn with J. L., an early riser, waking his grandson Hubbell Parker.

"Come on son! Are you going to sleep all day?"

"What time is it?"

"It's 4:30 already, Grandson," says Papa (as Hubbell Parker called his grandfather), standing by Hub's bed on the north porch. As he cuts open a garden melon, he says, "I'm having my dessert for breakfast, right now." (On the early winter mornings, J. L. roasted piñons by the fire.)

After Hub is up, Papa remarks, "Son, just remember this: early risers are conceited in the morning and dull in the afternoon."

Summer or winter, by six-thirty, the entire family is up—earlier still when they are irrigating the alfalfa fields. The sound of wood being chopped near the kitchen and at nearby hogans echoes around the ranch. Roosters crow from the chicken yard. Juniper smoke mixes with the morning dew. The noise of Navajos starting to irrigate the alfalfa mingles with the whinnies and braying of the draft animals, who graze on pungent alfalfa hay.

The tall Navajo cook, Loco or Hastiin Ne'e'y, arrives early and starts the kitchen fires. The family thinks Loco is a very good cook, though they have some concern about disappearing food, such as the squab they found once under his bulging jacket. After that discovery, Barbara kept the dining room cupboard, which contained their extra supplies, locked. (Considering that Loco's work hours began long before breakfast and ended with dinner for as many as thirty or forty people, he may have been attempting to balance an inequitable wage scale.) Loco's responsibilities end with the kitchen, as Barbara manages the

126

family home and often corresponds with employment agencies in search of household servants. Hubbell Parker described Loco as "a comic" who was "full of fun and enjoyed a good laugh." (This grandson also described J. L. as very strict about everyone doing what he or she was supposed to. He was a "benevolent dictator...[who] read a lot and educated himself...a very great public speaker.")

For breakfast, the family eats melons or dips into the root cellar for apples from the Ganado orchard. After breakfast, the Hubbell barn resounds with the yells of Mexican and Navajo freighters and animal snorts and brays. Dust is raised as the freighters round up horses and mules for the waiting wagons. The freighters have loaded the Gallup-bound freight wagons the night before with bundles of wool, hides, and blankets.

Wool being loaded at Hubbell's Ganado trading post.

Now they talk among themselves about crossing the treacherous Mexican Cry Wash east of Ganado or losing provisions at Black Wagon when their wagons bogged down in quicksand.

Long before the freighters leave, a silversmith and his weaver wife are on their way to Gallup with one of the Navajo mail-wagon drivers. There, the couple will board the train for Albuquerque or the Grand Canyon, where they are scheduled to demonstrate their art for tourists; the mail carrier will return to Ganado the next day.

These freighters, mail carriers, herders, and tour party cooks and roustabouts, who were generally Navajos, operated independently of the Navajos who worked for J. L. They braved Indian country's weather in their nights away from their homes. The night sky, or "rolling darkness," as the Navajos call it, substituted for their hogan ceiling, and the smells of tethered teams and sagebrush replaced the sizzling aroma of their wives' frybread.

While the freighters make ready to depart, one of J. L.'s grandsons shoots a cow. After it is butchered, Loco hangs the meat in wet gunny sacks in the meathouse. Other strips dry on the clothesline. Near the house, Hubbell grows a variety of foodstuffs; his April 1909 order from a Los Angeles seed company includes ox-heart and giant Australian carrots, cucumbers, radishes, beets, early Hubbard squash, melons, and winter rye. Some of this garden-fresh produce is laid away in the root cellar for the long winter months.

At the house, Loco or another baker starts the dough rising in bread bins as cedar logs burn to coals and ashes in the outdoor oven near the kitchen. In anticipation, the children hang around, watching the massive rounds of dough rise. The bakers, using long paddles to slide pans holding eight loaves each into the oven, often baked as many as four hundred loaves a week.

Hubbell's bakers at the ovens

Soon, the air is filled with the smell of fresh bread. As the baker removes the loaves from the oven, he rubs a little grease on each loaf. Hubbell Parker remembered tearing "the first loaves open...[taking] out the inside, [and putting] chile and beans in the fresh shell of crust. Some of this bread, wrapped in newspaper to keep it fresh, was sold in the trading post, two loaves for a quarter.

Milk cools in big pans on the south porch. Cream is skimmed off the tops and then churned for butter. The ranch's Jersey cow produced for many years and was regularly mated with the Presbyterian

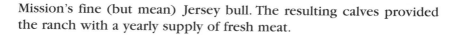

Mission's fine (but mean) Jersey bull. The resulting calves provided the ranch with a yearly supply of fresh meat.

Navajo laborers tend the family fields and garden plot north of the house, as well as working elsewhere on the trading ranch; wherever the family members go, they run into laboring Navajos. One Navajo woman, Asdzaa Dloo Holoni, recalled that Hubbell paid his laborers, such as her husband and others, with octagonal tin money, and she considered the farmland Hubbell developed to have been "[made] from his tin money." Another interviewee, Tsiniginie Nez, said that he did anything Hubbell wanted done,

> I worked inside, I swept and kept everything in order in the store-room...build a fire in the store. When I worked outside, I chopped and hauled firewood...[and] water for the Hubbell family.

Tully Lincoln, who was Loco's son, said the pay then was low, but food was inexpensive. From his youth, he planted and harvested hay, alfalfa, corn, and potatoes for Hubbell from six in the morning until six at night for one dollar and twenty-five cents a day (or four dollars, if he used his own horses). In a telling comment, Lincoln said that "everything around here [the trading ranch] was done by the Navajos for low wages."

Only a few Indians worked inside the house. Sometimes young Navajo or Hopi maids (for a while, Maria Antonia's daughter Marie was among them) dusted the ceiling baskets and books and made up beds under Adela's careful supervision. (Adela was such a perfectionist that Barbara would tell her to stay out of her room.) Some days, the sisters worked with the maids sweeping the rugs on both sides, mopping the floors, dusting the frames of pictures, washing the vigas with soapy water, applying a conditioner to all the books and chairs, and using a furniture polish made at home from boiled linseed oil and turpentine.

The Hubbell grandchildren and grandnephews attend school in a room adjoining the patio (later, in the manager's quarters). Maps hang on the south classroom wall and a blackboard on the north; the students turn their chairs to face the wall they need. The teacher gives the older students writing assignments while she teaches the younger ones to read. The first teacher at the trading ranch taught the children Greek myths.

From the classroom, the children can hear the thumps and cracks of handsome young *Des chii inii Neez* ("Whitehair's Son," reputedly one of J. L.'s Navajo children) chopping wood. In the fall, they listened to laughing and joking Navajos deliver wagonloads of piñon and juniper. The juniper was used in the cookstove, as it burned hot without the heavy carbon residue of pine. Piñon logs, which had been drying for a year, were burned in the fireplaces and heated the house's adobe walls.

The trading ranch resounds with the laughter of Cha (La Charles), Mudgy, Hub, and perhaps some cousins. Amid their childish pranks and goings—on, it is Cha, who described herself as a tomboy, who stands out. She is the only girl among a bunch of boys, and the family darling.

After school, the children play in the mammoth barn. Familiar noises mix with the children's screams and shouts: notes from a piano being played in the house; fragments of Navajo, English,

La Charles and her cousin in Halloween costume. A Navajo woman and her child, trading post customers, can be seen eating in the background.

Hubbell Parker and LaCharles in Navajo attire.

and Spanish conversations; the bleating and baa-ing of penned animals; the creak of the horses' harnesses and wagon wheels; the clanking of farm machinery; and the click of checkers being moved across a board.

At various times, the grandchildren's pets ranged from the exotic (eaglets, a crow called "Jimmy," a pet sheep named "Powhaton" who ate onions, a monkey named "Eva," and a briefly kept badger and bobcat) to the mundane (guinea pigs, canaries, guppies, turtles, a cat, and dogs). A little terrier, "Rover," was the only dog allowed in the house. A St. Bernard mix called "Big Ox" and the Airedales, "Hobo" and "Charlie," were outdoor dogs.

J. L. moves in and out of his office—a room that functioned also as a museum, bedroom, arsenal, and picture gallery—all day. High on the office walls are small paintings by his painter friends, depicting old textile patterns. Here, J. L. makes his deals.

A weaver carries in a flour-sack bundle and sits on the floor opposite his desk, her skirts in a circle around her. Hubbell treats the woman to canned tomatoes. As her daughter clutches her skirts, the weaver draws a tightly woven old-style blanket out of the sack: red terraces cut across blue and black stripes. In trader Navajo, guttural, clipped, and nasal, J. L. and the weaver negotiate. Once the parties reach a price, the weaver and her daughter go into the bullpen, where a clerk hands the little girl candy as a Navajo assistant, probably Joe Tippecanoe, helps the weaver trade out her credit.

An artist enters the office to complain about his bad luck trying to sketch a group of gambling Navajos. Barbara busies herself with post office duties in a corner of the room (she ran the post office there for nearly twenty-five years).

A streak of red dust moving below the Pueblo Colorado's eastern ridge announces incoming travelers. The new arrivals, tired and dust-covered, and their sweat-encrusted horses are greeted by J. L. with "*La casa es tuyo*," "The house is yours." Then he returns to his work as the travelers stretch their legs and rest in the cool dark inner room of the trading post before going into the house.

Ponies tied up outside the post stamp their feet and Navajos linger by the post door. The ratty-tap-tap of J. L.'s typewriter mingles with the soft sounds of the Indians' conversations. A flock of sheep criss-crosses the wash, grazing, drinking, and bleating. Barbara and a guest race their horses past the cornfields and over to the barn—Barbara wins the race.

As he did for all meals, Loco announces the evening meal by ringing the iron triangle hanging outside the kitchen door.

The Hubbell dining table at the end of the Hall.

Everyone gathers in the Hall, where J. L. sits at the head of the long table and serves while keeping the dinner conversation entertaining. Without a pause, he gives the cook instructions in Navajo, directs an instruction to a family member in Spanish, and talks to his guests in English. Barrel-chested, heavy shouldered, and thick-necked, jaw covered with a bristly gray beard (if he was in between political campaigns), Hubbell sprinkles his dinner conversation with Spanish sayings: "*Quien sabe,*" "Who knows?;" "*es costumbre,*" "the custom of the country;" "*Nada es verdada ni montira en este mundo traidor; todo es según el color del cristal con seq se mira,*" or "Nothing is true or false in this traitor world; everything partakes of the color of the crystal through which it is seen."

While Navajo fry bread was the plunk and plaster of the Indian world, the Hubbell daily fare was a mix of Hispanic and Anglo-American foods. Burdened freight wagons clanking to a stop in front of the post might interrupt a dinner of red chili, or a roast with garden vegetables. Guests recall the chili (hot red chiles simmered with meat or beans, or both). Meals featuring roast beef or lamb also included beans and corn on the cob from the family's garden and other assorted home-grown vegetables. Chickens provided fresh eggs, and turkeys were the centerpiece of birthday and holiday meals.

If J. L. was absent, Barbara acted as hostess, and if there were no guests, Barbara might question her father on family matters, such as the cost of "entertaining total strangers in the house." He would kindly quiet her concerns and respond in a low voice, "Daughter, you have not lived enough years yet to tell me what I should do and what I haven't done." To other questions from her or family members, she recalled that he would say "with a twinkle in his eye" that he just did not "want to talk about that," "that was the end of that," and sometimes, "that's enough for you to know."

After dinner, the guests wander over to the rug room and bargain with their host for blankets. The children climb into the big basket near the bookcase in the Hall. The Hall, high-ceilinged and thick-walled, is the heart of the residence. Visitors marvel at its pastiche of finely woven Navajo textiles, smoke-darkened oil paintings, deep-stained wooden chairs and tables, Spanish religious relics, Hopi mantas, and Plains Indians beaded storage bags. Leather-upholstered sofas are scattered around the room, and overhead, a mosaic of Indian baskets hangs between the ceiling beams. A faint odor of wool and the ghosts of many voices seem to have soaked into its walls.

In the evening, the Hall rings with music from the big Victrola gramophone, the piano, or Elias Armijo's violin, and guests and family dance to the music. Elias played so much that his bows gave out; a

J. L. in Hall

Chicago piano company once notified him that in addition to rehairing, his bows needed new frogs, leather grips, and brass tips.

The bookcase exhibits the breadth of J. L.'s interests. Works range from a six-volume set of Cervantes' *Don Quixote* (1787) to Washington Matthews' 1902 description of a Navajo healing ceremony, *The Night Chant*. History, Indian lore, government reports, and literature, plus autographed works by authors Hubbell knows—*Theodore Roosevelt:An Autobiography*, the Franciscan's *Vocabulary of the Navajo Language*, and Dane Coolidge's *Lorenzo the Magnificent*—press up against one another on the shelves.

At the end of the day, each person retires to his or her roomor to the cots for guests in the hall, and the trading ranch settles for the evening.

A Sense of Place

Whether one came into the Hubbell home from a bright summer day, a blinding sandstorm, or a heavy blizzard, its womblike and otherworldly qualities were immediately apparent. The variety, color, feel, and quantity of material goods indicated an eclectic male decorating touch. Hubbell seemed to have pulled richness from both Navajo country and the West into his residence, then amalgamated and reorganized this wealth into collections that had a distinctly European feel.

Elizabeth Hegemann said Ganado had "an aura of history and permanence" about it that was never achieved at the other posts. And while the Hubbells had lived in towns and did business there, they were not among those who wanted to retire from the reservation, who separated themselves from it. Hegemann grouped the Hubbells, the Days, and the Wetherills together "in [the depth of] their kinship and understanding" of Indian country, a closeness few traders experienced. Essentially, what she described was the sense of place that is so paramount in Indian cultures, including that of the Navajo. J. L. was aware of this as well, as is indicated by his comment that

> There is not an Indian trader now on this reservation that came here when I did, they come and go, the most of them are only here temporarily, make enough to start a business...and they shake the dust from their feet and then I never see them again.

Too, "come and go" aptly described the supplies coming to the post from Gallup and the Navajo goods going out. The lifeline for this activity was transportation.

CHAPTER NINE
Eighteen Thousand Pounds of Blankets

NAVAJO TEXTILES were the meat of J. L.'s trade, and transportation was the mutton fat that greased it.

The circa 1895 Ben Wittick photograph of J. L. examining a blanket with a weaver and her husband captures J. L.'s contributions to the Navajo economy in dioramalike fashion. The horse and wool sacks symbolize the transporting of Navajo goods and people off reservation. The photograph's focal point, the weaver with her textile, represents the women who wove for Hubbell in their hogans or through his arrangements at Fred Harvey Company's curio shops.

Between Two Points

In *The Santa Fe Magazine*, writer Harriet Mayfield described the years of growth and development at Hubbell's trading ranch, which the writer positioned at Indian country's "[commercial] strategic point." Just as merchandise moved into Indian country, Indian trade items streamed out in coast to coast patterns: wool to Albuquerque merchants, lambs to Colorado ranchers, piñon nuts to a Brooklyn candy company, and blankets and silver to curio shops from San Francisco to Boston.

Each fall, returning freighters filled the Hubbell warehouse with wooden buckets of mixed candy that tasted like sweet flour; Arbuckle coffee; Palm flour; cans of tomatoes, grapes, peaches, and pears; and sixty-gallon barrels filled with bot-

Piñon nuts being bagged at Ganado

tles of soda pop—strawberry, root beer, creme soda, and lemon. (The Navajos bought the soda pop at room temperature and the Hubbell grandchildren cooled theirs in a trough by the well.) On January 31, 1908, stock inventory alone was $14,461.87; the horses, wagons, and farm machinery were valued at $4,128.35.

Following is a typical order sent into Gallup in February 1913, and hauled back, more than sixty-five miles over rough reservation roads:

> a case of tow cards, twenty yards of zinc, milk, five cartons of sheep salt, six hams (good ones), baked beans, five boxes of yeast, six dozen cheap tin spoons, two cases of macaroni, four cases of eggs, two cases [each of] peaches, pears, cheese, jelly, small cabinet, jelly large cabinet, bottle ink, [a] case of small Karo syrup, send 5,500 pounds by Lame Jim, make up the load with Palm flour.

J. L.'s freighters primarily hauled wool and Navajo blankets out of Ganado, as well as piñon nuts in season. On a single July in 1902, Cotton reported twenty-three Indian freighters hauling 58,445 pounds of wool (an average of 2,541 pounds per wagon) from Ganado to Gallup. By 1909, J. L. was shipping 100,000 pounds of wool; it would take more than forty-five wagons to carry the equivalent of a year's shipment. In November 1911, he shipped 40,000 pounds of piñons to

Cotton, who complained that the Hubbells paid the Indians more than other traders did. In 1911, Hubbell handled more than 2,000,000 pounds of freight.

Wool shipment from Reservation arriving J. L. Hubbell post-warehouse in Gallup. Inset: Wool sacks stored at Keams Canyon shed trading post.

The Freighters and How They Hauled

Hubbell used independent haulers, usually Hispanic (sometimes a relative or in-law) and Navajo, to supplement his own wagons and teams. At any one time, he could have as many as fifty wagons on the road for him. After 1895, horses replaced oxen and mules, although as late as 1920, he owned sixty-six freight horses.

He also contracted to haul freight for others, including the reservation's government boarding schools.

In 1911, J. L. operated five mail routes in Indian country, and boasted in later years that Ganado had daily mail and freight service from Gallup (a statement that was true only when the weather was good). With the addition of a stage line from Gallup to

Hispanic employees at Hubbell's trading ranch. Some are farm hands. They could have doubled as freighters.

138

reservation destinations, Hubbell completed the web that connected his Gallup warehouse and mother trading post at Ganado to whatever satellite trading posts he had at the time—for instance, Nazlini and Black Mountain in addition to his core posts—and Indian agency sites such as Keams Canyon and Chinle.

Stopping points studded the main trade route between Gallup and Ganado. A stone dwelling at St. Michaels sheltered overnight stage line passengers and Hubbell family members; his freighters slept under their wagons after hobbling their animals and turning them loose to graze in the meadows. Freighters watered and rested their teams at the Cross Canyon Trading Post and again when they topped the Fort Defiance summit.

Hispanic freighters, who sometimes used their own draft animals, complained that the road conditions pulled the life out of their teams. A government report prepared after Hubbell's death described reservation roads as "unimproved and, though canyons and washes were numerous, bridges are relatively few." One tricky wash crossing about five miles east of Ganado was named *Naakaii Deïichahí*, the "Place Where the Mexicans Cry," "Where the Mexicans Cried," or "Mexican Cry Wash." There are several stories about how it earned this name. In one, Hispanic freighters, fraught with the difficulties of crossing, burst into tears. Another version has Navajos ambushing the stuck freighters, who pleaded for mercy. And in the last, Navajos hear the freighters camped at night at the place and interpret their guitar playing and singing as crying.

In the early years of Indian freighting, Navajos used farm wagons and their smaller ponies, which meant that they hauled smaller loads.

Twenty or so Navajos may have carried freight for J. L. at one time, but their compensation for this work was not well recorded. As early as 1902, Fort Defiance Agency letterbooks reference unfair labor practices—one letter includes comments indicating that traders forced Navajos to freight and transport supplies with payment in trade equivalents (probably tokens) at forty cents per hundred pounds.

It is likely that J. L. paid his freighters at least as much as Cotton paid them (though Hubbell may have paid in tokens); in November 1903, Cotton paid fifty cents per hundred pounds for shingles hauled by Indian freighters. In 1911, a Navajo who used the Franciscan's wagon for BIA labor received two and a half dollars a day from the government for his work. In the fall of 1912, with one hundred fifty thousand pounds of cement to be hauled, Cotton complained that no freighters were available since a job at Black Rock was paying seventy-five cents per hundred pounds (by implication, more than either Hubbell or Cotton). Traders often complained of short loads. It is possible that if short loads were indeed occurring, they were a predictable consequence of the freighters' low wages. Regardless of the weather and road conditions, freighting was tough work.

Rough Trips

Indian country's mesas and mountain ranges confined most wheeled traffic to the valleys, and valleys were not always idyllic places. The Fort Defiance Plateau-area valleys, which in spring were enameled with colorful wild flowers and spangled with hummingbirds, were shattered by inclement weather on a regular basis. Because visitors recorded their trips more consistently than did freighters, it is the visitors' memories that are best relied upon. However, the bad weather that made a visitor's trip unbearable would have affected the freighters equally. Hubbell himself seemed to glory in what others considered bad weather. For instance, in 1909, he wrote to his friend Burbank about Ganado's "elegant spring. Lots of snow and the ground is as wet as it can be. No danger this spring of scarcity of water." All that wet ground must have made it difficult to haul freight that year.

A run from Gallup through Ganado and on to Keams Canyon in the snow was described by Joseph Schmedding, who bought the Keams Canyon operation about 1918. Though this had been one of Hubbell's posts, it was actually Cotton who sold the post to Schmedding short-ly after acquiring it in payment of J. L.'s warehouse debts. (It is doubt-ful that Cotton ever ran this post, as its management appears to have transferred directly from Lorenzo to Schmedding.)

Schmedding, his wife, and their baby traveled by a heavy-duty open buckboard on one of J. L's mail runs. The driver stopped at Ganado and switched to a four-horse team, since snow drifts had obliterated the wagon trail. Schmedding and his family tried to stay warm with lap robes, woolen scarves, storm boots, and fur-lined gloves.

Freighting in the snow

The Indian agent for the Hopi, Leo Crane, described the same route during a severe snow storm. When Crane told J. L. that he had passed freight wagons loaded with hay headed for Ganado, the trader noted that he had loaned an Indian freighter a wagon to pick up twenty bales of hay. The freighter's livestock ate thirteen bales, and the freighter needed to borrow J. L.'s wagon to haul the remaining seven bales to his sheep camp.

In the 1920s, when J. L.'s staff freighted for the Ganado Presbyter-ian Mission, a cloudburst sank his wagons and three hundred dollars worth of mission and school supplies in Black Creek's water and quicksand. J. L. covered the loss by giving the mission a team of mules for plowing. In the winter of 1926–1927, the snow started the night before Christmas; by the time it stopped, the accumulation was five feet deep. No mail left from or arrived at Ganado for six weeks.

One of J. L.'s former employees, Cozy McSparron, proprietor of the famed Thunderbird tourist operations in Canyon de Chelly, said that J. L. himself ignored the weather. Traveling by buckboard or wagon, always with a driver, J. L. took on extra passengers, and more than once, even gave up the bed he expected to occupy at his destination, finding "what comfort he could standing or sitting all night by the fire." McSparron, who "never worked for a man" he liked so well, described J. L. as one who was never out of humor nor discharged a man except for a serious offense such as mistreating livestock.

Other Freighting Problems

Equipment and personnel problems augmented the challenges of inclement weather. Letters searching for wagon parts and even new wagons well into the automobile age can be found among the Hubbell Papers. In December 1913, Cotton complained about a bill for fixing one of Hubbell's "darned old wagons." He also relayed his suspicions that Navajo freighters were selling hides and Hispanic freighters were selling Navajo blankets, which Cotton suspected had been stolen from J. L.'s shipments.

To protect valuable goods or to foil theft, Cotton had his workers pack loads in ingenious ways: three dozen dynamite packages in butter-filled coffee pots, rifles in red boxes, and money in sacks of sugar. Sometimes, however, the wholesaler forgot to communicate that information promptly; on at least one occasion, a money-filled sugar sack was unwittingly sold once it reached the post.

Communication itself was often difficult. In one situation, Hubbell used horseback messengers, a letter, and the telephone to instruct Cotton to add items to his order before the freighters left the Gallup warehouse. In May 1909, during a month that J. L. said they had been keeping their noses to the grindstone, he wrote to one of the St. Michaels priests requesting that he telephone Cotton for one hundred fifty wool sacks (telephone lines had been strung from Gallup to Ganado by this time). J. L. further commented:

> If this Indian does not deliver this note in time to catch the telephone open, murder him for it, and we will attribute it to emotional insanity.

There were also many intra-post complaints about freight and mail: asking that teams hurry because inventory was down, blaming shortages on freighter theft, and objecting to the mail carrier's using the managers' comforters for bedding and their hairbrushes to curry the horses.

Motor Vehicles

J. L. started acquiring motor vehicles and setting up facilities needed to support their use, such as gasoline storage tanks, in 1912. At this point, the two-day trip between Gallup and Ganado became one that took only a few hours in good weather. In 1917, a new Franciscan father at St. Michaels noted that there were only five or six cars on the reservation and they belonged to the Hubbells, the agency superintendent, Sam Day, and Chee Dodge.

Many of J. L.'s personality traits can be seen in motor-travel anecdotes—his adventurousness, generosity, good humor, paternalism, and dash. According to Cozy McSparron, once J. L. began buying automobiles, he dedicated the best one for the family; he had a driver for his road car, which was a stripped-down skeleton of a vehicle. On the worst roads of spring, he traveled

> wrapped in an army coat, [his] face...[rough with] a seven-day growth of whiskers, [Hubbell toured]...the reservation sitting sound asleep at the side of his driver, with his feet braced against a [specially constructed] rod.

McSparron said that once, J. L. arrived mudcovered at an outlying post, shook hands all around, listened to Navajo troubles, opened a bag of his silver (probably tokens), and handed out money while he pinched the Navajo women and children's cheeks. Then he ate bacon and eggs, toast, and coffee and talked all night, in spite of his prior announcement about hurrying off to another post. As he left, he told McSparron

> take care of all the Indians. Pay the limit on everything you buy off them...and I will back you up. And don't let any Indian starve to death.

Another occasional post employee, Robert E. Karigan, recollected an occasion when Hubbell's vehicle passed through a narrow canyon between Sawmill and Nazlini in pitch darkness. Hubbell insisted that a car had passed them and stepped out of the vehicle to look for tracks, whereupon he promptly bumped his "nose against the canyon wall and lost his hat."

Lorenzo in the auto, Forrest standing next to it, and J. L. in the background.

On another outing, as Sam Day, Jr. (who often served as J. L.'s driver) ferried him across the mountains, the car lost its brakes. As the Ford gained speed, Day put the engine in reverse. J. L. woke to the landscape spinning past and commented, "That's what I call good driving."

As motor vehicle travel on the reservations increased, the outlying posts reported lost or stranded tourists. Even J. L. found himself on occasion joining the league of stranded motorists. In 1914, Hilda Faunce Wetherill described joining her husband, who managed J. L.'s isolated Black Mountain trading post, by a motor vehicle party. The expedition, led by J. L., included his daughter Barbara, Hilda, and probably Charlie Day as driver.

Hilda described the road as "two shallow trails running parallel over bunch grass and cactus" to the west. The car broke down, and as Charlie worked on it, J. L. "trudged away to a bluff and was out of sight." He reappeared two hours later with a Navajo holding a lantern. As J. L. and the Navajo guided the travel party to an abandoned trading post, J. L. scolded Charlie for not fixing the car. Once the group drank coffee and ate broiled meat, J. L. promptly fell asleep; the uncomfortable women did not rest as well. The next morning, when the party returned to the stranded car, they found a group of Indians there, one with his team harnessed to the front axle. The team owner positioned himself on the car's hood while J. L. insisted that all his passengers get in the vehicle. J. L. shouted instructions to the Indians, and eventually the car started and the party sputtered off.

Broken and stranded vehicles were common on the reservation.

Given the hazards of traveling by motor vehicle, Hubbell did not abandon his freight wagons, though he replaced their wooden hubs with steel. Even into the 1920s, when he operated a half-dozen Model T trucks, he went back to teams and wagons when reservation trails and roads disappeared in sand, snow, and mud. As J. L. often said, there is nothing sweet in the world without some bitter.

This theme of movement is also represented in his export of Indian arts and crafts.

Exports

In *Notables of the West*, J. L. said that his principal export was "the celebrated Navajo blanket." It was indeed these textiles that dominated his trading activities. He boasted that he had three hundred Navajo weavers weaving for him, and Ganado records show that he shipped thirty thousand pounds of Navajo weavings in 1903, forty-two thousand pounds in 1907, and, in just two consecutive days in August 1913, eighteen thousand pounds of woven goods.

The significance of the textile trade to his operations can be gathered from this 1894 income summary: a $1,087.61 profit on wool sales of $9,080.65; a $287.89 profit on goat-skin sales of $1,949; a $296.20 profit on sheep pelt sales of $973.59; a $4,073.98 profit on merchandise (store inventory); a measly $43.84 on horse team (shipping); and a $2,269.10 profit on blanket sales of $10,205.78. Not only were blankets more than twice as profitable as wool; he paid for them mainly in tokens.

In January 1908, the merchandise account for blankets-in-progress was $1,870.71, and for blankets on hand, $6,958.20. That same year, Hubbell wrote correspondents that he sold $45,000 worth of blankets, with only $3,000 in returns. The following year, 1909, he was "selling Navajo blankets to beat the band." By 1913, he said he sold $60,000 in blankets. Traders say they saved the Indians; the weavers reciprocated by saving the traders.

Textile Accounts

The weavers' share of Hubbell's textile pie can be calculated by a review of the trader's weaver account book. As of January 1, 1903, the trader paid out $890.79 to these eighty or so weavers (T. Baad Bama to T. B. Bitzie) on the account book's first two pages. The prices the weavers received per textile ranged from $3.02 to $40, though half fell under $10: Maria Antonia's Daughter received $3.10 for a blanket; *Hashque Ett Nuy* ("Bigue's Wife"), $9.99; Tonto's Mother, $9.02; and Crazy's Ex-wife, $15.75. The pay-outs included amounts traded, and in some cases, showed that Hubbell tokens made up the change. The odd sums also indicate that he paid for many blankets by weight, not quality. (Later Ganado-area interviews confirmed this.)

Clearly, the one who bought blankets called the economic tune. As textile authority Charles A. Amsden noted, traders profited doubly: they marked up the goods traded for a blanket and marked up the blanket on its sale. He also observed that the trader added a third profit level when he sold to the weaver "certain materials needed in weaving, such as dye, spun yarn, cotton twine for warp." Wryly, Amsden noted of the three transactions—and the three separate profits—that

[i]f one man thought of all that, his portrait, crowned with laurel,

should be over every trader's doorway. One man probably did not, but Messrs. Hubbell and Cotton in their store at Ganado were certainly among the pioneers of this ingenious plan for sharing with the Navaho [sic] some of the advantages of the American methods.

Publicly, Hubbell said he discouraged pound blankets, and most scholars agree that pound blankets encouraged the production of coarse textiles made from poorly cleaned wool. Yet Hubbell's 1902 catalogue had several blankets priced by the pound; for example, a cost of "$0.50 to $0.75" per pound was quoted. On February 11, 1909, J. L. wrote to a wholesale customer that he sold blankets at $1 to $2 per pound, depending on "the quality of weave and beauty of design," and had sold $6,000 in blankets that month compared to $1,300 for the same month in 1907. By 1914, he was pushing a new item, a six and one-half pound average-weight saddle blanket, at $.60 per pound.

According to the Hubbell account book for 1907 to 1910, Ganado weavers invested a hefty percentage of their rug earnings in their next textile. Stout Girl's Sister received $12 for a "Grey Blkt." From this, she got tokens of $3.70; wool, $2.20; yarn, 40 cents: flour, $1; sugar, 50 cents; "grub to mother," $1.50; cake, 60 cents; another entry for "grub to mother," 40 cents; and dyes, $1. Thus, $3.80, or 30 percent of the amount received, went into the next blanket. Another account for My Girl showed $39 received for a "grey blanket," with the following account notations: "Buy beads $28.00"; dyes, $2.50; merchandise, $3 and $3.25; cash, $2.25 less a $4 credit for a bracelet, with a diagonal scribble "Transferred to my acct."

Though the weavers themselves did not keep account books, there are many anecdotal records. Mrs. Etsitty said that she was about nineteen years old when she and her mother, Na-lli-yah-ni-baa', began to weave small rugs for J. L. After her mother and grandmother sold their rugs at the trading post, "they would bring back coffee, sugar, and flour. Coffee came in a bean," which they roasted and ground before using. "Naakaii Sání used to give us bread and canned foods to eat there before selling rugs. The price on the rugs ranged from ten to fifteen dollars." (As one of Hubbell's demonstrators, she traveled with her family to places like San Diego; San Francisco, where her family stayed two years; and the Grand Canyon.)

Even Navajo men like Pete Hubbard, born in 1916, equated weaving with food provisioning. He said his mother wove for groceries and wove the designs pictured in the rug paintings. She sold those textiles, aptly named "coffee rugs," as they were traded for groceries, for two or two and half dollars. Today, such a rug would cost at least a hundred dollars.

Mrs. Yazzie Holmes recollected weaving with wool Hubbell gave the weavers. She colored the wool using a blue dye she dug up near St. Michaels. When she took her rugs to Hubbell's Ganado post, her only outlet, he paid her five dollars for a saddle blanket-size textile. Another weaver complained about Hubbell's control of the market. Mrs. Frank Churchill, an Indian inspector's wife who visited Ganado in 1904, recorded in her diary,

> There are several Hogans near the store—one woman came into the store while we were there with a blanket. Mr. Hubbell was not willing to pay [the] price she asked. She said she could get much more in Gallup (60 miles distant)—she told him he had three partners in his business. He asked who they were and she replied, "cold, rain and mud"—if it wasn't for them she could get her price.

Hubbell and Navajo Silverwork

Hubbell applied his textile business formula to silverwork: selling supplies to the smiths, then buying the finished product. It has been acknowledged by most authorities that Hubbell (and perhaps Cotton) brought in Mexican silversmiths from Cubero, New Mexico, to teach Navajo men how to turn Mexican silver dollars, or *pesos*, into jewelry. Because they had less alloy, pesos were more easily melted than were American silver dollars. El Paso banks sold the pesos at less than one American dollar each. Hubbell located suppliers of turquoise, coral, and other semi-precious stones; he even found a source for a Czechoslovakian-glass trade bead that resembled spider web turquoise.

Silver- and textile-lined records metaphorically commemorate J. L.'s critical contribution to the Indian arts and crafts market. He arranged off-reservation venues for Navajo weavers and silversmiths and Hopi potters to demonstrate their crafts. He also supplied Indian clerks, janitors, and bellboys to be displayed in Indian attire at the Fred Harvey curio enterprises.

J. L. Hubbell and the Fred Harvey Co.

Just as the coming of the railway to the Southwest in the early 1880s changed the trading game, so did the birth of the Indian Department (formally, the Indian and Mexican Building and Museum) in 1902 at the opening of Fred Harvey Company's Alvarado Hotel in Albuquerque.

In 1876, founder Fred Harvey joined with the Atchison, Topeka & Santa Fe Railway to create a chain of restaurants and railhead hotels across the U. S. At his death in 1901, the restaurants numbered twenty-six; the hotel-restaurants, sixteen; and dining cars, twenty. Both the Santa Fe Railway and the Fred Harvey Company felt that advertising Indians and their arts and crafts stimulated tourist travel to the Southwest. In imitation of the world's fair approach, Fred Harvey Company also developed on-site attractions at specific tourist destinations.

At Albuquerque and the Grand Canyon, a museumlike curio shop displayed the artisans' output as well as other material-culture objects.

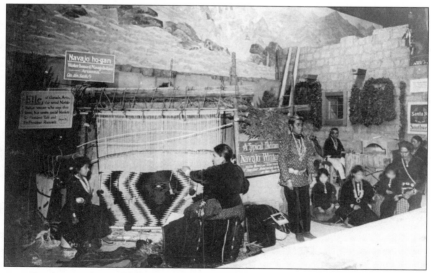

Posed against theatrical backdrops, the Indians created textiles, jewelry, baskets and pottery at Albuquerque, Grand Canyon, and the 1915 Panama-Pacific International Exposition in San Diego and San Francisco.

J. L. associated with John F. Huckel, the son-in-law of the company's founder, soon after Huckel opened the company's Indian Department at the Alvarado Hotel. Hubbell also worked with Herman Schweizer, a former news agent, who was Fred Harvey's Albuquerque Indian Department head. As early as March 1901, J. L. was promoting his Navajo textiles to the Fred Harvey Company; he described the all-wool-warped pieces, including Germantowns, ten dollar saddle blankets, fifteen to fifty dollar *portieres* (doorway covers), and "the old style Navajo blue and black striped blanket which is the best seller."

Over the course of their nearly thirty-year association, J. L. supplied the Fred Harvey Company with a substantial amount of Indian arts and crafts, including good quality Navajo textiles, retailing annually for up to twenty-five thousand dollars. In one order alone, the company requested one hundred small baskets priced from three to six dollars each, as well as some larger ones; another solicited two dozen of the very small Hopi baskets made at Mishongnovi, plus twelve of the next size up, and a dozen of the largest common green baskets, also called peach baskets. In 1906, the Fred Harvey Company purchased nearly thirty percent of their textiles from Hubbell.

When the Albuquerque Indian Department began selling silverwork, the Fred Harvey Company soon came to represent Hubbell's largest silver wholesale account. One large order included fifty-three swastika rings and numerous bracelets, silver trays, boxes, teaspoons, and rings. When the company requested special items for the silversmith demonstrators, such as old Navajo forges and stone molds for sandcasting, Hubbell would oblige.

Financial correspondence between Hubbell and the Fred Harvey Company highlighted Hubbell's operational problems. The company had its general offices in Kansas City, Missouri, and in 1906, employees in this office requested that J. L. send them itemized statements from as far back as 1901 in order to straighten out discrepancies. He ignored the request. Another letter included a triply underlined statement: "will you kindly send us an itemized statement at the end of each month covering that month's business." By February 1907, the general office complained that Hubbell, though promising to send monthly statements, had neglected to do so. In May 1907, the company reported receiving Hubbell's 1905 and 1906 statements.

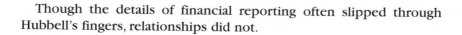

Though the details of financial reporting often slipped through Hubbell's fingers, relationships did not.

Provisioner of Demonstrators

It was Hubbell who, through personality and influence, played a pivotal role in Fred Harvey Company's Indian arts and crafts demonstrating arrangements. Anthropologists have observed that when corporate exhibitors displayed people at fairs or events, the corporation exercised its authority to establish special hours, places, and actions to be performed by the displayed persons. The exhibitors also attempted to control communication between the displayed persons and the viewers.

Among the Navajos and Hopis, however, there was little precedent for such an arrangement. Indeed, this, plus the nature of Indian country and the way things were done, meant that J. L. became more than the company's agent and personal representative. As though he were ordering common green peach baskets, Schweizer would demand that Hubbell send silversmiths, weavers, or "Get some Indians to the Canyon at once."

Not only was the company looking for quantity, it was looking for certain kinds of people. Huckel wrote to Hubbell on July 20, 1905, requesting "a couple weavers and one or two children.... I think I would just as soon have a silversmith as an extra attraction." A working silversmith augmented the sale of the silver goods.

Sometimes, though, Fred Harvey staff apparently just wanted Indians, as the staff would write asking the trader to "arrange it" or "send them [the Indians] the next time teams go out." "There will be over a thousand [people] at the [Grand] Canyon in one day so we must have Indians."

It was only J. L.'s standing and quarter of a century in the Navajo and Hopi communities that enabled the Fred Harvey Company to carry off such a vast and regular display of Navajos and Hopis at the beginning of the twentieth century. The recruitment of one of the Ganado-area interviewees substantiates the Hubbells' critical importance in this process. Charlie Ganado said Mr. Hubbell asked him if he would like to work in Albuquerque and he said he would "like it very much." Mr. Hubbell "trusted me, that's why he had me go there." As a

Hubbell mail carrier, Charlie Ganado earned a dollar token a day, while Fred Harvey Company paid him sixty dollars a month plus board for opening the store about seven in the morning, sweeping the floors, cleaning and stacking rugs, and sorting silver bars. He worked at Albuquerque for a while, then returned permanently to the reservation, where he apparently once again worked for Hubbell.

Generally, before the Indians left, J. L. explained their restrictions at the site; made their travel arrangements; and thereafter, along with the Fred Harvey Company, controlled their communications. Schweizer wrote "our Navajos are due to go home 2 weeks from date. Per our conversation I will let them go before the others arrive." The company expected the Navajos to stay "for 60 or 90 days" and wanted Hubbell to send three or four at a time, as that made loneliness less of a problem. Hubbell should provide them with provisions billed to the company and wool for weaving, with "one squaw working on a native [blanket] and the other on a Germantown" already started. The company had "plenty [of] cooking utensils, etc., all they need is their skins and blankets to sleep on." They would be paid satisfactory prices (satisfactory for whom is not specified).

The schedule, as Hubbell apparently explained it, was as follows: they were to work when the trains were in (the curio shops were at or near the train depots), or from about seven-thirty in the morning until noon. They could then either continue to work, or take the afternoon off and come back for the evening trains. They were forbidden to solicit money or sell their work directly to the tourists, though they could divide up the money thrown at them when they danced. (Schweizer condoned this practice but complained to Hubbell that some Indians used that time to solicit.)

On occasion, the company asked J. L. to manipulate certain Indians into staying. The most dramatic incident involved Miguelito. Either J. L. or Roman (Miguelito was his mentor) apparently talked him into staying in Albuquerque in May 1905, even though Miguelito wanted to go home before his pregnant second wife Ajibaa gave birth. Ultimately, Ajibaa became ill; Huckel hospitalized her, though he wanted to ship the family back to the reservation—a death in Albuquerque might lead other Indians to "think it was on account of their living here." When Ajibaa worsened, Miguelito took her out of the hospital and chanted over her. Irate, Huckel absolved the company of responsibility at that point. When Schweizer reported her death and burial at Albuquerque, he ignored the company's role in pressuring Miguelito to stay, and bid Hubbell to "tell Miguelito when he returns that there is no one to blame for her dying but himself."

Both Hubbell and the company were concerned the Indians not "get spoiled." The control issue, with its "how and when" transportation arrangements on both ends, meant that Indian families were discouraged from debarking anywhere but Gallup or returning on their own. Of those demonstrating, only a few, such as Elle and Tom Ganado and Capitan with his several wives, stayed long.

Miguelito

While working at the company sites, all the demonstrators relied heavily on Hubbell to problem-solve for them at Ganado, whether it was checking on livestock or family problems. If Hubbell did not do this, company staff wrote, the Indians would leave. For instance, on December 24, 1910, Schweizer wrote Hubbell that Joe wanted the trader to check on his wife's mother, as a silversmith who had just arrived at a demonstration site told Joe that his brother-in-law had chased her out. Joe and his family were worried and wanted Hubbell to fix the matter. Schweizer cautioned Hubbell that if the demonstrators did not hear something favorable, they would all go home.

Demonstrators frequently made other requests of Hubbell. Among the things they asked him to send them were *piki* (a Hopi bread, paper-thin and made from corn meal), all sizes of eagle feathers, Mexican silver dollars to make into a belt, bark to tan a buckskin, pistols, and clothing accouterments such as turquoise and buckskin.

For almost all the Indians who went to demonstrate or work for the Fred Harvey Company in those early years, the separation from their extended families and their familiar locale created hardships. This was particularly true for the women, who often were encouraged to leave some of their children behind. Too, although the company paid weavers for finished rugs, it may have been as late as World War I before they were paid a salary, reported to be thirty dollars a month (ten to twenty dollars less per month then the men). Some of the Indians thought they worked for Hubbell at these sites, and that was no wonder, since both Hubbell and Fred Harvey Company collected from the Indians for one another. Navajos working at company sites often sent tokens or money on Hubbell store accounts. Not only did the company ask Hubbell to collect small sums—fifteen dollars from Charley's wife—they even asked him to re-recruit demonstrators who still owed them money. While Hubbell sent families he knew well, the amount on a family's open account at the trading post could have been a factor. As early as the summer of 1903, Huckel was honoring Hubbell's request "not to pay Indians all their money, particularly Tom [Ganado]...as they owe you [Hubbell]."

Elle Ganado   Tom Ganado

Elle Ganado demonstrated her craft to thousands of tourists, who also photographed her at work. The Ganado-area Navajo interviewees remembered Elle Ganado as head of the weaving outfit in Albuquerque and elsewhere. Her husband Tom worked as greeter, sales clerk, janitor, and translator and also finished other Navajos' silverwork. In a moment of uncharacteristic generosity, Schweizer once loaned them one hundred fifty dollars to build a house. Sometimes Schweizer asked Hubbell's assistance in getting the Ganados back to Albuquerque when Schweizer thought they had "vacationed" too long.

March, 1917 cover for The Santa Fe Magazine, *Elle Ganado standing on right.*

In the early 1900's, another woman, the now-legendary Hopi-Tewa potter Nampeyo (called "Nanpea" in Hubbell's 1902 catalogue), who was probably the first Indian artist with name recognition, demonstrated through Hubbell's efforts. In the early 1900s, she worked at the company's Grand Canyon Hopi House. Once, the company prevailed upon J. L. to augment her clay supply, which involved having someone gather six boxes of clay on the Hopi reservation, haul the boxes to Gallup, and then ship them to the canyon (at Fred Harvey Company's expense).

It needs to be remembered that the demonstrators were working at a time during which Indians did not generally leave the reservations for employment. These individuals made possible the popularization of Navajo and Hopi arts and crafts with the traveling public.

These people, and their extended families, were closer to J. L.'s heart than were the fortunes of the Fred Harvey Company. In a similar fashion, the trader was loyal to Navajo country's non-Indians as well.

CHAPTER TEN
The Dyestuff: People and Places

IN NAVAJO WEAVING, the wool's hues come from dyes—vegetable matter like rabbit brush or packaged commercial colors. For J. L., the people and places that gave his life color throughout the seasons lived in or near Indian country.

A Community Forged by Friendship

Mountain ranges, buttes, and washes separated those who lived in or near Indian country from the services and amenities that most people took for granted. Still, for J. L., Indian country was a community forged by friendships, economic ties, and cooperation. Its non-Indian residents excelled at letter-writing and at frequent face-to-face contact. If competitors, they minded one another's business, sometimes literally.

Over the years, the numbers of traders on the reservation increased. In February 1909, Hubbell wrote two letters that seem to indicate his thinking on this increased competition. To George A. McAdams in Chinle, J. L. wrote about a competitor selling at cost. He advised McAdams to

> hang in there as trade is slow now and gets better and they can never monopolize trade and you will get some.... I...have lost all my trade, and it looked as if I never would get any yet after a while my opponent would get to sleep and it would all come back to me gradually.

To the Fred Harvey manager Herman Schweizer, he wrote about the "terrible scramble for trade this year," with everyone after his scalp. The bygone days of trading past looked "like child's play to what it will be like in the future. May the God of battles smile on us still."

Hubbell watched not only the activities of other traders, but what the government did through its local agents. Writing to the Commissioner of Indian Affairs in 1916, Hubbell said he made it a rule that when the Indian agent (and the Indian) made a request of him, he considered it a command, for his business was dependent on the

Navajo Indians, and their prosperity ensured his own.

Closer to Ganado, Hubbell sustained close relationships with the Navajo and Hopi agency superintendents. Hopi agent Leo Crane, for instance, was the most far-flung western member of Hubbell's non-family community. The most numerous of J. L.'s interactions with government agents were in nearby Fort Defiance, however. Too, Hubbell was heavily involved with H. F. Robinson, the District 5 supervisory engineer for the Indian Irrigation Service (Ganado was part of this district).

Indian Agents

Indian agent correspondence to J. L. often began on a friendly note—"My Dear Mr. Hubbell"—and repeated, like the stripes in a chief's blanket, everyday government concerns: provisioning the agency; detailing requirements for bonds, trader licenses, and government bids; requesting that the trader relay messages to Indian leaders; referencing employee accounts at the trading post; and ordering Navajo blankets, silverwork, and pottery. Since the turnover rate of Indian agents on the Navajo and Hopi reservations was high, Hubbell did an amazing of job keeping government-trader relations cordial.

One Navajo agent of the early 1900s, Reuben Perry, knew of Hubbell's investment in a preliminary irrigation system for the Ganado trading ranch, and much of his correspondence with Hubbell concerned this subject. Though Perry had trouble with other reservation residents (such as Hubbell's neighbor, trader Sam Day, Sr.), he always ended his letters to J. L. with "respects to your wife"; he sometimes requested the trader to kiss little Roman for him as well. On December 1, 1903, Perry wrote to Hubbell about an agency employee who was looking for pupils in J. L.'s area. In this letter, he made another request of Hubbell. "If [it is] not asking too much, would you induce the Indians to let her [Miss Shannon] have some of their children?" He also confided that Miss Shannon was "a lovely lady and I know that you will fall in love with her."

The Day Family

Though agents changed frequently, neighbors did not. J. L.'s longest, nearest neighbor was Sam Day, Sr. Following the Civil War,

Day ignored his wealthy family's interest in religion and college preparatory school; plagued with a restlessness similar to J. L.'s, Day moved to Iowa, and then Colorado. After fulfilling a government commission to survey extensions to the Navajo Indian Reservation, he brought his wife Anna and their three boys—Charlie, Sammie and Willie—to Navajo country, and settled at La Cienaga, a quarter-mile from the original reservation border.

Day ignored death threats made by Short Hair, the local headman. As Day explained to the Navajo agent who acted as the Indians' repre-

sentative, he left the water source unfenced and the valley's north end open to the Navajos. When this failed to satisfy the headman, Day offered to pay Short Hair and nine of his men a dollar-fifty a day each to help him build a fence. Day's "dollar diplomacy" worked.

Day, a Protestant, joined some other squatters in selling land at La Cienega to the Catholic Church, and regularly assisted the Franciscan fathers after their arrival there on

Sam and Anna Day about 1906.

October 7, 1898. This included working out an ingenious trade with the Franciscans to further his three boys' educations. His sons, who were then nineteen, sixteen, and fourteen, had grown up playing and working with the Navajos. In exchange for private instruction, the boys taught the Franciscans the Navajo language. In February 1899, the friars began translating a small Webster's dictionary with the boys' help: one team began with "z" and worked backward, the other with "a" and worked forward. The teams met on the letter "l" on April 26. After revising, the final written vocabulary contained 2,850 words and became the building block for Father Berard Haile's 1910 compilation, *An Ethnologic Dictionary of the Navajo Language.*

Though the Days and the Hubbells mingled with the same reservation residents and visitors—writer Hamlin Garland and merchant

Cotton, for example, who visited with both families in November 1899—the two differed in their daily activities.

Over the years, Mrs. Day wrote in her diary that she was "awfully tired of work-work-work." She might bake seven cakes or seventeen loaves of bread at a time, iron the men's shirts, and mop floors while her husband and boys (with rare assistance from Navajo laborers) hauled hay, oats, firewood, or otherwise labored for neighbors. Sometimes Anna Day visited Fort Defiance and played whist. Even after the Days left their trading post at Canyon de Chelly/Chinle (where they traded between approximately 1901 and 1906), the hardy Mrs. Day returned in the fall with camping equipment, a copper boiler, and a wagon to put up two hundred quarts of canned peaches from the orchards there. According to Dorothy Hubbell (Roman's second wife), no one topped Mrs. Day "on information about her neighbors far and near."

When motor vehicles came to Indian country, one of the Day boys might haul mail or chauffeur J. L. from post to post. No Hubbell ever worked for the Days, though the Day papers reflect bills, notes, and settlements of accounts with J. L.

A sense of the community atmosphere of the reservation (and the role of the Days and Hubbells in travelers' journeys) was captured in the first page of Mary Jeanette Kennedy's memoir. She described her departure from Gallup on July 4, 1913, to begin life as a trader's wife. Mrs. Kennedy and her husband set out from Gallup, had lunch with Mr. and Mrs. Sam Day, "pioneer traders on the reservation," and the next morning visited with Mr. J. L. Hubbell and his family. Hubbell welcomed them to the Indian trading business and commented that their location was a good one; he later became one of their first visitors.

Surviving Day-Hubbell correspondence is sketchy and most often concerned the comings and goings of family members. However, in the fall of 1911, the senior Day wrote a letter of apology to J. L. While Day's letter did not specifically describe his transgression, it revealed the regard he had for J. L.

> I come to you in "sackcloth and ashes" and on bended knee—when I wrote you the other day it was for the purpose of letting you know that Lorenzo had gone to Flagstaff and relieve your anxiety—I commenced to write in a spirit of raillery forgetting that a written word

is never received as a spoken one is—I confess I did not want to give you pain—I did not read the letter over or I probably should never have sent it—Forgive me—will you? You are more and nearer to me than any person on earth outside of my wife and boys and I would not knowingly do or say anything that would give you pain.

Day ended the letter with a flurry of family reminders and political reports. The letter implies that J. L. was touchy but reconcilable by appeals to his good nature, reason, and the past.

Rather than indulge in the liaisons preferred by the Hubbell men, Sam Day, Sr.'s son Sam married one of Manuelito's daughters in a Navajo ceremony. Sam Day III, the offspring of that union, recollected the two families' close relationship. The grandchildren played together at the Ganado post, and "old man Hubbell," as Sam Day III called J. L., admonished the children for throwing rocks at Mexican workers.

Hubbell and the Catholics

Both Day and Hubbell facilitated the religious entities that continue to thrive in Indian country today: the Franciscans at St. Michaels, and later, the Presbyterians at what became the Ganado Presbyterian Mission and Sage Memorial Hospital. Ultimately, these institutions were the means by which the federal government made inroads in their efforts to assimilate the Indians. The chronically short-funded Bureau of Indian Affairs used Christian organizations to inculcate Indians with the American values of education, individualism, self-reliance, monogamous marriage, the gospel, and the sanctity of private property.

Of all the Franciscans at St. Michaels, Father Anselm Weber, one of the original clerics, and Brother Simeon Schwemberger, stand out in the Hubbell correspondence—brown sheep in a Navajo flock.

Anselm Weber's intellect and sense of humor was a good match for J. L.'s own. Weber (the Navajos named him Chishchilli because he had curly brown hair) spoke for the Navajos often and pushed to enlarge their reservation. On August 12, 1899, nearly a year after Weber's arrival in Indian country, he met the entire Hubbell family at Ganado on his way to the Hopi snake ceremony. According to Weber's biographer, Robert L. Wilken, "Don Lorenzo was at his best and Mrs. Hubbell at her busiest...the children made an excellent impression."

Father Weber, left, a Franciscan at St. Michaels. Above, Brother Simeon who was at St. Michaels before he unceremoniously left the order with Father Weber's niece. He later worked for Hubbell at one of Hubbell's trading posts.

The presence of so many guests on their way to Hopi meant two seatings at the long table and more voices around the melodeon that night. English, Spanish, French, and German—the collective linguistic repertoire—must have energized Father Anselm after his long months of mission routine. The day and evening of conversation and song, the homeyness of it all, stood out as the highlight of the Weber's entire Hopi trip.

Even Mother Katherine Drexel, the former socialite and heiress who founded Indian Missions and St. Michaels, experienced the reservation community's camaraderie and ethic of assistance as she traveled from St. Michaels to Canyon de Chelly through Ganado. She commented on the trader's warm hospitality and the novelty of watching him

> pay out his own money "chips" for blankets, and scrip. It was so much more real for the Indians to barter with hard money than merely book credit.

St. Michaels

The next day, her party enjoyed mass at the Hubbell Hall's dining table and days later, borrowed a fresh horse from Hubbell.

Weber and Hubbell had mutual concerns. Weber often addressed J. L. in letters as the "Boss of Apache County." Once he teased that a telephone line would be strung from St. Michaels to Ganado by fastening the wire "to trees and sticks and rocks"; another time, he joked with Hubbell about his trips to the "effete East." The two argued, as well. According to one story, Hubbell lost his temper with Weber, who was visiting at Ganado, and threatened to cancel the mass Weber planned to hold in the Hall. The trader eventually calmed down, however, and is said to have told a joke about priests to break the tension.

In early 1905, on Weber's first trip to Washington, D. C., on behalf of the Navajos (some called Weber the Navajos' lawyer), he carried J. L.'s letter of introduction to the Indian Commissioner, Francis E. Leupp. Weber later said that the letter proved to be an "open sesame" to various executive offices in Washington.

J. L.'s friend Chee Dodge often traveled with Weber to plead for additional land for the reservation. Dodge impressed his fellow Navajos, as they felt his friendships with traders such as J. L., missionaries, and government officials helped persuade the government to act in the Navajos' favor on reservation-related issues. Weber, who served multiple roles with J. L., did the same with Chee Dodge; among them, legal advisor, investment broker, priest, and friend. The Franciscan kept an apartment at St. Michaels for Dodge and provided a waystation for J. L. as well.

All the Hubbells maintained close ties to Simeon Schwemberger, who arrived in 1901 to serve as a brother at St. Michaels Mission. The Navajos called Simeon *Anaa'tsoh*, meaning "big eyes" or "bulging eyes," referring perhaps to his camera. A visiting Catholic sister described Simeon as a "good hearted brother who is chief cook, singer in the choir, head housekeeper, farmer, poultry raiser, laundry man, baker, [and] alter server," with a tendency to tease. However, this short, stout, dark-complected brother disliked housekeeping chores, and his boisterousness made him unpopular with some of the priests.

In a May 1903 letter from Brother Simeon, we see again J. L.'s anger when he felt accused of prevailing upon others; we also see his likely misunderstanding of a friend's intentions. Apparently, Simeon had written (in a spirit of friendship, according to other residents of St. Michaels) about problems with J. L.'s mail carrier. J. L.'s haughty response, as Simeon characterized it in his letter, asked the brother not to presume that J. L. sent a mail carrier to be taken care of. Simeon said that he had heard the trader was "so very busy and likely you forgot to make arrangements." He pictured J. L. as red hot in writing his response, with "sweat...rolling down your face" as you pounded "the 'stuffings' out of the typewriter because no dog was near enough to kick." The episode reveals Hubbell's quick anger when accused of mooching; his tendency to forget to attend to details; and ultimately, his desire to maintain friendships once his anger had passed. When Simeon doffed his Franciscan robes—and vows—in about 1908, J. L. ignored Weber's ire and hired him to manage one of his trading posts, as he was fluent in Navajo.

Except for these and some other infrequent and relatively inconsequential incidents, J. L. maintained a close relationship with the Catholics at St. Michaels. This close relationship did not, however, abate his desire to have a mission, Catholic or otherwise, close to Ganado. By 1901, this goal was accomplished.

163

The Presbyterians

In the spring of 1901, a Flagstaff, Arizona, Presbyterian church party, representing both Arizona's Presbytery and the New York Board of Home Missions, was searching for a mission site. After camping along the wash at Ganado, they went into Hubbell's post for hay and water. He angrily refused their request and said "if you want to come in here and act like White people and be my guests, why I'll give you anything you want." Apparently, their camping-out was an affront to his reputation for hospitality; shortly thereafter, they became his guests.

In a not entirely altruistic gesture, Hubbell offered them a piece of his land for a mission site. While the trader expressed the opinion that the presence of a mission would draw more Indians and business and improve their access to education and health care (the nearest doctor was thirty-five miles from Ganado), these same benefits would also work to the advantage of his family.

Though Hubbell's offer was not accepted, the Presbyterian Home Board started the approval process for a mission site in the Ganado area with the Bureau of Indian Affairs. The Home Board wanted to build the Ganado Presbyterian Mission on a one hundred sixty-acre site two miles east and north of Hubbell's trading post. In the fall of 1901, they sent a newly graduated seminary student, thirty-one-year-old Charles H. Bierkemper, from Kittaning, Pennsylvania, as their pioneer missionary.

Ganado Presbyterian Mission and barn, circa 1929.

164

The Navajo agent visited the local headmen to obtain their approval; thirteen gave their permission on May 8, 1902, and Bierkemper then began constructing a two-room adobe residence and chapel on the site. In the interim, Hubbell provided housing (probably the old Leonard building) for the newly married Bierkempers, loaned them a buckboard and team of horses, and gave them a fine Navajo blanket as a wedding gift.

As historian Dr. Edgar W. Moore noted in his history of the Presbyterian Mission at Ganado,

> John Lorenzo Hubbell's approval and friendship were of major importance in beginning to foster Bierkemper's and the mission's relations with Navajos. But Hubbell's influence alone would have been a short-term asset had it not been for young Bierkemper's own character and abilities.

The Board of Home Missions transferred Bierkemper ten years later, ignoring J. L.'s meddling letters. The trader explained his interest as a natural concern, as "the mission was started at Ganado at practically my request." Further, he noted, his efforts to secure the Ganado irrigation project, which benefited the area Indians and the mission, meant he had "had the interest of the Ganado Navajos at heart for a great many years." Hubbell requested that if they replaced Bierkemper, they should "send a man of some sense and experience" as well as of "good temperament." (Though Bierkemper was indeed replaced, we do not know if Hubbell approved of the new missionary.)

Canyon de Chelly

Hubbell prized Canyon de Chelly's beauty and timelessness as much as he valued his friends and their Indian country establishments. His fascination with the area went beyond family memories and entrepreneurial flirtations, or its proximity to Ganado. Steep red cliffs pocked with Indian ruins lined the canyon's gigantic gorges; at one end of the canyon was the lofty nine-hundred-foot-high Spider Rock, and at the other, the magnificent White House ruins. In between, Navajos farmed its washes and called it home. Chinle, the settlement bordering this spectacular site, was thirty-two miles from

Photographs of unidentified visitors setting out for Canyon de Chelly. Some interesting comments on the photos—one says, "Tired after a heavy pull through the sands."

Ganado—fifteen miles north to Nazlini over rolling hills, then a steep drop and seventeen miles further over wide washes and hills to Chinle. J. L. enjoyed showing his numerous visitors around the Canyon de Chelly area, and was also entirely aware of its tourist potential.

The same confusion and contradictions that surround Hubbell's late-1800s tourist and trading activities in the Canyon de Chelly-Chinle area extend into the early 1900s. By 1900, it is said that J. L. may have had a place about two miles from today's Canyon de Chelly National Monument headquarters, in fact, at the site of the present-day Chinle post office. The Days were certainly actively trading there during this period as well.

Whatever J. L.'s entrepreneurial interests were in Canyon de Chelly during these years, he clearly considered it to be a valuable destination for visitors to the area. Stewart Culin, curator of the Brooklyn Institute of Arts and Sciences (now the Brooklyn Museum of Natural History), made a trip into the canyon in mid-July 1904; in his diary, he noted that he was traveling with the Days and J. L. as well as Adela, Forrest, Roman, Roman's friend, and a Mrs. Benjamin.

Probably to avoid the heat, the party stayed at the Days' residence and on July 20, arose at four in the morning to travel to Mummy Cave. According to Culin's diary notes, one of J. L.'s horses went lame that day, so the trader hired four Indian ponies and hitched them to the wagon.

The group then traveled up Canyon del Muerto and breakfasted at Antelope Ruin. Camp that evening was set up below Mummy Cave, and the entire party climbed up to explore the ruin. Charlie Day, who had been appointed as the canyon's custodian by the Navajo agent at Fort Defiance, made quite a discovery during this exploration: an unusual basket shield with a red disk center, outlined with two rings of black and yellow.

A group excavating ruins at Canyon de Chelly; photo undated.

On July 21, J. L. tried to make an early departure, but a sandstorm interfered; Culin, who had ridden out ahead of J. L.'s wagon party, missed the sandstorm only to be overtaken by a summer rainstorm instead. Culin reported that Hubbell was delighted with the rain, hoping that it filled his dam and reservoir so he could irrigate the new fields, some of which were planted with potatoes and corn, and others that were readied for alfalfa.

Throughout the early 1900s, Hubbell made arrangements for a variety of visitors to explore Indian country. Most notable were the extended arrangements Hubbell made (and charged for) at the request of eastern scientist Dr. Harold S. Colton and his artist wife Mary Russell-Ferrell Colton in the summer of 1913 to explore Navajo and Hopi country, including Canyon de Chelly. That trip was reportedly a contributing factor in the Coltons' move a few years later from the east coast to Flagstaff, Arizona, where they co-founded the Museum of Northern Arizona, which was dedicated to the Colorado Plateau region. (A half-century later, museum personnel helped J. L.'s descendants through the process of securing national historic site status for the trading ranch.)

Following the example of other tourists to the Ganado-Chinle area, the Coltons purchased a quantity of Indian arts and crafts from Hubbell and had them shipped back east. Dr. Colton wrote Hubbell that when they returned to Philadelphia, his wife left with thirty sketches and three canvases, one of which was of Canyon de Chelly.

Between 1913 and 1916, J. L. built a two-story stone structure in Chinle. Historian Frank McNitt described it as Ganado-style architecture built of massive, deep-red sandstone blocks, one hundred seven by thirty-five feet. The bottom floor housed the trading room and two warehouse rooms, while the second floor had eight guest bedrooms that opened off a long hallway, a guests' living/dining room, and the manager's quarters. Hubbell evidently anticipated both trade and tourists.

A post owned by Mike Kirk after he left Hubbell's employment

A June 24, 1915, letter from Mike E. Kirk, manager of the Hubbell post at Chinle (later, an independent trader and founder of the Gallup Intertribal Ceremonial) to Forrest at Ganado indicates that Hubbell's Chinle store charged for travel arrangements into the canyon: seven dollars and fifty cents for a day trip, ten dollars a day for overnight stays; the latter arrangement required bedding and the use of pack animals. (A few years later, Hubbell Trading Post quoted prices of thirty dollars a day for either a team and driver or an auto and driver.)

Not all visitors had to pay to visit the canyon. Hubbell made a distinction between tourists and his own artist friends who stayed at Ganado and took side trips to Canyon de Chelly; he provided these without charge for transportation or lodging. J. L. joked that even artists "were not able to spoil the canyon's beauty." Maynard Dixon wrote to his mentor and close friend Charles Lummis that his week-long trip to the canyon with photographer Ben Wittick was a painting failure, as a north wind fouled five days of painting. Another of Hubbell's artist guests, Henry J. Brown of San Francisco, was more fortunate in his 1916 visit—he had a week of fine weather and hospitable treatment by Hubbell's two employees, Kirk and McSparron. The artist left with "good sketches for three big pictures," and wanted Hubbell to have one of the pieces when it was done.

In 1916, the Chinle post made nothing; financial conditions worsened in both the tourism and trade businesses. By 1917, J. L. had sold out to Cotton (probably to offset his overextended account with Cotton's warehouse). The reason usually given for J. L.'s disposal of the Chinle operation was his disappointment in the low number of visitors and the harsh winters, which, it was said, worked against the tourist-trade profitability. However, Hubbell's ability to work well on a long-term basis with non-family post managers was also problematical. McSparron and Kirk, both capable men, went on to successfully manage their own trading operations.

J. L. emerges as a man on whom others in Indian country depended, a man who spun a web of connections to nearly every one of the region's communities. These attachments aided him in his political activities.

CHAPTER ELEVEN
A Good Grain of Wheat in a
Bushel of Rocks: Politics

AS A NAVAJO WEAVER retwists or respins yarn to strengthen and smooth it, so J. L. respun his political future, substituting the rough-and-tumble of territorial and state politics for his earlier interests in physical adventure.

"I've Wielded Considerable Influence..."

In the *Touring Topics* article, Hubbell summarized his political life as follows:

> In addition to being sheriff of Apache County for two terms, I served two terms as territorial assemblyman. Later I was elected to the State senate in 1912, and sat in the first senate that Arizona ever had. Since that time I've wielded considerable influence in various branches of State politics, and have been a member of several national conventions.

Although J. L. felt that his political activities gave him many intimate state and federal contacts (including personal acquaintances with every president from Grover Cleveland to Warren G. Harding), in reality, these presidential contacts were generally quite superficial—"Thank you" notes on White House stationery in return for a Navajo blanket or J. L.'s formal letters encouraging the appointment of this person or that person to a position constitute most of these "intimate contacts." Teddy Roosevelt's 1913 visit to Hubbell's trading ranch was the only true personal contact J. L. had with any of the country's presidents.

For J. L., politics usually had a real-life agenda. He claimed in *Touring Topics* that his political activities had

> no bearing upon Indian trading other than the fact that they enabled me to in some measure bring about a better understanding

between the Indian and the Federal and territorial governments. This also applied to the State government of Arizona, after Arizona became a State in 1912.

Nonetheless, Hubbell promoted the Navajos' causes only when they were closely connected to his own. In an April 6, 1912, letter to Carl Hayden (then Arizona's Congressional delegate) regarding the Ganado dam project, J. L. said he was glad to see something long-neglected finally remedied. He said that he viewed the Navajos as America's most progressive and industrious tribe, though in the letter he described himself as

> a little selfish about this matter to be frank as it will increase my business and make those neighbors of mine much more prosperous.... We cannot but hope that in the future we will all have neighbors who are not paupers to deal with.

When there was no benefit accruing to himself, J. L. was just as likely to oppose things that would benefit the tribe. For example, he was against increasing the Navajos' land by allotment in New Mexico. As he wrote to Father Weber on April 1, 1912, unless the Navajos lived on or occupied the land as they "have had time to do...the balance should be thrown open for the use of settlers." Had Indians had the right to vote, Hubbell may have been more concerned.

The Republican Party

Neither women nor Indians could vote in the late nineteenth and early twentieth centuries, and there were only a handful of male government employees, missionaries, and trading post owners and employees in J. L.'s voting precinct at St. Michaels. Add to that the fact that he was a Republican in a Democratic territory, and the trader's prominence in regional and national politics could be fairly described as miraculous.

In the West, the Republican party's popularity suffered after 1865 from land giveaways that benefited railroads, cattle barons, and timber-magnate monopolies. However, J. L., whose family had a long affiliation with New Mexico Territory Republicans, championed

Arizona's minority contingent. He looked consistently to the East, to the railroads, to Congress, to the offices of the Bureau of Indian Affairs and Postmaster General, and to the Republican party. In a March 10, 1909, letter to his friend Father Weber, he clearly stated a reason for supporting the GOP:

> The Democrats have been triumphing from that date [1886] until 1894. Every election, they reiterated the fact that no Republican would be again elected to office. I told them that I would live to see the day that there would be no Democrats left on the ticket to tell the tale that he also ran for Office.

He also outlined his goals for Arizona's Republican organization:

> In spite of the Educational Qualification Law, I am going to live to see this County Republican again and also the Territory send two Republican US Senators...you cannot keep a good man down or a people that fight for their rights.

When it came down to a choice between the personal and the political, however, J. L.'s loyalty transcended his political ambitions, just as considerations for family and close friends often overrode the need for changes in his business practice. In 1908, the governor and others dubbed him the strongest candidate for Congress, but his friend Ralph Cameron (considered a more viable candidate by Arizona Republicans) ran instead. In a June 11, 1912, letter to his son Roman, J. L. commented,

> while our friends here [in Phoenix] are thinking that I would make a good candidate for Governor, I believe I will make a better candidate to stay at home and you need not be afraid that the bee is flying around my head for I do not care anything for office, it is more the pleasure of conquering and winning under adverse circumstances that makes me stay in this political game.

Not only did party loyalty define Hubbell personally, but he often used it as a sign of a man's qualifications for office. On December 15, 1911, as chairman of the Republican Territorial Central Committee, he

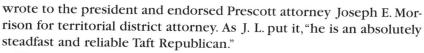

wrote to the president and endorsed Prescott attorney Joseph E. Morrison for territorial district attorney. As J. L. put it, "he is an absolutely steadfast and reliable Taft Republican."

His own political personality had blossomed when he reentered politics in the late 1890s.

The Political Bees Start Buzzing

According to Mormon diarist Fish, it was J. L.'s alignment (years after he lost his second bid for sheriff) with Apache County Mormons and their votes that relit the trader's political fire. Elected to the territorial legislature in 1893, J. L. was eclipsed by only two other legislative members in miles traveled to attend a session; his total was 799 miles to the territorial capital, which was by then in Phoenix. Boarding the train at Gallup, New Mexico, he went west to Ashfork, Arizona, then south to Phoenix. As on his trips to the East Coast, along the way, Hubbell abandoned his Ganado look—long, unkempt hair, raggedy beard, suspendered pants, and short-sleeved jacket— and emerged groomed for political battle. He was well read on issues of the day and smartly suited, hair clipped short and neatly parted and a mustache that copied Teddy Roosevelt's. (J. L. liked to be told that he looked like T. R., even though he did not always agree with him on political issues.)

His arrival did not go unnoticed in Phoenix, a city already heralded as the land of perpetual sunshine. On February 12, 1893, in an *Arizona Republican* column subtitled "Short Sketches of the Legislative Gentlemen from Abroad Now in the City," Hubbell was described as

> the only remnant of the late wreck in Apache. A worthier man could not have been saved. Republicans of Apache may congratulate themselves...the best was left there. Mr. Hubbell will occupy a prominent place in the council chambers, a place to which his natural abilities will lift him, assisted by the loneliness which will pervade the Republican side of the Chamber.

Two days later, the paper profiled him in a column titled "A Political Family." Reporting that J. L.'s brother, F. A. Hubbell, and his cousin, Colonel F. Chavez, led the Republican cause in New Mexico's territorial council as well, the writer went on to say that "Hon. J. L. Hubbell...is not...behind his distinguished New Mexico relatives in point of ability and sagacity," serving as sheriff and conducting a brilliant campaign to defeat "a popular Democrat in a Democratic County." The paper classified him as "one of the rising men of the territory, with a bright political future."

On February 14, 1893, the legislature's fifth day in session, a joint council and house, plus visitors, crowded into the Phoenix City Hall council chambers, where territorial legislative activities were held. J. L. was a member of several standing legislative committees, including Memorials and Petitions, Enrolled and Engrossed Bills, and Federal Relations. He introduced numerous bills, including one that defined office holders' qualifications and allowed a person literate in Spanish the same privileges as those who spoke English. He also submitted insurance bills requiring deposits, licensing, and taxing of insurance companies; an act for the just division of taxes; a bill requiring a two-year residency prior to holding a public or appointed office; an act to protect the interests of working men; and water rights legislation.

Politicking did not distract him from his interest in selling Navajo textiles, however. As the *Arizona Republican* of February 25, 1893, reported,

> Hubbell yesterday sold to Joe Alexander [another council member] one of the Navajo blankets he brought to the city with him for $100 which may seem a fancy price. However Mr. Hubbell has another which cannot be bought for $150.

A Topic of Debate

Members of the session argued vehemently over the women's suffrage question. According to March 10, 1893 issues of the local newspapers, the question

> lost by a strictly party vote which not only shows the hopelessness of women's suffrage, but also gives the Republican members of the council standing for gallantry.

Earlier, on February 23, 1893, the Arizona Republican had expounded a "cold business view" of the issue. Eastern states, "conservative and older settled communities," were the source of widespread opposition "among all classes"; if the territorial legislature adopted suffrage, an "incalculable injury" would occur "when so much now depends upon capital and immigration from those sections."

The suffrage movement was alive and well in Indian country as this 1910 photograph of suffrage activity at Keams Canyon shows.

Hubbell refused to support such a retrogressive position. In an undated letter to David K. Udall, of Hunt, Arizona, Hubbell wrote

> I hardly have the heart to write her [Miss Udall] about it. We did everything...[but] the cry of "rule of the people" is a cloak under which the greatest tyranny is used against a large number of our citizens.

Through the years, J. L. urged friends to join those supporting women's suffrage. On March 25, 1912, he congratulated an Arizona correspondent, Eli S. Perkins, for turning to women's suffrage. As he said in his letter,

> It has been one of my hobbies for a good many years.... People...are ready to grant that right which the female sex in Arizona should have had years ago. I do not know what effect it will have on our political career as Republicans but that is not the issue. The question is, is it right or is it wrong and I do not believe that there is a single argument that can be advanced against it.

According to the paper, Hubbell left the legislative session before it ended in order to attend to "important business" at Ganado. The paper rated him as an "untiring worker" and a "rising" man in the territory with promotion in the party ranks ahead. His energy, like that of others, made "fertile fields of deserts" in the Arizona Territory.

Statehood

During the early years of the twentieth century, Arizona's struggle for statehood took place against a backdrop of national and local political turmoil. Bryan's free silver campaign was hotly debated in the territorial legislature, and labor strikes in the territory's southern mining areas caused eastern Republicans to fear the largely Democratic-led Arizona Territory.

By the time Hubbell re-entered the political fray, the Phoenix area was bustling with construction and booming with modern conveniences—Victorian homes, the Arizona Canal, the newly opened Phoenix Opera House, a federal Indian school, parades, streetcars, German bakeries, and Italian ice cream wagons—and its residents regularly brought the issue of statehood before Congress. Two plans had long been offered; one required New Mexico and Arizona to be admitted as a single state, the other, that they be admitted as two separate entities. J. L. supported the former, but reversed his position after Arizona voters defeated the bill in 1906.

In 1908, when Arizona sent Republican delegate Ralph H. Cameron (another northern Arizona territorial entrepreneur) to Washington, D. C., eastern Republicans viewed this as a favorable change of heart for the territory. Though Cameron edged Hubbell out politically and received credit for keeping the territory's statehood interests alive with eastern Republicans after the labor faction took control of Arizona's legislature, the two worked as a team to push Arizona into statehood.

Cameron kept Hubbell abreast of statehood developments and asked Hubbell's advice on how to get matters through Congress. On one occasion, he invited Hubbell to come to Washington, D. C., after the busy trading season ended so that Hubbell could be there before the statehood matter came out of congressional committee. Reminding Hubbell that he could not take business with him when he died, Cameron also offered to pay J. L.'s hotel bill during his visit.

What survives of the men's correspondence rings with mutual confidence and intimacy. Among the topics covered in the letters are loans, Cameron's nearly annual Ganado visits, his son's summer-long sojourn there, and arrangements for visitors from the nation's capital including caveat's from Cameron to Hubbell for the trader not to go to extra expense for certain visitors.

On his part, Hubbell did not hesitate to seek Cameron's assistance; for instance, he asked Cameron to talk with the Commissioner of

Cameron trekked to Ganado in 1910 with Postmaster General Frank H. Hitchcock to partake of J. L.'s Hopi snake ceremony hospitality. Hubbell is on left; probably Hitchcock is next to him. Cameron is fourth from left.

Indian Affairs about increasing a Navajo agent's salary, the appointment of his brother Tom as U. S. Marshall, and the commissioner's approval of the Ganado irrigation project.

President William Taft's 1909 visit to the Southwest led to a 1910 enabling act that called for the two territories to become two separate states. J. L. was nominated to serve as part of Arizona's constitutional convention, but did not campaign. He lost by four votes. As Lorenzo wrote his to father on September 18, 1910, the election surprised me—I never thought for a moment that they would beat you; but then what do you expect when you don't do any electioneering.

Nonetheless, Hubbell was busy both that year and the next as chairman of Arizona's Republican Central Committee. There was extensive political maneuvering on issues as varied as the educational qualification act and the recall of judges. On November 18, 1911, for example, Hubbell sent thirty letters appealing for donations and urging the repeal of educational requirements for hazardous jobs, which included railway work.

In a January 2, 1912 letter to artist Albert L. Groll in New York City, J. L. said that he had been absent from Ganado for sixty days and was broke. However, finances aside, Hubbell's sojourn in the Phoenix area had a successful outcome; within a few weeks of this letter, on Valentine's Day, Arizona finally achieved statehood. None of Arizona's neighbors had held territorial status as long: California had achieved statehood in 1850, Colorado in 1876, Utah in 1896, and New Mexico a few days before Arizona.

In a commemorative photograph of President Taft signing the proclamation admitting Arizona as the forty-eighth state on February 14, 1912, J. L.'s position immediately behind the president represents the trader's contribution to Arizona's statehood struggle.

A Senator in the State of Arizona's First Legislature

In 1912, J. L. wrote that through some mistake, he had been elected to the state's first, and overwhelmingly Democratic, senate, which caused him to feel "like a good grain of wheat in a bushel of rocks." In another letter, Hubbell humorously reproached an Arizona newspaper whose writer had editorially roasted a fellow Republican, saying that he (Hubbell) "felt like getting up in the Senate and giving [the writer] a vote of thanks." The implication was that the writer's roast functioned as an endorsement. Hubbell commented that though his fellow Republican was hurt, he himself had been roasted so much and so forcefully that the writer should choose him as the target the next time. In reporting legislative activities to his friend Sam Day in an April 6, 1912, letter—addressing Day as "you old devil"—J. L. said "you can fill in the gaps with language that will be appropriate."

As a senator in Arizona's first state legislature, Hubbell brought all of his values to bear: friendship, loyalty, longevity, honesty, dedication, and humor. Arizona politician Solomon Barth characterized Hubbell as both his bitterest political enemy and warmest personal friend. On April 4, 1912, Hubbell wrote to George Curry, Arizona's first governor, regarding a political appointment; regardless of Curry's decision, the trader said, his feelings would not change towards the governor. "Do not think dear Governor that is simply bunkum that [I] am writing you, but it comes really from my heart." On the other hand, political dedication sometimes overrode even J. L.'s legendary hospitality and led to arguments with his guests. Burbank said he tired of Hubbell talking politics—in the artist's opinion, his host would rather talk politics than eat.

The first state legislature convened on March 1, 1912, and the laws passed that session included, among others, a child labor act; free textbooks in a free public school system; a working man's compulsory compensation act; creation or broadening of the powers of commissions; organization of irrigation districts; operation of motor vehicles; and maintenance of state highways and bridges. The legislature also petitioned Congress to open the rich mineral lands of the Colorado Indian Reservation for private development. Over strong protest, J. L. pushed to limit the sale of liquor to within six miles of any railroad, and worked (unsuccessfully) to pass a three thousand dollar appropriation that would enable the state to buy one of E. S. Curtis's photographic books on Indians.

Curiously, his Senate stationery read "Alonzo Hubbell, State of Arizona, First Legislature. Senate Chamber." It is not known if this was a printing error or if the party wanted to capitalize on J. L.'s Hispanic heritage. In an April 1912 letter to a Florence, Arizona correspondent with a Hispanic surname, J. L. explained his position opposing the Educational Qualification Act:

> Perhaps you do not know that I am half Mexican and could not speak any English until I was thirteen years old and was raised among Mexican people and have championed their cause in Apache County.

Following his first month in office as a state senator, J. L.'s political and business correspondence swelled. In April 1912 alone, J. L. nixed Roman's idea for blanket design cards, guided Forrest's proposed purchase of a drug store and appointment as postmaster, fought the Education Qualification Act and liquor sales, pushed for the Ganado Appropriation Act, instructed trading post managers on operational matters, penned family messages, lectured about the evils of alcohol, sent invitations to his chicken pull and the Hopi snake ceremony, and promoted mail route changes. He also wrote to a Washington, D. C. correspondent to collect a debt owed him, arranged to sell some land in Albuquerque, invested fifteen thousand dollars in the cancelgraph machine (an invention he hoped the post office would buy and in which he had invested heavily), stalled his bank, and tried to sell (for fifty thousand dollars) what he said was a painting by Raphael that had been in his family for three centuries.

Affairs in Ganado continued to nag him. As he wrote to Roman on April 19, 1912, "I feel kind of guilty that I attend more to politics than I do to our business." Hubbell also bemoaned his absence from Ganado to others. In an April 24, 1912, letter, he declined his friend Charles Lummis's invitation to meet in Santa Fe, saying that he had been absent from home so very long

> trying to keep down the Roosevelt microbe which is permeating

the Arizona Territory.... On the 15th of May I intend to go back home and attend to business. I have been attending to other people's business for so long that I will not know how to attend to mine.

Hubbell's reference to the "Roosevelt microbe" reflected his opinion of the presidential candidate's activities, including his recall of judicial decisions. As far as Hubbell was concerned, this destroyed constitutional government. Lummis responded that he was "glad to know that the Arizona Legislature has at least one good man in it." And, as Lummis continued in a postscript,

> Sorry you are fighting the Teddy microbe...that's just what we need in our blood. I hope we will get the nomination—am secure that if he does you will wallop the whole of Arizona into shape in his behalf. I will remember your gentle disfavor of the Damn Democratic Party—and I don't believe you would vote for God Almighty if he turned Jeffersonian!

Guilt about his absence was not apparent in the letter J. L. wrote to Lorenzo during the same period. The trader took a somewhat different tack in this April 27, 1912, missive.

> I don't think the trade would have been affected very much by my absence and I know very well if I had been home I would have been trusting the Indians too much, which is my great failing.

In a May 16, 1912, letter to Prescott colleague Frank A. Murphy, Hubbell had shared a Spanish proverb: "Those who have enemies should never sleep." He put this aphorism into practice during the 1912 Republican State Convention Conference. As he further commented to Murphy in his May letter,

> there is no doubt that the Roosevelt contingent is numerous enough for us not to sleep until June 3rd when we expect to give them the surprise of their lives.

Hubbell did indeed give the state's Roosevelt Republicans a surprise, as detailed in a June, 1912 letter. Using language reminiscent of his description of his St. Johns troubles, he described his convention activities:

> [We] had the pleasure of sending six regular delegates for President Taft. The Republican contingency, who were going to have 400 men in the hall, and who were going to throw me out...came to the Convention and sat in a corner and held a fake conference for about fifteen minutes and then adjourned.... Republican people have filed a contest against us.

According to the entry in *Notables of the West*, this kind of turmoil characterized Hubbell's political life. His machinations in winning the Taft delegation, "after one of most remarkable campaigns against overwhelming odds ever known to the party," represented the kind of challenge J. L. enjoyed. And he was rewarded: in "recognition of his victory at the State Convention, President Taft...sent to Senator Hubbell a personal letter of congratulations."

His old friend Burbank saw him at the Republican National Convention in Chicago, and wrote to Roman in August,

> I saw your Father in Chicago this week Tuesday, but he was so busy with political friends that I saw him for [only] a few minutes. He was looking better than I ever saw him. I guess the political life agrees better with him than an Indian trader's life.

Away from Ganado, J. L. spent all his waking hours with men who, unlike many of his Ganado guests, relished political discussions. Politics drew on his energy, resourcefulness, combativeness, gregariousness, and persuasive nature.

Warnings from Home

As political activities consumed him, the neglect that Hubbell himself noted began to jeopardize what he had spent his life developing. Cotton stressed the precariousness of J. L.'s situation. In a three-page letter addressed to J. L. in Phoenix, dated April 30, 1912, the Gallup wholesaler commented that Hubbell always bragged he could get a million goats; in Cotton's opinion, it would be "easier to get 2,000

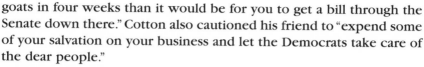

goats in four weeks than it would be for you to get a bill through the Senate down there." Cotton also cautioned his friend to "expend some of your salvation on your business and let the Democrats take care of the dear people."

As Hubbell continued to attend to politics at the expense of business, friction mounted between the wholesaler and the Hubbell post; charges of torn sacks of wool, misweighed potatoes, and wrong credit calculations abounded. Across the top of an argumentative letter from Cotton's wholesale outfit, J. L. boldly penciled a note to his staff to just "let it go."

In spite of his worries about how his businesses were faring in his absence, Hubbell felt compelled to attend the Republican convention conference in Tucson. He also traveled to Chicago for the national convention and to Washington, D. C., regarding his cancelgraph machine investment. Finally, he returned to Ganado in August 1912, just before the snake dance and chicken pull.

As Roman wrote to family friend Maynard Dixon in February 1913, J. L. had spent only two months at Ganado over the course of the previous two years. Not only was the trader physically gone, he was also depleting the company's cash reserves. On February 7, 1913, Lorenzo wrote to Roman with an uncharacteristic request: "[F]ather drew to the extent of $2,500 last month. I did not figure on that so I am that much in the hole with the bank...send money."

In an odd twist of fortune, a source of money was found. In March 1913, J. L.'s longtime Navajo friend Chee Dodge agreed to loan him thirty-two thousand dollars. In return, Dodge, familiar with the workings of the dominant culture, secured the loan with an all-encompassing mortgage on the Ganado real property, its water rights, and even the accounts receivable. In J. L.'s forty or so years of trading, Navajos had labored for him in subservient capacities for money he minted himself; now, the tables were turned.

Though Dodge's daughter, Dr. Annie I. Wauneka, who lived almost into the twenty-first century, once observed that her father and J. L. "were just like that [holding up two fingers pressed tightly together]," still, this transaction must have been a last resort. In many ways, the two men were more similar to one another than they were to their contemporaries. Both stood in two cultures; both, in the vernacular of the day, could be considered half-breeds; one of Dodge's parents was probably a slave, while Hubbell's maternal ancestors were slave owners. Both were leaders and politicians—while Dodge did not become the Navajos' first tribal chairman until 1923, the government and the Navajos had treated him for years as a spokesperson. Both J. L. and Dodge used language to achieve their ends. Dodge's lectures averted Navajo troubles during times of unrest, as had Hubbell's talks.

Without this and other cash infusions from Dodge, J. L.'s politicking would have ended, and it is possible that his trading empire would have collapsed as well.

Ambitions for the U. S. Senate

When Arizona became a state, its citizens elected two Democrats, Henry F. Ashurst and Marcus A. Smith, to the U. S. Senate; the latter drew the short term, which meant another election in 1914. By May 11, 1914, J. L.'s political correspondent Fred W. Nelson, county attorney for Apache County, wrote that he knew even before he got J. L.'s letter that "the political bee was buzzing in your direction, and that the United States Senatorship looked good to you." That same month, attorney and Republican Joseph E. Morrison solicited J. L.'s interest in purchasing the old Bisbee *Evening Miner*. Owning this newspaper would assure Hubbell of an editorial voice that supported his candidacy, Morrison noted, as the major Arizona papers routinely opposed Republicans. (Hubbell ultimately decided against buying the newspaper.)

The Republican State Committee met in Prescott on July 5, 1914, and Republicans signed J. L.'s nominating documents a few days later, a late start, it seems. The day before the primary, September 7, 1914, the Arizona Republican carried candidates' ads, which ranged from the index-card-sized ad for Eugene W. Chafen's Independent Progressive Party campaign to a multi-column ad run by the Mark (Marcus) Smith Club for the incumbent. Not a single ad endorsing Hubbell's candidacy appeared. Further, according to Washington, D. C. news correspondent Ira Bond, the Associated Press acted as though Hubbell lived in central Africa. Over the years, other political correspondents lamented Ganado's distance from Arizona's political base and felt that it weakened Hubbell's ability to keep close tabs on Arizona politics.

On Thursday, October 1, 1914, the newspaper advertised a City Hall

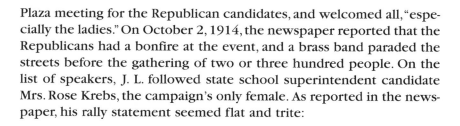

Plaza meeting for the Republican candidates, and welcomed all, "espe-cially the ladies." On October 2, 1914, the newspaper reported that the Republicans had a bonfire at the event, and a brass band paraded the streets before the gathering of two or three hundred people. On the list of speakers, J. L. followed state school superintendent candidate Mrs. Rose Krebs, the campaign's only female. As reported in the news-paper, his rally statement seemed flat and trite:

> [He] took a shot at the state administration; and at two subservient members of congress who regard their loyalty to the president above their loyalty to the people who send them to congress. Mr. Hubbell had in mind the Hon. M. A. Smith and his course with respect to the free tolls amendment. Mr. Hubbell resented the inter-ference of the president in the family quarrels of Arizona Democ-rats and he concluded with a prayer for the erring progressives.

In addition to Hubbell and Chafen, Socialist Bert Davis also ran for the incumbent's senate seat. Of the three, it appears that only Chafen challenged Smith to debates at five public meetings on the two big campaign issues: "Equal Suffrage, and the final solution of the alco-holic liquor [problem]."

The Republican candidates took their campaign to Arizona's rural communities—Ray, Florence, Sacaton, Mayer, Cherry, Jerome, and Flagstaff among them—speaking before large crowds about the need for a change from the Democratic administration's "extravagance and incompetency." Though a rural campaign just before the election may have set off political sparks, then as now, the state's small towns could not offset the votes of Arizona's largest cities, Phoenix and Tucson.

Nonetheless, Hubbell seemed to think that he would beat the odds, a challenge he relished. As he wrote to Cotton on November 1, the "election [is] so badly mixed that there is no telling what the outcome will be." Following the November 4 ballot, an article in Gallup's McKinley County Reporter placed J. L. with the Cotton family following the election, and reported that the trader believed himself to have won the election. In Phoenix, newspaper headlines shouted "State Vote Filters in Slowly—and State Returns Are Coming in Very Slowly." At the final count, Smith was swept into office with 25,790 votes; J. L. received 9,128 and Chafen, 7,248. The "Boss of

Apache County" missed carrying even Apache County by fifty-four votes, and Navajo County by one hundred fourteen.

In retrospect, it is possible to speculate that Republican rhetoric derailed J. L's campaign, aided by Democrat Woodrow Wilson's win over Republican William Howard Taft and Progressive Theodore Roosevelt two years earlier, Democratic control of Arizona, and the Republican's support of the unpopular issues of prohibition and suffrage.

The rough-hewn trader who posed in Ganado photographs was missing in the broadside J. L. used in this candidacy. Below his campaign photograph, which showed a slick urban businessman, he said, "As a constructive Arizona Business Man I Solicit Your Vote on November 3."

These factors may have closed the senate game to J. L. before he even got to play. Solomon Barth attributed J. L.'s defeat to a Democratic year paired with a party fight, which split the state's Republican Party wide open. And to his detriment, in the senate race, J. L. was less his feisty, personable self and more a gentleman politician. J. L.'s down-to-earth political bones may have warned him he could not win, yet he fancied winning. The fact that he might succeed in the face of such odds fit his view of himself.

Although at some point following the election fiasco, J. L.'s campaign expenses were designated as the culprit in his personal financial problems, campaign financial records do not support this, nor does the timing of the Dodge loans (the first of which was made before Hubbell declared his candidacy). His October 23, 1914, expense affidavit showed that he had spent $4,700.50, which included both his own personal campaign expenses and (typical of his generosity to friends) some of the other Republican candidates' travel expenses as well. Chafen spent $3,217.68 and Nelson, $335.15. The Mark Smith Club financed the incumbent's campaign.

Though J. L.'s political friends rallied around him, the trader withdrew after the loss. On November 7, 1914, Washington correspondent Ira Bond sent condolences, writing that Hubbell had "made a great fight and deserved success," and "you would have won but for the Socialist candidate." A year later, November 20, 1915, Bond wrote again complaining that "no one [had] heard" from J. L. Between January 2 and October 1915. Fellow Republican candidate Joseph E. Morrison wrote several letters commiserating with J. L. and complaining, "what the dunce has happened to you? None of us have heard from you in a coon's age." On October 11, 1915, after getting no response to a letter ordering blankets, he penned,

> Now, I know you have not answered my friendly letters, but I thought business matters would receive attention (ha-ha).... Why the —— don't you write your friends?

The defeat struck the sixty-one-year-old Hubbell a bitter personal blow. His post-election political correspondence withered. Like a fleece of wool rolled up and secured with cord, he withdrew, both personally and physically, from politics. He would never again hold a significant elected office. However, this political loss did not affect his reputation as one of the Southwest's premier hosts.

PART FOUR
DON LORENZO

Many years ago the Hubbell household instituted the custom of holding open house to all visitors and travelers in the country. I've spent tens of thousands of dollars feeding and entertaining people from every part of the United States and even from abroad and never charged anyone for a meal or a night's lodging.... In the vast majority of instances our hospitality was been appreciated, but we've also had a few experiences in having it sorely abused.

—J. L. Hubbell, *Touring Topics*

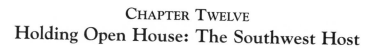

CHAPTER TWELVE
Holding Open House: The Southwest Host

J. L. COLLECTED VISITORS as a weaver collects rabbit brush to dye her yarn. And like the weaver's dye plants, the visitors colored the pattern of Hubbell's life.

The Host

In 1926, Gene Haldeman, a prospective employee for the Presbyterian Mission at Ganado, arrived by train in deserted, early-morning Gallup, New Mexico. Sitting on a bench was an elderly man, and Haldeman asked him about the Ganado Mission stage. The old man said that the stage would be leaving soon, and then invited Haldeman to "come down to the house [in Ganado].... It's not very much but it's comfortable and you're welcome to stay any time you've a mind to." The man identified himself as Don Lorenzo.

J. L.'s hospitable nature had secured him the title of "Don" in the Hispanic community at St. Johns as early as the 1880s. By the turn of the century, Ganado visitors, a few personal friends, and some Navajos who spoke English were calling him "Don Lorenzo" as well. (Only a few very close friends, such as Cotton, called him Lorenzo.)

Hubbell, like most non-Indian reservation residents, particularly traders, had an open-house policy, which may have had its genesis in loneliness and a hunger for news of the outside world. This hospitality and generous welcome to all newcomers also sprang from the sense of being engaged in a common struggle. It secured one's identity within a group and ensured that help would be offered in an emergency. In the West, a man gained prestige by opening his family home to travelers and strangers alike.

As family friend Henry B. [Bert] Coddington recalled,

> it was nothing for him [Don Lorenzo] to entertain one hundred and fifty people at his place at a time—Indians, Mexicans, bullwhackers, Eastern tourists, anthropologists, archaeologists, ethnologists—he was the most hospitable man in the world.

Historian Frank McNitt described Hubbell as "generous to a fault, [with a] large capacity for liking people, all kinds of people."

Writer Agnes Laut recalled him as a "courtly Spanish American gentleman...with a courteousness that keeps you guessing as to how much more gracious the next courtesy can be than the last one." Stewart Culin, the Brooklyn museum curator who visited several times, described J. L. at age forty-nine as "one of the most interesting characters on the Arizona frontier." Culin went on to say that Hubbell was a self-educated "half-Mexican" with such "courage, industry and intelligence" that every American, Mexican, and Indian in Navajo country respected and feared him. Indians, Culin said, traveled a hundred miles to trade with him and

> the Mexicans regard him as their best friend, and Americans, whether traders, artists, or investigator, find him ever the most cordial host in all this land of warm and unstinted hospitality.

As far as Hubbell was concerned, all comers were welcome.

Some of Hubbell's visitors arrived happenstance, others he solicited, and some he cajoled into coming. J. L.'s invitations were oftentimes condescending to the Indians. For example, Hubbell invited a Washington politician to Ganado in mid-August to see a chicken pull (originally, men on horseback attempting to pluck a live chicken out of the sand in which it had been buried up to its neck; later, a sack of money or trader tokens was the prize). He told him that two thousand Indians "composed of civilized, half-civilized, and the savage" would also be there. And at Hopi, the guests could view the "most astonishing and gruesome dance," the Hopi snake ceremony. Rather than emphasizing the religious aspects of the snake ceremony or that (like cowboys' rodeos) the chicken pull showed off Navajo stockmen's skills, his invitations instead lent to the events the same circus-midway atmosphere the Fred Harvey Co. invoked at its various displays of live Indian arts-and-crafts demonstrators. On other occasions, the trader dangled references to ruins at Canyon de Chelly and the Petrified Forest in front of his would-be guests as well.

To Hopi agent Leo Crane's accusation that he (J. L.) spent five thousand dollars a year hosting "bums, coffee salesmen, & other traveling

*Visitors standing with Hubbell (far right) in front of the Leonard building. Sign on ground says
"To The Moqui [drawing of snake] Dance or Bust." Lorencito sitting on ground on right.*

men" at the Ganado trading ranch, J. L. replied that it was at least that
much. What he failed to mention was that, as surely as sheep are
sheared in the spring, Don Lorenzo also extracted "fleece" from his
guests: sales of his arts-and-crafts inventory, political favors, and Southwestern fame.

Maynard Dixon labeled Hubbell a wolf when it came to sales of Navajo textiles. Turning away offers of payment for his hospitality, he would
say that he was in the blanket, not the innkeeping, business. "If you want
to spend your money, just come over in the blanket room with me and
watch me knock your eye out." Some guests became blanket brokers
and ambassadors, handling Don Lorenzo's Navajo textiles (and sometimes, jewelry) on consignment. Other guests facilitated his Ganado
dam and reservoir project, supplemented his art collection, and stimulated his passion for the Republican party and Arizona statehood. Some
just entertained him, satisfying his curiosity and his interest in people.

As Hubbell noted, he also had "a few experiences in having it [his
hospitality] sorely abused." One guest, ignoring J. L.'s admonition not
to pay for his stay, left a twenty-dollar bill behind, which an Indian
maid brought to Hubbell. When a flooded wash forced the man to
return to Ganado, he found himself sleeping in the store and taking

his meals with the help. Agnes Laut recalled the Berlin professor who arrived unannounced after midnight and said that he would take his breakfast later in the day. She also told of the drummer who ordered a Hubbell daughter to "hustle...fodder," and the government worker who demanded breakfast at three in the morning.

A visiting Eastern doctor irritated the locals with continual references to the East Coast's superiority and provoked Hubbell into issuing a swimming challenge. Sam Day II fished the spent doctor from Ganado Lake while old man Hubbell, a wonderful swimmer, floated on his back, spurting plumes of water into the air.

J. L.'s sense of humor and way of thinking are dramatically illustrated in two instances recalled by his grandson, Hubbell Parker. A basket connoisseur wanted to purchase one of the unique baskets attached to the ceiling, despite J. L.'s repeated statement that it was not for sale since it was "one of the personal household furnishings." The man persisted in his request, much to J. L.'s annoyance. After the man left, Hubbell had a clerk wrap up the basket and send it; when the man wired that no bill had been enclosed, Hubbell responded, "since you are so interested in baskets you can have it for nothing."

On another occasion, a debonair visitor dressed in riding clothes and puttees tried to debunk Hubbell's Wild West stories. J. L. bet him a ten-dollar gold piece that one of his muleskinners was so good with his blacksnake skinners' whip that he could nick the man's pants without touching him. The muleskinner laid the whip across the dandy's fanny. The dandy howled and swore at the muleskinner as Hubbell, laughing, gave the aggrieved "winner" the gold piece.

For Hubbell, the ideal guest bought Navajo blankets, appreciated the West, extolled his hospitality, accepted the family's generosity, distinguished between family and trading property, followed the house rules, demanded no special treatment, and sold Indian arts and crafts, particularly blankets, after his or her departure.

The Hubbell Papers are full of letters from former visitors. The letters often start off that the trader "may not remember," but five, ten, or twenty, years ago, the correspondent stayed at Ganado and experienced J. L.'s wonderful hospitality. Now, the correspondent wrote about his successful business or bad circumstances; if the latter, a loan was often requested.

First on the List of Visitors

Don Lorenzo's guest list started with presidents, followed by artists, then scientists, writers, and finally government officials and military officers. He considered President Theodore Roosevelt to be a long-time best friend, despite some differences of opinion. Nephew Phillip Hubbell recollected that the two men first met in Washington, D. C. Roosevelt had appointed some ex-Rough Riders to federal positions in the Southwest; among the appointees was a man Arizona Republicans did not endorse. The trader told President Roosevelt that the appointment was a mistake, and Roosevelt reportedly became angry, declaring that "I'm going to appoint him anyway. And I want to tell you to get out of my office." J. L. left the President's office, remarking, "It's your office...but your man is still a crook." Within a year, the questionable appointee was removed.

Some researchers have questioned J. L.'s inclusion of Roosevelt as a Ganado guest. However, various correspondence verifies at least a short visit. Nicholas Roosevelt, T. R.'s nephew, corresponded with J. L. in 1913 about outfitting his uncle's Utah hunting party once it crossed

Roosevelt on horseback at Keams Canyon.

195

into Arizona. The party was interested in visiting Rainbow Bridge and observing the Hopi snake ceremony as well. "Rosie," as Nicholas asked Don Lorenzo to call him, emphasized the secrecy of the arrangements, but promised the trader "you can at last have the opportunity of meeting Colonel Roosevelt man to man—regardless of past political differences." Rosie also noted that "the Colonel" preferred to stay in a tent in the trader's yard at Ganado; the ex-president felt this would safeguard his privacy.

Don Lorenzo sent two wagons and two men, including Loco, his own cook (Rosie later said that Loco was "one of the best"), for the Roosevelt party's Arizona travels. The Colonel liked J. L.'s suggestion that he go into the kiva to see the washing of the snakes, as it would be "one of the most interesting experiences of the trip." The trader charged Roosevelt only the actual cost of the teams, auto, and cook for the Arizona journey. In an August 28, 1913, letter to Roman, J. L. described Roosevelt as arriving at the snake ceremony clad in "old shoes, a flannel shirt, two-gallon hat, and his corduroy trousers stuffed into canvas leggings that laced down the sides." Roosevelt, he said, sat with his back against an old adobe wall and lifted himself with his hands to see better some of the "strange spectacle."

Roosevelt, speaking with J. L., leans against a wall at the Hopi village of Walpi.

In the *Touring Topics* article, Hubbell reported that the two men discussed politics and Indian affairs during Roosevelt's evenings at Ganado. He said that when Roosevelt exclaimed, "Mr. Hubbell you're a strenuous man!" he replied, "Maybe so, but if I am, I'm only following in your footsteps." One of the Hubbell grandsons recollected the pair's political arguments, which made him, as a child, think that "they were going to kill each other."

At the same time, Dr. Harold Colton and his artist wife Mary were also visiting the area as part of a tour arranged by Hubbell. They reported watching the snake ceremony at Walpi, sitting on a roof and dangling their feet over Roosevelt's head. The Coltons camped near Ganado when Roosevelt was at Hubbell's home, and said that Hubbell conveyed his feeling about Roosevelt's traitorous break with the Republicans to everyone but Roosevelt himself.

A letter from Teddy Roosevelt, dated September 12, 1913, thanked Hubbell for all the trader had done for the Roosevelt party that summer. T. R. also included his regards to Hubbell's daughters and commented that the "day at your house" was memorable. He went on to pay back the trader's hospitality in articles he later wrote for *Outlook* magazine (October 11 and 18, 1913) titled "Across the Navajo Desert" and "The Hopi Snake Dance." Roosevelt said that he motored

> across the desert with Mr. Hubbell to his house and store at Ganado, sixty miles away. Mr. Hubbell is an Indian trader. His Ganado house, right out in the bare desert, is very comfortable and very attractive, and he treats all comers with an open-handed hospitality inherited from pioneer days.

In an unwitting imitation of Bureau of Indian Affairs agents and Christian missionaries, Roosevelt went on to describe his host's "great influence among the Navajos...exerted to put a stop to gambling and drinking," his management of the Ganado trading business in such a way that it meant "the material and moral betterment of the Indians," and his championing of Indian rights whenever they were menaced. The advancement of the Navajos in the last fifty years, Roosevelt wrote, was "thanks to the presence of the white men in their neighborhood," such as traders like Hubbell.

Roosevelt seems to have validated J. L.'s view of himself as a national figure, an active man, and a risktaker. That Roosevelt, so well traveled and versed in the world's exotica, viewed his Arizona sojourn as adventurous and thrilling reinforced J. L.'s self-image. The trader was able to further flourish his generosity—even though he was financially strapped—by making a gift to Roosevelt of a dozen garnets; Hubbell even paid for a Boston jeweler to cut them for a necklace for Mrs. Roosevelt.

On November 1, 1915, a couple of years after Roosevelt's visit, one of Roosevelt's staff members wrote to Hubbell that Colonel Roosevelt was sending a bottle of Atlantic seawater and three hundred cowry shells by parcel post. Hubbell was to give them to the Hopi chief as Roosevelt had promised when Hubbell and Roosevelt attended the snake ceremony.

Through the Eyes of Writers

The Hopi snake ceremony was a sure draw for Ganado visitors, and Roosevelt was not the first Hubbell guest to write about it. Hamlin Garland, crusading author of political reform novels and autobiographical reminiscences, wrote in an 1896 issue of *Harpers' Weekly* that the ceremony was not revolting. He further observed that the "civilizing" of Indians should not be at the expense of interfering with native rituals, a view opposite that of missionaries and government officials, both of whom considered the rituals barbaric, immoral, and degrading. This latter viewpoint was capitalized on in some sensational reporting in the September 8, 1889 New York World, which was headlined "Barbaric Religious Festival of the Moqui Indians—Indian Braves Dance with Writhing Rattlesnakes in Their Teeth—Shocking Religious Rites in the Wilds of Arizona."

In his *Outlook* article, however, Roosevelt included an interesting description of the non-Indian audience, a potpourri of people with an affinity for Indian country. As he wrote,

> almost every other class of Americans was represented—tourists, traders, cattlemen, farmers, Government officials, politicians, cowboys, scientists, philanthropists.... Mr. Hubbell['s]...courtesy towards us was unwearied....

Roosevelt noticed others in the audience: Leo Crane; J. L.'s guest Geoffrey O'Hara, an ethnomusicologist, composer, and violinist; Father Weber, whom Roosevelt credited with great influence among the Navajos; and visitors from other tribes. One of them was a Navajo man named Clitso Dedman, who owned and drove the automobile in which J. L. traveled to Walpi. Dedman, an educated man, had worked in railroad machine shops, then returned to the reservation and purchased two stores.

Over the years, Ganado's other writer-visitors included Lew Wallace; Charles Lummis; Mary Roberts Rinehart; Louis B. Mervin; G. Wharton James; Carl Moon; Helen MacGowan Cooke; Kate T. Cory; and the aforementioned Hamlin Garland, whose 1895 stay with Don Lorenzo provided the genesis of "Joey the Navajo Teamster," which was published in *The Youth's Companion* in November 1897. A couple of years later, Garland again stayed at Ganado researching two stories of cross-cultural conflict—witchcraft and education—suggested by his host. These appeared in late 1900 in *The Independent.* The "Bad Medicineman" involved a medicineman who killed people by shooting poison pellets into their bodies. In "Big Moccasin," a Navajo headman refused the Indian agent's tools and clothing because attached to the goods was the condition that the headman's children attend school.

In Garland's book *Observations* (a collection of essays), he wrote that the Navajos left their distant hogans for a day at the store, to talk with the white man, "to see his house, to get, perhaps, a taste of his food or a whiff of his tobacco." Restating an American point of view on the nature and status of its native people as well as displaying a typical middle-class Anglo condescension, Garland said if the Indians believed in a white trader, they would travel hundreds of miles to his post, as his word was law. The Indians loved "to be silently in his presence like an intelligent dog." And even though a trader held no official capacity, he could do more than "a regiment to civilize the Indians."

Garland's last observation was echoed by another of his host's friends, Charles F. Lummis. In Lummis's opinion, Hubbell "had done more for the Indians than all the missionaries...[and] Indian agents."

The Trader and the Promoter

In many ways, Lummis can be considered one of the Southwest's master publicists. In his varied careers—journalist, editor, amateur ethnographer, photographer, librarian, museum founder (the Southwest Museum in Los Angeles), arts patron, poet, builder and preservationist, sculptor, and writer (four hundred fifty books, articles, poems, and translations)—he was instrumental in forming the nation's perceptions of the region. Between late 1884 and early 1885, the diminutive and energetic Lummis walked from Cincinnati to Los Angeles, thirty-five hundred miles, in one hundred forty-three days, writing romantic dispatches of his journey as he went. As he hiked across the Southwest, he stayed with a number of Hispanic families, including Colonel Manuel Chavez, one of Juliana's relatives.

Upon his arrival in Los Angeles, Lummis was made the city editor of the Los Angeles Times. Over the years, he continued to write romantic, idealized pieces about indigenous cultures in the overblown prose common to the nineteenth century.

Lummis also founded several Southwestern institutions. Hubbell joined his Southwest Society of the Archaeological Institute of America and the Sequoia League; the latter was established to promote justice for Indians. The trader wrote Lummis that he could provide "material assistance to any of the members who may visit this region." Hubbell also encouraged Lummis to visit, and commended him on his work with "the poor unfortunate Indians in California...who have no friends." (Obviously, Hubbell considered the Navajos and Hopis to be better off because of their friendship with him.)

When Lummis's party arrived in Gallup in 1906, Jesus, one of Hubbell's freighters, met them and took the group by buckboard through a sandstorm to St. Michaels. After spending the night at the mission, they proceeded to Ganado. Lummis described Ganado as "dominated by the most interesting character in Arizona, Don Lorenzo Hubbell," a man who had benefited art, artists, and scientists. His host gave Lummis two *zarapes magníficos* (magnificent wearing blankets) and a mountain lion fetish in recognition of Lummis's Mexican work.

Lummis with C. N. Cotton, circa early 1900s

The Lummis party left for Chinle, returning a week later in a fierce wind; by this time, the party's numbers were increased by Reverend Bierkemper and his family, and anthropologist and explorer Adolph

Bandelier. At the Ganado trading ranch, Lummis selected forty pieces of Hopi First Mesa pottery. Then, on the way back to Gallup, he stopped at Fort Defiance to interview other Hubbell friends, visiting U. S. Indian Commissioner Francis Leupp and Navajo leader Chee Dodge.

A July 5, 1906 letter to Hubbell from Maynard Dixon, friend of both Lummis and the trader, provides an interesting insight into the Lummis party. The group was minus Lummis's wife, but did include his illegitimate daughter and his secretary (who later became his second wife). Dixon noted that this probably struck a few as scandalous.

For the next two decades, the trader and promoter exchanged correspondence about the comings and goings of artists (Lummis knew most of them), dues and subscriptions for Lummis's organization, ads for *Out West* magazine, copies of old Spanish songs, political differences, and their respective health—Don Lorenzo's illnesses and Lummis's blindness. Lummis labeled the trader the "last of the Patriarchs—a Pioneer of the old Frontier."

George Wharton James, a Californian who succeeded Lummis as editor of *Out West*, called himself a professor and authority on Navajo blankets. Author of more than forty books by the time he published *Indian Blankets and Their Makers* in 1914, James counted nearly thirty years' association with Hubbell and Cotton. The fact that Hubbell was able to maintain friendships with both Lummis and James (Lummis's avowed enemy) is testimony to the trader's convivial skills.

James seemed to consider his "scholarship" as a source of income as well as information. As he wrote to Hubbell on July 11, 1913, "the only dealers I am going to mention in this chapter [in *Indian Blankets*] will be yourself, Cotton, Manning, Molokan, Benham Trading Co. and Fred Harvey.... I am charging each of these people $150 for this reference."

He asked Hubbell to write an article "telling your exceptional method of securing from them [the weavers]...[the] very best work" and to take out a yearly quarter-page ad in exchange for a full page ad for the heirloom painting Hubbell wished to sell. James further requested that the trader send to him "from 15 to 30 of the most representative designs that you have in your office, I will undertake to have them reproduced, giving you full credit for each one." He also

borrowed from the trader an old Navajo woman's dress, a Hopi ceremonial blanket, and a Cassidy Davis painting of a Navajo woman weaving to photograph for the blanket book.

Range Riders, Academics, and Collectors

Another Californian, Dane (Dana) Coolidge, also memorialized
Don Lorenzo Hubbell in print. This prolific Western novelist, photographer, and Arizona range rider first visited Navajo country in
1913 with his wife, sociologist Mary Roberts Coolidge. Their 1930
publication, *The Navajo Indians*, described the Hubbells' practice
of refusing to

> accept any payment for their whole-hearted hospitality, but the
> guest can always get his revenge by buying something at the
> store, and find a good bargain to boot.

Hubbell's interest in and collecting of Indian material-culture
objects, antiquities, and ceremonial or sacred objects drew others to
Ganado as well. As institutions and individuals became convinced
that Indians and their lifestyles were vanishing, collectors became
increasingly aggressive throughout the Southwest. They were aided
and abetted in this effort by traders such as Keam (the first trader to
support collecting efforts), Hubbell, and the Days. Hubbell shared
some of his collections; acquired cultural material to augment the
collections of others; and facilitated the sale of ethnographic material, even sacred items held by his friends such as the Days, to Eastern
institutions. Before the century turned, there were rumblings about
the impropriety of these practices.

These transactions seem to indicate that traders believed these non-
renewable resources to be inexhaustible. That belief was shared by
others as well. Stewart Culin, felt that the Southwest was littered with
enough ethnologic material to supply the world's museums, and may
himself have set a collecting record. In his eight summer sojourns in
the Southwest for the University of Pennsylvania and the Brooklyn
Institute, he is reported to have gathered some nine thousand objects.
These transactions also suggest an irreverence toward the Indians' cultural heritage, as well as an attitude of cultural superiority.

As one who believed that Indian ways were vanishing, Hubbell may have felt that it was entirely appropriate to provide items for museum display in order to benefit the progress and education of the larger population; on occasion, he donated pieces to institutions himself. Whatever his reasoning, Hubbell clearly facilitated the acquisition of the Indians' cultural property, including sacred ceremonial objects.

In addition to Culin, other prominent scientists and scholars stopped at Ganado. Many later acknowledged the trader's assistance in their work: John Gregory Bourke, soldier, ethnologist, naturalist, and orthographer; Dr. J. Walter Fewkes, the archaeologist who took over the Hemenway Southwestern Archaeological Expedition from Frank Hamilton Cushing and later worked on the Hopi mesas; Herbert E. Gregory, a geologist and geographer; and F. M. Palmer, the Southwest Society's director. In fact, Palmer attributed the 1906 Canyon de Chelly expedition's success in "the [collection of] handicrafts of Navajos, both ancient and modern" to "the courtesy and public spirit of the last Patriarch of the Western Frontier, Don Lorenzo Hubbell." At the same time, he complained that Eastern museums and scientists rewarded those who looted Canyon de Chelly's accessible ruins (probably a reference to the Days) by purchasing their spoils.

On one of his collecting trips, Culin wrote in his journal

> Upon my arrival [at Ganado], Mr. Hubbell had sent a message to Mr. Day telling him that I had come with the money [$400] and was prepared to close the purchase of his collection. Charles F. Day and his father...at once rode down to Ganado, followed shortly by a team with the remainder of their collection, the greater part of which was already at Mr. Hubbell's. The affair was quickly arranged.

Also in the collection of the Brooklyn Institute are the entire ethnologic contents of a cave near St. Johns, a find described as old sinew-stringed bows, obsidian arrowheads, turquoise beads, and pottery arranged in a semicircle, bowl piled upon bowl. Hubbell had purchased this material from local Mexicans for three hundred dollars.

The Sacred and the Profane

Too, the trader involved himself in moving sacred items used in a Navajo ceremonial, the Nightway, into non-Navajo hands. Navajos were reluctant to allow objects such as the masks (made from skins of deer that had been run down and strangled, rather than shot from a distance) used in their Nightway ceremony to be taken away from the reservation. On one occasion, J. L. wrote to Culin that he had visited a deceased medicineman's family and inquired about the masks. However, in anticipation of Hubbell's visit, the deceased's brother, Laughing Doctor, claimed the masks and took them away. The trader sent Culin to Father Weber, who knew Laughing Doctor well, and Weber accompanied Culin to Laughing Doctor's house. Once Laughing Doctor dismissed the interpreter, he sold the masks to Culin for two hundred dollars, with the stipulation that "no one should hear of the transaction."

Among Hubbell's own collection are more than a thousand ethnographic items: baskets from several tribes, Navajo quivers with bows and arrows, war dance shields, ceremonial lightning sticks, iron trade tomahawks, a rare Hopi *tableta*, Snake Society ceremonial attire, a Hopi butterfly dancer's headpiece, a fringed Apache rifle scabbard, a bone breast plate, and numerous Navajo textiles. (These objects, now part of Hubbell Trading Post National Historic Site, are in the care of the National Park Service.) Because Hubbell did not keep much in the way of records about how he acquired certain material goods, there is little provenance on the items he gathered.

J. L.'s passionate collecting of visitors and material objects extended to artwork as well. The rich amalgam that adorns the trading ranch's walls is representative of the creative energy of an era.

CHAPTER THIRTEEN
A Painter's Mecca

AS THE NAMES of individual rug styles—Burnt Water, Ganado Red, Wide Ruins—rolled off Hubbell's tongue, so did the names of the artists who discovered the Southwest at the Hubbell trading ranch or whose work hangs on its walls. Their art was woven into the fabric of Hubbell's life, a fabric the trader assiduously and deliberately created.

An Alphabet of Artists

J. L. did not store art; he literally papered his walls with it. On August 10, 1910, artist Sauerwein wrote a teasing letter to the trader; in it he said that Burbank had told him that J. L.'s art collection had grown so that the residence's "walls and halls and ceilings [were] fairly covered with paintings," and only the floor was left to show future accumulations.

That comment was a fair one—the Hubbell fine arts collection is a veritable alphabet of artists, with stuttering stops at the letters "b," "m," and "w." It includes photographer-writer Laura Armer; Hopi secret society initiate Louis Aiken; C. E. Barney; M. W. Batchellar; C. Bertram-Hartman; classic portrait painter H. H. Betts (who painted Hubbell's portrait); B. C. Boone; Edward Borein; Karl Oscar Borg; Conté crayonist E. A. Burbank (with one hundred seventy-five pieces in the collection); and Ferdinand Burgdorff.

Then there is Ohio painter and frequent correspondent Cornelia Cassidy Davis; co-founder of the Museum of Northern Arizona and member of "The Ten" Philadelphia Painters, Mary Russell Ferrell-Colton; Edward S. Curtis, photographer of the "vanishing" Indian; Lummis's friend Maynard Dixon; Frederick Melville Dumond; R. Ernesti; F. J. Fewa; H. Gorman; Eastern landscape painter Albert Groll; H. B. Judy, a friend of Stewart Culin who joined him on collecting trips; Edward H. Kemp; sculptor Emory Kopta; William R. Leigh; teacher Bertha A. Little; and Ferdinand Lundgren.

The list of contributors to the HTPNHS fine arts collection also includes H. G. Maratta; Xavier Martinez; Francis McComas; painter of Indian habitats and muralist Howard McCormick; Lon Megaree; medicineman Miguelito; Frederick I. Monsen; photographer of Indians for

Fred Harvey at the Grand Canyon, Carl Moon; W. Mootzka; F. Luis Mora; Jo Mora, artist and early visitor and resident at Hopi; J. W. Norton; Burt Phillips; Roland W. Reed; William Ritschl; H. F. Robinson; W. E. Rollins; California artist F. P. Sauerwein; P. A. Sawyer; Charles Schreyvogal of "My Bunkie" fame; Julian Scott; Joseph H. Sharp, the first Anglo artist to paint in Taos and one of the organizers of the Taos Society of Artists; J. Swinnerton; Southern California landscape painters Elmer and Marion Wachtel; Carl Werntz; Frederick Allen Williams; J. R. Willis; and Rising Wolf.

Most of these artists stayed at Ganado prior to 1930; many stayed for weeks, and one, Burbank, for months. For some, Hubbell arranged extended sojourns into Canyon de Chelly, the Painted Desert, and Hopi country. Most knew one another and provided other artist friends with letters of introduction to the trader. But whether or not an artist actually partook of Hubbell's Ganado hospitality, the trader's role as patron was a comfortable and familiar one.

Some, like Sharp (who attended a Munich art academy with Burbank) and Schreyvogal, probably never stayed at Ganado. Hubbell saw Sharp in New York and later traded for Sharp's work. Sharp, whose art was in the collections of both the Smithsonian and Andrew Carnegie, wrote to Hubbell on September 10, 1908, that he was pleased to add the trader as a patron, as Hubbell

> must be very popular and most certainly...in politics, for wherever and whenever we speak your name...everyone without exception has something fine to say about you [emphasis in the original].

Hubbell also sought out Charles Schreyvogal, an artist propelled into popularity with a painting entitled "My Bunkie." The artist wrote to Hubbell on September 24, 1910, with a wish to see him again in Hoboken, as the trader's "last visit was very short." He went on to thank the trader for his invitation to Ganado, and said that he wanted J. L. to have "one of my sketches for your collection." Schreyvogal later sent Hubbell a sepia-and-pencil drawing of cavalry men.

Except for a few scribbles relating to rug patterns, Hubbell apparently had no personal artistic aspirations, and he balked at requests to write articles. His predilection for working artists may have sprung from memories of his own early adventures. On a more pragmatic level, it is also possible that the name-dropping and social-climbing part of him realized that self-made Americans had art collections. However, a collection usually implies things brought together by choice of the collector, whereas in Hubbell's case, it was the artists who selected most of the pieces.

Financing the Collection

Though Hubbell frequently found himself in dire financial straits, he was faithful in his efforts to help his artist friends. Sometimes the trader's payment for art work made a critical difference; the seventy-five dollars Hubbell sent artists Elmer Wachtel and his wife Marion (members of "The Ten Painters of Los Angeles") in 1908 was gratefully acknowledged by Elmer. On December 6, 1908, Elmer wrote that "if some others would pay up we'd be out of the hole." If an artist sent Hubbell work with a cash price attached, Hubbell would return it if he was short of money.

More commonly, Hubbell financed his burgeoning collection by weaving a complicated system of barter with the artists. Artists became blanket brokers, trading and buying blankets and other crafts from him, most often on credit. In this way, the artists—like customers and laborers—became part of the Hubbell web. Before the great San Francisco earthquake of 1906, Maynard Dixon sold several blankets and some silver for Hubbell. Though the cataclysm cleaned out Dixon, he nonetheless managed to salvage all but two of Hubbell's consigned blankets. He asked the trader to shoulder that loss, which one assumes he did, as the friendship continued.

Hubbell often received letters from his artist friends detailing and bemoaning their financial woes. In November 1905, H. B. Judy wrote, "my debt to you will be cleaned out as soon as I can possibly get out of the present hole." Louis Aiken, who painted the famous "Storm Over the Grand Canyon," gave the trader a painting of a Hopi drummer, for "of many things—chief of which has to be an appreciation of you...this [painting] has been drifting around exhibitions." He also promised to paint something "that will settle the blankets for the season." One of the few women artists in the collection, and a correspondent from 1897 to 1912, Cornelia Cassidy Davis offered to satisfy her own and her husband's long-overdue bill with a painting titled "Three Moqui Maidens" (which can be seen today at HTPNHS).

One of the earliest references to Hubbell's art collection appears in Stewart Culin's 1902 journal. Culin noted the trader's painted copies of old blanket designs, as well other pieces. Among these was a painting his ancestors had brought from Spain three hundred years before, "a picture of the Holy Family, attributed to Corregio [also referred to as "the Raphael"], which has been highly valued by artists who have seen it."

The core of J. L.'s collection, comprising almost a third of it, in fact, was the work of Eldridge Ayer Burbank. Most of this representational work is executed in red Conté crayon (Indian portraits, referred to as "the redheads"), and the balance in oils and other media. The earliest Burbank work in the Hubbell collection is dated 1895, and the last, 1914, a period which also defines Hubbell's zenith as trader and politician.

Burbank's uncle, Edward E. Ayer of Chicago, said Burbank, was the first president of the Field Columbian Museum and owner of the "finest private library of Indian Americans." He turned his Munich-trained nephew from "studies of Negro types" "westward, commissioning him first to go to Fort Sill...and paint Geronimo's portrait." From then on, Burbank "lived and worked [among] one hundred and twenty-eight Indian tribes," doing portraits in red Conté crayon. His ultimate goal was to do portraits of all the tribes. Burbank completed, it is said, twelve hundred "redheads," a hundred of which were chiefs such as

Burbank

Geronimo, Red Cloud, and Sitting Bull. His most famous work, "Belle of the Kiowa," was sold for one hundred fifty dollars to a Chicago publishing firm, who in turn printed and sold over five million copies.

Burbank recollected first hearing of the trader "when I arrived at Gallup looking for Navajos to paint." Cotton told Burbank to go down to Ganado, see the trader, and "when you get there, give this [a razor] to him and tell him to shave himself." Burbank noted that the trader did indeed look like "a wild man, with a beard hanging to his belt...."

He refused to shave." It may have been Burbank who unlocked the trader's passion for art; prior to 1895, there are no written references to J. L. having any interest in art collecting or in artists themselves.

When Burbank tried to pay for his room, his host said, "I have been here for thirty years...and I have never yet charged anybody anything for either food or lodging." During his long stays, Burbank eased his conscience by giving the trader pictures and by copying rug designs. The artist later said that Hubbell "turned over his office for me as a studio," and with his influence, "I had little trouble getting the Navajos to pose for me."

In fact, Burbank's first Navajo subject was the trader's friend Many Horses, who posed wearing his colorful Navajo costume. Many Horses liked the drawing so much that he wanted to pose again. He appeared the next day wearing a tall stovepipe hat, which Burbank could not get him to remove. Many Horses left and returned, still wearing the hat, this time decorated with eagle feathers. And Burbank painted Many Horses again. The portrait so "delighted" Hubbell that he bought it and "had a cut made of the picture" to use on his Ganado letterhead; he called it "Chief *Tja-yo-ni*" (*Tyoni*, as spelled by the Indian agent).

The letterhead. It seems doubtful that Many Horses would have allowed such a silly likeness to be sent to Hubbell's correspondents if he had known that non-Indians would find it humorous.

Burbank seems to have been Hubbell's favored artist, as he paid and traded with him more than any other. In 1906, Hubbell spent at least three hundred twenty dollars for thirty-two pieces, and in 1909, three hundred twelve dollars for thirty-nine redheads. Burbank mailed these pieces to Hubbell from Laguna, California. Prior to buying Burbank's "Hopi Snake Dance" oil for five hundred dollars, Hubbell wrote to another artist, Ferdinand Lundgren, for an opinion on the piece. Lundgren responded that "you know what I think of his work and you cannot go very far wrong in buying anything of his." By 1909, Hubbell wrote a Salt Lake City correspondent that Burbank was

> the best Indian painter in existence. I have a collection of several drawings, red like the head on my envelope, about 125 of them. Also five or six of the oil paintings.

The Burbank pieces in Hubbell's collection dazzle by sheer variety alone: still lives of oranges and of onions, a portrait of the family dog, the trading post's bullpen, a seascape, an ocean shore, sand dunes, a Negro man shining his boots, the painted rug designs, the redheads, and the rather unique oil of Navajos gambling. This painting, "The Navajo Gamblers," which Burbank said took months to complete and cost him several hundred dollars in model fees, depicts some Navajos playing "Koon Can" in the old Leonard building amidst a group of male spectators. Most of Burbank's models worked for Hubbell at one time or another.

Since Burbank was the only artist to clerk at the post, he would have known that the Navajos bought playing cards there, and that they had quickly added poker and rummy to their gambling repertoire of stick-dice and shoe games. Burbank mentioned how touchy the missionary element was about drinking, so it is safe to assume that gambling out of sight might have been a precautionary measure. Government regulations made gambling illegal on most reservations as well, but those regulations were not applicable to private land. Gambling intrigued Burbank, perhaps because the games lasted for days and wagers were often made using Hubbell tokens.

While Hubbell was politicking furiously in early 1912, he warned Roman that Burbank had previously made a trading mistake, which, "if I had not been at home…might have been serious. Tell him to be very careful in case he buys wool." Not long after this, Burbank abruptly left the Ganado post. He attributed his departure to "nervousness," and indeed he spent nearly twenty years institutionalized at California's Napa State Hospital. In May 1912, Burbank wrote that he would like to be at the Ganado post, "selling some sugar to some old Navajo." The extensive Burbank-Hubbell family correspondence continued a decade past Hubbell's death. Burbank asked about people in Indian country and wrote about his art work, finances, lady problems, and artist introductions as well as his nervousness or breakdowns and feelings of being neglected. After J. L.'s death, much of the correspondence concerned the ownership of a painting Burbank said the trader was storing for him. Nearly every artist's letter, and some from writers, mentioned Burbank to J. L.

Unlike most of Burbank's correspondence, Jo Mora's and Maynard Dixon's letters sparkle with intellect and wit and exhibit a rapport with several generations of Hubbells. For these reasons, these two artists both starred in the constellation of artists collected by Hubbell.

Mora and Dixon

Joseph J. Mora's father was a Catalonian sculptor who had immigrated to Uruguay, studied gauchos, and imbued his son with the tradition of travel. As Mora himself traveled throughout the West, he observed its people and places and portrayed them in a variety of media and formats: painting, sculpture, photography, sketching, diorama, cartooning, and writing.

In August 1904, he trekked from Needles, California, by train, foot, and horseback, intent on sketching and photographing the Hopi snake ceremony. By then in his mid-twenties, Mora described the Hopi scene at Oraibi as being "from an artistic standpoint, paradise," with burros walking everywhere, chickens cackling, dogs

Mora in Lorenzo's office at Keams Canyon

211

climbing ladders, "naked potbellied cherubs," women loaded with wood and water trotting along, men in bright-colored blankets strutting on the housetops, then standing trancelike at sunset on the rooftops.

This paradise held him, and he stayed with the Hopis, sketching, painting, and photographing their lives. Mora also developed his friendships with Lorenzo at Keams Canyon and J. L. at Ganado during this period. In 1906, he hunted grizzly bears with J. L. in the White Mountains.

Mora's correspondence radiates the camaraderie he felt with J. L. Before leaving Hopi on an unexpected and hurried April 1905 trip to "hustle my avoirdupois away from the desert sands and turquoise skies to the hub of extreme culture and baked beans, sometimes known as Boston," he wrote to J. L. that he

> had no time to make the little sketch you asked for in return for the blanket, so give you a study I made of a Hopi mana. The larger picture I dedicate to you and hope you'll find an unoccupied nook for it in your office—or any old place where the wind sifts in. I expect to return sometime in July and shall certainly wind my way to Ganado for my delightful stay was all too short, for me at least.

In September 1905, Mora wrote that he felt lonely after his day's painting was done. As he sat on his "front verandah...punish[ing] a bit of weed," he wished for a magic carpet to "whiz over" to Ganado for a jolly, good chat with J. L. Mora signed the watercolors he gave to Hubbell "To the Boss of the Ranch with Remembrance of the Best Times," "*Al Buen Amigo—*J. L. Hubbell *Recuerdo De*." One given to J. L.'s oldest son was dedicated "To my Esteemed Friend Lorenzo Hubbell."

Maynard Dixon, born in Fresno, California, in 1875, was an illustrator for the *San Francisco Call*, the *Overland Monthly*, and the *San Francisco Examiner*; a leading painter of the Southwest; a member of San Francisco's Bohemian Club; and a muralist later in life. At the suggestion of Charles Lummis, known to Dixon as "Pop," the artist first traveled to the Southwest in 1900. He later commented that he "had to go east to see the West." After he had been there a while, Dixon expressed the opinion that the Navajos were "twice as Indian" as the Hopis, and said that they could "will themselves unsketchable." But what seemed to most captivate the artist was Indian country's saturation of sunlight and its blue and purple mesas.

Visiting Ganado in 1902, 1905, 1922, and 1923, Dixon kept his mentor Lummis informed of J. L.'s activities. In September 1902, he noted that J. L., who encouraged him to stay on at Ganado, was worried that the Navajos' poor crops would mean suffering when winter arrived. His host, wrote Dixon, treated the Navajos well and furnished a good market for their wares. He also profited "from 50 to 100 percent off them and that's what he's here for," according to the artist.

Four decades after Dixon's first stay at Ganado, he rated Hubbell's operation there as a real trading post, not a country store. J. L. was the "jovial dictator" of this kingdom, which was secured with barred windows, heavy doors and ready firearms. Dispensing both "droll anecdotes and a [dinner] fare of *carne seca, frijoles,* canned corn, and sourdough biscuits" to sena-tors, salesmen, and teamsters alike, J. L. offered courtesy and equality to all who sat at his table.

Dixon's letters start with colorful salutations that describe both the trader and the artist's relationship to him: "*Querido Patrón*" (Dear Boss), "Hubbell," "*Viejo*" (Old One), "*Querido Viejo*," "your partyman," "Senator," "Old Timer." His letters— in both Spanish and English and replete with slang, his comings and goings, his bout with the mumps, his financial woes, and his opinions

Maynard Dixon at Hubbell's trading ranch, circa 1900.

on social issues—demonstrate the warm relationship that existed between the two men.

Immortalizing the Collector

Given the popularity of photography in the early 1900s, it took a certain view of oneself to have a portrait painted in oil. Harold H. Betts, a Chicago painter and Ganado visitor in 1908 and 1909, painted J. L.'s portrait when the trader visited Chicago sometime in the teens. Betts made a career of portrait painting: a mutual friend, Chicago business-man J. W. Norton, wrote to Hubbell in the spring of 1915 that their friend Betts was "immortalizing some of the Chicago Club elite, sum-mering at Charlevoix, Michigan," and later, that he was capturing "some of the southern aristocrats on canvas." J. L. chose a profession-al to paint his portrait, although Betts himself wrote fifteen years later that he "was not satisfied with [it]—and wish[ed] now I had done it over better." The painting still hangs over the fireplace in the Hall of the Hubbell home; the eyes seem to follow one around the room.

The Lure of the Place

As California artist Frank P. Sauerwein wrote to Hubbell on Febru-ary 9, 1910, Ganado was "a painter's Mecca." If ill health had not prevented it, Sauerwein would have gorged himself on Hubbell's hospitality "until you would have Ganado fortified like a Gibraltar against painters and their scurvy tribe."

Another of the trader's guests, artist Frederick Melville Dumond, explained the area's attraction in an interview with a New York news-paperwoman: "No paint can be manufactured that is strong enough to give an adequate idea of the insanity of colors." Likening it to "painting with colored lights," Dumond commented on the startling contrasts of Indian country, which he called,

> my Navajo blanket landscape. Don't you see, where the Indians got their designs? Red and Black! That's practically the color scheme of this section. Red earth and black grass. The Navajos don't split hairs; it looks black to them with the shadows on it. And the serrated effect of the shadows give [sic] them the pattern they weave in their cloth.

In 1916, Dumond wrote Hubbell that he had pulled off a New York exhibit of his Ganado material, and that it had "opened the eyes of those of the east, to the mysteries and beauty of dear old Arizona."

Indeed, a stay in Ganado often provided artists with material for a successful exhibit. Albert L. Groll, an eastern landscape painter who

Brooklynite Herbert B. Judy, friend of Groll and Culin, is painting on the reservation. He gave Hubbell a sketch for his collection and congratulated the trader on acquiring a painting "from the brush of Groll."

accompanied Stewart Culin on his 1904 collecting trip, wrote to Hubbell on January 27, 1906, that his western paintings "have made a decided hit, both artistically and financially: in fact, my visit to the Southwest [has] been my lucky stars." The half-dozen Grolls in the collection include an oil, "Old Santa Fe Road," which the trader bought for four hundred fifty dollars. At Hubbell's request, Groll joined other of the trader's artist friends in a search for a "reasonable Remington."

Hubbell added his hearty invitation to those of his friend in a letter he wrote in May 1912 to W. R. Leigh (a well-known traditional Western painter, illustrator, and sculptor). It would be a pleasure, he said, to entertain the artist at Ganado and to send him to any locality he desired around Ganado, for

> I do not think you can go to any place in which you may have so many Indians and other things of interest to paint and you will find Indians of the old savage time within a short distance of Ganado.

On December 20, 1912, Leigh sent his host a little painting representing "pictures of like nature [that] have proven quite popular here [New York]."

Another artist whose Ganado stays translated into successful exhibitions was Howard McCormick, a New Jersey painter and one of Burbank's friends. He did murals of the Hopi, Apache, and Navajo for the American Museum of Natural History. As a sketching reference, Hubbell loaned the artist the Hubbell family's photograph album of Navajo ceremonial photos by Brother Simeon. Of the three McCormicks in the Hubbell collection—a pen drawing of President Taft, a small oil of Polacca Wash, and a watercolor of Hopi dancers—Hubbell said that the watercolor had "a place of honor in my collection."

Through the Camera's Lens

Photographers were equally enchanted by the Southwest's subject matter, color, and light. The hundreds of photographs sent to J. L. by named and unnamed visitors of reservation and trading post visits document the life and era of the trader and the region.

A group photograph, usually posed by the post door and including J. L. and often unidentified Indians, is a staple of the Hubbell photo collection.

Edward S. Curtis, long an icon in the pantheon of American photographers, visited the Hopi mesas early in the twentieth century. During his stays in Navajo and Hopi country, Curtis could count on aid from J. L. Once, the trader arranged for delivery of photographic plates to Curtis's camp near the performance area of the snake ceremony. On another occasion, he sent the photographer a Navajo blanket. And on May 10, 1912, Curtis wrote to Hubbell thanking him for marshaling a bill through the Arizona state legislature to authorize purchase of Curtis's Indian book (though ultimately, the bill failed to win approval).

While most of the correspondence between the artists and Hubbell has a cordial tone, some concerns problems. One artist, Gerald Cassidy of Santa Fe, wrote in October 27, 1915, about a check that had bounced. "No doubt you have thought 'here's another artist trying to get the best of Hubbell' and I wouldn't blame you if you had." Two artist brothers, Edward and Phillip A. Sawyer, enjoyed cordial relations with the trader for years before moving to Paris. One made the plaque of a Navajo man (some identified him as Many Horses, others as Bread-maker, or Red Point's father) that hangs above the entrance to Hubbell's trading-post bullpen. However, relations between Don Lorenzo and the Sawyers soured, apparently inexplicably as far as the brothers were concerned. And photographer and painter Carl Moon complained to family members that J. L. failed to acknowledge the oil painting he gave the trader.

Hubbell's art collection, a visual "guest book," is exceptional in relation to those of other Indian country entrepreneurs. In a sense, he shared his imagination with his writer and artist visitors, who then recreated or reinterpreted it in words and art. The pieces fall into three general categories, each of which reflects one of Hubbell's interests: portraiture, textile design, and landscapes. The number of Indian portraits that dominate the collection is a powerful reminder of trader Hubbell's relationships with Indians.

PART FIVE
NAAKAII SÁNÍ

I have been an Indian trader for fifty years, but I've dealt honestly with them. I've never taken a dollar from an Indian without giving the Indian value received, and I've given the Indians what should have been my own legitimate margin of business profit just to help them when they needed it....

They have philosophically accepted the fact that the white man can do anything under the sun, and are surprised at nothing. Their reasoning along such lines is simply: If you can build a wagon that runs better without a horse, why bother with the horse? If you can talk without wires, why go to all the trouble of stringing them? If you can fly through the air like a bird, why travel any other way?

—J. L. Hubbell, *Touring Topics*

CHAPTER FOURTEEN
A View From the Bullpen

WHEN A NEW and uneven Navajo blanket is first taken off the loom, it is buried in damp sand for several days, then wet down and pulled along its edges to improve its shape. Similarly, we can pull the edges of J. L.'s life blanket to even out Naakaii Sání's cultural portrait, particularly his relationship with Navajo families, with his weaver customers, and with community events—in a sense, to a view of him from the place where his customers congregated, the trading post bullpen.

Burbank reported on his arrival in 1897 that the Navajos already called Hubbell the "Old Mexican" or Naakaii Sání.

The Way to Navajo Wealth

Miguelito and his wife Maria Antonia exemplified the reservation's "getting ahead" formula: association with the trader. Miguelito pounded fences together for J. L., acted as foreman on his irrigation jobs and with his farm workers, and traveled with Maria Antonia to Fred Harvey curio sites.

While Maria Antonia did some domestic work for the Hubbells, it was her weaving that connected her to Hubbell's business operations. She was paid for her rugs in tin money, and credit was extended to Miguelito for purchases of up to three hundred dollars. As Mrs. Ben Wilson, their youngest daughter, observed, "My parents were able to obtain material wealth."

This wealth was largely four-legged; the family soon had a large herd of sheep, too large for one person to be responsible for and too large

221

for the place they were living. "So we moved to...White Sand Dunes. There the sheep multiplied even more." At one time, daughter Marie recollected, the family herded "one thousand six hundred head of sheep." Clearly, Miguelito shared J. L.'s knack for increasing his assets. And like J. L., both Miguelito and Maria Antonia strove for excellence, and matched him, though on a smaller scale, in family administration.

Mrs. Ben Wilson and baby on left, Atlnaba and Maria Antonia and Miguelito's grandchildren

Interchanges between the families were not confined to the adults, however, as Marie and Roman were playmates. In a sense, both Marie and Roman refashioned their lives, shifting from their own culture towards that of the other. Marie's family worried that she would abandon the Navajo way, as perhaps the Hubbell family worried over Roman's involvement with it. (Roman went so far as to have Miguelito perform a Nightway ceremony for him in 1922 in an attempt to cure his partial deafness.) Marie attended school and then worked for the Barths in St. Johns. Some summers, she worked for Mrs. Parker and Mrs. Goodman at the Hubbell home.

Mrs. Ben Wilson was apparently not as comfortable with the Hubbells, particularly the trader himself.

When I saw him [J. L.] in the store he used to just stare at me....
He would stand off at a distance and stare. This used to scare me
and I stayed away from the trading post altogether.

When questioned about whether J. L.'s Navajo was good, she said
"No, not really"; she was more positive about Roman's language abilities. "Just *Jai-kal* ["He Who Don't Hear," or "Deaf One"] spoke good
Navajo." Don Lorenzo knew some Navajo, she said "but not really
enough to carry on. But his son, Don Jr., really knew how to speak
it...knew more than his dad." Lorenzo also "spoke good Navajo." But
Naakaii Sání "never learned to speak Navajo well," which she speculated was due to his age. "He used to say *Yei-ah-day* instead of *Yei-
ah-tay*. He spoke like a baby. It was funny, I used to really be scared
of him...."

Much like J. L. in his trading life, Maria Antonia passed on her
weaving knowledge and its associated traditions not by showing or
teaching, but by her performance of the activity itself. Both perfec-
tionists, J. L. and Maria Antonia often lacked patience with those
around them. Maria Antonia did not want Marie to spoil her own
blanket weaving, and so did not teach her daughter to weave. In
spite of this, Marie made herself a little loom and learned to weave
while she watched the sheep, using wool filched from her mother's
supply. In taking matters into her own hands, Marie was behaving
similarly to Lorenzo, who ran off from his father's trading routine to
join in Navajo activities.

And like J. L., who dressed shabbily when at the trading ranch,
Maria Antonia had an equally plain but functional style when at home:
her washed-out twelve-yard velvet skirt had no nap and was riddled
with gashes. She would, however, dress up to go to the public sheep
dip, just as J. L. would present himself as a suave politician when the
occasion demanded.

Miguelito and Maria Antonia's home also echoed, in its way, the
wealth of material good in Hubbell's trading ranch home.

[It was a] large well-built hogan...a rich family's house with trunks
and suitcases filled with yards of cloth, velvet, baskets, and other
objects of bulk, surplus food, particularly flour, sugar and coffee....

Miguelito, who was also a medicineman (his ceremonial medicine-man paraphernalia was in evidence on the hogan walls), was described by ethnologist Gladys A. Reichard as a vibrant, energetic, mature man. This description was applicable to J. L. as well. Then in their early sixties, both men were patriarchs of extended families. Both were expansionists, one in the Navajo way, and the other in the Anglo/Hispanic tradition. Both parlayed their personalities, language skills, and cultural knowledge into successful associations with another culture.

This web of similarities extended into the community, for Maria Antonia claimed Chee Dodge as an uncle, and her family called both him and Many Horses "grandfather." In the Navajo way, this does not necessarily imply a direct blood relationship; a clan relationship grants the same status. Navajos are grouped into sixty or more matri-lineal clans. A Navajo baby is "born to" its mother's clan, and "born for" its father's clan. As there is a prohibition against marrying some-one from the same clan, the mother's clan and the father's are always different. In this case, Dodge's and Many Horses' "grandfather" desig-nation could have meant that the maternal or paternal grandfathers' clans were the same.

Burbank's memoirs provide numerous anecdotes about the rela-tionship between J. L. and Many Horses. On one occasion, a quarrel arose at the trading ranch when J. L. killed a Navajo's dog after it bit someone. The owner threatened to kill Hubbell in exchange, but Many Horses told the Navajo that if he did, then Many Horses would kill the Navajo. Apparently, the dog owner put down his gun and demanded payment for his dog (it is part of Navajo custom to be paid for a loss).

Burbank also described the following joking interchange between Many Horses and Hubbell.

> [Hubbell said] "If you die before I do...I will put a rope around your neck and drag you to the top of the hill...[and place] the largest stone...on top of you so that you can never go to the Happy Hunting Ground." Many Horses would laugh [and reply]. "You die first, and I do that to you."

The fact that, in general, Navajos then avoided contact with dead bodies makes it hard to believe that this anecdote is literally true.

However, while Burbank was at Ganado in the 1910s, Many Horses did indeed die; the artist helped bury the eighty-year-old man on Hubbell Hill where,

> [t]rue to his promise, the Indian trader put the largest stone he could find at the head of the Indian's grave, crying like a baby while he was doing so.

Many Horses represented a transition of leadership from older Navajo headmen, such as his father Ganado Mucho, to the much younger institution of a formal tribal chairmanship, which was ultimately held by Chee Dodge. Both Many Horses and Hubbell encouraged and valued industry, community, and cooperation. Both men had a sense of humor, an eye for justice, and a brotherly concern for one another's safety. And, finally, Many Horses' wife was also one of Hubbell's weavers.

Perspectives on Navajo Weaving

Weavers like Many Horses' wife and Maria Antonia and her daughters symbolize the larger relationship between the trader and the Navajos. To the Navajos, J. L. provided the economic underpinnings of the weaving trade. Weaving was, after all, a way for homebound women to contribute to the economic well-being of their families; the weaving process itself was also considered to be a nurturing one. Mrs. Wilson remembered that her mother Maria Antonia was "always weaving."

> At that time women folks didn't get any outside help.... Thinking about the hard times the early women had, I can't help but admire their endurance, they raised their family from what they could get off their rug sales. When I was small, there was no such thing as...extra money.

Weavers say that weaving is a way to Navajo spirituality—for example, packing the yarn down over the loom's warp with a wooden fork tool replicates the earth's heartbeat. The weavers sing to their rugs as they work, and many of the weavers interviewed at Hubbell Trading

Post "sang" very similar songs about the trader's influence on the craft of Navajo textiles.

To many non-Indians, Hubbell's historical prominence rests on what they consider his aesthetic and economic influence on the Navajo blanket, which evolved into the rug form during his lifetime. In conjunction with other early traders, J. L. is frequently given credit for fathering the Navajo rug by redesigning the blanket form's shape and weight; for getting it into the U. S. market by letter writing, advertising campaigns, and printing catalogues; and for wholesaling Navajo textiles to new markets.

Traders, including Hubbell, did indeed make their preferences known to the weavers. The weavers' expressions of these preferences were, in the words of silversmith historian John Adair in *Navajo and Pueblo Silversmiths*, "the Indian's idea of the trader's idea of what the white man thought was Indian design." Textile expert Amsden concluded that patterns standardized to the white man's preference for a "border and the use of isolated geometric figures" enclosed in a field were rarely used by the Navajos in earlier times. Amsden also acknowledged that J. L. encouraged those who wove for him to follow the "color paintings" done by his artist friends if a particular pattern proved popular with buyers. Textile authority Kate Peck Kent's assertion that weavers initiated innovations voluntarily from the selections of dyes, design ideas, and materials offered by the white culture somewhat modifies Amsden's position, however.

Anthropologists differ in their assessments of the traders' contribution to Navajo textiles. Gary Witherspoon has postulated that the traders might have unwittingly put the Navajo textile on the wall or floor; by virtue of this change of use, it went from a blanket to wall hanging or rug. According to Witherspoon, any notion that such a process destroyed Navajo aesthetics and creativity reflected the "exaggerated ego of the traders and the superficial analysis of rugs."

On the other hand, Kathleen M'Closkey, an American scholar in Canada, opined that traders devalued the Navajo textiles that were once the Southwest's most valuable trade item by treating them as a commodity, pricing them by weight rather than the quality or beauty of an individual piece. While Hubbell decried "pound blankets," his catalogue touted several categories of this very same blanket type, and his ledger books showed pound blanket trades. M'Closkey also argues that giving traders design credit ignores the size of the Navajo country and its inclement weather, which left Navajo women hogan-bound for months on end, designing and weaving one textile after another with few outside influences.

According to anthropologist Witherspoon, Navajo weaving may have adopted the same course as the rest of Navajo society and culture: specifically, that the Navajos, pragmatic and adaptive, absorbed without being absorbed and transformed without surrendering their identity and integrity. In weaving, the Navajo rug style known as the Ganado Red epitomizes Witherspoon's thesis. The red earth and black grass serrated by shadows, described by artist Frederick Dumond as the Navajo blanket landscape, is also the pattern of the rug type known as the Ganado Red. This red-and-black Navajo textile continues to represent the most common concept of a Navajo rug.

While the academic controversy over Hubbell and other traders' contributions to the Navajos' textile will continue, his customers' views of him as a trader (represented by the Navajo interviews) have few differences in opinion.

The First White Trader

Most of Hubbell's customers had high praise for the trader. Asdzaa Bekashi named J. L. as the first "*balagana* [white] trader at Ganado [when] famine came." Hubbell, she said, "was a great man...he passed out flour.... [W]e were starving and he saved us." She described the old days when the Navajos subsisted on a daily diet of small amounts of corn and a little meat from hunting. One ear of corn would be made into a gruel to feed everyone. To her,

Friday Kinlicheeny, a Hubbell employee, said, "Naakaii Sání was the one that saved us [economically]."

227

Ganado meant "the place of refuge, a place [that] never gives up [as] it protects friends." She felt that J. L. "was kind to the Navajos and helped everyone" and "paid quite a bit for his rugs...in tin money."

Both the Indians and J. L. worked on the principle of the importance of sheep in the Navajo world. Lacheenie Blacksheep said that everything the Navajos brought for trade—at the trading posts came from sheep-wool, rugs and lambs. J. L. repeated this perspective in the *Touring Topics* article:

> my post at Ganado for many years has done a business of more than quarter of a million dollars in wool and hides alone. The chief source of wealth among the Navajos is sheep and goats.

Hubbell understood the individual and community activity that Navajo animal husbandry represented. Herding, lambing care, and shearing were typically individual or household activities; dipping, counting, marking, and vaccination were community affairs. In the Navajo way, a sheep herd provided psychological and material security, created societal identity of wealth and respect, and incorporated basic Navajo values of community and individualism. Hubbell's trading ritual, which really represented cross-cultural courtesies, broke the ice through gift-giving. For instance, LaCheenie Blacksheep recollected that trader Hubbell always gave

> you food and invited you to eat first, after eating free, then you talked business with him...he would bring out his tin money and tell you what your wool was worth. If you asked for silver money, he would give you those big rounded silver coins in addition. That's what he paid.

J. L. benefited as well from the general flourishing of Navajo life, with its hundred-fold increase in population, reservation expansion, opposition to cultural onslaughts, maintenance of cultural beliefs, and transformation of tribal unity and organization.

Good Trader/Bad Trader: A Double-faced Token

When J. L. moved from St. Johns back to the reservation to trade, his reputation grew. Of all the reservation traders, Hubbell was the one on which the title of archetypal "trader to the Navajo" was bestowed. In fact, he himself said in *Touring Topics* that he was called "the King of Northern Arizona." Nonetheless, when area Navajos were interviewed, negative comments about the trader were sometimes made within the context of a positive interview. This contradiction represents the complexity of the times and of Hubbell himself, and can be likened to a token minted with Naakaii Sání's conflicting aspects. On one side was struck the "good trader" image, the man who helped many a lame sheep over an arroyo; the other showed a self-important exploiter who had his trading fingers into everything.

Joe Tippecanoe said Hubbell "always had a willing hand to help...giving you a small amount of groceries" like flour, sugar, potatoes, and small slabs of bacon. Hubbell, who Tippecanoe felt did not want anyone dying of starvation, once said, "I'll keep on helping even if I am starved doing it and then you can help me, too, bringing me some corn mush, too."

Navajos did reciprocate. Tippecanoe said if that they butchered a calf, they "brought him a leg or so" and brought him "roasted and mashed piñon nuts," pulverized and ground to the peanut-butter-type consistency that he liked.

Grover Cleveland, one of Hubbell's laborers (and therefore a customer), posing with his family, circa 1905.

Tully Lincoln, who made a comment about the low wages Hubbell paid, still portrayed the trader as a helper and a community resource.

Mr. and Mrs. Holmes recollected that Hubbell loaned them money to buy cattle. Mrs. Holmes explained that if you had Hubbell as a friend,

> it was rather good, for he took care of you like a mother or father; he used to make up little bags of sugar, coffee, and flour to give those who had no money.

Mr. Holmes added that in his opinion, no trader then or now matched his generosity.

Tom Morgan said "Old man Hubbell" loaned him goods which he traded for livestock; he then sold the good horses to Hubbell, and eventually increased his stock to two thousand sheep and forty cattle. T. Slivers considered that Hubbell's generosity exceeded what could be expected from other traders of the day. As an example, she said that one winter, he divided provisions equally among the Navajos when his freight wagon was mired in mud far from his post. (She probably did not know that Hubbell later billed the government for these provisions, although he may never have collected on the bill.)

Hubbell's largesse went beyond individual customers who traded at his post, often extending to the community as a whole in the form of entertainment and holiday celebrations.

Participants at chicken pull lined up for horse race.

230

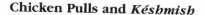

Chicken Pulls and *Késhmish*

In the summer, the trader regularly hosted a social event called the "chicken pull," an occasion for extensive socializing among Indians from far and wide. The chicken pull itself was inspired by Spanish tradition and based on *gallo*, a popular Sunday-afternoon horsemanship event in which the Hubbell brothers took part during their St. Johns days. In a description that echoed the prevailing American view, Hubbell described the Ganado event as a gathering of hundreds of "savages."

"Chicken pull" was in fact an all-encompassing term for a multi-day, multi-activity celebration on the order of the fur-traders' rendezvous. The U. S. Cavalry from Fort Wingate might show up to entertain the crowds with trick-riding demonstrations, and a visitor could count on opportunities to gamble and race horses as well.

Hubbell's chicken pulls became the stuff of local legends and were described by many Navajo interviewees. Mrs. Ben Wilson said,

> Navajos participate, no white men. Our events were horse races, footraces...tugs-of-war, chicken pulls. But they did not use live chickens. Instead, a gunny sack or a piece of leather was buried with a small piece sticking out. Men on horseback would alternate, each trying to see who could pull out the "chicken." When someone finally did, all the riders would then try to get it away from him. They'd gallop all over, fighting and chasing. The game was hard and brutal."

She also detailed the atmosphere of these sporting events.

> Back in those days, people used to come from miles around in covered wagons, on horses [and] the whole place was alive with people. In the evening, families would set up camps across and up and down the valley. They would build their campfires, and the whole place would light up just like the way Ganado lights up now.

Not only did Hubbell's post itself hum with activity, but the nearby visitors' camps droned with voices, and the blue summer sky was traced with fingers of smoke and dust. Mutton ribs and steaks sizzled

231

over campfires, and tokens and silver dollars clinked and jangled in the gamblers' hands. Buck Chambers recalled horse racing and heavy betting, and Tully Lincoln said that other events included tugs-of-war and the "saddle-the-horse-the-fastest-event." In this competition, saddles were placed at some distance from the men sitting bareback on their mounts. The men would then ride out, throw the saddles on their horses, remount, and race back to the starting point. All the Ganado interviewees emphasized horse racing and horse competitions as culturally important activities. Fifty years later, they still recalled the Navajos who rode the race horses using Jilhool's old track, and recounted their parents' ownership of race horses.

Hubbell's chicken pulls drew Indians from across Arizona and New Mexico's Indian country, including Crownpoint, Black Mountain, Chinle, and the Zuni Reservation. J. L. provided watermelon and cash prizes, and the Navajos bet on various events, backing up their wagers with tin money, saddle blankets, jewelry, and buckskins. Hubbell's post undoubtedly benefited, but the community's reputation was magnified as well.

Christmas provided another occasion for more local trader-customer socializing. The Navajo language lacks the sound for the English "r," so in Navajo, "Christmas" became *Késhmish*. The Késhmish celebration began during the Navajos' first year of incarceration at Bosque Redondo, when the fall supplies did not materialize until mid-December. The superintendent waited until Christmas eve to distribute the goods: bright red and blue blankets, awls, axes, buttons, hoes, knives, scissors, sheep shears, and shovels. Years later, traders often celebrated Christmas with their patrons in the same manner. Some, like George and Mary Kennedy at Salina Springs, provided a free meal of "a nice fat beef," bread, and coffee made in big cans. The Kennedys also passed out bags of fruit, nuts, and candy.

At some point in their dealing with Anglo Americans, Indians came to know of this important gift-giving occasion, this sharing of goodwill. Though no photographs record any of J. L.'s celebrations, his trading practice can be deduced through Lorenzo's correspondence and oral history accounts.

While at the Hopi posts, Lorenzo ordered candy, nuts, oranges, and apples for the boarding-school children; another year, he instructed his manager to give the "Indians some smoking tobacco, the kids some candy, and the squaws a bar of soap, or little something, if they come in Christmas Day."

In Annabel Hardy's oral history, she recalled visiting the Ganado post one Christmas at J. L.'s invitation; the trader offered the children gifts of shoes and clothing. Earlier that evening (in snow already three inches deep), Hardy's group had left for the party in a wagon. A young Navajo child, Tsitigai Yazhi', wanted to join in the festivities, but had no shoes or clothes to wear and so was left at home.

> We were almost halfway when he caught up with us barefooted in the snow, so my uncle chased him back. The second time he caught up with us he...was taken into the wagon. He received more gifts than anyone of us.

The scheduling, or even holding, of Christmas celebrations often depended on the weather, which was sometimes mild, but most often cold. Slushy wet snow or dry crusty-topped snowdrifts and hoarfrosted shrubs and trees shrouded in a soupy fog were common.

Though some of these festivities added social interaction to the economic exchange that took place between the Indians and Hubbell, the trader still held a myopic view of "his Indians."

J. L.'s Indians

Just as Hubbell, in the *Touring Topics* interview, called himself the "de facto czar" of Indian country, he saw the Indians as different, and lesser. Proprietary references to "my Indians" or "my Navajos" are scattered throughout the Hubbell Papers. Although he used the term "savage" rarely, it did appear in invitations sent to those in the East. Both designations reflected Hubbell's assumption of his culture's moral superiority.

Hubbell expressed both of these attitudes in his 1909 correspondence about Hastiin Bagodi, Ganado Mucho's son-in-law and an area leader, who attacked and nearly killed some people in Cincinnati. The trader's correspondence on the subject was initiated when he wrote to artist Cornelia Cassidy Davis and her husband that he had no idea "the man or Indian would do such a thing in his right mind," as he had known the "Indian for 37 years and a more honest man never existed." J. L. went on to spell his own Navajo name phonetically and to instruct Ms. Cassidy Davis's husband to take the letter to Bagodi. He was to tell Hastiin Bagodi that the letter was from him (Naakaai Sání) and that the Commissioner of Indian Affairs had taken up for him and he was not without a friend. When Cornelia Cassidy Davis wrote to J. L. about her husband's visit with the Navajo in jail, she asked J. L. to write the Navajo's attorney in his client's favor, as the "people here think them all a blood thirsty set of people."

Hubbell complied with her request. He said it was a

> very strange thing to me that the old man should be worked to such a frenzy as to commit the act that he did. While a savage himself, he has [been]...the leading champion of progress among these Indians.

Further, the trader believed that

> the foundation [of] this unfortunate affair has been caused by a constant agitation of an increase of the reservation and the failure to get what he wanted may have unhinged his mind.

Then, as though he were the government agent rather than the trader, J. L. complained that he was never consulted about Hastiin Bagodi's trip and wondered who was "responsible for sending an old savage like this one on a trip."

Hubbell regularly chided visitors and friends who, in his trader's eye, bestowed too-lavish remuneration for Indian services. He and his co-entrepreneurs, the Fred Harvey Company, fretted that the Navajo and Hopi demonstrators would become spoiled by their contact with sentimental Easterners, who did not know how to treat Indians.

J. L.'s biases, however they might be considered today, did nonetheless reflect contemporary views. In his *Touring Topics* interview, he does not mention individuals by name, but rather refers to them by a handful of tribal references: six Navajo, four Hopi, one Paiute (tribal affiliation is a critical issue among those generally lumped together as "Indians"). He flatly labeled the Indians as "notoriously improvident," although he had bragged earlier in the article about his own loss of sixty thousand dollars in a 1896 poker game. It should not be surprising that a nineteenth century man who prepared letters for the Navajo headmen that closed with "Your Navajo Children" used the word "savage." As Kirkpatrick Sales said in *Conquest of Paradise*,

> it all came down to this: the natives of the Americas were to be understood as LESS THAN HUMAN not in the literal sense...but still in some real and operative way that permitted the sort of psychological displacement we now know to be common in creating the image of the Enemy, the other [emphasis in the original].

J. L. did indeed imagine Indians as "the other," even though he was tolerant of their cultures and learned some of their ways and languages. In contrast, during Hubbell's trading era, the collective Navajo attitude towards non-Indians was primarily indifference, with an underlying current of hostility. From 1901 to 1934, this hostility had literal ramifications; Navajos killed twenty Navajo-country traders; one was Hubbell's favorite brother, Charlie. During the same period, a time when nationwide, non-Indian attitudes toward Indians ranged from patronizing to hostile, those on the reservation held the same diversity of views.

Nevertheless, more than most white reservation residents, J. L. championed the Indians. His friend and sometime-partner C. N. Cotton did not share J. L.'s generally benign outlook, however. Cotton once loaned three dollars to an Indian named Grover Cleveland, who claimed to be working for Hubbell; if Hubbell could not collect the sum, Cotton wrote on March 19, 1909, he (Cotton) would charge it to the "D. F. [damn fool] account." In a January 6, 1914, letter, Cotton wrote that "$180 for good teeth put in the head of Chischille is in my opinion $180 more than this lobster is worth"; Hubbell had footed the dentist's bill.

Most authorities agree that traders of unusual good character, the Franciscan fathers, and the Ganado Presbyterians, all of whom exhibited a kindness and devotion, earned the trust and loyalty of the Navajos. One of the Franciscans, Father Emanuel, described J. L. as one of

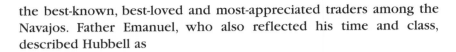

the best-known, best-loved and most-appreciated traders among the Navajos. Father Emanuel, who also reflected his time and class, described Hubbell as

> very kind to them...he could be strict with them, too. And his home was the home for everybody, anybody. I'm sure that he had a place where Indians could stay at his place, and if they were in need he was willing to help them.

As a patron to both his own extended family and to the Navajos, he was drawn closer to Navajo relative/kin status than other traders. At the same time as he was helpful and sympathetic, Hubbell avoided transculturation, the process through which an individual detaches from the birth group and enters the web of social realities that makes up another society, coming under its influence as to customs, ideas, and values. While J. L. lived physically apart from his own cultural heritage, he remained an emissary of it. Though he defined himself as culturally intimate with certain Hopi ceremonies or Navajo leaders, he also created in his Ganado homestead a replica of an Hispanic trading ranch. Throughout his life, Hubbell was convinced of the superiority of his own culture, as were the Navajos of theirs.

That Hubbell stood so tall in Navajo recollections meant that he in some way met Indian wishes and followed Indian values. Hubbell came close to what Gary Witherspoon described as the Navajo moral code: "what is good for the individual is good for everyone else, and what is good for everybody is good for the individual." J. L. articulated this premise as early as 1907 in an article in the *Indian School Journal*:

> [N]o intelligent Indian trader desires to live among a community of Indian paupers.... The first duty of an Indian trader...is to look after the material welfare of his neighbors.... This does not mean that the trader should forget that he is here to see that he makes a fair profit for himself, for whatever would injure him would naturally injure those with whom he comes in contact.

His premise echoed the Navajo belief that with cooperation, material goods increase for everyone, that another's success contributes to your own. Hubbell held, and generally acted on, other Navajo cultural values as well: positive behavior, productivity, dependability, helpfulness, generosity, and the ability to get along.

Though Hubbell lost the political games in which he participated, and would be harassed by financial troubles during his last fifteen years of life, in the eyes of the Navajos with whom he lived and worked, he was a "good trader."

PART SIX
LORENZO THE MAGNIFICENT

To a man who is not a judge of blankets this blanket looks well. Yet it is not a blanket that will wear [for if you will open a fringe end, you will see that] the warp is cut off...and the blanket will go to pieces with little wear. [The best quality blankets] have warp of one piece.

—J. L. Hubbell, 1901

[In a Navajo weaver's partially woven rug], one of the warp strands is holding by only the merest fiber. She inserts her batten, and snap! it has torn.... The weaver will be bothered frequently because of this weakness [and] before she is through...she...ties in a piece of new warp, making a small tight square knot at each end.

—Gladys A. Reichard, *Weaving A Navajo Blanket*

CHAPTER FIFTEEN
Snap! Snap! And Snap Again!

AS HE FACED lean times, the warp of Don Lorenzo's life often trembled and tore. It weakened when he politicked instead of trading. It weakened each time he borrowed and could not repay lenders. It tore when Navajos murdered his brother Charlie, snap! It tore as the importance of the customer-trader relationship declined, snap! Lorenzo, his oldest son, repaired warp after broken warp as Lorenzo the Magnificent's life unraveled.

Once Roman returned to the fold, J. L. gave up on politics and focused on his business and on the Ganado trading ranch. Farming and business west of Ganado were usually on the fuzzy edge of his focus, except when problems sharpened the contrast and brought them to the forefront. Such was the case in the spring of 1915, when a complaint was filed about Charlie, whose drinking had gotten him into hot water with Bureau of Indian Affairs.

Referring to himself as the senior partner of "J. L. Hubbell & Co.," J. L. wrote to the Assistant Commissioner of Indian Affairs about his brother's drinking. The introduction of alcohol on the reservations had never had his sanction or approval, he said. To his knowledge, his brother and partner, Charles (this was J. L.'s solitary reference to his brother having a partnership interest in the businesses) did not introduce liquor, but might have taken a drink when it was brought by others. In fact, Hubbell explained that Charlie had been addicted to drink but since he had been on the Moqui (Hopi) Reservation, had been a new man. Apparently, the complaint was favorably resolved, since Lorenzo wrote to his father in June 1915 that the bureau granted the trading license at Oraibi. Lorenzo said he would let his Uncle Charlie know that it paid to tell the truth.

That Charlie had problems with alcohol is not surprising—his letters are replete with complaints of tedium and isolation, and his loneliness was regularly expressed; "I suppose you have forgotten that I am in the land of the living," he once wrote to J. L. However, he stayed in the trading game all his life, while many of the relatives gave it up rather quickly. For example, Charles Rubi, trading at isolated

Sandwater, started off enthusiastically planting black locust trees around the post so that his family "would be in Paradise two years from now." When he requested bacon and a current newspaper from the Hubbell bookkeeper, he was told that there was no bacon and no mail delivery. Before the black locust trees had reached their two-year maturity, Rubi was gone.

J. L.'s politicking had put a serious financial burden on the trading operations, and these problems continued after he returned to trading. As the years passed, an increasing amount of the trading post-family correspondence concerned money. Hubbell post managers, complaining of competition, pushed Ganado continually for cash ("trade is going away for lack of cash"), wool sacks, and goods. By 1917, J. L., who himself pressed his Gallup bank for a twenty thousand dollar stock loan, found himself mired in business difficulties. One of the trader's ledgers (undated) lists notes with "Clinton N. Cotton, Co." totaling $30,092.75. Another undated document summarizes J. L.'s accounts with C. N. Cotton Co. at Merchant Bank of Gallup (Cotton's bank) for $130,578.62; in a notation, Hubbell wool, coming in at close to two hundred thousand pounds at thirty cents a pound, was pledged to paying off the indebtedness.

Though it was common for traders to pay off their large wholesale credit accounts with wool sales, in 1917, Hubbell's anticipated wool income amounted to less than half of what he owed. Hubbell gave Cotton an option on three of his reservation stores; this was followed by a sale to the wholesaler of several posts, including those at Chinle, Cornfields, Nazlini, Sheep Springs, and Keams Canyon. Technically, the Keams Canyon money went to Lorenzo and seems to have been applied to his father's bill.

In 1918, when Lorenzo moved from Keams Canyon to Oraibi, the center of the Hopi Reservation, fifteen of the seventeen licensed trading posts there were Hopi-owned. In time, from Oraibi, Lorenzo orchestrated a Hubbell trading renaissance using multiple strategies: outlying posts, increased Navajo trade from the western side of the Navajo Reservation, a Winslow-based wholesale operation, use of some non-family managers, and more modern business practices. Though he would have thrown in his trading towel to serve in World War I, he failed his physical. In the meantime, J. L. (due to what Forrest described as his father-in-law's "fighting blood") was urging Forrest to serve in the front.

The same year that Lorenzo moved to Oraibi (1918), Alma died in the influenza epidemic that swept the United States and J. L. seemed to be going downhill; as Forrest wrote, "your father has sold his sheep, but has no idea what he got for them." By 1919, the Battreall Shoe Co., a prospective supplier on credit, wrote to J. L. about his financial statement, saying that the "disquieting element was the fact...[that there is]

Lorenzo and Indian at Hopi

difficulty in retiring your obligations somewhere at maturity." The family was soon to face yet another "disquieting" situation.

Conflagration

"Charlie Hubbell is dead." The words spread over Indian country, and blazed into border towns and cities where Hubbell's friends lived. The words and deed choked the Hubbells, marking the end of a violence-free trading era for the entire family.

On March 22, 1919, wind-whipped flames at Cedar Springs were visible ten miles away at Billie Williams's trading post near Leupp, Arizona. When Williams arrived with Little Gambler, a Navajo man, only the chimney and the twisted remains of Charlie, his cookstove, and his bedstead stood in the smoldering ashes of Cedar Springs Trading Post.

When eight days had passed with the murderers still at large, Lorenzo wrote to Navajo friends Hastiin Nez and Adakai, reminding them of the many instances of his help. Then he said "two Navajos killed my uncle (*Ja-apeni*) and burned the store over him." He asked the men to trail the murderers. When a crime like this is committed, Lorenzo wrote, he knew that his Navajo friends would be against it. He offered to pay everyone trailing the murderers, as well as a two hundred dollar award to the first man giving information leading to their identification. He sent the letter via Hopi Superintendent Crane with a request that the agent send his interpreter to translate the letter "word for word" to Nez and Adakai. He signed his name "Lorenzo Hubbell (*Nakai Tso*) the Big Mexican."

In the meantime, newspaper reports emphasized the deceased's relationship to J. L., dramatized the murder, compounded the confusion over whether the murder happened on or off the reservation (and in which county), and variously reported the suspects as barricaded in a cave in the mountains or along the Little Colorado River. Meanwhile, surveyors tried to determine the post's county jurisdiction.

It was reported that Navajo trackers had followed the killers to

> their lair in the mountains, and a sheriff's posse set out to capture them, but two Indian policemen crossed the Little Colorado, surprised [them] and then made them swim the fresh swollen stream to the jail at Leupp, the policemen swimming along behind them to make sure that no attempt at escape was made.

They also noted that Charlie's brother, "former state Senator Hubbell, who spoke the Indian language fluently," planned to accompany a heavily armed posse to arrest the two murder suspects. By the time the posse—seventeen armed men in four automobiles—"left Winslow for a battle to the death with the pair," the suspects had been arrested.

After the late-March preliminary hearing, bail in the amount of twenty thousand dollars was established and the Indians were bound over for trial. By this time, Lorenzo had officially identified the remains as Charlie's; the newspaper said that Lorenzo's identification was made based on

> the frail form [the newspaper said Charlie weighed 103 pounds], the man's home, [and] the custom that no Indian trader leaves his premises without leaving someone else in charge.

While J. L. attended the preliminary hearing, only Lorenzo testified. Over the next few weeks, Lorenzo became his father's point man on this matter (presaging another shift that was taking place, the transfer of economic power from J. L. to his oldest son).

As the murder trial approached, a dozen leading Flagstaff citizens gave affidavits stating that they did not think the Indians could obtain a fair and impartial trial in Coconino County; these accompanied a July 7, 1919, motion for a change of venue. The court denied the motion and ignored the lurid newspaper articles, attached as exhibits, captioned "Confessed Slayers Barricaded in Mountain Cave," "Two Indian Police and Captives Risk Lives to Reach Jail," "Medicinemen Did Killing."

The last headline was apparently provoked by J. L. himself. On July 11, 1919, after the court continued the early July trial, the *Coconino Sun* reported that former Senator Hubbell said a murder may have been committed not for loot, but for a scalp. The reporter went on to say that J. L. Hubbell had been told that a medicineman needed a scalp of a non-tribal member to become a "full-fledged medicineman" (a whopping misrepresentation). In a more characteristic statement, J. L. said,

> there are good and bad Indians, the same as among the people of any other race, and knowing the friendly feeling [among] the Indians with whom my brother had lived for years, I doubt if any of the old men would ever have thought of murdering him.

That summer, the jury ruled at the older Navajo brother's trial that he (Ada toni Bigue No. l) murdered Charlie; Ada toni Bigue No. 2 then pled guilty before his trial began.

It seemed that Charlie had died in a dispute that started with a cookie. In their defense, the Bigue brothers said that Charlie Hubbell had refused them change after they purchased cookies, insisting they trade out the difference. Then Charlie's dog tore one of the Bigues' trousers. The Navajos demanded payment for the damage as well as change from the cookie transaction. Charlie told them to get out or he would kill them. The older brother and Charlie grabbed for Charlie's gun near the counter. When the Navajo got it, Charlie ran into his bedroom and came out with another gun. He shot at them. The older brother returned the shot and hit Charlie in the head. Then the brothers dumped coal oil on Charlie's body and around the post, grabbed jewelry and cash, ignited the oil, and rode off.

Dear Charlie. Beloved Charlie. Neglected Charlie. Frail Charlie. Bachelor Charlie. Troubled with drinking, his temper, and a knack for being in the middle of Navajo uprisings, Charlie led a lonely life. Sixty-three years old, Charlie died alone and perhaps sotted. Though no mention was made of Charlie's drinking in the newspapers or court proceedings, if the Navajos' story was true, it is perhaps the only explanation for his mishandling of the trade exchange.

On July 31, 1919, at the conclusion of the trial, Lorenzo wrote to his close friend and employee, Ed Thacker, that the jury was only out three minutes on the older brother's case, bringing in a verdict of first-degree murder. Eight wanted hanging and the others life, so his sentence was for life. As Lorenzo commented to Ed,

> it's too bad, but some people don't believe in hanging, though their own mothers were killed in cold blood, but it's best to be satisfied, as there is no comeback; every bit of evidence was presented, and the case was ably presented by Mr. Gold and Harben.

Lorenzo continued that the second Indian's age influenced a shorter sentence of 15 to 25 years

Following the trial, before he left for Ganado, J. L. gave an agitated statement to the paper, saying that travelers to the reservation should "follow the beaten paths," for Charlie's death was not "the end of such depredations."

The loss of Lorenzo's uninsured building and stock, and more importantly, the death of J. L.'s beloved brother, shattered what was left of the Hubbells' seeming invulnerability to misfortune.

By November 1919, Lorenzo was worried about his father. As he wrote to Ed Thacker, J. L. had gone into a "spell," which scared Lorenzo because the old man was "so sick." In various letters over the next few months, Lorenzo poured out his grief and the still-hurtful blow of Charlie's murder. (There are no surviving letters from J. L. concerning Charlie's death.) The flurry of letters to Lorenzo from Ganado—his sisters and his nephews and niece, in particular—indicate a pulling together of the family.

In her ten-year-old's scrawl, La Charles sent him birthday greetings and invited him for Easter, as they had not seen him in 1919. She reported on the Airedale puppies, the three piglets, and little Roman's tonsillectomy. In another birthday letter to Lorenzo, Roman's son John wrote about his duck hunting trip, saying, "I guess you know how many ducks we killed. There are six pens going in this room and five of the letters are going to you."

On June 9, 1920, Lorenzo wrote Barbara, "I certainly appreciate the love that you all have for me, whether I deserve it or not. I am not good, but I try." The same day, to his cousin Anita, he wrote that he classified himself as the family's black sheep and bemoaned his lack of courage, spirit, or responsibility to be efficient.

His opinion of himself does not seem to have been widely shared, however. George Hubbell, manager of the Black Mountain store, and his wife Madge, a likable and warm couple, treasured him. Their store orders to him frequently included endearments like,

> we are happy and thinking of you continually and pray that we will always merit the love you have given us. Some people, Lorenzo, think only of themselves [a probable reference to Roman]. It is too bad.

Family and Financial Ebb and Flow

Though J. L. had borrowed fifteen thousand dollars from Chee Dodge in March 1920, a financial crisis in August and September of that year caused Lorenzo (at Oraibi) to write to Adela. Saying that the family needed to get out of the "nervous stage," he continued that they must "slave and save for a couple years...[to] get our heads out of water." This crisis passed more authority from J. L. to Lorenzo, and slowly, Lorenzo moved into his father's role as the family's financial head.

Despite these periodic problems, Lorenzo financed Adela's vacation, paid her son Hubbell's military academy tuition, and encouraged his brother-in-law Forrest to come into business with him at a shop Lorenzo planned to open in Long Beach, California. Lorenzo, always considerate, wanted his father's approval before Forrest left Ganado. J. L. agreed and told Lorenzo to get a replacement for Forrest "right away" so the two men could gear up and purchase Navajo blankets to stock the new venture. By the spring of 1921, Forrest was operating the Arizona Navajo Indian Rug Co. in partnership with Lorenzo at Long Beach. Lorenzo commented in a letter to his father that having "no one over him [Forrest] there should bring him out."

Lorenzo's Hollywood operation represented at exhibit space.

During this difficult financial time, Adela thought her son Miles should return to Ganado and attend the mission's "high school for white children." She reported feeling "lazy," which was a problem, as they had lost their non-Indian cook at Ganado because of a fight. She felt, however, that they didn't "need a cook. I want to get busy, I cannot lay around.... I want to do my best in cutting down expenses." As early as 1914, correspondence mentioned she had "erysipelas [sic]," an acute skin infection. While indications are that she received the same type of family affection as had been given her mother, Adela seems to have lacked Lina's determination. The one exception to this generality involved her son. Forrest had sent the six-year-old on the train alone to Wichita, Kansas, where he would be attending school with the Parker children. He pinned a twenty dollar bill to the boy's shirt and admonished him "to stay close to the conductor." Adela threatened Forrest that "if anything happens to that boy, don't ever turn your back on me."

After Alma's death in 1918, Roman's family helped him care for his two small children. Gallup resident Clifton Farrar (C. N. Cotton's bookkeeper between 1920 and 1930) described Roman as a playboy who spent only brief periods at the Ganado store. Farrar had moved to

Gallup in March 1920 and made Roman's acquaintance at the city's Harvey House, a "hangout...for the ne'er-do-well, and the people that had a little political [pull]." Farrar said he went with Roman to old Fort Wingate for a party and Roman got involved in a big poker game in the officer's quarters. Nonetheless, Farrar thought that Roman was a fine person.

By July 1921, Roman had married Dorothy Smith, who had arrived from the East the year before to teach the half-dozen or so grandchildren, cousins, and nephews at the Ganado home. When she came to Ganado, two young Hotevilla women, Daisy and Elizabeth, were helping at the house; Edwardo took care of the gardening; and Loco cooked. Shortly after his marriage, Roman wrote to Forrest that he "was sure a lucky chap to be able to find Dorothy" (which over time proved to be an understatement). J. L. is said to have commented that he knew as soon as Dorothy stepped off the train in Gallup that Roman was "a goner."

Following their honeymoon, Roman wrote to Lorenzo; his letter, which fairly rang with self-satisfaction and importance, described the newlyweds' Mexico honeymoon. During part of trip, they met some wealthy Mexicans who in turn introduced them to Nuevo Leon's governor. Unfortunately, Roman, who counted on the Hubbell name and the doors it opened, lacked his father's ability to combine social contacts with business opportunity.

Dorothy, who was given "Lady" as a family nickname, was the source of many intimate recollections of J. L. and his family after Charlie's death (a death she said the family did not discuss in her presence). She described the elderly J. L., then in his sixties, as tall as her own five foot-six inches, chubby, and broad-shouldered, a strong man who dressed in dark clothes and always wore a necktie.

She also characterized him as being very gallant, and recalled his saying things to her such as, "Daughter-in-law, the day's brighter since you came in the room." Dorothy commented that her father-in-law could get Indian business through his gift of relationships, though he did not conserve money. She also admired him "as a very great reader," and one who never used slang. When a guest once said that she felt "lousy," J. L. thought she meant that she had lice. His conversation was often peppered with Spanish phrases, quotations from Keats to Shakespeare, and Bible verses. (She said that one of his often-used terms was "mollycoddle," by which he meant someone who did not behave or use good judgment.)

J. L. seems to have bloomed during a 1921 visit to Pancho Villa in Old Mexico. According to the *Gallup Independent* (December 29, 1921), J. L., who was by then sixty-eight, reported that Pancho Villa seemed to be a violent character, regardless of how his activities had been modulated by Democratic newspaper editors. While in Mexico, the old trader cast his entrepreneurial eye over the Mexican scene, and thought fortunes could be made in sheep or cattle if the animals could be kept until marketed. He was also quoted as saying that mining "insures the surest return [because nobody] can make off with your mine."

J. L.'s trip seems to have been precipitated by what he perceived to be the exhaustion of untrammeled opportunity in Indian country— figuratively, no more sheep to shear. The new posts that speckled its landscape and borders brought increasing competition for Navajo products among the traders.

As a tumbleweed is blown by the reservation winds, the hub of successful Hubbell family economic activity was shifting to trading ventures west of Ganado, ventures that were loosely affiliated with J. L. and dominated by Lorenzo.

Finally "Up Against It"

For Lorenzo, the year 1922 looked good. On June 30, 1922, Lorenzo painted a rosy picture of his financial situation when he tried to wangle a $50,000 line of credit from the First National Bank of Albuquerque: Assets $73,133.32, including cash; $30,000 in merchandise of rugs, skins, hides, baskets, plaques, pawn; Liberty Bonds and War Stamps, $4,525; accounts receivable (all good) $10,696.21 and "my slow" ones, $3,000; building, $15,000. His notes were all "taken up" (which probably meant paid), and he owed only $2,381.51. His personal life was looking up as well-Lorenzo married a much younger woman in 1922. There were no children born to his late marriage and it was later annulled.

In an apparent indication of the state of things in Ganado, Lorenzo

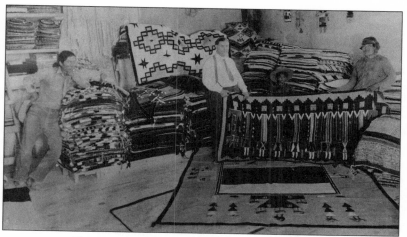

The rug room of Lorenzo's post at Oraibi; the Hopi Reservation was surrounded by Navajo country.

wrote to Roman on September 21, 1922, that he would "go through [Oraibi's] stock and see if they could spare goods." On September 27, his father asked Lorenzo "if he could spare any money." This letter was followed by another that arrived a couple of days later:

> I hope you will have the money by the first if possible but if there is none I would not worry about it. I certainly am up against it [but] it is better for me to be than all.

The family played Lorenzo's heartstrings much as Elias used to play the violin in the evening at Ganado: so long and hard that the strings and bow finally broke. An April 18, 1923, letter from J. L. to Lorenzo was uncomfortable and apologetic in tone.

> I...write you this letter in regard to something that I do not like to do but Henry [Chee] Dodge wants his interest and I do not blame him, it is $1,050 Dollars. Send him a check direct to St. Michaels.

The next day, his father wrote to Lorenzo again, mentioning the money already due Lorenzo from the family. In regards to Dodge, If Lorenzo could not pay him, J. L. said, "we will have to do something else, I do not like to make anyone promises for I have failed in every one."

251

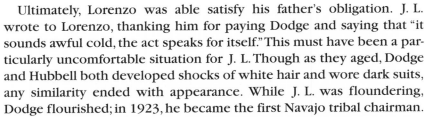
Ultimately, Lorenzo was able satisfy his father's obligation. J. L. wrote to Lorenzo, thanking him for paying Dodge and saying that "it sounds awful cold, the act speaks for itself." This must have been a particularly uncomfortable situation for J. L. Though as they aged, Dodge and Hubbell both developed shocks of white hair and wore dark suits, any similarity ended with appearance. While J. L. was floundering, Dodge flourished; in 1923, he became the first Navajo tribal chairman.

J. L., long the master of the grand gesture, is reported to have given Tom Dodge, Chee's son, a magnificent buffalo robe when Tom visited the trader at Ganado. Tom was directed to give the robe "to your father with my compliments, and tell him I still think of him." Chee Dodge was no slouch at making grand gestures himself. Once, according to Dr. Clarence Salsbury (J. L.'s last physician), Dodge kicked off a fundraising drive to buy an x-ray machine for Sage Memorial Hospital (part of the Presbyterian Mission at Ganado) with a five hundred dollar donation. On another occasion, when Dodge's grandson was in for a complete physical, Dodge told the doctor to "order five hundred dollars' worth of whatever equipment I needed, and send him the bill."

In April 1922, J. L. found a buyer for the Black Mountain post, which he was offering for sale at a price of seventy-five hundred dollars. By summer's end, the old trader was ill again. On August 22, 1923, Lorenzo reported to Ed Thacker that he had traveled to Gallup to see "my father who was dangerously ill...[but is] now recovering." (Six weeks later, Thacker himself died of heart failure while dipping Lorenzo's sheep at Weepo Springs—another grievous loss for Lorenzo.)

By 1924, Lorenzo was being increasingly squeezed between J. L. and Roman. J. L. pushed the sheep business—selling sixty-five hundred lambs to pay his taxes, and not losing as much as "earlier reported." He also wrote at length to Lorenzo about hard economic times in Gallup. In a June 1924 letter, Roman insisted that he was on the verge of a "big season" in sheep if Lorenzo could invest twenty-five thousand dollars, or invest five thousand dollars to buy wool. After ten days had passed, Roman followed up with a letter complaining that he had not heard from Lorenzo; he also expressed the hope that his brother was going to take care of him, as often Ganado was "out of groceries and nickel stuff."

Though money was being eaten up like free crackerjacks in the bullpen, Lorenzo ignored J. L.'s advice and purchased a wholesale house in Winslow, Arizona. To manage it, he hired "Dad" Hibbens. Hibbens, as Lorenzo wrote to his father in December 1924, was "a crank on having things right, the most particular man I have seen with books." Shortly thereafter, Lorenzo packed Hibbens off to a Los Angeles Shriners Convention with money, a white flannel suit, a red fez, silver beads, and silver bracelets. The relationship between Lorenzo and the older man grew; Hibbens was a man with whom Lorenzo took one of his two vacations in twenty-five years, a man Forrest could not work with, and probably most significantly, a man who gave Lorenzo fatherly attention.

By the summer of 1925, the tone of Lorenzo's letters is a curious mix of family love, disappointment, hurt, tentative advice, and preliminary limit-setting. In late July, Lorenzo wrote to a friend that his father had spent had the night with him, but "not long enough to take up anything." According to Lorenzo, J. L. looked well and seemed enthusiastic about various business prospects.

On March 6, 1926, Lorenzo, whose heart was as big as his forty-four-inch waist, wrote his father two more checks for five hundred dollars each, bringing the total owed by J. L. to his son to four thousand dollars. These loans were to be paid back by the end of wool season, Lorenzo said, and shared his philosophy with his father:

> I have a growing business...that can fall away at any time, if I mismanage; I am in fine shape now, but that is when a man must be careful, I never was full of confidence, as I believe that to succeed you must do right and work every day, and take your future seriously.

By May 14, 1926, the son was advising the old trader not to contract for lambs unless he got eleven cents or better per pound; and even then, he was to write to Lorenzo before closing any deals.

On May 30, 1926, J. L. seemed to be acknowledging Lorenzo as the family head when he wrote another request for money in his sprawling hand: "Dear Son: If you send the money [$3,300] to buy the auto I'll finish up in good shape." The old trader signed the letter to Lorenzo "your loving son, J. L. Hubbell." Lorenzo, who obviously noticed his father's closing declaration, sent J. L. the funds he had requested, along with a letter. Lorenzo addressed his letter to "Dear Father," included several references in the letter to J. L. as "Papa," and ended with "your son" and an instruction to READ AND DESTROY. Beneath the ignored instruction, in a peevish gesture, J. L. scratched a note "to [sic] many irons in the fire."

Chapter Sixteen
The Old Blankets Are Passing Away

THE WORDS that J. L. wrote in his 1902 catalogue about Navajo textiles, "The old blankets are passing away in the nature of things," are also a fitting epitaph for the trader's last years.

A Family Sketch

Lorenzo painted a particularly rosy picture of the Hubbells in 1927 when he wrote a friend in February that

> father is well but as usual is a very busy man, he has several mail contracts, the principal one is from Gallup to Shiprock, N.M., he is on the job to see them start in the morning and at the Post office when they come in the evening, he is well, better than he has been for years.

Lorenzo went on to note that Roman was in charge of the Ganado trading ranch, which had been improved with the addition of running water and baths.

An elderly J. L. at his Gallup post-warehouse.

Except for his removal of the "old stake house" (probably the Leonard Building), Roman had improved the area considerably— Ganado looked beautiful, Lorenzo noted. His sister Barbara had remarried, and (following the closing of the Long Beach business) Adela and Forrest were in Winslow managing his (Lorenzo's) wholesale house, "selling merchandise and curios." His nephew Hubbell was attending the University of Southern California in Los Angeles and Miles was in high school in Winslow.

There was a flurry of correspondence between Oraibi and Winslow after Lorenzo's February 1927 letter. Forrest asked Lorenzo for advice on Roman's request for three thousand pounds of flour in addition to one thousand pounds of oats, two hundred pounds of sugar, one hundred pounds of ground coffee, and other items. In return, Roman would send some large rugs to Winslow as payment on Ganado's warehouse bill. Forrest declined to fill Roman's order "until I hear from you [Lorenzo] to do so." Piles of unsold Navajo blankets, more than fifteen hundred textiles, already took up space in Lorenzo's Winslow warehouse. On March 3, 1927, Lorenzo wrote Forrest

> Conditions are such that I am very glad you wrote Roman as you did. I am unable to carry the load, and if it keeps up I rather think I will have to cut out even the good accounts, but that are slow to pay. If I remember rightly Roman had already drawn what the blankets would come to.

Financial pressures mounted; six weeks later, in April, he wrote Forrest that he had enclosed a check for three thousand dollars. In the letter, he fretted "how much more do you [Forrest] need, my goodness it is getting beyond my capacity."

Lorenzo's letters to his father took a more gentle tone. He wrote that he had been busy, "though I should not have neglected writing you." Business had been slow, though not desperate, he explained, and "it takes considerable financiaring [sic] to keep my business up. I have a lot of Navajo rugs, enough to supply the whole country." If he could sell them, all would be well. Lorenzo said that Barbara and her new husband had visited him briefly, and reminded his father that he had promised to visit Oraibi. "I hope you have not changed your mind and that you will soon do so."

On May 18, 1927, as if underscoring the old trader's diminishing powers, the Gallup store's bookkeeper reported—probably to Lorenzo at the Ganado trading ranch—that Mr. Hubbell had sold a blanket, one "C. N. C. would not take...[even] for $17.50," for a quantity of candy, but did not recollect the name of the company he sold it to. On August 1, 1927, another twenty-five thousand dollars had to be borrowed from Chee Dodge.

That same year, competition came to Ganado when Albert H. Lee (a descendant of John D. Lee) opened the Ganado Trading Post. As George Hubbell, manager of the Piñon store and a man rarely given to advice, observed in a letter to Lorenzo, it was "too bad about the competition Ganado will have to buck....The Indians like Ganado but to hold them, their sistem [sic] must be changed."

In the 1927 to 1928 outgoing Hubbell correspondence file, there is an undated letter to Roman written by someone for J. L. To it was attached a note for five thousand dollars in favor of Chee Dodge, dated July 14, 1927, due July 14, 1928. The old trader boasted that this was the first Dodge note paid in full, which contradicts the beliefs of some Navajo interviewees, who thought that the Hubbells never repaid the money J. L. borrowed from Chee. (Even Burbank, miles away and years removed from the reservation scene, heard a rumor that "Chee Dodge, the Navajo, owns the Hubbell store and all its contents at Ganado.")

By the late 1920s, J. L.'s correspondence was reduced to a few brief letters lacking in wit and solely focused on money. Often written by another in a grade-school-like hand, only a few of these letters carry J. L.'s signature. Though he did not write as he once did, J. L. maintained close personal relationships, such as the one with Cotton. Cotton's bookkeeper, Clifton Farrar, described J. L. as an educated and soft-spoken "old gent" who was articulate in both English and Spanish. He recalled that the two always visited first, then did business. Cotton supplied J. L. with

> any merchandise he wanted...unlimited credit. He [Cotton] thought the world and all of old Hubbell... [He would] get mad at him and cuss him out, and say "I'm not going to have him another sack of flour till he pays his bill." That afternoon the old man would come around, have some sob story. "Well, this is your last load now." [Cotton would say] That's the way it went for years.

Farrar recalled J. L.'s getting big freighting checks when he contracted for the Farmington-Gallup and Gallup-Ganado mail runs. J. L. was "foxy," the bookkeeper said; he would buy cheap apples, ship them parcel post to Ganado, then dump the apples in the arroyo. He made his "money on postage and on parcels hauling the freight." (Apparently, the freight charges for weight and distance carried exceeded the value of certain items shipped; nonetheless, it is hard to believe that J. L. would condone destroying produce.) When a check came in, J. L. would give Cotton only two-thirds of it "cause he'd have to have a little of it, he'd say, for the other fellows."

Herman W. Atkins, an attorney who arrived in Gallup in 1923 and represented both Cotton and Hubbell, characterized J. L. as a gentleman, a non-aggressive man, who entertained lavishly at Ganado, though he was not wealthy. Atkins noted that Hubbell "always owed Mr. Cotton...a lot of money... [a] lot of people when they get old, do that." Atkins frequently attributed Hubbell's lack of affluence to his "getting up in years" and recollected Dr. Salsbury's comment that late in his life, Hubbell had lost eighty thousand dollars in wool one season. In fact, the attorney said, neither J. L. nor Roman was a good businessman.

Another slant on J. L.'s financial situation comes from his grandson Hubbell Parker, who described the early trading post's barter-trading style as reflective of the "personalities who ran the store." His grandfather,

Cotton in 1927 with Barbara Seymour, his daughter.

258

1929 photo of Hubbell

always paternalistic, "couldn't continue that way," and yet, Parker said, J. L. thought that "those Indians must have their income protected and he would run the risk of it and...the wool market would drop."

Bert Coddington's father, who came to Gallup in 1893 to run the Home Ranch Stables, thought that Hubbell "was such a fine fellow." Bert remembered feeling awed on his first meeting Don Lorenzo. One day in the late 1920s, Coddington's father met the trader, who was dressed in an "old wool suit and threadbare old overcoat" on a snowy, windy Gallup street. J. L. is reported to have said to him, "Coddington, I'm broke." The same day, the story goes, some wealthy Easterners invited J. L. to join them for dinner that evening at El Navajo, Gallup's finest restaurant. The elder Coddington watched as, at the meal's conclusion, the Easterners either "reached for their glasses...and Don Lorenzo reached out and took the check," or "[t]hey walked off leaving Hubbell to pay the bill!" (The ending depended on who was telling the story.)

Illness

In 1928, J. L. suffered a stroke and was taken to the Gallup hospital, where the doctors "gave little hope he could live beyond a few days." He was given last rites by a Catholic priest and the family brought him back to Ganado, where "he wanted to die." It was apparently not quite his time. Though he never regained "full power of distinct speech," he recovered sufficiently to borrow another twenty-five thousand dollars from Chee Dodge in October; the following year, he made a five thousand dollar loan, again from Dodge.

J. L. seems to have been failing as 1929 progressed. On April 23, one of the California Hubbells wrote that the family "sincerely hope[s] he is muchly [sic] improved by now." On May 16, George Hubbell wrote to Lorenzo that he (George) saw Roman in Gallup for "a few minutes...[and he said that] Papa is getting along nicely." Days later, George's wife Madge reported to Lorenzo that Roman had said that "Papa is not good now, he is in bed most of the time."

Last family photo in front of the house with J. L. flanked by his daughter Barbara, his son Roman, Roman's wife Dorothy, and grandson John.

On May 31, 1929, Barbara wrote to "Lala," (her sister Adela):

> There isn't much I can tell you. Papa yesterday and today has been feeling pretty poor. But he just will not go to bed at night. Sleeps in the chair. Last night he was in bed only 2:15 minutes and then I just stood over him and made him stay and pretty soon he was asleep. He gets up before he is fully awake.

She also recounted a trip to Nazlini with Dorothy, "the first I had been away from the house in a month."

La Charles Eckel recollected that for "a year and a half...[J. L.] was so ill that he couldn't function, really, in the store or anyplace." He also displayed other eccentricities, such as insisting that Barbara, whom he called *mi hita* (my little daughter), bring him his hat so he could go to the "privy"—the new indoor bathroom next to his bedroom.

In what would be the last year of J. L.'s life, a veteran press photographer named Newcomer was visiting Polacca, the village at the bottom of First Mesa on the Hopi Reservation. Newcomer, who had been to Ganado and the Hopi mesas a few years earlier, recalled that while he was there, "an old Walpi village Snake Clan Chief, Harry Shupla," came to him. Shupla had heard that the old trader was sick, and wanted "to see him before he goes away, before he is *moki* [dead]." Newcomer agreed to take Shupla from Walpi, the old village on the mesa above Polacca, to Ganado; bad weather made the journey into a two-day trip. Once at Ganado, "the two old men sat and talked in the Hall. Don Lorenzo sat in a high back chair and the Snake Clan Chief beside him."

A young mission friend, Gene Haldeman, said that in his last year, J. L. "liked to lie on the north porch swing [and] spin yarns by the hour and I liked to listen to him." Occasionally, J. L. would lapse into Spanish, which Haldeman did not know. The old man also enjoyed basking in the sun on a bench near the trading post's entrance, telling stories to anyone who joined him. Many of the tales published in journals and magazines about J. L.'s life originated during this time, a time of mellow recollection and some embroidering of an already-adventurous life.

Infirm or not, Hubbell was still the master of his house. As Haldeman remembers, J. L. was

> a strong-willed old fellow. He said something was going to be done and it was done.... No matter what their ages, Roman and the rest of them, it was "Papa" this and "Papa that"...what he said...was done.

Colors and Shadows

From his porch swing, through a screen of vines and flowering Virginia creepers, J. L. could look toward Hubbell Hill, the family burial ground. Across the Pueblo Colorado Wash, that intermittent stream he had struggled to harness, he could see a swish of color—an elderly woman dressed in sun yellow and dark blue herding a flock of sheep—and hear the sheep baa-ing. Near the porch was a wall made from sandstone, its striations and colors providing a representation of Indian country. The roses and yucca that cast their shadows against the wall and the tall corn growing from mail-order seed in the adjacent field were botanical metaphors for the cultural mix Hubbell had created at Ganado. The flagstone pathways crossing the sandy yard echoed his stage and mail routes.

There on the porch, surrounded by all that he had found and all that he had made, J. L. could recreate the world in which he had traded and politicked. He could varnish his stories, and often did (he sometimes laughed so hard that he left them unfinished). J. L. probably spoke of smelling the soldiers' alcohol as he dropped it in the wash, feeling the cold Colorado when he swam it, hearing the soft shuffle of Hopi kachinas dancing, tasting the corn kneeldown bread, and seeing hundreds of Indians milling around Hubbell Hill during one of his chicken pulls.

By late 1929, J. L. was the last living link to Santiago and Juliana. Frank Hubbell's daughter Anita died in July 1929, followed by Frank himself in August. Juan Lorenzo Hubbell turned seventy-six in 1929. Elderly Navajos trace their age by calculating the number of years prior to or after a major event. In J. L.'s case, there would have been a number from which to choose: *All Quiet on the Western Front* had become a bestseller, the stock market crashed, the first musical Mickey Mouse films were shown, "Singing in the Rain" was a popular melody, and newspapers were full of Chicago's bloody St. Valentine's Day Massacre.

Sometime in late summer or fall of 1930, John Edwin Hogg, journalist and photographic illustrator from Alhambra, California, visited J. L. During the visit, the writer collected the material from which the *Touring Topics* biography was written. Hogg wrote to Hubbell's daughter Barbara on November 1, 1930, thanking her for her cooperation and "the characteristic Hubbell hospitality enjoyed by Mr. Toms" and himself during their "brief sojourn at Ganado." Hogg went on to say that he had found "a number of photos taken of Don Lorenzo... about 1890" by the late Dr. Frederick Monsen, and commented,

> In writing the biographical sketch of J. L., I have endeavored to portray him as the grand old man and virile character that he has

obviously been. I feel that I have done this in a way that will do credit to him, and all members of your wonderful family.

And indeed, the interview replicated J. L.'s voice. About a quarter of the published piece emphasized his youthful adventures; another quarter, trading; and about a sixth, politics. There was a mere paragraph about his current condition. The Hogg article, which came out in November 1930, after J. L.'s death, included the old trader's last words to the public. In it, he tied up the loose ends of his life's wool sack.

> The passing of the last few years have rested increasingly heavy upon me...[I am] old...in poor health...[with] no future. My life is all in the past. But, by los todos santos [by all the saints], what changes, and what times I've seen! You who are younger by many years will live to see even greater changes. We've only seen the beginning.

Dr. Clarence Salsbury of the Ganado mission hospital treated J. L. during the last year of his life, and recalled being distressed "to see how little we could do. The strains of an incredibly active life and the infirmities of age were too much." J. L.'s condition seems to have worsened in the fall, for in mid-September 1930, Lorenzo made two requests of Roman: "[a] list [of] all of my father's indebtedness... including the balance due me on September 1st, which is $46,129.00, not including any interest," as well as the leases held, real estate owned, inventory, and Indian accounts owed.

During these last days, J. L. was confined to what the family called the "Teddy Roosevelt" room, the middle room on the south side of the Ganado house. This single-windowed, dark, twelve-by-seventeen

J. L. nods in his wheelchair while his grandson John is flanked by his pet crow and monkey

263

foot space with steep sloped ceilings was cool in the summer and warm in the winter. From the wrought iron bed, J. L. could watch the light move across the room's burnt sienna walls; bright, white painted windowsills; and dark, nearly maroon, flooring. He could look up at the water-stained knotty pine ceiling boards, six to ten inches wide and aged like dark oak. He could also see the log beams, eighteen inches in diameter, carved from giant pines that had grown on the Fort Defiance Plateau. The sagging ceiling boards and the beams were Pueblo Colorado Wash-colored—russet, taupe, salmon, and gray—dimpled and shadowed by the hand tool that had been used to scrape off the bark.

During violent reservation sandstorms, the windowpanes vibrated and thin spirals of dust fell on the bedcovers. More often, it was quiet. Bird songs and voices were faint. This room, the place of his last illness, resonated with the texture of J. L.'s life, a life that he had spun and twisted as Navajo women spin and twist wool for their weavings. It was an interior reflection of his life's exterior composition; a palette of objects, colors, hues, textures, and sounds.

Lorenzo the Magnificent died in that middle bedroom of his trading ranch home on November 12, 1930, a few days short of his seventy-seventh birthday.

CHAPTER SEVENTEEN
By *Los Todos Santos*—By All the Saints

J. L. WOULD HAVE relished the headlines that his death generated, headlines that reduced his life to a few words and were as fanciful as a pictorial rug, as colorful as a Ganado Red.

"King Hubbell Dies at Post"

One of the accounts of J. L.'s funeral, written by Joseph Emerson Smith, was headlined "Greatest Patron of Navajo Artistry in Rug Weaving Dies: News of Lorenzo Hubbell's Death Causes Mourning in Studios of Painters in New York, Paris and Rome; Arizona Indians Beat Funeral Dirge," (*Denver Post*, November 23, 1930). In the article, the journalist constructed a fanciful view of Hubbell's death celebration, one that included word of his death being spread by drum beats from Ganado's skyline, and Navajos in the hundreds viewing the body of "the little god" and offering prayer chants for the safe passage of their friend.

Harriet Mayfield, in an article titled "Great Southwest Pioneer Passes On: Death of Lorenzo Hubbell, Last of the Dons of New Spain, Closes an Eventful and Picturesque Career," (*The Santa Fe Magazine*, January 1931), "revealed" Navajo customs to her readers. According to Ms. Mayfield, a leader's death required deliberations, which, once completed, were followed by

> the Indians filing *en masse* over to the Hubbell home, [where they] stood in dignified silence while their headman figuratively speaking, bestowed the cloak Don Lorenzo had worn to the shoulders of Roman.... They expected him to carry on in the same way his father had done, and that he might count on their support.

As his last public statements about his life were rife with myth, so he went out in myth. Mayfield reported a most touching tribute (if true) made by his Navajo friend Loco:

> You wear out your shoes, you buy another pair. When the food is all gone, you buy more. You gather melons, and more will grow on

the vine. You grind your corn and make bread, which you eat, and the next year you have plenty more corn. But my friend Lorenzo is gone, and none to take his place.

Regardless of the episode's literal truth, its essence was certainly accurate: this old trader, with his unique background, was not a renewable resource.

Lorenzo described his father's death and funeral in letters to the old trader's friends. To Dane Coolidge, he wrote that his father was buried on November 14, 1930, on Hubbell Hill "in the kind of weather he liked so well, sleet and snow; there he rests leaving a memoir of his kind deeds that will never be forgotten." To artist W. R. Leigh, Lorenzo wrote that his father was "now buried by mother's side on Hubbell Hill, his old Navajo friend, Many Horses is also buried there."

Ganado trader Albert H. Lee remembered that on the day of the funeral, roads to the trading ranch were "rutted and slippery from a cold, sleeting rain...and wind-driven snow" from the season's first storm. Dr. Salsbury, who served as a pallbearer, described sliding in the muddy clay: "You'd go ahead one foot and back about three, it seemed almost impossible" to get up to the top of Hubbell Hill. Even this final ceremony offered just the kind of challenge J. L. liked.

Condolence letters poured in. On November 16, 1930, once-wild nephew Tom Hubbell wrote his cousin Lorenzo that "Papa was the only father that I really remember having." In a letter to Barbara, Tom's wife Eleanor conveyed her sorrow and her knowledge that Barbara would "miss him, as you were so devoted and faithful during his long weary illness." George and Madge Hubbell at Piñon wrote to Lorenzo that Papa's passing was

> well, for his last year of life was full of agony and suffering.... He was a thoughtful, kind and generous friend, and I shall never forget the many times his generosity and thoughtfulness helped us.

Madge also offered Barbara comfort with the thought that

> you have nothing to regret how you have been a wonderful daughter to Papa in his last illness and I am glad not only for you

but for dear Papa that he is out of all his sufferings.

By way of condolence, Dr. Gary R. Burke of California sent a copy of the book *Trails Plowed Under* by Charles Russell, inscribed for "Auntie Bob, Roman and Mrs. Parker." Dr. Burke said in his cover letter (dated November 29, 1930) that

> Good men are scarce there.... The Lord probably had a lot of Navajos who needed a friend. Probably a doctor or two who needed to be helped around the reservation, and who needed a bit of advice on how to handle the government. Perhaps he needs a mail carrier who will always see the mail gets through no matter what the weather is.

Mora, who had been notified by wire of J. L.'s death, wrote that the telegram had shocked him as much as if he "had received one [about]...my own family." Expressing a sentiment shared by J. L., the artist said that "grief should be taken with but one philosophy—that same which allows us to reconcile to the bitter as we accept the joys of life."

A Life in Review

While geographically, J. L. Hubbell had moved less than two hundred miles from Pajarito to Ganado, socially, politically, and intellectually, he was oceans beyond his Pajarito origins and siblings. From his childhood in an Hispanic/Anglo milieu through Civil War days, to the Great Depression, J. L. had constructed a life for himself, his family, his friends, and even his customers.

He composed his own life by unraveling his father's endeavors, stringing them out, and re-plying them on the cultural loom of the Southwest. He chose an area even more rural and isolated than that of his birth, a country of little rain and intermittent streams, of few people who lived even farther apart on a high desert plateau. He wound his home, business, and political life around the warp of a one hundred sixty-acre homestead.

In this spartan physical and social landscape, the man born Juan Lorenzo Hubbell (and finally known as Lorenzo the Magnificent) achieved success, fame, and his own following. He accomplished this largely on the strength of his amiability, energy, honesty, and imagination. In J. L. Hubbell's life journey, the myths of the West's frontier lawmen, the fearless and honest man, the Indian and Mexican friend and defender, the self-made man, the art patron, the grassroots politician, and family progenitor add color and texture.

Hubbell prospected Indian country much as a goldminer would, looking for spots that lent themselves to other ventures. With tokens, Mexican silver dollars, groceries, and occasionally a little cash, he wrapped his Indian customers and laborers in a tight economic warp. The feudal nature of Hubbell's operations was coupled with his capitalistic belief in free enterprise and the self-made man. He spared no effort in developing a dependent community around him, both at Ganado and at his other trading posts.

Hubbell's interests went beyond developing a single trading ranch; he was an estate builder as early as 1879 when he juggled his time and attention between Ganado and St. Johns. In his fifty years of trading, he owned or had an interest in (sometimes for just a season and sometimes more than once) trading posts at Blue Canyon, Black Mountain, Cedar Springs, Chinle, Cornfields, Gallup, Ganado, Ganado Dam, Keams Canyon, Manuelito Camp (Navajo City), Mud Springs, Nazlini, and Oraibi, as well as the St. Johns Mercantile. One reference shows fleeting interests in Washington Pass in 1884 and Sin-let-za-he in 1886.

Historian Frank McNitt assessed J. L. as a man with feet of clay, but such an assessment ignores some of the trader's unique characteristics. Although he owned homes in Albuquerque and Gallup in later years, he preferred the isolation of Ganado, punctuated by the visitors he drew to him. He balanced conviviality and introspection, relishing involvement in the world of events and people on one hand, and of thoughts and feelings on the other.

When presented with difficult situations, J. L. sprang into action. Tough, poised, alert, decisive, and restless, he could be emotionally detached in all but family matters. He expected assertive, aggressive, and perhaps even daring behavior of his male relatives, while at the same time taking a paternalistic approach to all his family members. Unfortunately, his sense of noblesse oblige was not coupled with independent means. A quick starter and a slow, careless finisher, he sometimes formulated decisions without the skills to successfully execute them.

Competitive in the extreme, to the point of winning at all costs, J. L. was also able to freely give time, money, and resources to casual guests. In fact, he did this so freely that former visitors seemed to have no hesitation in turning to him for financial aid in their own bad times.

His home was his stage, allowing him to play out his personal dramas to an audience of family, friends, and guests. A nineteenth-century man, he fared well until Arizona sprang belatedly into statehood. Even without his fifty years of trade and numerous trading posts, J. L. would have been the dean of Southwest traders on personality alone.

When he wrote about pioneer mercantile operation in post-Civil War America, historian Irvin G. Wyllie was in effect describing Hubbell. In *The Self-Made Man in America,* Wyllie said that these ventures had been handled by "practical, strong willed men" of rugged character with "abundant opportunities, daring, coupled with rule-of-thumb methods." Once pioneering diminished in importance at the end of the century, the game became one of expansion and maintenance of complex business empires, and indeed, Wyllie's observations on this situation also ring true for Hubbell. "It was not easy to sustain and operate giant corporations on the basis of hunch and mistake...[in the] corporate age." Hubbell's nineteenth-century patrón and benevolent dictator approaches did not work as Arizona and the reservations moved into the twentieth century.

As he became older, he became increasingly rigid and inflexible. Even with this, he wore the laurel of foremost trader due both to timing—his business life spanned the trading post era—and to personality. A former employee, Robert E. Karigan, who later operated a trading post at Fort Defiance, characterized J. L. as "a brilliant, energetic, forceful man; always on his toes, shrewd, ambitious to extend his control over the whole Navajo country, able to drive a sharp bargain, but never dishonest or oppressive."

However, Hubbell could not shake the village-community tradition of his childhood. With the sole exception of C. N. Cotton, he held to the adage that family members can be trusted more than outsiders. Though he instilled respect in his children for his trading operations, he undermined the family success with his Old World views, his maintenance of control, and poor financial practices. His very different sons—Lorenzo the older, hardworking and self-directed; and Roman the younger, too much under his father's thumb, too much caught up in the Hubbell mystique—were unable to sustain a dynamic Hubbell dynasty.

His daughters lacked clout within the family. Unlike Navajo women who enjoyed head-of-the-household status and its accouterments of economic and social prestige, they were subservient to the men in their families. Their father often treated them like children even after they were grown.

While second- and third-generation Hubbells were drawn to Ganado, none made a living there. Of the five grandchildren, only one, Roman's son Monnie, seemed attuned to trade and Navajo culture; however, he died during World War II.

The willy-nilly growth of the family's enterprises multiplied personal tensions in an already-difficult business setting. For those family members who stayed on at Ganado, Hubbell provided affection and attention. Those who lived elsewhere (whether through choice or need) received only sporadic and brief notice. J. L. saved his parental adoration not for Lorenzo, the oldest, but for Roman, so masculine and handsome, perhaps a reflection of J. L.'s view of himself.

Monnie

In his trader-centered world, he relied on the federal custodianship of the reservations to reduce competition, yet resented the government's dominance. For Indian and trader alike, the dependence on federal spending and regulation created problems as well as benefits. In his milieu, any debate about the ravaging of the Americas would have been unimaginable. Domination of nature—deforestation, building, water manipulation, farming—was his life theme. He considered the reservation as a land of adventure and romance, and was keen to harvest its resources. Wool, piñons, rugs, and pottery: Indian country's natural cornucopia spilled into his trading post.

In "helping" the Navajos develop massive flocks, he contributed to the degradation of the land; overgrazing transformed sheep herding into an extractive industry. Related to this was Hubbell's signature trade product, the Navajo textile, which served both as a cultural and individual mark. Herman Schweizer said Hubbell did more to stabilize and standardize the Navajo blanket industry than anyone else in the industry, and gave J. L. credit for being "the premier Indian trader."

Two geographic factors, land and water, enabled him to succeed at trading, defining success by longevity and number of trading posts. He welded together several not-quite-livelihoods—trade, curio sales, stage lines, farming, freighting, job agent—into one living.

Just as land in America went beyond being a symbol of national identity and became a commodity used to determine social status, economics, and political power, in the same manner, Hubbell took his mere one hundred sixty acres, and by the legal principle of usufructs (the right of enjoyment of another's property, in this case, livestock trails, wagon roads, irrigation ditches, and tourist routes), enlarged it to a Texas-size cattle ranch.

In the American West, the flow of water and the flow of power are one. Federal oversight of Indian country checked J. L.'s plans. He described the Ganado irrigation project as benefiting the Indians and only incidentally, himself. According to J. L., he "labored to interest the Indian office in the matter...[with] tacit understanding [that other than water sufficient to irrigate my 160 acres], I do not desire special privileges." But he did. Always, and on every level, he expected special privileges. Because of his longevity in Indian country and in the Southwest. Because he curried favors. Because he was J. L. Hubbell.

The Shadow Side

Indians have always symbolized that something was wrong with the American dream. Something was also wrong when J. L. fought the educational qualification act in Arizona so Hispanics would not be disenfranchised but never promoted Indian enfranchisement. Something was wrong when traders such as Hubbell were able to benefit from use of Indian reservation land without paying the tribe anything for that use. Something was wrong with certain of his trade practices: payment in tokens for goods and labor, buying blankets by the pound, collecting money for Fred Harvey Co., marking up inventory (sewing

271

needles sold singly for the cost of a package), and having poor Indian labor conditions. He underwrote his collections, and indeed, his reputation for hospitality, by paying low wages to his Indian laborers. (J. L.'s labor standards continue to haunt Navajo country a hundred or so years later.) And what an irony to have Chee Dodge save him from ruin and then become one of the Hubbells' most dogged creditors!

The chiaroscuro of his presence swirled across Indian country. As these dynamic and challenged Indian cultures confronted difficult times and refocused their worlds, his shadow fell across Indian life. The panoply of trader practices became so fine-tuned and oppressive that in 1973, four decades after Hubbell's death, the Federal Trade Commission issued a report damning these practices. While dollops of generosity and goodwill diluted their impact during J. L.'s lifetime, many of the objectionable practices had their genesis during his trading era and were refined and extended once transportation improved on the reservation and competition escalated.

Icons of a Life

His collections (textiles, basketry, ethnological articles of material culture, paintings, drawings, sculptures, photographs, books, and thousands of visitor letters) constitute a bulky guest book. Ever the gambler, Hubbell shook all of these individually, like dice, and threw them out on the dry, sandy floor of Pueblo Colorado Wash. This array represented a maplike biography—a sculptor in Paris, a weaver at Kinlichee, an artist in Hoboken, a writer in Berkeley, a postmaster general in Washington, a basketmaker at the bottom of the Grand Canyon, and a silversmith from Piñon.

Like icons of his life, the objects he collected hung on his walls and ceilings. These led his visionary son Roman and Roman's wife Dorothy, as well as former acquaintances, to think of his collection and post as permanent memorials to him and to the trading era.

Navajo interviewees spoke of non-Indian visitors looking at the material J. L. collected. For the Indians, however, the emphasis was on the creation of art—the process, not the product of the activity, nor its preservation, display, and possession. In the interviews, the Navajos talked also about the process of Hubbell's life—his words, deeds, and relationships, not his material goods—and recognized him for the way he lived.

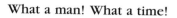

What a man! What a time!

Hózhǫ́ǫ́jíí na'shad. He traveled in beauty.

EPILOGUE

WHEN A NAVAJO WEAVING has advanced three-quarters of its length, the warp becomes exceedingly tight and the weaver is forced to use a variety of skinny tools (such as umbrella ribs) to thread loose yarn into the piece. Likewise, J. L. Hubbell's heirs resorted to various strategies as their trading world narrowed.

Settling the Estate

Attorney Atkins did not remember Hubbell's estate as being difficult to settle because "he [J. L.] didn't have too much, as he didn't seem to care too much about money, he just liked to operate." Before his death, J. L. had turned over all of his property and business to his four children under the Bulk Sales Act, which meant the business would continue operation under the name "J. L. Hubbell Trading Post Inc."

At the end of November 1930, Lorenzo assured a Gallup creditor that he had not bought out his father's Ganado store.

> [Business will be] conducted under my managership, with General Power of Attorney, given to me by Mrs. Parker, Mrs. Goodman, and Roman Hubbell. No member of this new firm takes on any personal liability...[but] will...see that no creditors take a loss.

Lorenzo started off 1931 by instructing Roman, through Forrest, to add ten per cent interest to all charge accounts (these amounted to $46,318.08) and call it an "overhead charge." Though trade dropped off during Roman's absences, Lorenzo was able to deposit monies to the credit of J. L. Hubbell Trading Post; in April 1931, for example, he made a $10,000 deposit. In mid-summer, Lorenzo, his trading skills to the wheel, wrote Roman about various business deals and reminded him that "Work and Economy is [sic] what we must adhere to."

And the family did. As already mentioned, Hubbell descendants were involved in a string of trading posts in addition to those at Oraibi and Ganado; there were other business ventures as well. There were good years and bad years in wool, lambs, piñons, and textiles, and there was a great deal of competition in these commodities. Debt levels fluctuated; some represented the usual debts involved in a trading-oriented business and some carried over from J. L.'s time. After much struggle, J. L.'s heirs finally paid off the debt to Dodge's heirs.

Regardless, Lorenzo traded and traded with a single-mindedness unknown to both his father and his brother. While Roman's life could be compared to a colorful multi-strand Zuni fetish necklace (car salesman, movie picture producer and consultant, tour-resort operator, ersatz trader, dabbler in Navajo life, and consultant to anthropologists), Lorenzo's would be more akin to a single strand of the flat brown and white shell beads known as heishi. Phillip Hubbell considered his uncle Lorenzo to be a natural-born trader and Roman, an attractive, quixotic man with none of his brother's business acumen.

As the last-born and locked between his father and brother, two consummate traders, Roman played a supporting actor's role in the Hubbell trading drama (though not in the ultimate disposition of the Ganado trading ranch). David M. Brugge, one of the first curators at Hubbell Trading Post National Historic site, said both brothers appreciated the intricacies of Navajo culture more than their father, and that Roman appeared to be a romantic figure caught between two cultures.

The years of trading drained Lorenzo physically as well as financially. In 1939, in a letter regarding Lorenzo's medical tests, his doctor warned him about his kidneys and heart. The doctor recommended that Lorenzo discontinue his "native work...live in a low altitude in a warm... climate, under proper care." His trading post days numbered, Lorenzo made his will shortly thereafter, naming Forrest M. Parker as his administrator and leaving his interest in the Ganado post to his sisters. The will also offers

Lorenzo and Roman at a 1933 conference in Fort Defiance.

evidence that Lorenzo followed his father's practice of running high accounts-receivable with Indian customers, as he left forty thousand dollars in uncollectible accounts on his death in 1942.

After Lorenzo's death, Roman and Barbara petitioned the court to remove Forrest as executor of their brother's estate. Their litany against Forrest included charges that he had sold assets without their knowledge, failed to pay La Charles Eckel or Dorothy Hubbell for inventory work or Roman for his work as New Mexico ancillary administrator, neglected to communicate with post managers while he spent two months in Phoenix, and paid his wife Adela for Winslow office duties for which she had no qualifications. The most damning charges, the ones that summed up Forrest's long-term association with Hubbell enterprises, was the complainants' statement that they had

> known Mr. Parker for more than 30 years, he had never made a success in any business...Mr. Parker is habitually intoxicated...[They] knew and at least four other disinterested parties heard Lorenzo Hubbell say that he intended changing the executor...when Mr. Lorenzo Hubbell was very ill in bed, he received a letter from Mr. Parker begging him to send $250...Lorenzo said he was tired of supporting Forrest Parker and refused to send the money.

Dorothy and Roman in front of the barn doors
at the trading ranch, circa 1935.

With this petition, decades of family tension exploded.

In the years between Lorenzo's death and Roman's, other managers floated in and out of Ganado as Roman and his wife Dorothy moved about like a nervous sheep in search of good range. The couple worked first at Winslow, then Marble Canyon, then returned to Ganado. In the end, Roman's strengths—managing the ranch as farm property and turning his father's guests into paying tourists—were not enough, and the corporation filed bankruptcy. However, the Hubbells were as good as J. L.'s word and eventually paid all of the creditors. When the legal and financial dust had settled, a single Hubbell asset remained: the trading ranch at Ganado.

Throughout their lives, Dorothy and Roman had often visited the Wetherills in Kayenta. When they visited after the Wetherills' demise, they found that all the property, including the family's significant ethnographic collection, was gone and questions about its whereabouts unanswered. Like an exposed warp in a Navajo rug, this troubled Roman and Dorothy. In 1957, Dorothy talked to a National Park Service employee passing through Ganado about ways to preserve the Hubbell trading ranch intact. Roman, a visionary like his father, also discussed this issue with Dr. Harold S. Colton, director of the Museum of Northern Arizona and an old friend of J. L.'s, and with Dr. Edward B. Danson, the museum's assistant director. In September 1957, Danson wrote to Arizona's Congressional delegation, Representative Stewart Udall and Senators Carl Hayden and Barry Goldwater, about getting the Hubbell Trading Post into the National Park Service system.

It is doubtful that Lorenzo, who was almost entirely business-oriented, could have imagined the trading ranch as a viable part of the National Park Service. To their lasting credit, Roman and Dorothy were the ones to make the leap from business to history.

Roman died on October 14, 1957, the day after his sixty-sixth birthday. He made his will literally on his death bed; family attorney Atkins came out from Gallup with his wife, who typed the will in the trading post office. Roman's signature is the awkward scrawl of a dying man.

As a weaver struggles to finish the last few inches of her rug, Roman's widow, ex-school teacher Dorothy, mustered her skills with a tenacity that her father-in-law would have respected. This gracious, bright woman kept the Hubbell Trading Post at Ganado intact for a decade, until the 89th Congress approved the purchase of the property and designated it as a national historic site (a story in itself). Until her death in 1993, Dorothy Hubbell shared her recollections of her father-in-law and of the Hubbell Trading Post operation from the 1920s to 1967 with all researchers.

Today, the National Park Service operates the Hubbell Trading Post National Historic Site with rangers, interpreters, and curators. The Southwest Parks and Monuments Association, a non-profit organization that supports scores of National Park Service units in the region, operates the still-functioning trading post itself, with the help of a resident trader, now Bill Malone. Store clerks are all local Navajos, people for whom the post has always been a part of life. The rhythm of the Hubbell post is maintained: the bullpen shelves are well-stocked, the rug room is piled high with rugs. The parking lot is filled with buses and vehicles, tourists and Indians.

The operation of Hubbell Trading Post National Historic Site, with its emphasis on the process of buying arts and crafts from the Indian community (it no longer buys wool), continues to be in sync with one of J. L.'s goals. According to Lorenzo in a 1940 *Desert* magazine interview, his father "never wanted money for money's sake. Rather his idea was...to bring about the preservation of native arts and crafts."

The trading post commemorates not only the trading era in the Southwest, but also its founder and his family, Brahmins of Southwest trading.

To paraphrase J. L., "What times it's seen."

APPENDICES

APPENDIX ONE

J. L. Hubbell Trading Posts, 1915: Manager List (annotated)

The outline for the Hubbell Papers (Colby/Special Collections, University of Arizona, Tucson) contains a complete list of the employees/managers at the five trading posts mentioned in the 1915 article in *Notables of the West* about J. L. Hubbell.

Cedar Springs Trading Post

1909
Claudio Romero
Jim C. Karigan

1909-1911
Charles Hubbell

1910
J. F. Alkire

1912-1915
S. Schwemberger (Sim or Simmy)

1912-1913
J. E. Owen

1912
Indelicio (Andy) Romero

1913
Harry W. Wetsel (perhaps H.C. Wetsel)

1918-1919
Charles Hubbell

Cornfields Trading Post (Perhaps owned as early as 1902)

1905-1908
Julius Neubert

1905
Antonio Armijo
Sam Day II
Thomas Edward (Ed) Thacker

1909-1911, 1913, 1916-1917

J. C. Karigan (could be the same as Jim C. Karigan)

1910

Paul Campbell

1913-1915

H. C. Wetsel (perhaps H. W. Wetsel)

1924

Youngblood

1928

Eugene V. Smith

Ganado

(Originally, Pueblo Colorado; later, J. L. Hubbell Trading Post)

1878, 1883

Charles Hubbell

1881

Hubbell (?)

1882-1885

J. L. Hubbell

1884, 1887

S. Pillsbury

1884-1885

September 23, 1884, Clinton N. Cotton bought half-interest from J. L. Hubbell; "bought" the remaining half interest June 22, 1885

1886-1897

C. N. Cotton

[Note: Colby lists J. L. Hubbell as clerk for 1888-1889 and 1892-1897]

1899, 1901-1906, 1908-1910

J. L. Hubbell

1912-1913

Roman Hubbell

1913

J. L. Hubbell

1913-1914
F. M. Parker

1915-1919
J. L. Hubbell, with F. M. Parker as manager

1920-31
Roman Hubbell
Followed by F. M. Parker, Ed Morris, Epimenio Armijo, A. A. Romero, Charles E. Rubi, H. W. (see note above) Wetsel, La Charles Eckel, Dora W. Balcomb, Bob and Betty Dillon

1955-1957
Roman Hubbell

1957-1967
Dorothy S. Hubbell

Keams Canyon Trading Post (According to Colby/UA Special Collections, purchased from Thomas V. Keam by Lorenzo Hubbell, Jr., on May 17, 1902; in author's opinion, purchased by J. L. Hubbell and run by family. See Colby for list of clerks.)

1902-1918
Lorenzo Hubbell, Jr.

August 20, 1918
Sold to Schmedding
(probably after the Hubbells used it to satisfy debt to Cotton)

Oraibi Trading Post (Established by William Volz, ca. 1897)

1905
Purchased by J. L. Hubbell

1908-1910
Antonio Armijo

1910
J. F. Alkire and Claudio Romero

1911-1916
Charles Hubbell

1916

Ed Thacker

Ben (?) A. Wetherill

1918

R. R. Mahan

Elias Armijo

Ed Morris

Sold to Lorenzo Hubbell, Jr.; managers as follows

1920

F. M. Parker

1922

Ed Thacker

1923

E. H. Armijo

1924-1940

Fletcher Corrigan

(See Colby list for clerks and post-1940 period for these trading posts and all other posts in Appendix Two.)

APPENDIX TWO

Hubbell Trading Business Enterprise Sites

Big Mountain, AZ (1935-1946)
Black Mountain, AZ (1914-1937)
Blue Canyon, AZ (1886-1887; 1928)
Canyon Diablo, AZ (1929-1932)
Cedar Springs, AZ (1909-1919, and later)
Chinle, AZ (1885-1888; about 1915-1917)
Cornfields, AZ (turn of century-1928)
Cow Springs, AZ (1935)
Dilcon, AZ (1935—ownership interests vague)
F. O. Natural Bridge (unknown)
Gallup, NM (1914-1943)
Ganado, AZ (1876 or 1878-present)
Ganado Dam, AZ (1912-1918)
Greasewood, AZ (1928-1936)
Hollywood, CA (1926-1928)
Keams Canyon, AZ (1902-1918)
Kinlichee/Red House, AZ (1934-1938)
Long Beach, CA (1921-1922)
Manuelito Camp/Navajo City, NM (1878/1880-1882)
Marble Canyon/Lee's Ferry, AZ (1929-1945)
Mud Springs/Hashtl'ish, AZ (about 1900-1902)
Na ah tee Canyon, AZ (1933-1949)
Nazlini, AZ (1915-1923)
Oraibi/Kykotsmovi, AZ (1905-1948)
Piñon, AZ (1916-1949)
Piñon Springs, NM (1916; 1920-21; 1925)
Polacca Cable Crossing, AZ (unknown)
St. Johns, AZ (1879-1887, multiple stores)
Sand Springs, AZ (1922-1945)
Sin Let Za He (1886-unknown)
Steamboat Canyon, AZ (1912-1915/1917)
Washington/Narbona Pass, AZ/NM (1884)
Winslow, AZ (1924-1953)

APPENDIX THREE

[The following three maps are from *Hubbell Trading Post National Historic Site: An Administrative History* by Albert Manchester and Ann Manchester, Southwest Cultural Resource Center, Professional Papers No. 46. Santa Fe, New Mexico, 1992.]

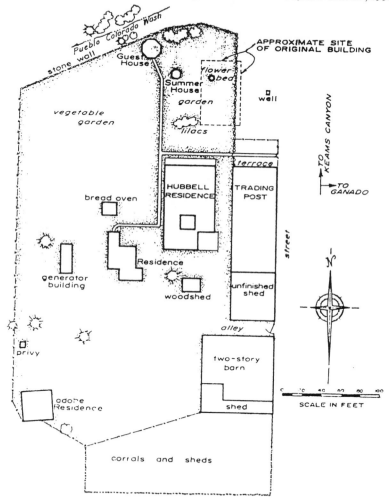

BUILDINGS & GROUNDS LAYOUT
J.L. HUBBELL TRADING POST
ARIZONA

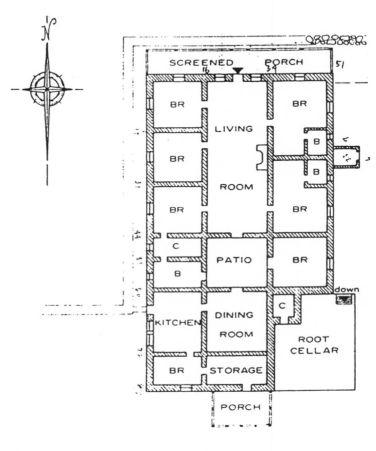

LEGEND

BR   BEDROOM

B   BATH

C   CLOSET

SCALE IN FEET

HUBBELL RESIDENCE

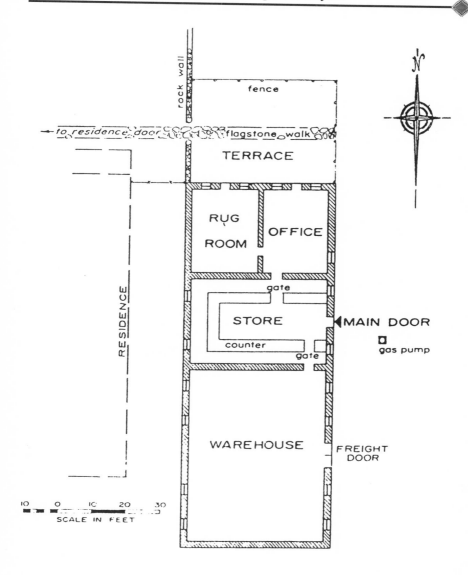

rock wall

fence

to residence door · flagstone walk

TERRACE

RUG ROOM

OFFICE

RESIDENCE

gate

STORE

counter

gate

MAIN DOOR

gas pump

WAREHOUSE

FREIGHT DOOR

10 0 10 20 30
SCALE IN FEET

N

J.L. HUBBELL TRADING POST

287

NOTES AND REFERENCES

This work is intended primarily for the general reader and secondarily for the researcher/specialist. Given the primary reader, and in the interests of space and aesthetics, I have chosen to use an informal notation style (one without superscripts in the text). References can be gleaned from the notes.

Those with an interest in a particular aspect of Hubbell's life will find references to further readings, and researchers can locate primary records, if they so desire, and from there isolate the specific information the researcher is interested in. For example, anyone interested in J. L.'s uncle, Charles M. Hubbell (who served with Kit Carson in the Navajo roundup), will learn that primary records concerning his service can be found in the McNitt Collection at the New Mexico State Archives.

The references referred to in the source notes are not a complete record of all the works and sources I consulted while conducting research for this book, however. In addition, I drew upon the numerous books, articles, and reports that I have read over the past thirty-plus years, and my family trips to Indian country, which began in the 1950s. My professional association on various levels with tribal governments, courts, legislative bodies, and Indian clients have also assisted me in the development of ideas expressed in this work.

The source of quotations not attributed in the text is referenced in the source notes which follow the annotated list of source abbreviations.

CNT

Liz Bauer, "Research for a Catalog of the Navajo Textiles of Hubbell Trading Post." (National Endowment for the Humanities, Grant No. GM-22317-84; July 4, 1987). This lucid 219-page manuscript and its approximately 100 pages of appendix by a former HTPNHS curator is the definitive source for Navajo textile material from the Hubbell Papers. It includes a narrative of correspondence and catalogues, drawings of rug designs and elements, and a chronology of the family emphasizing matters significant to Navajo textiles. It represents an exhaustive gleaning of the subject of textiles vis-a-vis the Hubbells.

H&F

Dr. Charles S. Peterson, "Homestead and Farm: A History of Farming the Hubbell Trading Post National Historic Site." (prepared for Southwest Parks and Monuments Association, Tucson, AZ, March 1986). This premium manuscript provides an important perspective on Hubbell's farm operation by setting it within the Southwest's farming tradition/experience. Peterson was the first researcher to make extensive use of the Navajo oral histories, and he took a revisionist view of the Hubbells' operation at the Ganado trading ranch (including Roman Hubbell's era).

HFP

Hubbell Family Papers. Located at the New Mexico Commission of Public Records, State Records Center and Archives, Santa Fe, New Mexico. Includes the Pajarito Grant

Claim No. 157. The Claimants' Petition (September 10, 1887) includes documents and title abstracts dating back to 1746. The papers are a valuable resource and provide a glimpse of both the early days of the Gutierrez family (those who examine these papers will note that the family name originally ended in "s" rather than "z") and the American era in New Mexico.

HP (sometimes referred to as HPAUL by other researchers)
Hubbell Papers. Located in Special Collections, University of Arizona Library, Tucson. These papers were deposited with Special Collections at the University of Arizona Library on July 1, 1971.

The processing of the papers was a Herculean task for the university's archival staff; the finding outline that resulted is itself 141 pages. Sorted into 573 archival boxes, the material is grouped into the following categories: Correspondence (Incoming, boxes 1 to 90, alphabetically arranged by originating correspondent; Outgoing/Intrapost, boxes 91 to 123, arranged chronologically; and Indian Letters); Vendor Files; Business Books and Records; Legal Matters; Banking Matters; Personal Materials; Post Office Materials; Sales Books; and Advertisements, Price Lists, and Catalogs. This mass of material spans the 1880s to 1967. (The University of Arizona Special Collections staff deserves recognition for their fine job.)

I did not examine each item in the collection; rather, I concentrated on the Outgoing/Intrapost and the Incoming correspondence. I also examined numerous other boxes at random.

For microfiche users, a reference to HP, Box 46, for example, indicates that the information comes from an of microfiche sheets. Each envelope contains several microfiche sheets marked consecutively—46(1), 46(2), and so forth. Each sheet holds 50 to 70 documents, depending on document size, and is organized both alphabetically and chronologically within that arrangement. As an example, correspondence from J. E. Hogg starts with the earliest date and ends with undated letters, if any. In the notes that follow, I have in some instances referenced both box number and microfiche sheet number; in other instances, I have not. However, the researcher would know that Hogg belongs in the Incoming Correspondence file and can use the HP inventory to locate specific boxes in which Hogg's letters are located.

While a good portion of the papers deal with the day-to-day, sometimes rather boring, affairs of various Hubbell enterprises long gone, or matters with which the trader was not personally connected during his lifetime, almost every box examined yielded a clue to his life. Almost the first outgoing letter is one from J. L. Hubbell and his then-partner C. N. Cotton; they wrote to a Mrs. H. C. Mason in October 1884, asking her to send bills for meals given to the mail carrier.

These papers are a goldmine of information for studies relating to almost any aspect of late-nineteenth to mid-twentieth century business and life in and near Indian country.

HUTR
Every National Park Service unit has a four-letter administrative abbreviation that is

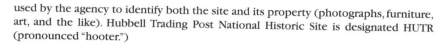

used by the agency to identify both the site and its property (photographs, furniture, art, and the like). Hubbell Trading Post National Historic Site is designated HUTR (pronounced "hooter.")

IT

Frank McNitt, *The Indian Trader* (Norman: University of Oklahoma Press, 1962). Among secondary sources, this is the only overview that is specific to the Southwest and examines the network of traders and their families. While McNitt's interviews with old trader families cannot be duplicated, it should be remembered that (at least in regard to Hubbell), some anecdotal information is presented as fact.

McN

The Frank McNitt Collection, New Mexico State Records Center and Archives, Santa Fe. Includes not only the material McNitt used in researching the aforementioned book and other of his works on Navajo history, but also his research for works-in-progress, one of which was a biography of J. L. Hubbell. Much of McNitt's research on the Hubbells in New Mexico was particularly helpful. Unfortunately, McNitt suffered a heart attack and died before he could begin drafting the biography. Given McNitt's stature as a scholar in the field of trader and Navajo history, the biography would have been an exceptional contribution to the literature, and I recognize and thank him for his phenomenal work.

Among the most helpful of McNitt's twenty-two boxes of research files are those covering National Archives records, Indian traders, Navajo historical material, Bosque Redondo, Don Lorenzo Hubbell I and II (see particularly boxes 18 and 19), and maps. The research file inventory is fifteen pages long, while that for his publications is fourteen pages in length. Here, when I refer to his published works, I include his full name; when I cite McN (the McNitt papers), please check boxes 18 and 19.

NOW

Press Reference Library, *Notables of the West: Being the Portraits and Biographies of Progressive Men of the West Who Have Helped in the Development and History of Making This Wonderful Country*, Western Edition (New York: International News Service, 1915), vol. 3, pp. 187 to 188 is a two-page biographical sketch of J. L. Hubbell, which was apparently prepared from information he provided when he was in both his political and trading prime, is a chatty account that, in most instances, tracks the documented details of his life.

OH

Some confusion exists in the individual interviews generally conducted between 1969 to 1972 which are listed in an undated document, six pages in length, titled "Interviews in HUTR Files" beginning with "#1 Ya Na Bah Winker" and ending with "#55 Joy B. Patterson." My copy I obtained in the late 1980s, so list may now be expanded. Some were made under various oral history projects like the Doris Duke Oral History Project and some were reprinted in professional journals. Please see the list. The ones used heavily in this work were taken primarily by David M. Brugge and

Roberto Tso.

HUTR also includes interviews by Frank McNitt of Hubbell family members and other non-Navajos which have made their way into the HUTR files. I refer to these interviews/ histories from this time period as the first set of interviews to differentiate them from other interviews done in the mid-1980s.

Within this amazing early interview/historical record are approximately fifty-five oral histories taken primarily from Navajos but also from a few of the Hubbells or Euro-Americans associated with the Hubbells. They include direct translations where appropriate and an unedited body of detail and information. Interviews with J. L.'s daughter-in-law, Dorothy S. Hubbell, dominate accounts by Euroamericans, both in length and substance. In the category of Navajo interviewees, LaCheenie Blacksheep's account stands out. Both interviewers and interviewees made a significant contribution to the understanding of the trading post era in the Southwest. The interviewees were elderly and most are now deceased.

Researchers should note that some topics are scattered throughout a number of interviews; a few interviews lack page numbers, dates, and/or birthdates; some were translated twice; and many are short. Therefore, I identify the interviewee as best I can and include a page reference if the subject is isolated in the interview or if it is in a long interview.

Of less importance are the mid-1980s interviews conducted with female and male Navajo weavers that were made as part of the Hubbell Rug Study. These interviews concentrated on who sold rugs to HTPNHS in the 1980s, thus historical information on the trading post era appears only sporadically in the accounts of the older weavers.

HTPNHS has a list for the first set of interviews (Interviews in HUTR); to my knowledge, there is no complete summary available or a list of the second set of interviews done in the mid-1980s. The Interviews in HUTR list indicates the name of the interviewee, often the date of birth, present residence, date of interview, number of tapes, and where the interview was published, if at all.

SR

Robert Utley, "Special Report on Hubbell Trading Post, Ganado, Arizona." (Santa Fe, New Mexico: National Park Service, Region Three, 1959). This report later appeared as "The Reservation Trader in Navajo History," *El Palacio* XVIII:1 (Spring 1961), pp. 5–27.

TT

J. L. Hubbell and John Edwin Hogg, "Fifty Years an Indian Trader," *Touring Topics* XXII (December 1930), pp. 24–51. In *Hubbell Trading Post National Historic Site* (Tucson, AZ: Southwest Parks and Monuments Association, 1993), author David M. Brugge said that J. L. Hubbell, knowing the end of his life was near, was selective in the facts he revealed; consistent with human nature in general, he also omitted "his sins and mistakes. If his memory was not perfect, the magazine article that J. E. Hogg was to write was even less so." Hogg, who in his letterhead described himself as a "journalist and photographic illustrator," said in a November 1, 1930, letter to Barbara Goodman, J. L.'s daughter (HP, Box 40) that in "writing the biographical sketch of Don Lorenzo, I have endeavored to portray him as the grand old man and virile character that he has obviously been. I feel that I have done this in a way that will do credit to him, and all the members of your wonderful family." While the overblown emphasis on and the obvious embellishment of J. L.'s Utah trip; his adventures while sheriff in St. Johns, Arizona; and the whiskey incident with the army may reflect Hogg's artistic license, visitors to Ganado in the late 1920s heard J. L. reel out similar tales. He often used the same turns of phrase as Hogg includes in the article. At any rate, Hubbell's matter-of-fact accounts of various aspects of Indian trading match more-or-less the biographical material he had earlier provided to the Press Reference Library.

WP

Working Papers, HTPNHS (sometimes referred as the Historical Files, though this category includes the oral histories referenced earlier). One list includes categories as diverse as "Louis Aiken" and "Domestic Water Supply." This random collection of photocopied, typed, or handwritten papers seems to have been assembled primarily from original documents that are rarely cited as to source or author. Though the collection includes a great deal of information that is also in the Hubbell Papers in Special Collections at the University of Arizona Library, it also includes material from a variety of other sources; these sources are not consistently identified.

This collection grows as researchers submit their working notes to HTPNHS. To the best of my knowledge, the collection is presently located in the library (the old root cellar) at HTPNHS rather than in the curatorial offices. For distinct subjects, this ersatz collection of research material provides the quickest access to the Hubbell Papers.

Throughout this work, I have not provided a source for every statement, since some of the text (Hispanic and Navajo history in the Southwest for instance) presents the very general information necessary to understand J. L.'s life and times. In those cases, I indicate good sources for further reading. In other areas, I draw upon my several decades of contacts and observations.

For source references, I state the page number and key words in their textual order (e.g., *mustered into the army*), and give a general source reference. If the same reference would be cited later in the same chapter, then I usually add the second group of key words in the opening key phrase, as well (see for example, *Spanish frontier...colonizer...Navajos pushed* in Chapter One). References to particular persons or places are located at the topic's first mention only (see Chee Dodge reference in Chapter One), as most of the references are repetitive.

PART ONE: JUAN LORENZO

For background on Hispanic and Anglo-American occupancy of the Southwest, see Howard R. Lamar, The Far Southwest 1546-1912, A Territorial History (New Haven, CT: Yale University Press 1966); Carey McWilliams, North from Mexico (New York: Monthly Review Press, 1961); and Jerry L. Williams, ed., New Mexico in Maps

(Albuquerque: University of New Mexico Press, 1986). These are indispensable sources on the history of New Mexico. For a treatment of Hispanic daily life, see Louann Jordan and St. George Cooke, El Rancho de las Golondrinas: Spanish Colonial Life in New Mexico (Santa Fe, NM: Colonial New Mexico Historical Foundation, 1977). I am particularly indebted to David M. Brugge for his comments on my initial (and much longer) discussion of Hubbell's ancestry and early years.

Chapter One
Eighty-Four Pairs of Ears

3 *Blood sprayed* OH #4, T'iis Yazhi (b. 1887, residing Burnsides, AZ), April and November 1971; OH #32, Amos Johnson (b. 1913, residing Ganado, AZ), June 1970. See further references in Martha Blue, *The Witchpurge of 1878: Oral and Documentary History in the Early Reservation Years* (Tsaile, AZ: Navajo Community College Press, 1988). Note the press name is now Diné College Press.

3 *Hombro* Navajo names are variously spelled in historic documents; this is sometimes spelled "Hombre."

3 *Navajo...managing conflict* Mark Bauer and Frank Morgan, "Navajo Conflict Resolution," *Diné Be'iina*, I:1, Spring 1987.

3 *Big House* Charles S. Peterson, "Big House at Ganado: New Mexican Influence in Northern Arizona," *The Journal of Arizona History* 30:1 (Spring 1989).

4 *Spanish frontier...colonizer...Navajos pushed* See general discussion in the short publication by Robert W. Young, *The Role of the Navajo in the Southwestern Drama* (Gallup, NM: Gallup Independent, 1968).

5 *Pajarito...Spanish legacy* HFP, transcript of the Pajarito Land Grant No. 157 proceedings (dated September 10, 1887, filed September 16, 1887) pp. 2,432-2,491. Signatures on this document represent a dozen descendants, including "Julianita [Juliana] Gutierrez," daughter of Clemente Gutierrez, who died in 1785 in possession of the Pajarito tract. Description of Juliana and information about James found at HTPNHS in interviews of Phillip Hubbell, son of J. L. Hubbell's younger brother, Felipe. The interview with Phillip Hubbell by Frank McNitt in Albuquerque on May 16,1973 is 23 pages (copy of it at HTPNHS OH #46 and two other interviews listed in HUTR list that apparently were done by others than McNitt and Brugge dated October 16, 1969, and November 12, 1971 which I do not have.) My reference to the Phillip Hubbell interview is solely to the McNitt interview. Also, see the L. Hubbell Parker interviews by McNitt of 38 pages May 12, 1973 and Brugge of 9 pages April 11, 1973 both at HUTR but no interview /OH number in list in my possession. Reference will be to McNitt interview Hubbell Parker or Brugge interview Hubbell Parker. For more family history, see Carol N. Callary," Political Biography of Frank A. Hubbell 1862-1929." Master's thesis, University of New Mexico, 1967).

5 *annulment of peonage* Based on Phillip Hubbell's interview, the Pajarito grant

proceedings, and New Mexico history.

6 *Hubbell was born* For a thorough extended-family chart, see HTPNHS curatorial offices; and for a shorter version, see front matter in this book. Also scan of Walter Hubbell, *History of the Hubbell Family Containing Genelogical Records of the Ancestors and Descendants of Richard Hubbell from A.D. 1086 to A.D. 1915,* 2nd ed. (New York, perhaps self-published, 1915).

7 *Spanish clash* See the Navajo version of this 1805 Spanish expedition in Campbell Grant, *Canyon de Chelly: Its People and Rock Art* (Tucson: University of Arizona Press, 1978), pp. 84–90. The Spanish-language report of this expedition is found translated by David M. Brugge in Frank McNitt, *Navajo Wars* (Albuquerque: University of New Mexico Press, 1972), pp. 431–433, which also has the Narbona quote. See also Young, pp. 4, 12, and 14. Don Lorenzo Gutierrez may have kept Navajo captives from the 1805 expedition; the last Spanish census listed three Gutierrez servants who could have been Indian captives.

7 *Slave trafficking* For more information on this complicated subject, see Lynn R. Bailey, *Indian Slave Trade in the Southwest: A Study of Slave-taking and the Traffic of Indian Captives* (Los Angeles: Westernlore Press, 1966) and David M. Brugge, *Navajos in the Catholic Church Records of New Mexico 1694–1875* (Tsaile, AZ: Navajo Community College Press, 1985). Between 1700 and 1870, New Mexico church records indicate that more than 1,600 Navajos were baptized (the individuals were referred to as slaves, *genizaros* or half breeds, *indios, coyotes,* or servants, though they were often baptized as captives.) In 1790, the Spanish census for San Ysidro de Pazarito, (later known as Pajarito) listed a Gutierrez widow with one male servant designated as a *coyote* and a female servant listed as Indian-Ute.

8 *patrón, persons of* Callary, discussion of *patrón* system in the Hubbell context, pp. 150–156.

8 *property statement* HFP, Pajarito Land Grant proceedings, pp. 2,469–2,470.

9 *yankee traders* Williams, pp. 102–104.

9 *mustered into the army* HFP and McN and particularly the government records, newspaper clippings and census documents for an overview of activities and whereabouts of J. L. parents, uncles, and siblings.

10 *Fort Defiance in 1851* McNitt, *Navajo Wars,* p. 195, and Will C. Barnes, *Arizona Place Names,* revised and enlarged by Byrd H. Granger (Tucson: University of Arizona Press, 1960), p. 10.

10 *pursuit of the raiders* J. Lee Correll, *Through White Man's Eyes: A Contribution to Navajo History: A Chronological Record of the Navajo People from the Earliest Times to the Treaty of June 1, 1868,* 6 vols. (Window Rock, AZ: Navajo Heritage Center, 1979), vol. 1, pp. 282 and 288. Also, McNitt, *Navajo Wars,* pp. 171–172. The Correll volumes are enlightening, as he includes verbatim excerpts from correspondence and reports of the Spanish, Mexicans, and Americans through August 22, 1868, as well as illustrations of historic

events by Jack Phasteen and archival photographs, paintings, drawings of relevant individuals. The appendix material is vast and includes treaties, slave records, and the like. See vol. 2, pp. 290-293, for the September 1859 incident and photograph of James Hubbell.

10 *freighted heavy mining equipment* Henry P. "Pick" Walker, "Wagon Freighting in Arizona," *Smoke Signal* 28 (Fall 1973), p.185; and OH, Phillip Hubbell.

10 *James drove* Katharine Jones Moore, "The Odyssey of James Hamilton," *Westport Historical Quarterly* V:3 (December 1969), based on diaries and letters of James Hamilton's drive of cattle to California accompanied by a "Mr. Hubbell," who was driving sheep over the same route.

10 *slave blankets* Kate Peck Kent, *Navajo Weaving: Three Centuries of Change* (Santa Fe, NM: School of American Research, 1985), pp. 69-77. In these pieces, weavers mixed Navajo and Spanish design, color, and size elements.

10 *stockings with feet* Charles A. Amsden, *Navaho* [sic] *Weaving: Its Technic* [sic] *and Its History*, (1934; reprint, Glorieta, NM: Rio Grande Press, Inc. 1972), p. 108.

11 *killing herders* McNitt, *Navajo Wars*, pp. 371-372.

11 *matriarch* OH, Phillip Hubbell, pp. 6 and 7.

11 *Civil War* HFP; and McN, Box 18, for both James and Charles.

13 *Attendance at St. Michaels* See "Boarders Accounts & Registration 1859-1865," p. 25; Students St. Michaels Book 1, 1859-1905 and Prospectus," found in the archival records of the St. Francis Cathedral, Sisters of Loretto Chapel, Santa Fe, New Mexico.

13 *roundup the Navajos* See Lynn R. Bailey's books, *The Long Walk, a History of the Navajo Wars, 1846-1868* (Los Angeles, CA: Westernlore Press, 1964) and *Bosque Redondo: An American Concentration Camp* (Pasadena, CA: Socio-Technical Books, 1970); and Lawrence C. Kelly, *Navajo Roundup: Selected Correspondence of Kit Carson's Expedition Against the Navajo, 1863-1865* (Boulder, CO: Pruett Publishing, 1970). These sources provide an expanded view of the conditions and dynamics surrounding this period of Navajo history, the turbulence of which ultimately opened up trade opportunities for J. L. Hubbell. See McN and HFP for correspondence during this time. Also, Gerald Thompson, *The Army and The Navajo: The Bosque Redondo Reservation Experiment 1863-1868* (Tucson: University of Arizona Press, 1976), pp. 40, 45,49, 54, 73, details the enormous plum that Bosque Redondo represented for New Mexican contractors. For example, in January 1865, sheep for Bosque cost the government $3.50 each, up a dollar over 1864.

14 *Henry Chee Dodge* See David M. Brugge, "Henry Chee Dodge: From the Long Walk to Self-Determination," in L. G. Moses and Raymond Wilson, eds. *Indian Lives: Essays on Nineteenth- and Twentieth-Century Native American Leaders* (Albuquerque: University of New Mexico Press, 1985), pp. 91-112. Larry Evers, ed., *Between Sacred Mountains: Navajo Stories and Lessons from the Land* (Tucson: University of Arizona Press, 1982), pp. 136-141, 146, 151, 160 and 168;

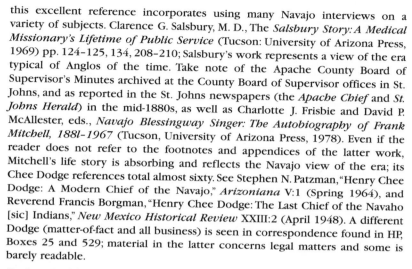

this excellent reference incorporates using many Navajo interviews on a variety of subjects. Clarence G. Salsbury, M. D., The *Salsbury Story: A Medical Missionary's Lifetime of Public Service* (Tucson: University of Arizona Press, 1969) pp. 124–125, 134, 208–210; Salsbury's work represents a view of the era typical of Anglos of the time. Take note of the Apache County Board of Supervisor's Minutes archived at the County Board of Supervisor offices in St. Johns, and as reported in the St. Johns newspapers (the *Apache Chief* and *St. Johns Herald*) in the mid-1880s, as well as Charlotte J. Frisbie and David P. McAllester, eds., *Navajo Blessingway Singer: The Autobiography of Frank Mitchell, 1881–1967* (Tucson, University of Arizona Press, 1978). Even if the reader does not refer to the footnotes and appendices of the latter work, Mitchell's life story is absorbing and reflects the Navajo view of the era; its Chee Dodge references total almost sixty. See Stephen N. Patzman, "Henry Chee Dodge: A Modern Chief of the Navajo," *Arizoniana* V:1 (Spring 1964), and Reverend Francis Borgman, "Henry Chee Dodge: The Last Chief of the Navaho [sic] Indians," *New Mexico Historical Review* XXIII:2 (April 1948). A different Dodge (matter-of-fact and all business) is seen in correspondence found in HP, Boxes 25 and 529; material in the latter concerns legal matters and some is barely readable.

15 *Barboncito* Thompson, *The Army and the Navajo*, pp. 152–153 and Broderick H. Johnson, ed., *Navajo Stories of the Long Walk Period* (Tsaile, AZ: Navajo Community College Press, 1973), John Tom contribution, pp. 178–179. This is very readable compilation of Navajo recollections of this period.

15 *treaty...returning Navajos* Garrick Bailey and Roberta Glenn Bailey, *A History of the Navajos: The Reservation Years* (Santa Fe, NM: School of American Research, 1986), pp. 25–28, 38. This unusual reference work culls economic and other data from a variety of sources.

16 *remodeling* McN, particularly newspaper clippings; OH #46, Phillip Hubbell; and McN business files for mining ventures. According to Phillip, Santiago carried his family through hard times with hoarded gold.

Chapter Two
Adventures Similar to Marco Polo

19 *muscular* IT, p. 200.

17 *post office* Civilian Personnel Records, St. Louis, Missouri, correspondence to author dated December 10, 1987, indicated that no personnel records were found for Juan Lorenzo Hubbell or John Lorenzo Hubbell. A telephone contact with the Civil Archives Division, National Archives and Records Administration, Washington, D. C., yielded the same response. In any event, the post office department then had a tightly regulated operation that would have afforded some training to J. L. in recordkeeping and the like. Take note of Harriet Mayfield's "Great Southwest Pioneer Passes On," *The Santa Fe Magazine* XXV:2

(January 1931).

18 *John D. Lee* SR; see also Robert Class Cleland and Juanita Brooks, eds., *A Mormon Chronicle: The Diaries of John D. Lee 1848-1876* (San Marino, CA: Huntington Library, 1955); and James H. McClintock, *Mormon Settlement in Arizona: A Record of Peaceful Conquest of the Desert* (Phoenix, AZ: Manufacturing Stationers, Inc. 1921). Other versions of Hubbell's coming-of-age appear in Albert H. Lee, *Gaamaliitsho Indian Trader: An Autobiography of Albert Hugh Lee 1897-1976* (Mesa, AZ: Lofgreens, Inc., c1982) p. 190 et. seq.— Lee was a Mormon and a trader at Ganado; Salsbury, *The Salsbury Story*, pp. 137-138; and the interview by David Brugge in Flagstaff with J. L.'s Euro-American friend Gene Haldeman, November 29, 1972, p. 13, in which Haldeman gave J. L.'s version: after he decided not to marry a girl he was courting and to leave Utah, he was followed on his departure, forded the Colorado River, got outfitted at a Navajo hogan, and went on his way. Interview is at HTPNHS, though not on my list.

19 *Hopis live in* Survey various issues of *Plateau* (Flagstaff, AZ: Museum of Northern Arizona) for information on Hopis and Hopi autobiographies; see also Alfonso Ortiz, ed., *Southwest*, vol. 9 of *Handbook of North American Indians*, (Washington, D. C.: Smithsonian Institution, 1979), pp. 514-603 (henceforth cited as Ortiz, vol. 9). Within that volume, take note particularly of J. O. Brew, "Hopi Prehistory and Hopi History to 1850," p. 515; John C. Connelly, "Hopi Social Organization," p. 551; Edward A. Kennan, "Hopi Economy and Subsistence," p. 557; and Frederick J. Dockstader, "Hopi History: 1850-1940," p. 525. Scan Laura Graves, *Thomas Varker Keam, Indian Trader* (Norman: University of Oklahoma Press, 1998), pp. 11-26, for a comprehensive view of the Hopis. See also Jesse Walter Fewkes, *Hopi Snake Ceremonies* (Albuquerque, NM: Avanyu Publishing Inc., 1986), which has selections from the Bureau of American Ethnology Annual Reports for the years 1894-1895 and 1897-1898. David M. Brugge's excellent article, "Navajo and Western Pueblo History," *The Smoke Signal* 25 (reprinted 1981), includes a good bibliography for Hopi and Navajo history.

21 *Bureau of Indian Affairs* See Wilcomb E. Washburn, volume editor, *History of Indian-White Relations*, vol. 4 (Washington, D. C.: Smithsonian Institution (1988), Donald J. Berthrong, "Nineteenth Century United States Government Agencies," p. 257. The Bureau of Indian Affairs was transferred from the War Department to the Indian Department in 1849. It was referred to as the Bureau, though in letters etc. of the times Indian Service and government service were common synonyms.

22 *Reed's posts* In the Albuquerque Sunday *Herald* (June 11, 1922), Nathan Bilbo, an early Euro-American Southwest pioneer, recollected that in July 1868, when the Navajos passed through Fort Wingate on their return from Fort Sumner (Bosque Redondo), Fort Wingate had two stores, Spieglebergs (Jewish pioneer merchants) and Waters. Bilbo recalled that "J. L. Hubbell, now at Ganado, then in his teens, clerked for Waters at the time."

22 *Government service* See the National Archives, Letters Received by the Office

of Indian Affairs, New Mexico Superintendency, 1874 and 1875, specifically letters dated 12/29/1873, 4/24/1874, 9/2/1874 (voucher for payment to J. L. for June); many vouchers for services performed in 1873 and 1874 (though the date of completion of the vouchers is unclear); and 7/15/1875 petition addressed to President Grant by Navajo leaders.

22 *Agent W. F. Arny...Thomas Keam guaranteed* For a more thorough treatment of Arny in general and J. L.'s involvement with the Navajo leaders, see IT, pp. 143–156, 165. Also, Graves, pp. 69–91. For a view of Arny as a reformer with a philanthropic interest in the Indians, look at Lawrence R. Murphy's *Frontier Crusader—William F. M. Arny* (Tucson: University of Arizona, 1972).

23 *Keam...married...Navajo* See Graves' work regarding Keam's efforts to become agent and the effect of his Navajo marriage on this desire.

24 *naat'áanii (headman)* The oral histories have scattered references to both these leaders, particularly Ganado Mucho. See, too, in WP the three-article series in the *Navajo Times* (December 1967), on Ganado Mucho by Lee J. Correll, which can be in WP; Richard F. Van Valkenburgh, "Navajo Naataani," *The Kiva* XIII (January 1948); and Bailey and Bailey, *A History of the Navajos*, pp. 28–36.

26 *treaty reservation's original* For extensive general treatment of Navajos, their history, and other issues, see Alphonso Ortiz, vol. ed., *Handbook of North American Indians* (Washington, D. C.: Smithsonian Institution Press, 1983), vol. 10, *Southwest*, pp. 489 to 683 (hereafter cited as Ortiz, vol. 10). For reservation expansion in particular, see Robert A. Roessel, Jr., "Navajo History, 1850–1923," Ortiz, vol. 10, p. 521.

22 *language* For Navajo language set in the traditional Navajo culture of the early Reservation days and J. L.'s active years of trading, the Franciscan Fathers, *An Ethnologic Dictionary of the Navaho* [sic] *Language* (1910, reprint St. Michaels, AZ: St. Michaels Press, 1968) is a gem. It's organized by a narrative discourse on Navajo culture with Navajo and English word lists for subject areas. Some Navajo spellings (included in my definition of spelling are diacritical marks, as well) come from the Franciscan's publication, as it was contemporaneous with Hubbell's life. Please, remember that many Navajo words are built around a stem with prefixes and the like. So it's not just a matter of looking up a word in the alphabetical listing of a Navajo dictionary, since several factors change how a word is spelled. In this work, Navajo words in quotes, taken from historical documents and the like appear as they were phonetically written at the time. Some words have always been spelled with almost equal frequency two or more ways like the word for white man. Often I've listed the alternate spellings so that the non-native speaker will recognize the word when it appears in other works. Due to the foregoing I've not put a [sic] designation after the older or less common variation of the Navajo spelling of a word. For a more current work on the Navajo language, indeed considered the bible by some, see Robert W. Young and William Morgan Sr.'s *The Navajo Language, Grammar and Colloquial Dictionary*, Revised Ed., Albuquerque, the University of New Mexico Press, 1987. Its prefatory material

includes excellent references to other Navajo dictionary works , plus a history of the Euro-American's interest in Navajo and the development of Navajo grammars and dictionaries. Too, for the reader interested in language and grammar this work includes the phonemes of Navajo (the vocal length, nasality, and tone for sounds) and the diacritical marks (subscript nasal hooks, acute accent marks, glottal stops, and the like.) A rather lengthy language discussion appears in Clyde Kluckhohn and Dorothea Leighton, *The Navaho* [sic] rev. ed. (Natural History Edition, 1962 and Cambridge, MA: Harvard University Press, 1946), pp. 253-293; "elephant," p. 299; and verbs, pp. 263-270 (p. 269, poem). Also, see Gary Witherspoon, "Language and Reality in Navajo World View," in Ortiz, vol. 10 pp. 570-578. This article also discusses *hózhǫ́*, which is mentioned toward the end of this chapter. For verbs, see Gary Witherspoon, *Language and Art in the Navajo Universe* (Ann Arbor: University of Michigan Press, 1977), pp. 48-52.

27 *Amsden Navaho* [sic] *Weaving*, pp. 168-170.

27 *attire* Quotes and descriptions found in Bailey and Bailey, *A History of the Navajos*, pp. 70-73, and Amsden, *Navaho* [sic] *Weaving*, p. 186.

28 *taller* Kluckhohn, *The Navaho* [sic], pp. 84-86.

28 *kinship* See particularly Gary Witherspoon's chapter on "Navajo Social Organization," in Ortiz, vol. 10, pp. 524-535.

29 *Sheep* Perhaps the Navajos' adaptability, a theme that appears in most works about them, shows up readily in sheepherding. See R. W. Young, "The Rise of the Navajo Tribe," in *Plural Society in the Southwest*, ed. by E. H. Spicer and R. H. Thompson (Tucson: University of Arizona Press, 1972). For a thorough treatment of sheep in Navajo history, see Lynn R. Bailey, *If You Take My Sheep: The Evolution and Conflicts of Navajo Pastoralism, 1630-1868* (Pasadena, CA: Westernlore Publications, 1980) p. 271, for part of Barboncito's quote (cited hereafter as IYTMS). The other part is found in Ruth M. Underhill, *The Navajo* (Norman: University of Oklahoma Press, 1956), p. 152.

30 *excess* Underhill, *The Navajo*, p. 181. Underhill's book is a rather dramatic read, one in which Navajos are often the subjects rather than the objects of the story.

30 *Tully Lincoln* OH #11 (b. circa 1902, residing Ganado), May 1972, p. 5. This is a lengthy interview that gives a good overview of Navajo life. Mr. Lincoln's father was Loco, J. L.'s cook.

31 *hogans* See Stephen C. Jett and Virginia E. Spencer, *Navajo Architecture* (Tucson: University of Arizona Press, 1981) for a thorough discussion of the hogan.

31 *1874 annual report* Bailey and Bailey, *A History of the Navajos*, p. 67.

31 *Navajoland* This geographical summary comes from a variety of sources, including Young, *The Role of the Navajo*; B. Youngblood, "Navajo Trading, A Report to the Office of Experiment Stations, U. S. Department of Agriculture, 1935" (a good discussion of the geography and roads) and cited in SR as

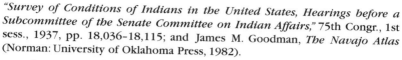

"Survey of Conditions of Indians in the United States, Hearings before a Subcommittee of the Senate Committee on Indian Affairs," 75th Congr., 1st sess., 1937, pp. 18,036-18,115; and James M. Goodman, *The Navajo Atlas* (Norman: University of Oklahoma Press, 1982).

33 *sacred mountains* See Evers, pp. 2-3.

33 *Earth's feet* Witherspoon, *Language and Art*, p. 26.

34 *Van Dyke's book* Van Dyke was the recorder of *Son of Old Man Hat* (1938, reprint Lincoln: University of Nebraska Press, 1966), and with his wife Ruth Van Dyke, editor of *Lefthanded: A Navajo Autobiography* (New York: Columbia University Press, 1980). These are excellent sources of information on the daily life of a Navajo man in the post-Fort Sumner period.

34 *motion* For a thorough and fascinating discussion of the motion and the principal Navajo verb, see Margaret Astrov, "The Concept of Motion as the Psychological Leitmotif of Navajo Life and Literature," *The Journal of American Folklore* (1950) Vol. 63, pp. 45-56.

PART TWO: WEARING SPECTACLES

Chapter Three
Lok' áahnteel: Place of Wide Reeds

As background for the material presented in this chapter, see David M. Brugge, "The Valley of the Red House," July–August 1972, draft and unpublished history prepared while he was curator at HTPNHS (article cited earlier) and available at the site. Also, see references cited in this chapter particularly Basso and Kelly for an Indian perspective on behavior and place.

37 *date he started trading* IT, p. 201; CNT, Hubbell Chronology, p. 1.

37 *Manuelito Springs* IT, pp. 203-204. See also CNT, Hubbell Chronology, p. 1 et. seq.

37 *Lok'áahnteel* This term is variously spelled: —*Lok'aaniteel, Luka'antquell, Luka'nt-quel* (in TT), *Luka ntqel*; it is referred to as either "wide reeds," or *Luka Knintqel,* "the wide ruins in the reeds."

37 *Hubbell's granddaughter* La Charles G. Eckel, "History of Ganado," *Museum Notes: Museum of Northern Arizona* 6 (April 1934), pp. 48-50.

37 *trail running* IYTMS, p. 84; and H&F, pp. 16-17.

38 *Two washes* See H&F generally, particularly pp. 56-61; and Goodman, pp. 30-31, 44-45.

38 *Thirteen ... archeological sites* See report by Albert Manchester and Ann Manchester, "Hubbell Trading Post National Historic Site: An Administrative History" (Santa Fe, NM: Southwest Cultural Resources Center, Professional Papers No. 46, 1992).

38 *gigantic Navajo chieftain* See Eckel; also, for the giant and Hopi stories, OH #4,

T'iis Yazhi, pp. 20-22.

38 *raiding Apaches* T'iis Yazhi, OH # 4, April 27, 1971, pp. 1-3.

38 *picture of an event* Klara Bonsack Kelly and Harris Francis, *Navajo Sacred Places* (Bloomington: Indiana University Press, 1994), pp. 1-11, 198.

39 *Escalante* Amsden, *Navaho* [sic] *Weaving*, plate 57a.

39 *black slave* McNitt, *Navajo Wars*, p. 325.

39 *the fall of 1860* IYTMS, p. 213; McNitt, *Navajo Wars*, pp. 391-398; Bill P. Acrey, *Navajo History: The Land and The People* (Shiprock, NM: Central Consolidated School District No. 22, 1988), pp. 30-31; Brugge, *Navajos in the Catholic Church Records* 1985, p. 89; and Bailey, *Indian Slave Trade in the Southwest*, p. 213.

39 *Joseph C. Ives's* Joseph C. Ives, *Report Upon the Colorado River of the West Explored in 1857 and 1858,* 36th Cong., 1 sess., Hse. Exec. Doc. 90 (Washington, D. C.: GPO, 1861), pp. 128-131.

39 *Mrs. Yazzie Holmes* OH #33 (b. 1890, residing Ganado, AZ), September 1970, pp. 1, 18-19, 33-34, and 42.

39 *Dolth Curley* OH #3 (b. 1884, residing Ganado, AZ), November 8, 1971, p. 12.

39 *Friday Kinlicheeny* (also spelled Kinlichii'nii) OH #31, (b. 1895, residing Ganado, AZ), September 1970, pp. 3, 4, and June 1972 interview.

40 *Crary...Leonard building* IT, pp. 200-202.

40 *Blacksheep* (in HUTR list, Hastiin Dibetlizhini) OH #18, (b. 1876, residing Ganado, AZ), January and February, 1972; (see especially, January, p. 10).

41 *said no twice* Robert L. Wilken, *Anselm Weber, O. F. M.: Missionary to the Navajo 1898-1921* (Milwaukee, WI: Bruce Publishing Co., 1955), p. 19.

41 *T'ahasbaa' Slivers* OH #40 (b. 1886, residing Snake Flats, AZ), August 1972, p. 4.

41 *Nák' ee sinilí* (also rendered as Nakeznilih, Nikhaeznili, Nakhaeznili) See Franciscan's dictionary, p. 126.

41 *naalyehe* Irene Silentman of Newcomb, NM, provided the literal translation of the Navajo words for trading. Martha Blue, "A View from the Bullpen: A Navajo Ken of Traders and Trading Posts," *Plateau* (MNA), 57:3 (1986), pp. 10-17.

42 *Coolidge, in their work* Dane and Mary Roberts Coolidge, *The Navajo Indians,* (1930; reprint New York, Ames Bros., 1979), pp. 65-69.

42 *"Navajo Shoguns"* Ruth Underhill, *The Navajo* , p. 177.

42 *Schmedding, who traded* Joseph Schmedding, *Cowboy and Indian Trader* (1951; reprint Albuquerque: University of New Mexico Press, 1974), p. 346.

42 *wood cups* Clyde Kluckhohn, W. W. Hill, and Lucy Wales Kluckhohn, *Navajo Material Culture* (Cambridge, MA: Harvard University Press, 1971), pp. 136-137; this is a fascinating and informative text on a wide range of cultural material.

43 *trading tents* IT, p. 72.

44 *"customers won't buy"* I have heard this adage repeated by traders numerous times over the years; see also Adams, p. 181.

44 *Anglo Sam Day II* Samuel Day II interview April 1-2, 1960 at Carrigon's [sic] Trading Post, conducted by Bernard L. Fontana, Field Historian, University of Arizona Library and archived there and at HTPNHS. Note McNitt interviewed Day as well the same year and place Day at Karigan's Trading Post, north of St. Michaels.

45 *Frank Mitchell* Frisbee/Mitchell, see pp. 50-54, 56, 117, 238, 250-256, 262-264, 271-72.

45 *"Store food"* OH #1, Ya Na Bah Winker (Mrs. Kirk, b. 1897), Ganado, AZ, November 1971, p. 12.

46 *Agent John E. Pyle* From Pyle's diary, dated January 1-November 27, 1878, in the collection of the Bancroft Library, University of California, Berkeley, CA. Pyle, who died in 1879, served as Navajo agent during the time he kept his diary. This document provides a critical look at the BIA as well as the activities of the U. S. Army at Fort Wingate and some of the personalities of the times, such as Manuelito, Ganado Mucho, Arny, and trader William Leonard.

46 *An 1886 order* HP, Outgoing Correspondence, April 9, 1886. Those items ordered in small quantities can be identified from the paperwork included in this file.

47 *tin money* Martha Blue, "Money Made of Tin," *Coins* Vol. 35, No. 10, (October 1988), pp. 66-68.

47 *tobacco* IT, pp. 75-76; Brugge interview, L. Hubbell Parker, p. 6.

49 *Franciscan* OH #51, Father Immanuel Trocker, OFM, St. Michaels, June 1970, which is a copy of an interview done by Arizona Historical Society. The first name is spelled differently in various references, the surname the same so I assume given the time period interviewee was at the Mission that it is the same person. There is another interview with Father Emanuel, #76/Doris Duke/1967, at St. Michaels Mission, by D. Cordyn Hammond; see pp. 48 and 49 in that interview for the Navajos' view of traders. Also the Franciscan Papers at Special Collections, University of Arizona, Box 47, lists two oral histories taken by representatives of the University of Utah in August 1967 and September 1970.

49 *bull snake* Brugge interview L. Hubbell Parker, p. 6.

49 *Lefthanded* Van Dyke, *Son of Old Man Hat*, pp. 67-69.

49 *bordered on ridicule* See Keith H. Basso, *Portraits of "the Whiteman": Linguistic Play and Cultural Symbols Among the Western Apache* (Cambridge, England: Cambridge University Press, 1979). See entire text, most especially Chapter Three. While critics have pointed that these linguistic plays represent only the Apaches' view of whites, both the foreword by Dell Hymes in Basso's book and Alan Wilson, *Navajo Place Names: An Oberver's Guide* (Guilford, CT: Jeffrey Norton Publishers, 1995) point out that these attitudes

have analogies elsewhere in Indian country. In my sustained relationships with citizens of Arizona's Indian country, I have found Basso's observations consistently borne out.

50 *Navajo trading behavior* See generally, William Y. Adams, *Shonto: A Study of the Role of the Trader in a Modern Navaho* [sic] *Community*, Bureau of American Ethnology, Bulletin 188 (Washington, D.C.; GPO, 1963) for a discussion of trade with the Navajos historically and trading practices specifically.

50 *Schmedding* Schmedding, *Cowboy and Indian Trader*, p. 143.

50 *Hamlin Garland* Lonnie E. Underhill and Daniel F. Littlefield, Jr., *Hamlin Garland's Observations on the American Indian 1895-1905* (Tucson: University of Arizona Press, 1976), p. 86.

51 *Coolidges* Coolidge, pp. 65-69.

51 *sales of dead pawn* WP, in an unpublished short piece by Maynard Dixon.

52 *Indian novelist* Paula Gunn Allen *The Woman Who Owned the Shadows* (San Francisco, CA: Spinsters Ink, 1983), pp. 139-140.

52 *paid-out tokens...collection plate* IT, pp. 83-86; WP, Intrapost correspondence; HP; OH #47 and Dorothy S. Hubbell interview, October 1969, p. 55; and Blue Interview, 1986 and 1988.

52 *hired Indians* H&F, pp. 83-91.

52 *vassalage* H&F, p. 166.

54 *"trader Navajo"* Adams, p. 214.

54 *a few Navajos opined* OH #12, Asdzaa Dloo Holoni, (b. 1880, residing Ganado Lake), January 1972, pp. 25-27; see several interviews over several dates with long-time Hubbell employee Joe Tippecanoe, (OH #7, b. 1876, residing Ganado).

54 *"his whoring mistress"* Undated notes by David M. Brugge on an early draft of the manuscript for this work.

54 *Mrs. Ben Wilson* OH #14 (b. 1906), Ganado, AZ, January 1972, p. 30-31. This interviewee is the youngest daughter of Miguelito and Maria Antonia.

54 *overworked Navajo* Frank C. Lockwood, "John Lorenzo Hubbell: Navajo Indian Trader," *More Arizona Characters* General Bulletin No. 8 (Tucson: University of Arizona, 1942), p. 58; at least a portion of this article appears in Frank C. Lockwood, ed., "John Lorenzo Hubbell," *Pioneer Portraits: Selected Vignettes* (Tucson, AZ: University of Arizona Press, 1968), pp. 128-159.

Chapter Four
Witches Shot Stones Into Their Bodies

55 *a band of Navajos* For multiple versions of these "Wild West" yarns, see Dorothy Challis Mott, "Don Lorenzo Hubbell of Ganado," *Arizona Historical Review* 4:1 (April 1931), pp. 45-51; Lockwood; and Dorothy E. Albrecht, "Vignettes of Arizona Pioneers: John Lorenzo Hubbell, Navajo Indian Trader,"

Arizoniana IV:3 (Fall 1963).

56 *undesirable non-Indians* IT, pp. 159 and 175.

57 *smallpox* See TT for Hubbell's statements. See Franciscan Fathers, *An Ethnologic Dictionary*, p. 107 for a discussion of Navajo views toward smallpox in the early twentieth century.

58 *Witchpurge and Trading* See citations for Chapter One on this subject.

59 *avoid the dead* Witherspoon, in Ortiz, Vol 10, p. 571. Navajos do not fear death or the dead per se; rather, the behavior is a practical response to the danger of illness or other potentially fatal contagious disease.

60 *Navajo weaving history* See Amsden, *Navaho* [sic] *Weaving* ; Gladys A. Reichard, *Spiderwoman: A Story of Navajo Weavers and Chanters* (1934; reprint, Glorieta, NM: The Rio Grande Press, Inc., 1968) and *Weaving a Navajo Blanket,* (1936; reprint, New York: Dover Publications, Inc., 1974); Mary Hunt Kahlenberg and Anthony Berlant, *The Navajo Blanket* (New York: Praeger Publishers, Inc., in association with the Los Angeles County Museum of Art, 1972); and Alice Kaufman and Christopher Selser, *The Navajo Weaving Tradition: 1650 to the Present* (New York: E. P. Dutton, Inc., 1985). For the Navajo weavers' perspective, see Ann Lane Hedlund, *Reflections of the Weaver's World* (Denver, CO: Denver Art Museum, 1992), which includes thirty-eight interviews with weavers, as well as a culturally sensitive look at weaving by Hedlund; and CNT, pp. 147-178. For Euro-American and a few Indian perspectives on Native American arts and crafts (including the Navajo textile), see the essays collected in Marta Weigle and Barbara A. Babcock, eds., *The Great Southwest of the Fred Harvey Company and the Santa Fe Railway* (Phoenix, AZ: The Heard Museum, 1996) and Kathleen L. Howard and Diana F. Pardue, *Inventing the Southwest: The Fred Harvey Company and Native American Art* (Flagstaff, AZ: Northland Publishing Co., 1996). Liz Bauer's previously cited publication and weavers' oral histories at HTPNHS provide a specific look at J. L. Hubbell and HTP's involvement with the Navajo rug.

60 *Spanish Governor* Kaufman, p. 11.

60 *weaving origin story* Reichard, *Spiderwoman*, title page.

60 *a 1909 interview* Edgar K. Miller, "The Indian and the Trader," *Indian School Journal* VII:8-9 (June–September 1907).

61 *pound blankets* See Hubbell's 1902 pamphlet, "Navajo Blankets and Indian Curios: Catalogue and Price List. Ganado, Apache County, Arizona" (Chicago, IL: Press of Hollister Brothers, 1902) for pound blankets. Hubbell both bought and sold certain Navajo textiles by the pound.

61 *In 1884* George Wharton James, *Indian Blankets and Their Makers* (1914; reprint, New York: Dover Publications, Inc., 1974), p. 47.

61 *Cotton* CNT, pp. 27-30. For general information about Cotton, see John Kevin Fell, "The Role of C. N. Cotton in the Development of Northwestern New Mexico," *New Mexico Historical Review* 55:2 (1980); and Lester L. Williams, "C.

N. Cotton Indian Trader," *Denver Westerner's Roundup* 33 (May/June 1977) and *C. N. Cotton and His Navajo Blankets* (Albuquerque, NM: Avanyu Publishing, 1989). HP also contain letterpress copies of Cotton's correspondence while he was at Ganado (1884–1889).

My rather critical attitude toward Cotton comes from my reading of the correspondence among J. L., his sons, and Cotton. These letters indicate that Cotton took business advantage of J. L., perhaps playing on the trader's proclivity for standing by old friends. This assessment, which was supported by Dorothy Hubbell who said that both J. L.'s sons held the opinion that Cotton took business advantage of their father. Cotton, does not, however, match the opinions of former HTPNHS curators David M. Brugge and Liz Bauer.

62 *Miniature rug designs* HP, Box 12, Burbank, and Box 52, Bertha Little; CNT, pp. 59–87.

62 *Burbank later said* See the rather disappointing, nearly childlike perspective of Indians in E. A. Burbank and Ernest Royce, *Burbank Among the Indians* (Caldwell, ID: Caxton Printers, 1946), p. 206.

63 *oral histories* Several of the oral histories relate weaving information throughout the interview, such as the places the weavers traveled for Hubbell, what they wove, and the prices they were paid. See also OH #27, Annabel Hardy (b. 1906, residing Ganado, AZ), April 1972; OH #1, Ya Na Bah Winker, pp. 12–13; OH #2, Asdzaa Bekashi (b. 1891, residing Ganado, AZ), November 1971, p. 14; OH #40, T'ahasbaa' Slivers; OH #12, Asdzaa Dloo Holoni; OH #25, Marie Etsitty (b. 1900, residing Ganado, AZ), August 1969 and April 1972, pp. 1–3.

64 *Hubbell revival* CNT, pp. 47, 49, 59–77.

64 *By 1890...In 1899* See Bailey and Bailey, *A History of the Navajos*, pp. 60, 152; and Amsden, *Navaho* [sic] *Weaving*, 193–194.

PART THREE: J. L. HUBBELL

Chapter 5
St. Johns: A Kettle of Fish

For a general discussion of St. Johns history from a Mormon perspective (with an emphasis on the political-economic forces at play in Apache County during the last two decades of the 1800s), see Joseph Fish, John H. Krenkel, ed., *The Life and Times of Joseph Fish, Mormon Pioneer* (Danville, IL: Interstate Printers & Publishers, 1970); *Mormon Settlement in Arizona*; Charles S. Peterson, *Take Up Your Mission: Mormon Colonizing Along the Little Colorado 1870-1900* (Tucson: University of Arizona Press, 1973) and *Apache County Centennial Memento Booklet 1879-1979; Apache County Historical Quarterly* 4 (July 1978); and Wayne Davis, ed., *St. Johns Arizona Stake Centennial 1887 July 23, 1987* (St. Johns, AZ: The Church of Jesus Christ of Latter-Day Saints, St. Johns Arizona Stake, 1987). The last three works contain information regarding gambling in St. Johns. I am also indebted to Steve Udall, an attorney from St. Johns, for his insight into the issues of gambling in that era and the St. Johns-Hispanic-Mormon relationship during the nineteenth and early twentieth century.

The information on the Hubbell family in St. Johns was generally gleaned from the Department of Library, Archives, and Public Records [DLAPR], State Capitol Building, Phoenix, Arizona which holds the older county records, including lawsuits, marriage licenses, voter registration, election results and the like. These include the Apache County Great Registers and the supplemental registers, as well as court records. Only a small portion of St. Johns' early records are at the Apache County Courthouse.

An important document regarding the family generally is David M. Brugge's "Hubbell Trading Post National Historic Site, Furnishings Study, The Hubbell Home" January 1972. A copy of this unpublished document is at HTPNHS.

67 *Fish gives* Krenkel, *Life and Times*, pp. 200, 201, 215, 247, 255, 256, 361 for various references relative to this chapter.

67 *Cruz Rubi...St. Johns...Solomon Barth* McN, interviews with St. Johns settlers' descendants such as Jacob Barth (April 28, 1972); the *St. Johns Herald Observer*, usually referred to as the *St. Johns Herald*, newspaper clipping file, particularly November 1928 and June 20, 1942; and Thomas E. Farish, *History of Arizona*, vol. VI (San Francisco, CA: Filmer Bros. Electrotype Co., 1915–1918), an eight-volume collection. See Rubi in "Notices Effecting Real Estate," Book #1, Apache County Recorder's Office, St. Johns, Arizona.

67 *Apache County* See Henry P. Walker and Don Bufkin, *Historical Atlas of Arizona* (Norman: University of Oklahoma Press, 1979), particularly pp. 30–32 for maps and description of county development.

68 *leader David K. Udall* Located by Librarian at the Arizona State Library, Phoenix, with under Ariz. q979.155, s14b on the document.

68 *Lina Rubi* TT, lineage discussion; DLAPR for court proceeding *Lina Rubi de Lucero v. Encamacion Lucero*, 68 (December 26, 1884), Alfred Ruiz, Clerk [a relative], C. L. Gutterson, Attorney for Plaintiff. Several pleading documents were filed through September 1885. As the divorce proceedings appear in the text, please refer back to this citation.

69 *wearing-blanket fragment* Marian E. Rodee, *Old Navajo Rugs: Their Development from 1900 to 1940* (Albuquerque: University of New Mexico Press, 1981), p. 2.

69 *baptismal records* WP, copied and translated by curator David M. Brugge, HTPNHS, in St. Johns, AZ, April 17, 1972, and translated.

70 *reservation border* Goodman, pp. 56–57.

70 *Navajo City...wide-ranging commercial interests* HP, Box 95, National Archives, per David M. Brugge.

71 *trading post ledgers* HP, Box 327.

71 *Board of Jail* Minute Book for the summer of 1885, Apache County Board of Supervisors' records in the office of the County Clerk for the Board of Supervi-

sors in St. Johns.

71 *building up* William J. Robinson, "A Construction Sequence For Hubbell Trading Post and Residence," *The Kiva* 50:4 (1985).

71 *Sam E. Day, Sr.* IT; see also the Samuel E. Day, Sr. (or Day Collection) at Special Collections, Cline Library, Northern Arizona University, Flagstaff; Clifford E. Trafzer, "Sam Day and His Boys: Good Neighbors to the Navajos," *Journal of Arizona History* 18:1 (Spring 1977); and HP, Box 23, Day letters.

71 *a local newspaper* Microfishe of *Apache Chief* and *St. John's Herald* available at Special Collections, Cline Library, NAU, Flagstaff. Refer to papers on dates indicated in the text regarding J. L. Hubbell's problems as sheriff.

72 *sheriff of Apache County* See Larry D. Ball's readable and thorough book, *Desert Lawmen: The High Sheriffs of New Mexico and Arizona 1846-1912* (Albuquerque: University of New Mexico Press, 1992) for general information about territorial sheriffs as well as some specific information about Hubbell's term (pp. 63-64, 191, 266, 286).

72 *Navajo oral histories* Lockwood, 1968, p. 139. See also OH #5, Yazzie Holmes (b. 1884, residing Ganado AZ), November 1971, p. 7, for recovery of Navajo horses stolen by whites.

73 *Solomon Barth's son* McN and HUTR #52. Notes from interview with Jacob Barth by Frank McNitt in St. Johns, April 28, 1972.

74 *entertained...board of supervisors...Huning* J. L.'s problems as sheriff are taken from contemporary newspaper reports in St. Johns; extant summary minutes of the Apache County Board of Supervisors. See also notes of McNitt and Brugge regarding Apache County Records which were apparently sent by Clint Colby to HTP on August 31, 1970, and taken from the Minute Book, Apache County Courthouse; and a two page undated typed list by Brugge of all papers at the Apache County courthouse related to individuals with the last name of Hubbell.

74 *nepotism was the rule* Ball, *Desert Lawmen*, pp. 33-34.

75 *selling-on-paper* In my July 29, 1988, interview with Dorothy S. Hubbell in Sun City, Arizona, I asked about the Cotton buyout and raised the question of the source of the funds that J. L. would have needed to buy Cotton out on that date. She thought that Hubbell's resources were generally taxed. Hubbell's sheriff salary, irregularly paid, was often delayed by the Board of Supervisors and he was buying livestock/wool too. It is my opinion that the two men continued in some loose business arrangement regarding Ganado and that the sale of the remaining half of the trading ranch was a political ruse.

78 *letterhead* HP, Box 95.

79 *re-election difficulties* Ball, pp. 63-64, and the *St. Johns Herald*.

80 *Navajo agent advised Owens* See at various depositaries (I used Bancroft Library, University of California at Berkeley) the Navajo Indian Agent Letterbooks, Fort Defiance, AZ, 1880-1905. Owens confiscated on 3,982 of Frank's sheep in June 1887, and Frank then sued Owens (Docket #109—number has been cut off

of the papers). In August 1889, Apache County sued Frank regarding a judgment involving two Hispanic-surnamed men. Those who investigate this source will note that some of the pleadings made during this era have no docket numbers.

80 *Hubbell's defeat* See earlier cites to local Mormon historians as well as the *St. Johns Herald.*

80 *Arizona Mercantile Company* McN, in notes by David M. Brugge at HTPNHS, HP records.

81 *lawsuits* For example, records listed above generally in the Superior Court, some at DLAPR: *Eiseman Bros. vs. J. L. Hubbell and Pedro Montano,* 121, Court Records, Apache County, regarding failed wool delivery; *Territory of Arizona, ex. rel. vs. J. L. Hubbell and His Sheriff Sureties* for sums not collected or tendered during his tenure as sheriff, 7/5/1887, with amount in dispute taken out his salary on 7/11/1888; and *J. C. Wahl vs. Roman Lopez, Bengio Lopez and J. L. Hubbell* 117, 119, 450, and others, involving horses, sureties, execution of judgments, and failure of the defendants to appear. The matters went on for years and it is not possible to determine final resolutions from extant documents.

Chapter Six
Long a Tremendous Gambler

82 *Cotton as tall* CNT, pp. 27–30 includes a detailed discussion of Cotton's business activities relative to the Ganado trading ranch and tied to HP. See also the Hubbell Chronology. See HP, Boxes 91 through 95, Outgoing Correspondence/Cotton at Ganado, roughly 1884 to 1889, sometimes referred to as "Cotton's Letter Book."

82 *trade in Chinle* See Charlotte J. Frisbie, "On the Trail of Chinle's 'Big House,'" in *Diné Bíkéyah: Papers in Honor of David M. Brugge,* Meliha S. Duran and David T. Kirkpatrick, eds. The Archeological Society of New Mexico 24 (1998), which covers the two-story trading post built by J. L. in the mid-1910s. The 1885 Chinle license was not renewed, (IT, p. 214). Check further: H&F, pp. 25–26; WP, undated list of licenses to trade with the Navajo in the nineteenth century; and IT, pp. 213–224 (though McNitt was in error when he wrote that the Hubbells' two-story Chinle post-tourist hotel was established in the early 1900s). Note Laura S. Harrison and Beverly Spears, *Historic Structure Report, Chinle Trading Post, Thunderbird Ranch, and Custodian's Residence Canyon de Chelly National Monument, Arizona* (Santa Fe, NM: National Park Service, Southwest Regional Office, 1989), pp. 1–26.

82 *Charles (Charlie) Hubbell* Often referred to as "Charlie" (he signed his letters "Chas."); he managed to be involved in both the witchpurge of 1878 and the 1892 Round Rock confrontation between Black Horse and the Navajo Indian agent. Both involved military intervention, and the latter included Chee Dodge, who co-owned the Round Rock trading post with a non-Indian partner. A reference to Charlie's Navajo name appears in Navajo Land Claim papers.

See also references to Charlie in IT, pp. 78, 214, 279, 281, 338; McN; and HP, Outgoing Correspondence, which contains numerous business and personal letters from Charlie to family members (primarily to J. L.) at other posts. For some of Charlie's problems, see HP, Box 33, and Intrapost Correspondence; see also OH #35, Buck Chambers (b. 1902, residing Ganado Lake), May 10, 1972, p. 13 and OH #3, Dolth Curley, p. 18.

83 *improvements at Ganado* See Robinson, "A Construction Sequence..."

83 *Ganado land claim* See H&F, pp. 22-61, for a thorough narrative on this subject. For primary records on Hubbell's efforts to acquire title (and water matters), see *Rights of Settlers on the Navajo Reservation, Arizona,* 56 Cong. 1 Sess., Sen. Rept. 699 (Washington, D. C.: GPO, 1900); *Adjustment of Rights of Settlers on the Navajo Reservation,* 57 Cong., 1 sess, Sen. Rept. 2042 (Washington, D.C.: GPO, 1902); WP, letter from C. E. Vandever, 9/25/1890; and H&F, p.30.

84 *separate letterheads* HP, Box 95, May 1890.

84 *wholesale catalogue* Clinton N. Cotton, *Wholesale Catalogue and Price List of Navajo Blankets* (San Francisco, CA: H. S. Crocker Co., 1896) prepared by G. Wharton James.

84 *J. L.'s granddaughter* Eckel, "History of Ganado".

85 *draw heavier...exaggerated prices* HP 19(7) and 21(5), Cotton correspondence to Hubbell.

86 *former husband: gambling* See citations at beginning of Chapter Five.

87 *Francis E. Leupp* HP, Box 51

87 *painting of Hopi girls* HP, Box 23, 1902 correspondence.

87 *first visit* HP, Box 12, Burbank correspondence.

87 *"Lorencito"* Mrs. White Mountain Smith, "He is Our Friend", *The Desert Magazine* 4:1 (1940).

89 *Washington, D. C.* HP, Outgoing Correspondence Box 95-100 summarized from a variety files.

90 *first bill* H&F, particularly p. 37 and earlier cites to land claim.

91 *Big House* See Robinson, "A Construction Sequence..."

92 *cottonwoods* See Hubbell family interviews at HTPNHS.

92 *Cornfield is in* See H&F, pp. 130-136 for discussion of this area, p. 133 for Robinson quote and more complete citation.

92 *struck by lightning* Burbank, *Burbank Among the Indians,* p. 47.

93 *friend Manyhorses* OH #3, Dolth Curley, pp. 21-22.

93 *Keam, trading post* IT, Graves, pp. 124-199; Richard Van Valkenburgh "Tom Keam, Friend of Moqui," *The Desert Magazine* 9:9 (July 1946).

94 *water frontier* H&F, for an especially detailed look at this topic see pp. 41-142; Peterson not only covers Hubbell's acquisition of water rights, he has an excellent discussion of the Winters doctrine, regional water development, homesteading,

irrigation projects, and specific government agencies/agents involved in same.

94 *extreme weather* See generally Youngblood, "Navajo Trading, A Report..."

95 *C. M. Supplee* Lieutenant W. C. Brown Survey, *Report on Conditions of the Navajo Country 1893.*

95 *Rufus Eley* Rufus Eley, "Ganado: The Arizona Home of J. L. Hubbell," *The Irrigation Age* (July 1903), pp. 269–271.

96 *own canal system valued* H&F, p. 93; HP, Box 346.

96 *agents' annual reports* The Arizona Historical Society, Tucson, has several Navajo agents' annual reports in their archives. See also Bailey and Bailey, *A History of the Navajos*, the first two chapters and part of the third, for information gleaned from various government reports of the period; see same text for the Panic of 1893.

97 *Chee Dodge* See earlier cites in Chapter One.

97 *Navajo Agent Hayzlett* H&F, December 1899 correspondence, p. 35, see full quote and citation.

97 *Joe Tippecanoe*: OH #7, November 15, 1971, interviewer David M. Brugge, pp. 3–6. Note a half dozen interviews listed.

98 *Other Navajo men:* OH #28, Jim James (b. 1893, residing Ganado Lake, AZ), May 1, 1972, p. 2; OH #36, Net Slivers (b. 1897, residing Ganado, AZ), June 14, 1972, p. 1; OH #39, Charlie Ganado (b. circa 1884, residing Cross Canyon), August 2, 1972, pp. 1–4; Kinlicheeny, pp. 1–11; and other scattered references to working for Hubbell; OH #26, Sam Taliman (b. 1896, residing Cornfields, AZ), April 26, 1972, pp. 1–2.

98 *taught Loco* See Hubbell family oral histories for information about Loco, also called Hosteen Nez.

99 *Miguelito or Red Point...Mrs. Hubbell* For background on this entire section, see HTPNHS, David M. Brugge, "Miguelito, Navajo *Hatali*," 20 pp. unpublished manuscript dated June 1972; also, OH #14, Mrs. Ben Wilson and OH #17, Marie Curley (b. 1901, residing Ganado, AZ), September 10, 1970, pp. 23–26 (regarding Lina); and Gladys Reichard's works regarding the Miguelito family.

99 *'Old Mexican'* Burbank, *Burbank Among the Indians*, p. 41.

Chapter Seven
A Man Has to Have Some Vices

A good detailed report about the lives of individual Hubbell family members and daily life at Ganado can be found in David M. Brugge, "Hubbell Trading Post National Historic Site: Furnishings Study, the Hubbell Home," January 1972. General information is found in the Hubbell family interviews (OH) and some of the outgoing correspondence in the HP.

101 *mother died* According to the *Albuquerque Journal-Democrat* 12/10/99,

Juliana died on December 8, 1899, with all her sons by her side; at her funeral, the village church bell tolled as the hearse carried her magnificent floral-covered casket to a requiem mass celebrated by priests from Isleta Pueblo, oldAlbuquerque, and Belen. By the terms of his mother's will, J. L. received a one-sixth interest in land in Pajarito between the Rio Grande and the Rio Puerco (approximately 806 acres total parcel size).

101 *Havailand china* OH #47, Dorothy Hubbell, October 10, 1969, p. 14.

102 *remembered...Lina* OH #46, Phillip Hubbell, pp. 4–6; McNitt interview Hubbell Parker, pp. 4–6.

103 *she handled her mother'* HP, Boxes 95–106, Outgoing/Intrapost Correspondence; all immediate-family correspondence surviving through 1931 is arranged chronologically.

103 *Frank who stayed...Felipe* HP, Box 41, see correspondence from J. L.'s brothers in Albuquerque to J. L. Note that the correspondence to the Albuquerque brothers is scattered through the Outgoing HP Boxes 95–106. Also, the Bernalillo County probate records, located at the Probate Court for the County in Albuquerque, for Frank, Tom, and Felipe shed interesting light on the brothers' lives. Also see Callary, "A Political Biography..." for information on the Hubbell brothers (particularly Frank) who returned to Albuquerque.

105 *Adela and Forrest* Hubbell Parker interviews for information regarding his father particularly McNitt interview p. 2, for gun incident, plus other Hubbell family interviews; interview by David M. Brugge (anthropologist/curator, Southwest Regional Office) with Wilmer C. Roberts, Jeddito trader, conducted in Albuquerque, NM, 1977 on file at HTPNHS though not on Interview List. See also WP, the Dixon material, including *Chi 'ndih,* the short story that features the dynamics between Forrest and J. L.

106 *"Dear Little Roman"* HP, Box 25, Drachman.

106 *went to Notre Dame* HP Box 94–97 for family correspondence relative to Roman's education and problems.

107 *formal homestead entry* H&F, pp. 39–40; note that the Sam Day survey was not correct and the property had to be resurveyed and a new patent issued in 1917. On his arrival at Ganado in the 1870s, Hubbell did not homestead; the homesteading (and proving up of same) occurred years after President Roosevelt signed the bill excepting lands claimed by settlers from the 1880 executive order expanding the Navajo reservation.

107 *summer of 1911* HP, Boxes 96 through 99, Outgoing Correspondence, for the period between 1911 and early 1915. J. L., active in politics and absent from his Ganado trading ranch, attempted to run his operation by letters sent primarily to his youngest son Roman. These files contain a wealth of information about trading post operations as well as details about the family.

108 *Alma Doer* (Sometimes spelled Doerr or Dorr); HP, Box 23, Cassidy See also Elizabeth Compton Hegemann *Navaho* [sic] *Trading Days* (Albuquerque: Universi-

312

ty of New Mexico Press, 1963), pp. 201–204; this absorbing book introduced me to trading life from the insider-outsider perspective.

110 *Keam* Cathy Viele, "Thomas Keams [sic]: Squaw Man, Gentleman," *Northlander* (Thursday, August 30, 1979), pp. 162–165. See also Graves biography of Keam for a detailed look at the issue.

111 *St. Michaels birth records* Certified copies of St. Michaels Mission census records listing J. L. Hubbell as the father of children provided to author, placed on file with HTPNHS. These records are discussed at length later in this chapter.

111 *Eleanor, the wife* Correspondence 11/15/30. HP, Box 106.

111 *Ed Sawyer* HP, Box 73; WP.

111 *Dixon...Jones* WP.

111 *resources in Indian country* Kirkpatrick Sales, *The Conquest of Paradise: Christopher Columbus and the Columbian Legacy* (New York: Alfred A. Knopf, 1990), p. 141.

112 *Underhill said* Ruth Underhill, *The Navajo*, p. 170.

112 *Curt Cronemeyer* IT, pp. 274 and 327–331.

112 *Navajo oral histories* OH #11, Ya Na Bah Winker, p. 12; OH #2, Adszaa Bekashi, p. 9; OH #13, Elsie Yazzie (b. 1901, residing Cornfields), January 14, 1972, p. 4 (like Burbank, Mrs. Yazzie said that J. L. and his sons went for young Navajo girls); OH #12, Asdzaa Dloo Holoni, pp. 26–27.

113 *Day granddaughters* Interview, Sam Day III by author at St. Michaels, March 22, 1986.

113 *account books* HP, Box 523 (weavers) and HP, Box 344 (Ganado Indian accounts).

114 *words of a* The bulk of this section is based on numerous conversations with Ganado-area residents; National Park Service staff, past and present; Peggy Scott of Chinle (she provided information on flour or baking powder blankets); and an attorney representing Dorothy Hubbell during the National Park Service acquisition of HTP.

114 *further exploration* While most of the mother/grandmother names in the Navajo oral histories bear little to no resemblance to the names in the Franciscans' records, there are a few that do, and a few that are consistent with the clans indicated in the records. Someone fluent in Navajo needs to listen to the original recordings to determine the appropriate spelling of the maternal ancestors' names and then interview the families involved. I noticed the most consistency in the names of Navajo families with close ties to the Hubbells.

117 *dam at Ganado Lake* H&F, p. 86. See earlier cites & p. 96 et seq. plus H. F. Robinson discussion p. 103.

118 *Charlie* IT; McN; Brugge passim. HP, Outgoing Correspondence, has business and personal letters from Charlie; these were usually addressed to J. L., though sometimes to other relatives as well. See HP, Box 33 for official complaints against

Charlie.

120 *governor of Arizona* HP, Box 42, George Hunt.

120 *aunt wrote* HP, Box 22, Lola Creague. Interesting correspondence regarding family dynamics, distrust of Ganado post office run by Hubbells, poor view of Roman and Adela, and favoring of Barbara and Lorenzo.

121 *last borns* See post-Freudian theorist Dr. Alfred Adler's work; for overview, see Heinz and Rovena Ansbacker, eds., *The Individual Psychology of Alfred Adler: A Systematic Presentation in Selections from his Writings* (New York: Harper & Row,).

Chapter Eight
The Big House

Again, most of the information in this chapter regarding the residence's interior and the trading post operation comes from numerous family interviews; for the function of the rest of the buildings and grounds, from Navajo oral histories as well as my personal observations.

122 *business in Gallup* See Brugge, site specific unpublished history, 1972, p. 34.

122 *His letterhead* HP, Box 101, 2/1/16.

122 *as a familial group* See HP Index for more complete list.

124 *Eley, editor* Passim.

124 *writer, Agnes* Agnes Laut, *Through Our Unknown Southwest* (New York: McBride, 1915), pp. 103–133.

125 *husband managed one* Hilda Faunce Wetherill, *Desert Wife* (reprint, Lincoln: University of Nebraska Press, 1981), pp. 64–65.

126 *Day at the Trading Ranch:* The description of a typical day at the Hubbell trading ranch draws on several Hubbell family member interviews and the Incoming/Outgoing Correspondence in the HP. Particularly, see McNitt and Brugge interviews with Hubbell Parker (May 1972). Refer to WP, especially Maynard Dixon's unpublished manuscripts. An untitled site guide to HTPNHS, written by Kathy M. Anderson, also gives a good overview. Note that classes were sometimes held in the manager's residence and that as additions and remodeling were done, some of the building functions changed. See also Hegemann, *Navaho* [sic] *Trading Days*.

126 *Loco* OH #47, lists several interviews with Dorothy Hubbell at Ganado with David M. Brugge (October 13–24, 1969 pp. 1–2, 23–26 and with McNitt (May 2, 1972, pp. 4–5 and May 6, 1972, p. 8) at her home in Sun City; some of the other oral histories contain limited references to Loco.

127 *benevolent dictator* McNitt interview with Hubbell Parker, p. 27.

127 *Mexican Cry Wash* Alan Wilson with Gene Dennison, *Navajo Place: An Observer's Guide* (Guilford, CT: Jeffrey Norton Publishers, 1995), p. 67. An excellent

book that includes a cassette tape of place names spoken in both Navajo and English. See also, Richard F. Van Valkenburgh, L. W. Adams and J. McPhee, eds., "Diné Bíkéyah," (Window Rock, AZ: The Navajo Nation, 1941), an unpublished work with Navajo stories of place in and around Navajo country.

128 *smell of fresh bread* Brugge interview Hubbell Parker p. 5

129 *Tsiniginnie Nez:* Interview by Vernon Morgan (not in HUTR interview list and no date). See pp. 1 & 3. Nez thought he was 99 when he was interviewed. Indian labor is discussed in H&F, pp. 84-87, and Youngblood, "Navajo Trading, A Report...," p. 12.

129 *Tully Lincoln* OH # 19, Tully Lincoln, pp. 13 and 14; good interview about working for Hubbell.

129 *attend school* McNitt interview May 2, 1972 with Dorothy Hubbell, pp. 7-9; second interview same date see p. 1. See also, Hubbell Parker's interview Brugge, p. 2.

133 *daily fare...question her father* McNitt interview with Hubbell Parker, pp. 27, 36-37.

134 *bookcase exhibits* See HUTR records.

135 *an aura of history* Hegemann, *Navaho* [sic] *Trading Days* p. 204.

135 *shake the dust* HP, Outgoing Correspondence, Letter to Commissioner of Indian Affairs, 2/12/16.

Chapter Nine
Eighteen Thousand Pounds of Blankets

136 *Between Two Points* WP, Dr. Edgar W. Moore, "Commerce in the Southwest: The Indian Trader, A Review of the Literature" unpublished paper given at the Great Lakes Historical Conference, April, 1979 (Moore affiliated with Indiana University of Pennsylvania). See also, H&F pp. 209-250 Harried Mayfield, "Great Southwest Pioneer Passes On," *The Santa Fe Magazine* XXV (January 1931).

136 *Ben Wittick* Wittick, a well-known Western photographer who often photographed Hubbell family members.

137 *1908 and 1913* H&F, p. 231; HP, Box 96(1) et seq; Outgoing Correspondence (1908 to 1913).

138 *mail routes* HP, Outgoing Correspondence (for general information).

139 *road conditions* See Youngblood, "Navajo Trading, A Report..." for description of reservation roads the time of J. L.'s death.

139 *Freighters and how* H&F, pp. 209 to 250 (emphasis on pp. 232-235); Frisbee/Mitchell, *Navajo Blessingway Singer*, pp. 113 & 161; and Bailey and Bailey, *A History of the Navajos*, p. 162.

139 *Mexican Cry Wash* Passim.

140 *short loads...Rough Trips* Schmedding, *Cowboy and Indian Trader*, pp. 325

and 311–313.

140 *Thank God* Lockwood, *Pioneer Portraits*, p. 145.

141 *cloudburst...snow* OH, Gene Haldeman, November 29, 1972, interviewed by David M. Brugge (much of the discussion concerns weather on reservation, especially pp. 49–50); OH #51, Father Immanuel Trocker, OFM, taken for Arizona Pioneer Historical Society by David M. Brugge and Victoria Best.

142 *equipment and personnel* HP, Incoming Correspondence, for instance Box 20 and Outgoing Correspondence 96.

142 *McSparron...army coat...Karigan* Lockwood, *Pioneer Portraits*, pp. 146–147, 148, 149.

142 *ingenious ways* HP, Box 19 (7).

143 *six cars:* Father Trocker, passim.

144 *motor vehicle party:* Faunce Wetherill, *Desert Wife*, pp. 66–72.

145 *Ganado records* HP, Box 523 Lists, Weavers. See also weaver accounts in HP, Box 344.

146 *profited doubly* Amsden, *Navaho* [sic] *Weaving*, p. 179.

147 *Etsitty* An unnumbered, undated interview with David Brugge, p.3. Interviewee related by clan to Red Point.

148 *Pete Hubbard* OH #16, Peter Hubbard, Sr. (b.1916, residing Ganado), January 23, 1972, pp. 45–46.

148 *Mrs. Yazzie Holmes* OH #33, Mrs. Yazzie Holmes, pp. 25–31.

148 *Mrs. Frank Churchill* WP. The original is located at the Hood Museum of Art, Dartmouth College, Hanover, NH, with Clara G. Churchill's journal, December 5 to December 21, 1903 (Kansas City to Keams Canyon, vol. I).

148 *Navajo silverwork* John Adair, *The Navajo and Pueblo Silversmiths* (Norman: University of Oklahoma Press, 1944), pp. 8 and 135; this absorbing work relies heavily on Indian interviews. See also, Van Valkenburgh, *Diné Bikéyah*, p. 64; Ruth Roessell, "Navajo Arts and Crafts," Ortiz, Vol 10, pp. 599–601; and Larry Frank with Millard J. Holbrook II, *Indian Silver Jewelry of the Southwest, 1868–1930* (Atglen: Pa: Schiffer Publishing, 1990).

149 *Fred Harvey* For an overview of this topic, albeit one slanted toward the prominence of Fred Harvey staff, see Howard and Pardue, *Inventing the Southwest*, and Weigle and Babcock, eds., *The Great Southwest*. See also HP, Boxes 36–38, Fred Harvey correspondence; most of the text for this section came from the Correspondence/Incoming from Fred Harvey Co. or /Outgoing from the Hubbells and can be tracked by dates.

151 *Anthropologists have* See Burton Benedict, *The Anthropology of World's Fairs: San Francisco's Panama Pacific International Exposition of 1915* (Berkeley, CA: Lowie Museum of Anthropology, 1983) for an excellent discussion of this phenomenon.

151 *little precedent* Acrey, *Navajo History*, p. 114.

151 *Schweizer would demand* Kathleen L. Howard, "'A Most Remarkable Success': Herman Schweizer and the Fred Harvey Indian Department," in *The Great Southwest* p. 87.

151 *Charlie Ganado* OH #39, Charlie Ganado, pp. 1–4.

155 *Elle...Nampeyo* Pardue and Howard, "Making Art, Making Money: The Fred Harvey Company and the Indian Artisan," in *The Great Southwest*, pp. 168–173.

Chapter Ten
The Dyestuff: People and Places

For information on the Day family, I consulted the Anna B. Day diary, transcribed by Jewell Adams and part of the St. Michaels Records, Special Collections, University of Arizona Library, Tucson. Quotes from the diary retain Anna Day's spelling and punctuation. According to Jewell Adams, the Days arrived at Cienago Amarillo (now known as St. Michaels) on March 9, 1887. An excellent biography with much detail about other members of the reservation community is Robert L. Wilken, *Anselm Weber, O.F.M.: Missionary to the Navajo 1898–1921* (Milwaukee, WI: Bruce Publishing Co., 1955).

The Franciscan's correspondence with J. L. Hubbell is found in HP, Box 30. For the Bierkempers and the Ganado Presbyterian Mission, see Dr. Edgar W. Moore's excellent article, "The Bierkempers, Navajos, and the Ganado Presbyterian Mission, 1901–1912," *American Presbyterians: A Journal of Presbyterian History* 64:7 (Summer 1986). Also, see Salsbury's autobiography (cited earlier). HP, Box 9 contains the Bierkemper incoming correspondence. Incoming correspondence from the Indian agents is found in HP, Boxes 43 and 44. Incoming Cotton correspondence starts in HP, Box 19. See prior citations to Cotton references.

158 *taught the Franciscans* Wilken, *Anselm Weber, O.F.M.*, pp. 43–44; see also The Franciscan Fathers, *An Ethnologic Dictionary of the Navaho* [sic].

158 *Garland* Anna B. Day diary, notes throughout.

159 *Dorothy Hubbell* Interview with author previously cited.

159 *first page* Mary Jeanette Kennedy, *Tales of a Trader's Wife: Life on the Navajo Indian Reservation 1913–38* (Albuquerque, NM: Valliant Co., 1965), pp. 1, 2.

159 *letter of apology* HP, Box 23 September 14, 1911.

160 *grandchildren played* Author interview with Sam Day III.

161 *Drexel* Wilken, *Anselm Weber, O.F.M.*, p. 22; see also general newspaper articles on the Franciscans in Special Collections files at University of Arizona, Tucson.

161 *on way to Hopi* See Wilken for general information; quoted material for 1899 visit, pp. 53–54, 1902 visit, p. 97.

163 *"big eyes"* Paul V. Long, *Big Eyes: The Southwestern Photographs of Simeon Schwemberger, 1902–1908* (Albuquerque: University of New Mexico Press, 1992); see p. 10 for sister's description. J. L. released Simeon from his job managing a

Hubbell trading post after the latter charged Claudio Romero, a Hubbell relative employed in the family operation, with mishandling the mail (HP, Box 97).

164 *Presbyterian Church party* Moore, "The Bierkempers, Navajos...," p. 131; see p. 128 for reasons Hubbell wanted a mission in Ganado.

166 *Culin's diary* WP.

167 *Colton* HP, Box 18 for undated letters; see also Jimmy H. Miller, *The Life of Harold Sellers Colton: A Philadelphia Brahmin in Flagstaff* (Tsaile, AZ: Navajo Community College Press, 1991), pp. 62, 63.

168 *two story...Chinle* Frisbie, "On the Trail of Chinle's 'Big House'...," pp. 69-85.

168 *Kirk* HP, Box 99.

169 *Dixon...Brener* HP; copies of both artists' correspondence can be found in this collection.

169 *made nothing* HP, Box 101.

Chapter Eleven
Politics

The letters of J. L. Hubbell, his sons, and brother Charlie are found in HP/Outgoing Correspondence and can easily be located by the date indicated in the text; the microfiche material in the Hubbell Papers is arranged by date rather than by writer.

As J. L.'s absences increased, the frequency and sometimes the length of the letters correspondingly increased. The period 1911 to 1914 provides an excellent overview of J. L.'s trading post operations. Letters from this era also give insight into J. L.'s thirty years of trading; the strengths and the weaknesses of his operation (and of himself); and to a lesser extent, his politics. The letters he received and contemporary newspaper accounts flesh out the story of this very political period in his life.

Several general books on Arizona history were consulted for background: Walker and Bufkin, *Historical Atlas of Arizona*; Hubert H. Bancroft, *History of Arizona and New Mexico* (Albuquerque, NM: Horn & Wallace, 1962); Lynn I. Perrigo, *The American Southwest: Its Peoples and Cultures* (Albuquerque: University of New Mexico Press, 1971), specifically, pp. 323-325 for the statehood struggle; and Odie B. Faulk, *Arizona: A Short History* (Norman: University of Oklahoma Press, 1970). Consulted as well were the Session Laws of the 16th Legislative Assembly (Phoenix, AZ: Phoenix Herald Book and Job Office, cal892), pp. 15-16 and 119; and the Journals of the 17th Legislature of Arizona (Phoenix, AZ: Phoenix Herald Book and Job Office, 1893), pp. 87, 91, 145, 344, 358, 359. See Calvin D. Linton, ed., *The American Almanac: A Diary of America* (Nashville and New York: Thomas Nelson, Inc., 1977) for national politics generally, and specifically, pp. 280-283 for the Bull Moose party.

From all of these, a summary of the brief political history covered in this chapter was constructed. Though the statehood period has been heavily studied, the wealth of material in the HP concerning politics dictated a rather broad approach to the general subject of Arizona history.

173 *799 miles* See DLAPR, Phoenix, Az. for political documents.

174 *Arizona Republican* Taken primarily from the newspaper reports cited.

176 *Ralph H. Cameron* HP, Box 14. Cameron mimicked Hubbell's territorial entrepreneurism by establishing mines at the Grand Canyon and mercantile and sheep operations in the Flagstaff, Az. area. In 1890, he widened an old Havasupai Indian path into what became the first trail into the Grand Canyon; he later charged visitors a dollar a head to use the trail, which he named Bright Angel). At one point, Cameron claimed 13,000 acres of Arizona land, far more than his friend's claim to a mere 160 acres.

179 *Barth* Issac Barth, interview in the *St. Johns Observer* (July 10, 1937).

180 *Alonzo Hubbell* HP, Box 99, letter to son Roman (April 16, 1913).

180 *first month in office* HP, Box 547 for information on the cancelgraph matter; for Raphael-related issues, see 1912 general Outgoing Correspondence, particularly to and from Cornelia Cassidy Davis.

180 *Charles Lummis's* HP, Box 53.

183 *Chee Dodge* See earlier Dodge citations. Chee Dodge and his wives regularly brought their wool to Hubbell. In January 1912, Cotton's staff wrote to HTP at Ganado about Chee Dodge's 78 bags of wool a credit total $2,886.75. Dr. Wauneka's comment was made at a Hubbell Friends event in the 1990s at Ganado. See Lockwood's comment in *More Arizona Characters*: "Chee Dodge told me that Hubbell spent so much money on his candidacy for the United States senatorship (legitimately) he was so embarrassed financially that Dodge loaned him thirty thousand in cash. He [Dodge] added that just then he was the only friend who could and would advance that much cash to relieve him [Hubbell] from the strain." (p. 77).

The money Hubbell used for living expenses and travel during the approximately three years he was heavily involved in politics, his absences from the post at its busiest time, his inability to pass control to his sons/managers and his investments in the cancelgraph, all seriously impacted the Hubbell enterprises' which already had a shaky cash flow.

185 *final count...campaign financial* Department of Library, Archives and Public Records, Phoenix, Arizona, and the report of the 1914 election results by county (vote tallies).

PART IV: DON LORENZO

Chapter Twelve
Holding Open House: The Southwest Host

Any reading of the HP Incoming Correspondence files yields innumerable letters from former and prospective guests. The WP at HTPNHS contain copies made from the HP as well as articles, copies of book pages, reports, and materials related to individual visitors. Sometimes these materials are referred to as extract copies of an original manuscript in another museum or library collection. The extract copies are found in HUTR historical files (also called WP).

191   *himself as Don Lorenzo* Brugge interview with Haldeman, pp. 1 and 2.

191   *Coddington recalled* IT, p. 217.

192   *Writer Agnes* Laut, *Through Our Unknown Southwest*, pp. 126, 127.

192   *Culin said* WP, quoted in Brugge's unpublished "The Hubbell Home" 1972; WP, Culin, 1902 journal, p. 21. Journal probably obtained by HTPNHS from the Brooklyn Museum and added to the WP.

192   *Washington politician* HP, Box 97(6), April 17, 1912.

192   *bums, coffee salesmen* Lockwood, *Pioneer Portraits*, p. 156.

193   *Dixon labeled* WP.

193   *blanket brokers* HP, Boxes 1 and 24. See also HP, Box 41, Ada Hubbard 1903 correspondence, for a fairly thorough overview of a long-term rug ambassador relationship.

193   *sorely abused* Laut, *Through Our Unknown Southwest*, pp. 106–107.

194   *swimming challenge* Sam Day II, Fontana interview. See generally for examples of Hubbell's behavior with contemporaries, and pp. 65–66.

194   *basket connoisseur...muleskinner* McNitt Interview Hubbell Parker, pp. 14–16.

195   *President Theodore Roosevelt* HP, Box 23, artist Cornelia Cassidy Davis (later divorced and Cornelia Cassidy) letter dated September 18, 1902, for "look-a-like" observation. Correspondence from the Roosevelts is found in HP, Box 71. See McNitt interview, Hubbell Parker; HP, Box 97, J. L.'s letter to Roman; and other letters in Intrapost Correspondence regarding the 1913 Hopi Snake Ceremony.

195   *Nephew Phillip* McNitt interview, Phillip Hubbell, pp. 16–17 and 20–22.

197   *Colton* Miller, *Life of Harold Sellers Colton*, pp. 62–63.

199   *Other writer-visitors* See profiles of many of Ganado's noted visitors (including writers) in Dan L. Thrapp, *Encyclopedia of Frontier Biography*, 3 vol. (Lincoln: University of Nebraska Press, 1988). Also, the WP contain copies of most of the articles by the various authors about Hubbell and his adventures.

199   *Garland's book* Lonnie E. Underhill and Daniel F. Littlefield, Sr., *Hamlin Garland's Observations*, p. 86.

199   *Charles F. Lummis* WP; selected material includes some translation of Lummis's Spanish journal entries about his Ganado trip. See also, HP, Box 53, Incoming Correspondence.

201   *George Wharton James* HP, Box 46.

202   *Western novelist* HP, Box 18; see also, Coolidges, *The Navajo Indians*.

203   *Stewart Culin felt* WP for journal etc.; see also Grant, *Canyon de Chelly*, pp.

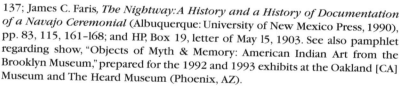

137; James C. Faris, *The Nightway:A History and a History of Documentation of a Navajo Ceremonial* (Albuquerque: University of New Mexico Press, 1990), pp. 83, 115, 161–168; and HP, Box 19, letter of May 15, 1903. See also pamphlet regarding show, "Objects of Myth & Memory: American Indian Art from the Brooklyn Museum," prepared for the 1992 and 1993 exhibits at the Oakland [CA] Museum and The Heard Museum (Phoenix, AZ).

203 *F. M. Palmer* WP, 1906 report to the Honorable Chairman of the Executive Committee of the Southwest Society. Note that Hubbell's catalog lists "a rare collection of genuine pre-historic pottery: $2.50 to $10.00 each."

204 *thousand ethnographic items* See HUTR records and reports. Specifically, what is referred to as the museum collection consists of 16,800 artifacts, including 200 or so oils and pastels, 4,000 photographs, 500 Indian baskets, 200 Navajo rugs, 200 pieces of pottery (both prehistoric and historic), several farm wagons, and various machinery and parts.

Chapter Thirteen
A Painter's Mecca

There exist two primary catalogues/lists for the Hubbell Fine Art Collection. The first (possibly prepared early on at the establishment of the site by one of the first curators) consists of twenty-one pages of legal-size paper with typed entries divided into Art Objects (artist, media, title, size, and location at site); Photographs (photographer, title, size, and site location); Ethnological Articles; Guns; Furnishings; and Books (listed alphabetically).

The second, titled "Database Inventory of Fine Arts Collection HTPNHS Museum Collection, 1992," was ably compiled by NPS curator Ed Chamberlin and staff and is an exquisitely detailed catalogue of the fine arts collection. It includes not just additional detail (such as markings on a work of art), but also includes each painted rug design. It adds Christmas cards as "works of art," as well as several works dated post-1930. When the two lists are compared, it is easy to see that there is a difference in the number of pieces.

Anyone interested in what J. L. acquired during his lifetime will need to consult the list of artworks at HTPNHS kept by Dorothy Hubbell, which does not account for all work that appears in the HP as bought, traded, or given to the Hubbells. My list of visual image makers is from the combined catalogue/lists.

A reader with research interests in a particular artist can consult the HP Index for relevant letters; in most instances, these letters will generally be found in Incoming Correspondence (check for Dumond, Sauerwein, Groll, McCormick, Curtis, the Sawyers, and Moon, for example). The WP at HTPNHS is a quicker source of this information. The space that I was able to allocate to the three individual artists whom I felt were of most importance to Hubbell is merely an introduction to both the artist and the artist-trader relationship. I encourage those who are interested in further detail to review the

WP as well as the following references.

Burbank is well represented in literature concerning Western artists: his own account, *Burbank Among the Indians*; Charles F. Lummis, "Painting the First Americans," *Land of Sunshine* (May 1900); G. W. James, "A Noted Painter of Indian Types," *The Craftsmen* (December 1904); Everett Maxwell, "The Art of Elbridge A. Burbank," *Fine Arts Journal* XXII:1 (January 1910); and August 1966 notes compiled by Thomas S. McNeill, "Painter of Indians," located at Braun Research Library, Southwest Museum, Los Angeles, California.

From the HP, the second half of Box 12 (beginning with frame 6) contains Burbank's correspondence. There are numerous references to Burbank in much of the correspondence from other artists, writers, and visitors, as well.

In addition to the Dixon correspondence in the HP, there is a wonderful collection of Dixon-Hubbell correspondence in Bernard L. Fontana, *Querido Patrón: Letters From Maynard Dixon to Lorenzo Hubbell* (Tucson: Friends of the University of Arizona Library, 1987).

The WP contain several of Dixon's typed and handwritten notes in which he mentions incidents occurring at Ganado. The Dixon folder also contains a typewritten "Chronology Outline" for a Maynard Dixon biography compiled by Grant Wallace in 1936.

See also Wesley M. Burnside, "Maynard Dixon, Artist of the West" (Ph.D. diss., Ohio State University, 1970), archived at the Braun Research Library. Finally, see Peggy and Harold Samuels, *Samuels' Encyclopedia of Artists of the American West* (Secaucus, NJ: Castle, 1985), a comprehensive reference to Western American art; most of the artists who visited Hubbell are listed in this work.

208 *"arrived at Gallup"...Many Horses* Burbank, *Burbank Among the Indians*, pp. 41 to 56. There is some confusion between Many Horses and a man called Tyoni (variously spelled). Hubbell's letterhead designates the hatted figure as Tja-Yo ni. Some interviewees refer to the two (Many Horses and Tyoni) as brothers, but Tyoni is not listed in Ganado Mucho's family chart. Regardless, it seems doubtful to me that Many Horses, or Tyoni, if he's a separate person, knew his likeness would be ludicrous in non-Navajo eyes.

210 *Hubbell spent* HP, Box 12(7). Burbank sporadically summarized the annual exchange between himself and Hubbell, what he sent to Hubbell, and what Hubbell paid (usually, between five to ten dollars for each piece).

210 *"Hopi Snake Dance"* HP, Box 97, 2/12/07.

210 *family dog* Burbank, *Burbank Among the Indians*, pp. 203-204.

210 *Navajos gambling:* OHs of Tully Lincoln, Tsinijinnie Nez, T'ahasbaa' Slivers, and OH #34, John Kiiya'aanii (b. 1898, residing Cornfields, AZ), May 1972; Lockwood, *More Arizona Characters*, p. 61; WP.

211 *Joseph J. Mora's* WP; HP, Box 60; Samuels, *Encyclopedia of Artists...*, p. 331-332. See Mora's book, *Trail Dust and Saddleleather* (New York: Charles Scribner 1946).

212 *Maynard Dixon* Passim and WP.

213 *Harold H. Betts* HP, Box 9 and WP.

214 *Frederick Melville Dumond* See article by Eleanor Bradley, "An Artist Two Years Alone in the Desert," *True West* (September–October, 1978), p. 37.

217 *plaque of Navajo man* For instance, OH, #26, Sam Taliman (b. 1895, residing Cornfields), p. 35.

PART V: NAAKAII SÁNÍ

Chapter Fourteen
A View From the Bullpen

221 *Maria Antonia* See Reichard, *Spiderwoman*, pp. 37–43 for reference on Marie learning to weave; p. 96 for Maria Antonio's remark about teaching Reichard; and p. 146 for Miguelito's (or Red Point's) house.

221 *Mrs. Ben Wilson* OH #14, Mrs. Ben Wilson, pp. 2–3, 5, 31, and intermittently throughout the rest of her interview.

224 *Dodge as an uncle* OH #17, Marie Curley, pp. 40–41.

224 *grandfather* For information on Navajo clan structure, see previously mentioned general Navajo references; see also Gary Witherspoon, "Navajo Social Organization," in Ortiz, Vol. 10, p. 524.

224 *killed a...dog* Lockwood, *Pioneer Portraits*, pp. 139–140.

224 *Happy Hunting* Burbank, *Burbank Among the Indians*, p. 43 (both quotes).

225 *"always weaving"* OH, Mrs. Ben Wilson, p. 14.

225 *Navajo spirituality* Navajo Studies Conferences attended by author; author's personal conversations with weavers; and Lena Shondee interview, "Spinning Cultures," in *Navajo Times*, November 27, 1985.

226 *Traders, including* Amsden, *Navaho* [sic] *Weaving*, pp. 189–190; Kate Peck Kent, *Navajo Weaving: Three Centuries of Change* (Santa Fe, NM: School of American Research, 1985), p. 83; Gary Witherspoon, "Navajo Weaving: Art in Its Cultural Content," *Museum of Northern Arizona Research Paper 36* (Flagstaff, AZ: undated), pp. 58–77; and Kathleen M'Closkey, "Myths, Markets and Metaphors: Navajo Weaving as Commodity and Communicative Form" (Ph.D. diss., York University, Toronto, 1996) pp. 195–223. Other background information on this subject comes from the several-years-long correspondence between Kathleen M'Closkey and the author.

227 *high praise* OH #2, Asdaa Bekashi, a short interview with many references. See OH #18, LaCheenie Blacksheep, pp. 10–11, 40. OH #7, Joe Tippecanoe, pp. 23–2;. OH #19, Tully Lincoln. Also, OH #33, Mrs. Holmes, pp. 19–20; OH #8, Tom Morgan (born 1879, residing Ganado), November 19, 1971 and April 25, 1972), see p. 5 of second interview. OH #4, T. Slivers, p. 4.

228 *Double-faced Token* See Kluckhohn, *The Navajo*, 1946, 1962, p. 311 for a

discussion of two-sidedness.

231 *"chicken pulls"* OH #14, Mrs. Ben Wilson, pp. 39–42; OH #35, Buck Chambers; and OH #19, Tully Lincoln, pp. 61–63. Callary, "A Political Biography...", p. 6, for reference to *gallo.*

232 *Keshmish* Thompson, *The Army and the Navajo*, p. 66; Kennedy, *Tales of a Trader's Wife*, pp. 14, 41–44; Annabel Hardy, pp. 3–4.

233 *Hastiin Bagodi* HP, Box 95, J. L.'s letters to John H. Lloyd (2/28 and 3/9/09) and Mr. McPherson (3/11/09); see also WP, Cassidy Davis letter (February or March 1909).

235 *natives of the Americas* Sales, *Conquest of Paradise*, p. 281.

235 *From 1901 to 1934* IT, p. 322.

236 *strict with them* See earlier citations for Franciscans.

236 *avoided transculturation* See Helen M. Bannan, "Newcomers to Navajoland: Transculturation in the Memoirs of Anglo Women, 1900–1945," *New Mexico Historical Review* 59:2 (April 1984).

236 *Navajo moral code* Witherspoon, Oritiz, ed. Vol. l0, p. 535; Witherspoon quotes philosopher John Ladd, who had studied the Navajo moral code.

PART VI: LORENZO THE MAGNIFICENT

Chapter Fifteen
Snap! Snap! And Snap Again!

This chapter deals with J. L.'s last dozen or so years as an Indian trader. Because I chose to concentrate on Hubbell's working life, rather than his decline or fallow years, the reader will find a certain amount of chronological compression in both this chapter and the one following.

241 *"land of the living"* HP, Box 99, June 10, 1914.

241 *Charles Rubi* HP, Box l02, April 24, 1923.

242 *trader's ledgers* HP, Boxes 529–530 for legal matters and summary pages of mortgages and related information.

242 *Hopi owned* See Chapter Two citations related to Hopis; Ortiz, vol. 9, pp. 526–529, 559.

243 *Charlie...is dead* See *State of Arizona vs. Adeltoni Bigue #1 and Adeltoni Bigue #2,* Superior Court of Coconino County (no docket number), particularly the record of the preliminary hearing (in microfiche form at Coconino County Courthouse, Flagstaff), the newspaper exhibit attachments to a Motion for Change of Venue, the *Coconino Sun* articles found at Special Collections, Northern Arizona University; and HP, Box 101, March through December 1919. Also, Billie Yost, *Bread Upon the Sands* (Caldwell, ID: Caxton Publishers, 1958), pp. 221–238; and Bailey and Bailey, *A History of the Navajos*, p. 222, for a discussion

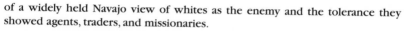

of a widely held Navajo view of whites as the enemy and the tolerance they showed agents, traders, and missionaries.

243 *Lorenzo financed* HP, Boxes 103, 104.

248 *Wichita, Kansas* McNitt interview, Hubbell Parker, p. 4.

249 *Dorothy Smith* Taken from various interviews with Dorothy Smith Hubbell and other family members conducted by Brugge and McNitt.

250 *Pancho Villa* HP. See McN for newspaper articles and passport.

250 *"Up Against It"* HP, Boxes 101 to 106, Outgoing/Intrapost Correspondence, provides a good view of Hubbell family enterprises after Charlie's death as well as glimpses of J. L.'s decline.

252 *first...chairman* During this period, the Navajo perspective on both the chairmanship and the tribal council (which was formed at the same time) was that they would behave cooperatively, in effect rubber-stamping Bureau of Indian Affairs decisions.

252 *Tom Dodge* Lockwood, *Pioneer Portraits*, p. 155.

252 *fundraising* Salsbury, *The Salsbury Story*, pp. 124-125, 134.

Chapter Sixteen
The Old Blankets Are Passing Away

257 *"old gent"* OH #49 Clifton Farrar, Arizona Historical Society, taken by David M. Brugge and Victoria Best (1970), pp. 1-2, 23-24.

258 *Herman W. Atkins* OH #54, Herman W. Atkins (b. circa 1887) 1972, interview with McNitt.

258 *financial situation* McNitt interview with Hubbell Parker, p. 20.

259 *Coddington's father* Henry B., "Bert" Coddington, Gallup, NM, May 10, 1972, by McNitt, pp. 4, 11. McN and copy at HTPNHS.

259 *suffered a stroke* Lockwood, *More Arizona Characters*, p. 79.

260 *insisting that...Barbara* OH #53, La Charles Eckel at Ganado, June 26, 1979, interviewed by Lawrence C. Kelly, pp. 24, 25.

261 *named Newcomer* Burke Johnson, "Story of Don Lorenzo," Arizona *Days and Ways* (December 26, 1965), pp. 4-11. Newcomer is the only name given in article.

261 *mission friend* Gene Haldeman interview, pp. 12-13.

262 *Frank himself* HP, Box 41, Summer 1929.

262 *last year* Salsbury, *The Salsbury Story*, p. 137-141.

Chapter Seventeen
Los Todos Santos, By All the Saints

Condolence letters are archived in HP Box 106 for some family members and others under Hubbell in HP Box 41 in the Incoming Correspondence which is alphabetized. Check for post-November 1930 letters by sender's name.

266 *Albert H. Lee Gaamaliitsho Indian Trader*, p. 195.

266 *Salsbury The Salsbury Story*, p. 140.

269 *Irvin G. Wyllie The Self-Made Man in America: The Myth of Rags to Riches* (New York: The Free Press, 1954), pp. 107–108.

271 *Indian enfranchisement* WP, newspaper article regarding voter registrar Dorothy Hubbell's opposition to Indians voting.

272 *Federal Trade Commission* U. S. Federal Trade Commission Staff Report, "The Trading Post System on the Navajo Reservation" (Washington, D. C.: Government Printing Office, 1973).

Epilogue

See the HP Outgoing/Intrapost Correspondence; OH Dorothy Hubbell interviews; probate of Lorenzo Hubbell's estate in Navajo County, some is in WP; WP file on National Park Service Acquisition and Albert Manchester and Ann Manchester, Hubbell Trading Post National Historic Site: An Administrative History, Southwest Cultural Resources Center, Professional Papers No. 46, (Santa Fe, N.M., 1993). Documentation on repayment of Dodge loans can be found in HP, Box 529; Interview by author with Dorothy Hubbell, July 29, 1988 along with supplementary typed notes by Dorothy Hubbell. Benjamin J. Dodge, Mary Dodge Peshlakai, and Annie Dodge Wahneka (usually spelled Wauneka) transferred their interests in the Hubbell mortgage in 1949 to Rico Motors. Later the mortgages were cancelled and released by Merchant's Bank in Gallup on January 27, 1967. The owner of Rico Motors was an officer of the bank.

BIBLIOGRAPHY

Acrey, Bill P. *Navajo History: The Land and The People*. Shiprock, NM: Central Consolidated School District No. 22, 1988.

Adair, John. *The Navajo and Pueblo Silversmiths*. Norman: University of Oklahoma Press, 1944.

Adams, William Y. *Shonto: A Study of the Role of the Trader in a Modern Navaho* [sic] *Community*, Bureau of American Ethnology, Bulletin 188. Washington, D. C.; GPO, 1963.

Albrecht, Dorothy E. "Vignettes of Arizona Pioneers: John Lorenzo Hubbell, Navajo Indian Trader," *Arizonian* IV:3 (Fall 1963).

Amsden, Charles A. *Navaho* [sic] *Weaving: Its Technic and Its History*. 1934; reprinted, Glorieta, NM: Rio Grande Press, 1972.

Ansbacker, Heinz and Rovena, eds. *The Individual Psychology of Alfred Adler: A Systematic Presentation in Selections from his Writings*. New York, NY: Harper & Rowe.

Astrov, Margaret. "The Concept of Motion as the Psychological Leitmotif of Navajo Life and Literature," *The Journal of American Folklore* (1950).

Bailey, Garrick and Roberta Glenn Bailey. *A History of the Navajos: The Reservation* Years. Santa Fe, NM: School of American Research, 1986.

Bailey, Lynn R. *Bosque Redondo: An American Concentration Camp*. Pasadena, CA: Socio-Technical Books, 1970.

—-. *If You Take My Sheep: The Evolution and Conflicts of Navajo Pastoralism, 1630-1868*. Pasadena, CA: Westernlore Publications.

—-. *Indian Slave Trade in the Southwest: A Study of Slave-taking and the Traffic of Indian Captives*. Los Angeles: Westernlore Press, 1966.

—-. *The Long Walk, a History of the Navajo Wars, 1846-1868*. Los Angeles, CA: Westernlore Press, 1964.

Ball, Larry D. *Desert Lawmen: The High Sheriffs of New Mexico and Arizona 1846-1912*. Albuquerque: University of New Mexico Press, 1992.

Bancroft, Hubert H. *History of Arizona and New Mexico*. Albuquerque, NM: Horn & Wallace, 1962.

Bannan, Helen M. "Newcomers to Navajoland: Transculturation in the Memoirs of Anglo Women, 1900-1945," *New Mexico Historical Review* 59:2 (April 1984).

Barnes, Will C. *Arizona Place Names*, revised and enlarged by Byrd H. Granger. Tucson: University of Arizona Press, 1960.

Basso, Keith H. *Portraits of "the Whiteman": Linguistic Play and Cultural Symbols Among the Western Apache*. Cambridge, England: Cambridge University Press, 1979.

Bauer, Liz. "Research for a Catalog of the Navajo Textiles of Hubbell Trading Post." National Endowment for the Humanities, Grant No. GM-22317-84; July 4, 1987.

Bauer, Mark and Frank Morgan. "Navajo Conflict Resolution," *Diné Be'iina* I:1 (Spring 1987).

Benedict, Burton. *The Anthropology of World's Fairs: San Francisco's Panama Pacific International Exposition of 1915*. Berkeley, CA: Lowie Museum of Anthropology, 1983.

Berthrang, Donald J. "Nineteenth Century United States Government Agencies," in the *Handbook of North American Indians* series, Alfonso Ortiz, vol. ed., vol. 9 *Southwest*. Washington, D. C.: Smithsonian Institution, 1988.

Blue, Martha. "A View from the Bullpen: A Navajo Ken of Traders and Trading Posts," *Plateau* 57:3 (1986).

—-. "Money Made of Tin," *Coins* (October 1988).

—-. *The Witchpurge of 1878: Oral and Documentary History in the Early Reservation Years*. Tsaile, AZ: Navajo Community College Press, 1988.

Borgman, Francis (Reverend). "Henry Chee Dodge: The Last Chief of the Navaho [sic] Indians ," *New Mexico Historical Review* XXIII:2 (April 1948).

Bradley, Eleanor. "An Artist Two Years Alone in the Desert," *True West* (September–October, 1978).

Brew, J. O. "Hopi Prehistory and Hopi History to 1850," in Ortiz, ed. *Southwest*, vol. 9 of *Handbook of North American Indians*. Washington, D. C.: Smithsonian Institution, 1979.

Brown, Lieutenant W. C. Survey, *Report on Conditions of the Navajo Country* (1893).

Brugge, David M. "Henry Chee Dodge: From the Long Walk to Self-Determination," in L. G. Moses and Raymond Wilson, eds., *Indian Lives: Essays on Nineteenth- and Twentieth-Century Native American Leaders*. Albuquerque: University of New Mexico Press, 1985.

—. "Hubbell Trading Post National Historic Site, Furnishings Study, The Hubbell Home" January 1972 (also cited as Historic Preservation Team: Denver Service Center).

—. "Miguelito, Navajo *Hatali*," Unpublished manuscript. June 1972.

—. "Navajo and Western Pueblo History," *The Smoke Signal* 25 (reprinted 1981).

—. "The Valley of the Red House," July-August 1972, draft and unpublished history.

—. *Hubbell Trading Post National Historic Site*. Tucson, AZ: Southwest Parks and Monuments Association, 1993.

—. *Navajos in the Catholic Church Records of New Mexico 1694-1875*. Tsaile, AZ: Navajo Community College Press, 1985.

Burbank, E. A. and Ernest Royce. *Burbank Among the Indians*. Caldwell, ID: Caxton Printers, 1946.

Callary, Carol N. "A Political Biography of Frank A. Hubbell 1862-1929." master's thesis, University of New Mexico, 1967.

Cleland, Robert Class and Juanita Brooks, eds. *A Mormon Chronicle: The Diaries of John D. Lee 1848-1876*. San Marino, CA: Huntington Library, 1955.

Connelly. John C., "Hopi Social Organization," in the *Handbook of North American Indians* series, Alfonso Ortiz, vol. ed., vol. 9 *Southwest*. Washington, D. C.: Smithsonian Institution, 1979.

Coolidge, Dane and Mary Roberts Coolidge. *The Navajo Indians*. 1930; reprinted New York: Ames Bros., 1979.

Correll, J. Lee. *Through White Man's Eyes: A Contribution to Navajo History: A Chronological Record of the Navajo People from the Earliest Times to the Treaty of June 1, 1868*, 6 vols. Window Rock, AZ: Navajo Heritage Center, 1979.

Cotton, Clinton N. *Wholesale Catalogue and Price List of Navajo Blankets*. Prepared by G. Wharton James. San Francisco, CA: H. S. Crocker Co., 1896.

Davis, Wayne ed. *St. Johns Arizona Stake Centennial 1887 July 23, 1987*. St. Johns, AZ: The Church of Jesus Christ of Latter-Day Saints, St. Johns, Arizona, Stake, 1987.

Dockstader, Frederick J., "Hopi History: 1850-1940," in the *Handbook of North American Indians* series, Alfonso Ortiz, vol. ed., vol. 9 *Southwest*. Washington, D. C.: Smithsonian Institution, 1979.

Eckel, La Charles G. "History of Ganado," *Museum Notes: Museum of Northern Arizona* 6 (April 1934).

Eley, Rufus. "Ganado: The Arizona Home of J. L. Hubbell," *The Irrigation Age* (July, 1903).

Evers, Larry, ed. *Between Sacred Mountains: Navajo Stories and Lessons from the Land.* Tucson: University of Arizona Press, 1982.

Faris, James C. *The Nightway: A History and a History of Documentation of a Navajo Ceremonial.* Albuquerque: University of New Mexico Press, 1990.

Farish, Thomas E. *History of Arizona,* vol. VI. San Francisco, CA: Filmer Bros. Electrotype Co., 1915-1918.

Faulk, Odie B. *Arizona: A Short History.* Norman: University of Oklahoma Press, 1970.

Fell, John Kevin. "The Role of C. N. Cotton in the Development of Northwestern New Mexico," *New Mexico Historical Review* 55:2 (1980).

Fewkes, Jesse Walter. *Hopi Snake Ceremonies.* Albuquerque, NM: Avanyu Publishing Inc., 1986.

Fontana, Bernard L. *Querido Patrón: Letters From Maynard Dixon to Lorenzo Hubbell.* Tucson: Friends of the University of Arizona Library, 1987.

Franciscan Fathers. *An Ethnologic Dictionary of the Navaho Language.* 1910, reprinted St. Michaels, AZ: St. Michaels Press, 1968.

Frank, Larry with Millard J. Holbrook II. *Indian Silver Jewelry of the Southwest, 1868-1930.* Atglen, PA: Schiffer Publishing, 1990.

Frisbie, Charlotte J. "On the Trail of Chinle's 'Big House,'" in *Diné Bíkéyah: Papers in Honor of David M. Brugge*, Meliha S. Duran and David T. Kirkpatrick, eds. The Archeological Society of New Mexico 24 (1998).

—- and David P. McAllester, eds. *Navajo Blessingway Singer: The Autobiography of Frank Mitchell, 1881-1967.* Tucson, University of Arizona Press, 1978.

Goodman, James M. *The Navajo Atlas.* Norman: University of Oklahoma Press, 1982.

Grant, Campbell. *Canyon de Chelly: Its People and Rock Art.* Tucson: University of Arizona Press, 1978.

Graves, Laura. *Thomas Varker Keam, Indian Trader.* Norman: University of Oklahoma Press, 1998.

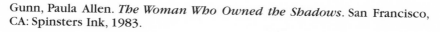

Gunn, Paula Allen. *The Woman Who Owned the Shadows*. San Francisco, CA: Spinsters Ink, 1983.

Harrison, Laura S. and Beverly Spears. *Historic Structure Report, Chinle Trading Post, Thunderbird Ranch, and Custodian's Residence Canyon de Chelly National Monument, Arizona.* Unpublished. Santa Fe, NM: National Park Service, Southwest Regional Office, 1989.

Hedlund, Ann Lane. *Reflections of the Weaver's World.* Denver, CO: Denver Art Museum, 1992.

Hegemann, Elizabeth Compton. *Navaho* [sic] *Trading Days*. Albuquerque: University of New Mexico Press, 1963.

Howard, Kathleen L. and Diana F. Pardue. *Inventing the Southwest: The Fred Harvey Company and Native American Art.* Flagstaff, AZ: Northland Publishing Co., 1996.

Hubbell, J. L. "Navajo Blankets and Indian Curios: Catalogue and Price List. Ganado, Apache County, Arizona" (pamphlet). Chicago, IL: Press of Hollister Brothers, 1902.

Hubbell, J. L. and John Edwin Hogg. "Fifty Years an Indian Trader." *Touring Topics* XXII (December 1930).

Hubbell, Walter. *History of the Hubbell Family Containing Genelogical Records of the Ancestors and Descendants of Richard Hubbell from A.D. 1086 to A.D. 1915,* 2nd ed. New York, 1915.

Ives, Joseph C. *Report Upon the Colorado River of the West Explored in 1857 and 1858,* 36th Cong., 1 sess., Hse. Exec. Doc. 90. Washington, D. C.: GPO, 1861.

James, George Wharton. *Indian Blankets and Their Makers.* 1914; reprint, New York: Dover Publications, Inc., 1974.

—-. "A Noted Painter of Indian Types," *The Craftsmen* (December 1904).

Jett, Stephen C. and Virginia E. Spencer. *Navajo Architecture.* Tucson: University of Arizona Press, 1981.

Johnson, Broderick H., ed. *Navajo Stories of the Long Walk Period.* Tsaile, AZ: Navajo Community College Press, 1973.

Johnson, Burke. "Story of Don Lorenzo," Arizona *Days and Ways* (December 26, 1965).

Jordan, Louann and St. George Cooke. *El Rancho de las Golondrinas: Spanish Colonial Life in New Mexico.* Santa Fe, NM: Colonial New Mexico Historical Foundation, 1977.

Kahlenberg, Mary Hunt and Anthony Berlant. *The Navajo Blanket* New York, NY: Praeger Publishers, Inc., in association with the Los Angeles County Museum of Art, 1972.

Kaufman, Alice and Christopher Selser. *The Navajo Weaving Tradition: 1650 to the Present.* New York: E. P. Dutton, Inc., 1985.

Kelly, Klara Bonsack and Harris Francis. *Navajo Sacred* Places. Bloomingdale: Indiana University Press, 1994.

Kelly, Lawrence C. *Navajo Roundup: Selected Correspondence of Kit Carson's Expedition Against the Navajo, 1863-1865.* Boulder, CO: Pruett Publishing, 1970.

Kennan, Edward A., "Hopi Economy and Subsistence," in the *Handbook of North American Indians* series, Alfonso Ortiz, vol. ed., vol. 9 *Southwest.* Washington, D. C.: Smithsonian Institution, 1979.

Kennedy, Mary Jeanette. *Tales of a Trader's Wife: Life on the Navajo Indian Reservation 1913–1918.* Albuquerque, NM: Valliant Co, 1965.

Kent, Kate Peck. *Navajo Weaving: Three Centuries of Change.* Santa Fe, NM: School of American Research, 1985.

Kluckhohn, Clyde and Dorothea Leighton. *The Navajo* rev. ed. Cambridge, MA: Harvard University Press, 1946.

—-, W. W. Hill, and Lucy Wales Kluckhohn. *Navajo Material Culture.* Cambridge, MA: Harvard University Press, 1971.

Krenkel, John H. ed. *The Life and Times of Joseph Fish, Mormon Pioneer.* Danville, IL: Interstate Printers & Publishers, 1970.

Lamar, Howard R. *The Far Southwest 1546-1912, A Territorial History.* New Haven, CT: Yale University Press 1966.

Laut, Agnes. *Through Our Unknown Southwest.* New York: McBride, 1915.

Lee, Albert H. *Gaamaliitsho Indian Trader: An Autobiography of Albert Hugh Lee 1897-1976.* Mesa, AZ: Lofgreens, Inc., ca. 1982.

Linton, Calvin D., ed. *The American Almanac: A Diary of America.* Nashville and New York: Thomas Nelson, Inc., 1977.

Lockwood, Frank C. "John Lorenzo Hubbell: Navajo Indian Trader," *More Arizona Characters,* General Bulletin No. 8. Tucson: University of Arizona, 1942

Lockwood, Frank C., ed. "John Lorenzo Hubbell," *Pioneer Portraits: Selected Vignettes.* Tucson, AZ: University of Ariona Press, 1968.

Long, Paul V. *Big Eyes: The Southwestern Photographs of Simian Schwemberger, 1902-1908.* Albuquerque: University of New Mexico Press, 1992.

Lummis, Charles F. "Painting the First Americans," *Land of Sunshine* (May 1900).

—-. "Swallow-Nest People," *Out West* XXXI:6 (June 1907).

M'Closkey, Kathleen. "Myths, Markets and Metaphors: Navajo Weaving as Commodity and Communicative Form." Ph.D. diss., York University, Toronto, 1996.

Manchester, Albert and Ann Manchester. "Hubbell Trading Post National Historic Site: An Administrative History" Report. Santa Fe, NM: Southwest Cultural Resources Center, Professional Papers No. 46, 1992.

Maxwill, Evertt. "The Art of Elbridge A. Burbank," *Fine Arts Journal* XXII:1 (January 1910).

Mayfield, Harriet. "Great Southwest Pioneer Passes On," *The Santa Fe Magazine* XXV:2 (January 1931).

—-. "Great Southwest Pioneer Passes On," *The Santa Fean Magazine* XXV (January 1931).

McClintock, James H. *Mormon Settlement in Arizona: A Record of Peaceful Conquest of the Desert.* Phoenix, AZ: Manufacturing Stationers, Inc. 1921.

McNitt, Frank. *Navajo Wars.* Albuquerque: University of New Mexico Press, 1972.

—-. *The Indian Trader.* Norman: University of Oklahoma Press, 1962.

McWilliams, Carey. *North from Mexico.* New York: Monthly Review Press, 1961.

Miller, Edgar K. "The Indian and the Trader," *Indian School Journal* VII: 8-9 (June-September 1907).

Miller, Jimmy H. *The Life of Harold Sellers Colton: A Philadelphia Brahmin in Flagstaff.* Tsaile, AZ: Navajo Community College Press, 1991.

Moore, Edgar W. "Commerce in the Southwest: The Indian Trader, A Review of the Literature." Unpublished paper in WP/HTPNHS.

—-. "The Bierkempers, Navajos, and the Ganado Presbyterian Mission," *American Presbyterian History* 64:7 (Summer, 1986).

Moore, Katharine Jones. "The Odyssey of James Hamilton," *Westport Historical Quarterly* V:3 (December 1969).

Mott, Dorothy Challis. "Don Lorenzo Hubbell of Ganado," *Arizona Historical Review* 4:1 (April 1931).

Mora, Jo. *Trail Dust and Saddleleather*. New York: Charles Scribner, 1946.

Murphy, Lawrence R. *Frontier Crusader—William F. M. Arny*. Tucson: University of Arizona, 1972.

"Objects of Myth & Memory: American Indian Art from the Brooklyn Museum," prepared for the 1992 and 1993 exhibits at the Oakland [CA] Museum and The Heard Museum (Phoenix, AZ).

Patzman, Stephen N. "Henry Chee Dodge: A Modern Chief of the Navajo," *Arizonian* V:1 (Spring 1964).

Perrigo, Lynn I. *The American Southwest: Its Peoples and Cultures*. Albuquerque: University of New Mexico Press, 1971.

Peterson, Charles S. *Take Up Your Mission: Mormon Colonizing Along the Little Colorado 1870-1900*. Tucson: University of Arizona Press, 1973.

—-. "Big House at Ganado: New Mexican Influence in Northern Arizona," *The Journal of Arizona History* 30:1 (Spring 1989).

—-. "Homestead and Farm: A History of Farming the Hubbell Trading Post National Historic Site." Unpublished. Prepared for Southwest Parks and Monuments Association, Tucson, AZ, March 1986.

Press Reference Library, *Notables of the West: Being the Portraits and Biographies of Progressive Men of the West Who Have Helped in the Development and History of Making This Wonderful Country*, Western Edition. New York: International News Service, 1915.

Pyle, John E., diary (January 1-November 27, 1878). Collection of the Bancroft Library, University of California, Berkeley, CA.

Reichard, Gladys A. *Spiderwoman: A Story of Navajo Weavers and Chanters*. 1934; reprint, Glorieta, NM: The Rio Grande Press, Inc., 1968.

—-. *Weaving a Navajo Blanket*. 1936; reprint, New York: Dover Publications, Inc., 1974.

Robinson, William J. "A Construction Sequence For Hubbell Trading Post and Residence," *The Kiva* 50:4 (1985).

Rodee, Marian E. *Old Navajo Rugs: Their Development from 1900 to 1940*. Albuquerque: University of New Mexico Press, 1981.

Roessel, Robert A., Jr. "Navajo History, 1850-1923," in the *Handbook of North American Indians* series, Alfonso Ortiz, vol. ed., vol. 10 *Southwest*. Washington, D. C.: Smithsonian Institution, 1983.

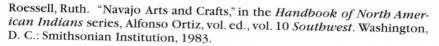

Roessell, Ruth. "Navajo Arts and Crafts," in the *Handbook of North American Indians* series, Alfonso Ortiz, vol. ed., vol. 10 *Southwest*. Washington, D. C.: Smithsonian Institution, 1983.

Sales, Kirkpatrick. *The Conquest of Paradise: Christopher Columbus and the Columbian Legacy*. New York: Alfred A. Knopf, 1990.

Salsbury, Clarence G., M. D. The *Salsbury Story: A Medical Missionary's Lifetime of Public Service*. Tucson: University of Arizona Press, 1969.

Samuels, Peggy and Harold. *Samuels' Encyclopedia of Artists of the American West*. Secaucus, NJ: Castle, 1985.

Schmedding, Joseph. *Cowboy and Indian Trader*. 1951; reprinted Albuquerque: University of New Mexico Press, 1974.

Shondee, Lena (interviewee). "Spinning Cultures," *Navajo Times* (November 27, 1985).

Smith, Mrs. White Mountain. "He Is Our Friend," *The Desert Magazine* 4:1 (1940).

Spicer, E. H. and R. H. Thompson. *Plural Society in the Southwest*. Tucson, AZ: University of Arizona Press, 1972.

Thompson, Gerald. *The Army and The Navajo: The Bosque Redondo Reservation Experiment 1863-1868*. Tucson: University of Arizona Press, 1976.

Thrapp, Dan L. *Encyclopedia of Frontier Biography,* 3 vol. Lincoln: University of Nebraska Press, 1988.

Trafzer, Clifford E. "Sam Day and His Boys: Good Neighbors to the Navajos," *Journal of Arizona History* 18:1 (Spring 1977).

U. S. Federal Trade Commission. Staff Report, "The Trading Post System on the Navajo Reservation" Washington, D. C.: Government Printing Office, 1973.

U. S. Government. *Adjustment of Rights of Settlers on the Navajo Reservation,* 57 Cong., 1 sess, Sen. Rept. 2042. Washington, D. C.: GPO, 1902.

—-. Bureau of American Ethnology Annual Reports, 1894-1895 and 1897-1898.

—-. *Rights of Settlers on the Navajo Reservation, Arizona,* 56 Cong. 1 Sess., Sen. Rept. 699. Washington, D. C.: GPO, 1900.

Underhill, Lonnie E. and Daniel F. Littlefield, Jr. *Hamlin Garland's Observations on the American Indian 1895-1905*. Tucson: University of Arizona Press, 1976.

Underhill, Ruth M. *The Navajo*. Norman: University of Oklahoma Press, 1956.

Unknown. *Apache County Centennial Memento Booklet 1879-1979*; *Apache County Historical Quarterly* 4 (July 1978).

Utley, Robert. "Special Report on Hubbell Trading Post, Ganado, Arizona." Unpublished. Santa Fe, New Mexico: National Park Service, Region Three, 1959.

—-. "The Reservation Trader in Navajo History," *El Palacio* XVIII:1 (Spring 1961).

Van Dyke, Walter and Ruth Van Dyke, eds. *Lefthanded: A Navajo Autobiography*. New York: Columbia University Press, 1980.

Van Dyke, Walter, ed. *Son of Old Man Hat*. 1938, reprinted Lincoln: University of Nebraska Press, 1966.

Van Valkenburgh, Richard. "Tom Keam, Friend of Moqui," *The Desert Magazine* 9:9 (July 1946).

—-. "Navajo Naataani," *The Kiva* XIII (January 1948).

—-, L. W. Adams, and J. McPhee, eds., "Diné Bikéyah." Unpublished. Window Rock, AZ: The Navajo Nation, 1941.

Viele, Cathy. "Thomas Keams [sic]: Squaw Man, Gentleman," *Northlander* (Thursday, August 30, 1979).

Walker, Henry P. and Don Bufkin. *Historical Atlas of Arizona*. Norman: University of Oklahoma Press, 1979.

Walker, Henry P. "Pick" "Wagon Freighting in Arizona," *Smoke Signal* 28 (Fall 1973).

Weigle, Marta and Barbara A. Babcock, eds. *The Great Southwest of the Fred Harvey Company and the Santa Fe. Railway.* Phoenix, AZ: The Heard Museum, 1996.

Wetherill, Hilda Faunce. *Desert Wife*. Reprint, Lincoln: University of Nebraska Press, 1981.

Whiteley, Peter. *Deliberate Acts: Changing Hopi Culture Through the Oraibi Split*. Tucson: University of Arizona Press, 1988.

Wilken, Robert L. *Anselm Weber, O. F. M.: Missionary to the Navajo 1898-1921*. Milwaukee, WI: Bruce Publishing Co., 1955.

Williams, Jerry L., ed. *New Mexico in Maps*. Albuquerque: University of New Mexico Press, 1986.

Williams, Lester L. *C. N. Cotton and His Navajo Blankets.* Albuquerque, NM: Avanyu Publishing, 1989.

—-. "C. N. Cotton Indian Trader," *Denver Westerner's Roundup* 33 (May/June 1977).

Wilson, Alan with Gene Dennison. *Navajo Place Names: An Observer's Guide.* Guilford, CT: Jeffrey Norton Publishers, 1995.

Witherspoon, Gary. "Navajo Social Organization," and "Language and Reality in the Navajo World View," in the *Handbook of North American Indians* series, Alfonso Ortiz, vol. ed., vol. 10 *Southwest.* Washington, D. C.: Smithsonian Institution, 1983.

—-. "Navajo Weaving: Art in Its Cultural Content," *Museum of Northern Arizona Research Paper 36* Flagstaff, AZ: n.d.

—-. *Language and Art in the Navajo Universe.* Ann Arbor: University of Michigan Press, 1977.

Wyllie, Irvin G. *The Self-Made Man in America: The Myth of Rags to Riches.* New York: The Free Press, 1954.

Yost, Billie. *Bread Upon the Sands.* Caldwell, ID: Caxton Publishers, 1958.

Young. Robert W. *The Role of the Navajo in the Southwestern Drama.* Gallup, NM: Gallup *Independent*, 1968.

Youngblood, B. "Navajo Trading, A Report to the Office of Experiment Stations, U. S. Department of Agriculture, 1935" *Survey of Conditions of Indians in the United States, Hearings before a Subcommittee of the Senate Committee on Indian Affairs*, 75th Congr., 1st sess., 1937, pp. 18,036–18,115.

PHOTOGRAPHIC ACKNOWLEDGEMENTS

The majority of the photographs are from the photographic collection archived at Hubbell Trading Post National Historic Site, Ganado, Navajo Indian Reservation, Arizona. These photographs are identified as HUTR with a specific number or by a letter number combination, such as HUTR RP 3. I am indebted to Curator Ed Chamberlin at HTPNHS and his assistant Kathy Tabaha for their enthusiastic and able assistance with the photographs, as well as my husband Oliver W. Johnson who shot many of the old photographs in the collection at HTPNHS.

A word is in order about the extensive collection of photographs at HTPNHS. The size of the collection perhaps is due to friends/visitors of the Hubbell family gifting the family with photo albums. Some photographs at HTPNHS also are in other collections as the photographer printed duplicates. Generally printed material about HTPNHS over the past thirty some years have utilized collection photographs without identification numbers. This has been burdensome when the curator's office has been asked to locate a given photograph which appeared in a publication. Therefore at their request, the identification number in the HTPNHS collection is indicated where known.

Front Cover: J. L. outside buying rug HTP-PP-38.71

p. 104 Frank HUTR 9644;   Tom HUTR RP 220

p. 108 Alma and baby Jack HUTR 7074

p. 109 Alma & Roman HUTR 4976

p. 117 Chee Dodge older HUTR 2126;
group Navajos HUTR 9408

Chapter Eight
p. 123 Trading Ranch with horsemen HUTR 4407

p. 127 Wool bags loaded HUTR 22919

p. 128 Bread oven HUTR 8656

p. 130 Halloween photo HUTR 9576

p. 131 Grandchildren "Navajo style" HUTR 9283

p. 132 Hubbell Hall's dining function HUTR 4487

p. 134 Hall HUTR 4963/4532

Chapter Nine
p. 136 Buying rug Ben Wittick photographer, HUTR 2165

p. 137 Pinon nuts bagged HUTR RP 186

p. 138 Wool at Gallup HUTR 11517;
Wool at Keams Canyon HUTR 9000

p. 138 Hispanic employees 9341

p. 139 Navajo wagon HUTR 4477

p. 141 Freight snow HUTR 4475

p. 144 Hubbell men & auto HUTR 4767

p. 145 Stranded vehicle HUTR 9306

p. 149 Demonstrators #5012 From the Fred Harvey Collection,
Courtesy Special Collections, University of Arizona, Tucson, Arizona.

p. 153 Miguelito HUTR 9233

p. 154 Elle Ganado, Tom Ganado, *The Santa Fe Magazine*, Feb-Mar, 1924.

p. 155 Elle with Mary Pickford, *ibid*. Photos on pp. 154 and this page
courtesy Kansas State Historical Society, Topeka, Kansas.

Chapter Ten
p. 158 Days HUTR 4837

p. 161 Weber HUTR 5310 ;
Simeon HUTR 4829

p. 162 St. Michaels HUTR 5327

p. 164 Presbyterian Mission HUTR 7560

BOOK VI
Chapter Fifteen

Chapter Sixteen

Chapter Seventeen

Epilogue

INDEX

Note: Italicized page numbers indicate pictures. Citations mentioning "Hubbell" or "J. L." refer to Juan Lorenzo Hubbell. Relationships indicated in parentheses are to Juan Lorenzo Hubbell unless otherwise specified.

Index

Index